The Next Generation

The Next Generation

Immigrant Youth in a Comparative Perspective

EDITED BY

Richard Alba and Mary C. Waters

NEW YORK UNIVERSITY PRESS
New York and London

NEW YORK UNIVERSITY PRESS
New York and London
www.nyupress.org

References to Internet websites (URLs) were accurate at the time of writing.
Neither the author nor New York University Press is responsible for URLs
that may have expired or changed since the manuscript was prepared.

Library of Congress Cataloging-in-Publication Data
The next generation : immigrant youth in a comparative perspective /
edited by Richard Alba and Mary C. Waters.
p. cm.
Includes index.
ISBN 978-0-8147-0742-5 (cl : alk. paper) — ISBN 978-0-8147-0743-2
(pb : alk. paper) — ISBN 978-0-8147-0762-3 (e-book)
1. Children of immigrants—Social conditions—Cross-cultural studies.
2. Children of immigrants—Economic conditions—Cross-cultural studies.
3. Children of immigrants—Education—Cross-cultural studies.
4. Assimilation (Sociology) 5. Group identity—Cross-cultural studies.
I. Alba, Richard D. II. Waters, Mary C.
JV6344.N49   2011
305.23086'912—dc22   2010039829

New York University Press books are printed on acid-free paper,
and their binding materials are chosen for strength and durability.
We strive to use environmentally responsible suppliers and materials
to the greatest extent possible in publishing our books.

Manufactured in the United States of America

c   10 9 8 7 6 5 4 3 2 1
p   10 9 8 7 6 5 4 3 2 1

Contents

PART III: THE ROLE OF LOCAL CONTEXT

PART IV: IN CLOSING: COMPARATIVE STUDIES

Acknowledgments

The essays in this book were first written for a conference held at the Radcliffe Institute for Advanced Study at Harvard University in October 2004. This conference was part of the activities of a cluster of scholars at the institute working on immigration in the United States and western Europe. Katherine Newman, now at Princeton but at the time the dean for the social sciences at Radcliffe, was instrumental in bringing the cluster together and securing generous funding from the Mellon Foundation and the Foundation for Child Development. We are very grateful to Kathy for her leadership and vision in bringing together scholars to work on this important issue. We are also grateful to Harriet Zuckerman, vice president of the Mellon Foundation, and Ruby Takanishi, president of the Foundation for Child Development, for their generous support. The Radcliffe cluster was co-led by Mary Waters and Jennifer Hochschild and included Richard Alba, Riva Kastoryano, Reuel Rogers, Luis Fraga, and, in its planning stages, John Mollenkopf. The immigration fellows played a large part in the design and implementation of the conference on the second generation in Europe and North America and a companion conference on political integration of immigrants in Europe and North America, many of the essays of which have now appeared as the book *Bringing Outsiders In: Transatlantic Perspectives on Immigrant Political Incorporation,* edited by Jennifer Hochschild and John Mollenkopf. The luxury of having a year to do scholarly work at Radcliffe was very helpful to both the editors, and we would like to acknowledge Drew Gilpin Faust, Judy Vichniac, and the staff at Radcliffe who helped us with the conference and provided a nurturing environment for scholarly work during our year there as scholars.

We would like to thank the two anonymous reviewers and Peter Wissoker, who gave us valuable feedback on an earlier version of the book. We are very fortunate to be working with Ilene Kalish at New York University Press, who has been an enthusiastic and supportive editor for this project. We are grateful to Dorothy Friendly and Despina Papazoglou Gimbel, who helped in the preparation of the manuscript. We are also both extremely grateful to our generous families, who allowed us to steal away time to complete the book.

1

Dimensions of Second-Generation Incorporation

AN INTRODUCTION TO THE BOOK

Richard Alba and Mary C. Waters

Immigration is transforming the societies of North America and western Europe in ways that could not have been predicted a few decades ago. The roots of this population movement extend back to the middle of the twentieth century—a period of world war and recovery from wartime destruction—and they have been nourished subsequently by decolonization, economic development, and political instability in the Third World, along with the steadily shrinking significance of distance in human affairs, a development often referred to by the term *globalization.*

One consequence of these population movements has been the rise of ethnic, religious, and racial diversity in societies that previously thought of themselves as homogeneous, along with its permanent expansion in societies where immigration was already part of the national story. There is some degree of historical role reversal in this development, as countries such as Germany and Italy that previously were the source of many immigrants going elsewhere have become places where immigrants now settle in large numbers.

The second generation occupies a key position with respect to the future of the new groups and the societies where they reside, for this generation, born and/or raised in the host society, has a far greater capacity for integration than does the immigrant one. The term *second generation* is often taken in a broad sense to encompass the children who grow up in immigrant homes, whether they are born in the receiving society or enter it at a young age. In the more precise language of social-science research, the term *second generation* is usually reserved for those children of immigrants who are born in the host society, while the children who arrive at a young age and thus receive part or all of their schooling in the new society are called the *1.5 generation,* a term invented by the sociologist Rubén Rumbaut. In this introduction, however, we use *second generation* in the broader sense.

Because of differences in national systems of statistical accounting for immigrants and the second generation, it is impossible to give commensurate figures for all the societies involved, but a few illustrative ones suggest the magnitude of the developments. In the United States, a common estimate (as of 2006) is that more than a fifth of the population belongs to the immigrant or second generations, with the two very roughly of the same order of size; a similar fraction of school-age children lives in immigrant households (Hernandez, Denton, and Macartney, chap. 3 in this volume). The United States is generally thought of as the immigration society par excellence, but numerically at least, it now has a number of rivals in Europe. In Switzerland, for instance, nearly a quarter of the population is foreign-born; and the children of the immigrants account for almost 40 percent of the overall child population (Innocenti Research Centre 2009). In Germany, where according to the scrupulous accounting of Rainer Münz and Ralf Ulrich (2003) about one-sixth of the German population as of the late 1990s was born outside the boundaries of present-day Germany, the 1.5 and second generations now amount to 26 percent of all children. Even in Italy, which has not appeared to be central to the immigration flows transforming western Europe until very recently, the children of immigrants are already a tenth of all children (Innocenti Research Centre 2009).

The comparative study of the second generation is in its infancy, despite the critical importance of clarifying the uncertainties that surround the trajectories of the children of immigrants in contemporary immigration societies. At one vertex of a triangle of possibilities lies assimilation, associated with gradual cultural, social, and socioeconomic integration into the mainstream society. Although assimilation is prevalent among the descendants of past immigrants (Alba and Nee 2003; Noiriel 1988), its applicability to contemporary immigrations has been called into question. At another vertex is the possibility, increasingly raised, that the value of ethnic social and cultural capital, combined with transnational connections on a scale never before seen in human history, will sustain ethnic pluralism to a new extent (Glick Schiller, Basch, and Blanc-Szanton 1995; Levitt 2001; Portes and Zhou 1993). The final vertex is occupied by a special form of assimilation, associated with the theory of "segmented" assimilation: assimilation into a racial or ethnic minority status that entails systematic disadvantage vis-à-vis members of the societal mainstream (Portes and Rumbaut 2001)

Because segmented-assimilation theory explicitly addresses these three modes of incorporation, it is an important reference point for any comparative examination of the second generation. This theory, formulated in the

U.S. context, poses starkly different possible outcomes for the second generation: upward assimilation, downward assimilation, and a combination of upward mobility with persistent biculturalism. These paths correspond to three processes that summarize the relations between immigrant children, their parents, and the wider ethnic community: consonant, dissonant, and selective acculturation. Consonant acculturation occurs when the children and the parents learn American culture and gradually abandon their home language and "old country" ways at about the same pace. Thus, as children enter the American mainstream, they achieve upward mobility with the support of their parents. Dissonant acculturation occurs when children's learning of the English language and American ways outstrips that of their immigrant parents. Portes and Rumbaut (2001) argue that this process can lead to downward assimilation, as young people confront racial discrimination, bifurcated labor markets, and an often nihilistic inner-city youth subculture on their own, without strong parental authority and resources and with few community supports. The third process, selective acculturation, is the one that leads to upward assimilation and biculturalism. Selective acculturation occurs when parents and children both learn American ways gradually while remaining embedded, at least in part, in the ethnic community. Portes and Rumbaut (2001, 54) argue that selective acculturation is especially important for those groups who are subject to discrimination.

Segmented assimilation also takes into account background factors such as parental human capital (including parents' education and income), modes of incorporation (state definitions of immigrant groups, eligibility for welfare, degree of discrimination and antipathy toward immigrant groups), and family structure (single-parent versus married-couple families as well as multigenerational versus nuclear-family living arrangements). Although less explicitly stated, the model also points to the varying degrees of transnational connection among immigrant groups as an important element of the context of reception. This theory has helped to organize and systematize a large volume of work on immigrant incorporation. The concept of *modes of incorporation,* for instance, has been extremely useful in systematizing the relationship between varying political and cultural reactions to immigrant groups and the experiences of acceptance or resistance of individual immigrants themselves. In the United States there is close to universal agreement that American society and the American economy do not make up an undifferentiated whole—and in that sense the experience of assimilation is clearly *segmented.* Virtually all studies show that the children of immigrants do not follow a single trajectory and that second-generation outcomes are highly contingent on the segment of American society into which they are being incorporated (Greenman and Xie 2008).

Other authors have argued that they do not find evidence of segmented assimilation because they generally do not find second-generation decline or downward assimilation. Farley and Alba (2002), Hirschman (2001), Smith (2003), Waldinger and Feliciano (2004), and Kasinitz et al. (2008) all find evidence of progress for the second generation vis-à-vis the first generation, and this evidence is sometimes interpreted as disputing segmented assimilation. For instance, Boyd (2002, 1037) finds no support for segmented assimilation in Canada and concludes that "contrary to the second generation decline or the segmented underclass assimilation model found in the United States, adult immigrant offspring in Canada who are people of color (visible minorities) exceed the educational attainments of other non-visible minority groups." This pattern of second-generation advantage, in particular in educational attainment, is a key theme in Tariq Modood's chapter on Britain in this volume (chap. 9).

Segmented assimilation was raised first in the U.S. context as a prospect for groups that face especially high barriers to their entry into the mainstream, as appears to be true for groups deemed phenotypically black by North American standards (Portes and Zhou 1993; Waters 1999a), and its relevance for other national contexts has been widely discussed since then. The question of how relevant segmented assimilation is for the European context is explicitly raised in several of chapters in this volume, most notably Roxane Silberman's chapter on France (chap. 14), Fibbi, Lerch, and Wanner's chapter on Switzerland (chap. 6), and Phalet and Heath's chapter on Belgium (chap. 7).

But the question about the trajectories of incorporation of immigrant groups in contemporary societies hovers over all the essays in this volume. It is most usefully addressed within a comparative frame because of the strong likelihood that features of the receiving society interact with characteristics of the immigrant group to determine the latter's trajectory. In the remainder of this introductory essay, we sketch some of the major axes of difference among immigrations and among the societies of North America and western Europe that are widely thought to bear on processes of incorporation and hence on the life chances of the second generation. We view four in particular as primary: the character of the immigration; the citizenship regime, whose scope extends, according to the famous formulation of T. H. Marshall (1964), from the basic political rights understood as part of citizenship narrowly construed to the socioeconomic rights embedded in social-welfare systems; the institutions of the host society that the children of immigrants must pass through; and the local contexts within the receiving society where the children of immigrants grow up and whose features impact on their opportunities. We consider also how the essays in this volume contribute empirically to our knowledge about the role of these dimensions.

Types of Immigration

All immigrations are not the same when it comes to their impact on societal diversity, for some are easily absorbed into the societal mainstream because of ethnic proximity to natives, whereas others can lead to longstanding, if not permanent, majority-minority divisions. In the United States, western European and Canadian immigrants, though making up a small fraction of the whole, are rather invisible in ethnic terms and generally blend easily into the white-dominated mainstream. The same cannot be said for the more massive immigrations from Asia, Latin America, and the Caribbean. In most of western Europe, the intra-European immigrations made possible by the European Union, though not invisible, nevertheless do not stand out as problematic in their incorporation, whereas most of the non-European groups do. In France, for instance, Portuguese immigrants and their children are viewed as immigration successes, while the North Africans, sub-Saharan Africans, and Turks are not (see Silberman, chap. 14 in this volume). The implications of the immigration mix for societal diversity are hardly limited to racial visibility, as Tariq Modood describes for Great Britain in chapter 9 in this volume.

Though we do not discuss in depth the role of state policy and law in shaping the volume and mix of immigration streams flowing into a society, it is obviously consequential and thus to some extent agenda setting for second-generation integration. To be sure, the impact of states is never as absolute as they would like—prospective immigrants, usually in collaboration with their already settled relatives and contacts, can often use immigration law and policy in ways unforeseen by policymakers to gain entry. Yet the differences between the immigration streams into receiving societies seem, at least in some cases, undeniably related to state policies. Canada and the United States offer an informative comparison, for despite their geographic proximity, Canada takes in relatively little of the low-wage immigration, especially from Latin America, that looms large in the United States; plausibly, this difference is related to the occupational selectivity entailed in the Canadian point system as compared to the predominance of family relationships in the U.S. immigration system (Boyd and Vickers 2009; Reitz 1998), although the long land border between the United States and Mexico also plays an important role.

Of the major types of immigration, labor migrations hold a fundamental importance for the ethnic and racial divisions that have emerged in North America and western Europe; and most of the essays in this volume focus largely or exclusively on the second generations from these migrations, typified by the Turks of Europe and the Mexicans of the United States. Generally large in size and usually coming from Third World countries whose citizens are perceived as culturally different from the mainstream of the countries of reception and frequently as racially different too, the labor migrations of the post–World War II era have created new minorities in many countries or expanded old ones. Though often conceived as temporary by the governments that promote them, labor migrations generally lead to permanent settlement by some portion of the immigrant group, which finds the opportunities in the new society, however humble, preferable to those it would face upon return. Most of the groups whose second generations face incorporation difficulties have arisen from this form of immigration.

Though labor immigrations have been promoted by profound economic and political changes in both source and receiving countries, they typically require legal and policy steps in both countries in order to take place (Sassen 1988; Massey et al. 1993). For this reason, they often develop in fits and starts, synchronized with political decision-making. In the United States, the beginnings of the contemporary labor immigration can be spotted in the "bracero" program, which was initiated during World War II to fill the need for labor at a time when many American men were in uniform. The bracero program, which gave several million Mexican workers their first taste of life in "El Norte," led to a rise in immigration from Mexico that predates 1965, the date of changes in immigration law that are often cited as the moment of birth of contemporary immigration to the United States.

In Europe, too, the labor needs that gave rise to large-scale labor migrations came after the war, when additional labor was needed to reconstruct damaged infrastructures and economies, especially given the massive losses of manpower due to the war itself. France, for instance, established its office of immigration (ONI) in 1945. Germany had perhaps the exemplary program during the postwar period, recruiting so-called guest workers, who were expected to come without their families and to work for predetermined periods and then return home (Bade 1994). Initially, many were housed in barracks by the companies they worked for and took jobs at the bottom rungs of the labor market.

Often what started as a temporary immigration initiated by the state turned into permanent settlement. Family reunification has been the key policy provision that has catalyzed this process and allowed labor immigration to continue to grow in many countries. In the United States, a series of critical laws established family reunification as the primary principle that would govern legal admission: it was a centerpiece in the watershed 1965 act, which has shaped the landscape of immigration ever since its passage. In Europe, active recruitment of low-wage immigrants came to an end in most countries in the early 1970s when their economies were rattled by the shock of oil-price rises. However, labor-immigrant populations have continued to grow as a result of the family-reunification parts of immigration law, which are found in all countries (although there have been some recent efforts to narrow them). Indeed, the end of active recruitment precipitated a process of settlement for many immigrant groups. The Turks in Germany are a case in point: Many of the guest workers did not return home but found ways to stay and to bring their families. Family reunification accelerated with the official halt to guest-worker recruitment in 1973, when the immigrants realized that entry into western Europe would become more difficult. The Turkish population continues to grow through family-reunification immigration, which now often occurs in the form of marriages between second-generation Turks in Germany and partners from the home regions of their parents (Kelek 2005). Maurice Crul's chapter in this volume (chap. 13) discusses the immigration dynamics of the Turks in Germany and in three other west European countries.

In both the United States and Europe, labor immigration also persists in unauthorized ways, with undocumented immigrants after a period of residence and work often receiving legal sanction through amnesties and regularizations, which have occurred in the United States and in several western European countries. In the United States, studies have shown that undocumented immigration occurs both as a result of clandestine border crossing, especially at the Rio Grande, and visa overstaying. As of 2008, the total number of the unauthorized was estimated at twelve million, truly an astonishing figure in a nation with a population of about three hundred million—according to this accounting, one of every twenty-five to thirty residents lacks the legal right to live and work in the United States (Passel and Cohn 2008). The United States has had one previous amnesty, which was legislated in the 1986 Immigration Reform and Control Act (IRCA) and which resulted in about three million grants of permanent residence to previously undocumented residents. Whether and under what conditions currently undocumented residents can gain legal status is the subject of current debate in the U.S. Congress and in the media. Chapter 2 in this volume, by Susan Brown, Frank Bean, Mark Leach, and Rubén Rumbaut, addresses the impact of immigrant legal status on the socioeconomic position of the second generation.

The unauthorized population is almost certainly not as large in western Europe as it is in the United States, in part because a number of major European countries have much tighter internal controls—for example, requiring the regular presentation of identity documents—than the United States does. Nevertheless, there is a significant unauthorized population in western Europe also, albeit one that is less settled than that in the United States. Much of this population comes from the Mediterranean region or from sub-Saharan Africa. It is thought to be particularly large in the countries of southern Europe, Greece, Italy, and Spain. Several of the European countries with sizable undocumented populations have had fairly frequent regularizations—this is true of Spain, for instance, which in 2005 decreed a large-scale regularization that gave legal status to some seven to eight hundred thousand immigrants, including some from Latin America.

The groups that have originated from low-wage labor migrations are the ones that stand out whenever immigration is discussed in North America and western Europe—especially Mexicans and Central Americans in the United States and Turks and North Africans in western Europe. Yet not all migrations are of humble workers with limited educations seeking jobs that natives are reluctant to take. Many states are currently seeking to expand their intake of immigrants with high educational diplomas, professional qualifications, or unusual skills. The presence of a highly skilled stratum in the immigration stream gives the immigrant populations in many countries a bimodal appearance: along with the low-skilled workers who fill jobs at the bottom are high-skilled ones who take well-paid jobs and live in middle-class, if not wealthy, neighborhoods (Portes and Rumbaut 2006). This bimodal division in skills and wages is accentuated by ethnic difference. Generally speaking, the low-skilled immigrants and the highly educated ones do not come from the same countries, creating an ethnic division of considerable consequence within the foreign-born and then the second-generation population. In the United States, for instance, Indians are concentrated in the ranks of engineers, physicians, and other highly trained immigrants.

States also seek out entrepreneurs, although many small-business owners enter receiving countries initially as labor or professional immigrants. The

United States, for example, has a provision to admit "investors" who bring significant financial capital and intend to funnel it into businesses that will provide employment. However, many immigrant entrepreneurs arise from the ranks of labor immigrants, and in fact the larger the immigrant group, the greater the chance for enterprising individuals to establish businesses that initially depend on servicing the needs of coethnics. In Germany, for example, the Turks are well known for the many businesses they have established, often in ethnic neighborhoods. The Mexicans in the United States, who have a very low rate of self-employment, demonstrate that not every labor immigration gives rise to a sizable entrepreneurial stratum.

The position of the second generation of professional and entrepreneurial migrations is very different from that of its counterparts issuing from labor immigration, and it therefore is not addressed much in this volume. The difference is due not simply to the generally superior economic position of families headed by professionals or entrepreneurs. On average, the educational attainments and other human capital of these immigrants are much higher than those of labor-seeking migrants, and thus the endowment of the second generation for progressing through educational systems is more favorable. It also appears that some immigrant entrepreneurs view the demanding efforts they make to run successful small businesses as the sacrifice of one generation to give the next a head start in the attainment of high educational and professional qualifications—this is famously the case with many Korean small-business owners in the United States. Such immigrant parents emphasize for their children the central goal of educational success.

Other sorts of immigration complicate the picture further, in ways that cannot be addressed in detail here. If labor, professional, and entrepreneurial immigrants can be regarded on the whole as individuals who have "chosen" to leave their countries of origin and migrate abroad, usually in an effort to improve their economic situations and their children's opportunities, that is not true on the whole for the most important of the remaining types of immigrants. Refugees by definition are individuals who have been forced to flee their countries of origin because of imminent threat—generally of a political, religious, or ethnic nature. Because they are usually unable to plan their departure and their economic entry into the new society, refugees are typically extended significant financial support by the countries that receive them. How such immigrant groups subsequently fare is highly variable and depends on the trauma associated with their departure, the human and even financial capital they are able to flee with, and their reception in the host society.

The Citizenship Regimes of Receiving States

The rules of access to, and the nature of, the rights that host societies accord automatically to their native-born citizens potentially impact profoundly on the integration of the immigrants and the second generation. These rights determine the abilities of the members of immigrant-origin groups in numerous domains of life in the new society, which, depending on the country, may include return from travel abroad; assistance to family members who want to immigrate; voting and political expression; parity with natives in the labor market, especially in the civil service, often a highly protected sector; and financial assistance from the state at times of need. We think of the rules of access and the nature of these rights as the *citizenship regime,* in accordance with the expanded concept of citizenship famously introduced by T. H. Marshall (1964). To be sure, citizenship laws and policies constitute a central portal to these rights, but not all of them are granted only in this way (Bloemraad 2006; Soysal 1994). This is particularly true for the social rights associated with the welfare state, for which the rules of access and the benefits to be obtained vary considerably across countries.

When it comes to citizenship itself, a key distinction is often made between *jus soli* and *jus sanguinis* regimes (Brubaker 1992). The former, exemplified by Canada, France, Great Britain, and the United States, gives citizenship to individuals based on their birth on a state's territory, regardless of the citizenship of their parents. (Not all the *jus soli* states attribute citizenship to such individuals at the moment of their birth, and they may qualify the offer in other ways. The United States is at one extreme, attributing citizenship at birth regardless of the legal situations of a child's parents. France, by comparison, provides birthright citizenship at the age of majority and allows individuals to opt out.) The *jus sanguinis* system was epitomized by Germany until the 1999 change in its citizenship law. Prior to that point, the German-born children of immigrants inherited the citizenship of their parents, which meant that the great majority of the descendants of the largest immigrant group, the Turks, remained noncitizens even into the third generation and could only obtain German citizenship by a naturalization procedure little different from that faced by the immigrants themselves (Diehl and Blohm 2003). Despite the 1999 law, which allows the German-born to hold dual citizenship—German and that of their parents—until the age of twenty-three, the adult second generation there grew up under a very different regime of citizenship, which has shaped its life chances and orientation toward the society of reception. Among the countries considered in this volume, Switzerland still employs the *jus sanguinis* principle, and the attainment of citizenship by the second generation is far from universal, as described in chapter 6 by Rosita Fibbi, Mathias Lerch, and Philippe Wanner.

Political rights loom foremost among the rights associated with citizenship, but there has been some decoupling of the two in Europe. Under EU law, citizens of one EU state who live in another have the right to vote in local elections where they reside (and also in elections to the European Parliament). In the interests of equity, some European states also grant local voting rights to noncitizen immigrants from outside the European Union, and these include, of course, the groups of most interest to our authors (Groenendijk 2008). For example, in the Netherlands, immigrants can vote in local elections after five years of residence, and they can even stand for election themselves, with the result that large numbers of immigrant representatives are found on the councils of the larger Dutch cities (Alba and Foner 2009). However, in the Netherlands, as elsewhere, in order to vote in national elections and help determine the political orientation and policies at the national level, immigrants must become Dutch citizens.

For some children of immigrants, what matters is not so much citizenship but their parents' legal status. Its critical role is demonstrated by chapter 2 in this volume, by Susan Brown, Frank Bean, Mark Leach, and Rubén Rumbaut. They examine the consequences of parental legal status for outcomes among the second generation in the United States, and their essay suggests the costs of having undocumented parents for the second generation, even for children who are themselves U.S. citizens by birth. Drawing on the Immigration and Intergenerational Mobility in Metropolitan Los Angeles (IIM-MLA) data, Brown and her colleagues find that a little less than half of all the Mexican mothers and fathers in this representative sample of 1.5- and second-generation Mexican Americans in Los Angeles came to the United States as unauthorized or undocumented migrants. Most were able to legalize as a result of the 1986 IRCA law, which provided a path to citizenship. For those who grew up in homes where one or both parents remained undocumented, however, the costs to their own adult status, reflected in educational and economic outcomes, are substantial. Their chapter has strong public-policy implications for the current debates in the United States over what to do with the millions of undocumented immigrants currently in the country, suggesting that there will be huge negative costs imposed on the next generation if a path to citizenship is not provided for the parental generation.

There has been a tendency to see the differences in citizenship rules and access to political rights as indicative of something much larger, which could be described as national paradigms of integration. These paradigms, according to the common view, couple configurations of state policies with well-established societal understandings about the nature and course of integration (Brubaker 1992; Favell 1998). The citizenship rules do seem to correspond in a very rough way with dominant ideologies concerning the incorporation of immigrants and their children. Some of the *jus soli* countries are home to strongly assimilationist ideologies, though there are significant differences in this respect among them, as between France and the United States. The United States has often been characterized as a nation that regards all immigrants as potential members of the American nation and is rather quick to extend the identity of "American" to new arrivals and certainly to their children without demanding their complete acculturation to American norms. In public discourse, France adheres mostly to what has been called the "Republican" ideology, which, while accepting that anyone can become French through the acquisition of citizenship, still expects an acculturation to a French identity and, concomitantly, a muting of ethnic characteristics, at a minimum in public spheres (Schnapper 1991). (The 2004 French law banning headscarves and other visible signs of religious affiliation in schools is one indication of the differences between U.S. and French understandings of incorporation.)

A *jus sanguinis* citizenship regime is more likely to correspond with an ethnically inflected understanding of "membership," which can operate as a barrier to the easy incorporation of new immigrant populations. Germany, at least in the recent past, does seem to illustrate this linkage. Germans were slow to recognize that groups that had entered as "guest" workers had turned into more or less permanent settlers; for a long time, the mantra of many major German politicians was that "Deutschland ist kein Einwanderungsland" (Germany is not a country of immigration), and the widespread expectation was that the Turks and other guest-worker groups would eventually return to their countries of origin (Bade 2004). Even after the recognition that an immigration situation had taken hold, there was not a clear, widely accepted view of how to integrate the new groups into German society.

In similar fashion, one could argue that the Dutch approach of extending local voting rights to noncitizens is emblematic of the multicultural orientation toward the incorporation of new groups that prevailed there until recently. Dutch multiculturalism has been seen as the product of an emphasis on "tolerance" in the national self-identity and of an institutional heritage of "pillarization," whereby the key religious groups in the population have possessed their own state-supported institutions, including schools. The understanding has been that immigrant groups would not be required to acculturate fully to the existing Dutch society and could preserve a large degree of cultural and social independence but that they could still be full participants in the receiving society. This generous view has suffered major body blows during the past few years, as the depth of the problems faced by some in the second generation has become apparent. The most damaging blow was the murder of the filmmaker Theo van Gogh, which made manifest the rejection of Dutch society by a segment of second-generation Muslim youth (Buruma 2006).

However, we take the position that these paradigms are not in general good overall guides to the comparative study of incorporation (Freeman 2004). Our reasoning is that incorporation is fundamentally a matter of integration experiences in a variety of domains, such as residence, education, and the labor market, each of which has its own institutional logic, often the result of arrangements that were established long before the new waves of immigrants. The chances of immigrant-origin students in education, for instance, are likely determined far more by longstanding features of national and local school systems, as we will shortly point out, than by overarching, national-level integration paradigms.

Moreover, the access to, and the nature of, what T. H. Marshall referred to as "social citizenship," the supports provided by the social welfare system, vary across countries in ways that do not correspond with their citizenship laws; social citizenship and political citizenship are not tightly linked. These social supports no doubt play a part in the differing outcomes among the second generation, but surprisingly little research has focused on the topic.

Scholars who study the different types of social welfare provisions available in advanced industrial countries note large differences in the types of benefits available, in the degree of universality of access to benefits and in the relationship between the market and the state. At one end of the spectrum, the United States typifies what Esping-Andersen (1999) calls the liberal welfare state, where people are responsible for their own welfare, and the state provides only for those who cannot provide for themselves. In this system, assistance is means tested, social insurance is modest and limited, and entitlement to government benefits is strictly controlled. At the other end of the spectrum are countries with a social democratic welfare state, where universalistic benefits are provided to the entire population, the state plays a strong role in redistributing income, and social equality is a strong goal. This system is most closely approximated by the Scandinavian countries. The middle group—what Esping-Andersen calls the corporatist welfare state—includes countries such as Germany, France, Italy, and Austria, where the state provides welfare benefits based on contributory social insurance. The state provides welfare benefits to all, but the levels of support vary on the basis of social class and income levels in a way that preserves status and class differences. As Freeman (2004) argues, these welfare regimes form integral parts of national political economies and no doubt influence patterns of immigrant incorporation.

Perhaps surprising to Americans, some of the same European countries that restrict citizenship rights for immigrants and later generations are very inclusive with regard to the social welfare rights of immigrants and their offspring. For instance, countries such as Germany and Switzerland that do not have histories of birthright citizenship generally confer eligibility for benefits on noncitizens. This inclusiveness stands in sharp contrast with the United States, where recent decades have seen restrictions on the eligibility of legal immigrants for welfare benefits. The 1996 Personal Responsibility and Work Opportunity Reconciliation Act, or welfare reform act, specifically targeted the eligibility of legal immigrants for welfare payments. Immigrants who entered after 1996 were made ineligible for most types of public assistance. The ban is lifted when the immigrant becomes an American citizen (a minimum of five years after entry as a legal immigrant). This law controls federal aid to legal immigrants and remains in force. Most states with large numbers of immigrants passed laws making legal immigrants eligible for assistance from the state to make up for some of the harshest consequences of the law. Illegal immigrants in the United States are eligible for almost no government aid. The only exceptions are emergency medical treatment and schooling for undocumented children through the twelfth grade. Thus, the country with the least generous social welfare system—the United States—is also the country that is most restrictive in conferring welfare benefits on immigrants and noncitizens.

Scholars have not explored the implications of these different welfare regimes and their degrees of inclusiveness for immigrant and later-generation outcomes, but some have speculated that the inclusivity and generousness of some welfare policies in Europe have fed anti-immigrant backlashes or eroded support for the welfare state itself. The national variations in access to health care, day care, safe and affordable housing, and unemployment insurance would logically have an effect on the development of second-generation children in immigrant families. It remains a topic for further research.

Key Institutions of the Receiving Society:
Schools and the Labor Market

The institutions of the receiving society—most notably, the educational system and the labor market—obviously affect the incorporation of the immigrant and second generations, but the precise features and configurations of these institutions that count most for incorporation are a continuing matter for debate.

The educational system has a powerful impact on the life chances of the second generation and of that part of the first generation that arrived during the ages of schooling. In general, the children coming from low-wage immigrant households are disadvantaged in schools when compared with the children from native homes. However, when compared with their own parents, who typically bring educational levels from their home societies well below those characterizing the host mainstream, the second generation generally makes a substantial leap forward. This conjunction has led some researchers to judge that, when native and immigrant-origin students of similar class backgrounds are compared, the immigrant-origin disadvantage disappears. However, we reject this conclusion, in part on the grounds that the educational backgrounds of native and immigrant parents, acquired in different systems, are rarely commensurate (Feliciano 2005). The degree of disadvantage that the children of immigrants face in the educational system—owing to such factors as coming from homes where languages other than the dominant tongue are in daily use, having parents who lack fundamental knowledge about the options in the educational system and their long-run significance or who are unable to help with schoolwork and may even be illiterate, or facing discrimination because of racial, religious, or immigrant origins—is significant but variable in a complex fashion. Nevertheless, the Programme for International Student Assessment (PISA) reports on the levels of school-taught skills among secondary-school students in the countries of the Organisation for Economic Co-operation and Development (OECD) make clear that the disadvantage is usually not small (e.g., OECD 2001, 2004).

Three chapters in this volume illustrate the challenges involved in any assessment of the educational advance or disadvantage of the descendants of immigrants. It can be difficult to measure the status of postimmigrant generations because national data sets often lack information on generations apart from the foreign-born. This is a problem with the U.S. Census, which in 1980 stopped asking about the birthplaces of parents, the information necessary to identify the second generation. In chapter 4, Joel Perlmann deploys a methodological innovation to address the often-feared possibility that the Mexican American second generation will assimilate "downward" and develop into an underclass. To solve the problem of measuring the characteristics of the second generation in decennial census data, Perlmann uses a proxy group, defined by individuals who arrived in the United States as very young children, before the age of three. Based on data for this group, he finds that the high-school dropout rates for the Mexican second generation are quite high but that indicators of involvement in risky behaviors—for example, incarceration rates and low sex ratios, an indication of missing men—are relatively low. Consistent with this picture, the rates of labor-force attachment are high, and consequently the earnings payoff to efforts to improve the high-school graduation rates of Mexican Americans would be substantial, according to Perlmann's calculations. The benefits to families would also be considerable because of the relatively high rate of intact families among Mexican Americans.

Chapter 5, by Richard Alba, Dalia Abdel-Hady, Tariqul Islam, and Karen Marotz, is the only chapter in this volume to examine the third generation, the grandchildren of immigrants. The authors focus on Mexican Americans, since a frequent claim is made that the educational progress of this group stalls after the second generation (e.g., Telles and Ortiz 2008). However, the generational analysis of this group is complicated by its long history of immigration to the United States, which implies that different generations at a single point in time may originate in distinct immigration streams. Hence, rather than compare second and third generations directly—the conventional approach—these authors compare each to its parents. They find that in general Mexican Americans, even in the third generation, make a substantial educational leap beyond their parents; this advance is greater on average than is its equivalent among non-Hispanic whites. However, Mexican Americans of the third generation still have lower educational attainment than do their white peers. Their educational leap implies that their second-generation parents had low educational outcomes, to which the institutional discrimination that they faced in the mid-twentieth-century United States contributed. History, in other words, matters very much for any evaluation of the Mexican American case.

In chapter 9, Tariq Modood examines an unusual case: the overrepresentation of ethnic minorities in British higher education. He shows that ethnic minorities—many of whom belong to the second generation—attend universities at higher rates, sometimes much higher rates, than do native whites. This surprising advantage cannot be accounted for by social class, although there are some class influences, but rather, he argues, by the strong ambitions that parents hold for their children and the robust ties between parents and children within communities that reinforce these ambitions. Modood argues that this explains why racial discrimination and socioeconomic disadvantage do not lead to an underrepresentation of ethnic minorities in higher education, as some scholars had predicted. Modood's argument alludes to the notion of "immigrant optimism"—that immigrant parents tend to have expectations about their children's advance that are significantly higher that those of native, working-class parents (Kao and Tienda 1995). In addition, he draws on notions of social capital to put forward the idea of "ethnic capital," which consists of relationships, norms, and norm enforcement and is posited to explain the remarkable intergenerational education mobility of many groups in Britain. Modood finds these concepts to be directly useful in the British case and ends on a hopeful note about the possibility of an inclusive Britain, which provides the opportunity for recent nonwhite immigrants and their descendants to develop a strong sense of belonging in Britain without having to disavow their ethnic identities.

Yet, in the more usual case, the disadvantages of the children of immigrants stand out, and a number of aspects of educational systems could in principle contribute to these disadvantages. Two clusters of interrelated features have been much discussed: one, the degree of internal stratification and the age at which it is imposed on students by the system; and two, the system of school financing and how it interacts with the degree of residential segregation of immigrant populations.

A contrast in the first cluster is marked by the German and U.S. systems: the German system is highly stratified, and the separation of students into different tracks begins early, after the fourth grade; the U.S. system is rather loosely stratified, with more possibilities of changing tracks, and stratification sets in gradually, becoming most formal during the high-school years. In Germany, students' trajectories diverge in the fifth year of schooling along three basic pathways: the *Gymnasium,* which ultimately prepares them for the university system; the *Realschule,* the middle track that provides training for many white-collar jobs; and the *Hauptschule,* the least demanding track that leads typically to less skilled blue-collar positions. Once students embark on these tracks, they find it difficult to change from one to another and especially to go from a lower to a higher one. The two lower tracks are also coupled with the apprenticeship system to determine the labor-market possibilities for the young people who emerge from this educational formation. In such a complex system, which imposes critical choices so early in youngsters' lives, a great deal of weight falls on the knowledge and strategizing of parents, who must guide their children and also negotiate on their behalf with representatives of the system, such as teachers. For obvious reasons, immigrant parents, especially those who have entered through a low-wage labor migration, are generally unprepared for this responsibility, at least relative to middle-class native parents.

In the United States, there is certainly tracking, which begins with ability grouping in primary school, but there is less formal separation among the tracks and greater possibility for moving upward. Indeed, tracking often takes place within school buildings rather than between them, which implies that students can shift among tracks by moving from one classroom to another. The primary manifestation of tracking has to do with the academic rigor of the classes that students take, and this can vary enormously depending on the population served by the school—it is usually lower in schools that serve poor, minority, and working-class students—but it also varies within schools. In many American high schools, the same subject is taught at various levels of difficulty, with students placed according to teacher perceptions of their abilities but also according to the students' ambitions. The strongest high-school students take academically enriched programs featuring college-level courses in at least some subjects. Counterbalancing to some extent this academic differentiation, which correlates strongly with students' social class and minority status, is the relative openness of the postsecondary system, itself strongly differentiated according to the quality or rigor of the education provided. Any student who possesses a high-school diploma—and even many of those who do not but who have earned its "equivalent" through examination (the so-called GED)—can enter some postsecondary institution and persevere to a university-level degree.

There is evidence that these structural features of educational systems make a difference for second-generation outcomes. The PISA studies reveal that average achievement differences among schools are quite large in countries such as Germany and Austria that have more formally stratified school systems. In chapter 13, Maurice Crul addresses in four national contexts—Austria, France, Germany and the Netherlands—how such institutional features affect the educational outcomes of second-generation Turks. A comparison of only educational outcomes seems in one way to favor France and the Netherlands, where the second generation goes further in school, an advantage that seems attributable to differences associated with formal stratification—for example, the later age of selection into vocational tracks in these two countries. However, early departure from school—that is, dropout before any secondary credential is earned—is also higher in France and the Netherlands, and the risk of unemployment for dropouts is very high; in Austria and Germany, by contrast, the apprenticeship system provides a stronger link to the labor market for those with limited educations, and this has favored the emergence of a large skilled blue-collar stratum in the second generation. In the end, which type of system will foster more successful integration in the long run remains unclear.

If the U.S. system is unusual for the extent to which it offers such second chances, it is also unusual for an organizational feature with much more negative implications for immigrant minorities. American schools vary considerably in quality from one location to another, and this inequality interacts with extensive residential segregation. That is, the funding of schools is heavily dependent on locally and regionally raised taxes, and this produces marked inequalities among schools in resources and in the characteristics of teachers (e.g., Orfield 2001). These inequalities impact negatively on minorities, both native and immigrant, because of residential segregation, which tends to concentrate them in places that are relatively impoverished. Generally speaking, the European systems are more uniform by comparison because they are more centrally financed. In the French system, for example, the role of the national state, both in financing and regulation, is relatively strong, and it is a matter of policy to treat schools more uniformly and to reduce the opportunities for affluent areas to provide their schools with greater resources. Moreover, the French government in 1981 put in place a policy, the ZEP (Zones of Educational Priority), to provide additional funding to schools in difficulty according to criteria that include the percentage of immigrants in the catchment area. Much more than is the case in the contemporary United States, then, France has overtly attempted to redress inequalities through the school system.

The implications of systemic differences in the way schools are funded are hard to pin down in quantitative terms. Alba and Silberman (2009) found similar magnitudes of disadvantage in educational outcomes for second-generation Mexican Americans in the United States and North Africans in France. Chapter 3, however, addresses some of the drawbacks of the U.S. system of funding. Donald Hernandez, Nancy Denton, and Suzanne Macartney investigate educational enrollment at the preschool level for three-, four-, and five-year-olds in the United States to explore racial, ethnic, and nativity differences in these beneficial programs. Despite the fact that preschool programs could be especially valuable for children from immigrant homes, these children are less likely to be enrolled than native-born children. The authors analyze the factors associated with enrollment in order to explain the immigrant-origin disadvantage. They conclude that socioeconomic differences matter more than culture and immigrant status do in explaining low prekindergarten enrollment. Especially relevant are the elevated poverty rates among many immigrant groups and the high cost of nursery school and preschool, which is not uniformly provided free of charge by the state.

The opportunities available in the labor market of the receiving society also shape strongly the pathways followed by the children of immigrants. Access to some parts of the labor market depends on the citizenship status of the second generation. Since this generation, broadly defined, can include immigrants' children born in the country of origin and brought to the receiving society at a young age, its citizenship status is mixed, depending on birthplace and the citizenship rules of the host country. Especially in the United States, it may even include individuals who are "undocumented," that is, lacking the legal right to reside and work in the host country; these individuals are probably as disadvantaged in the labor market as are undocumented immigrants who arrive as adults. Even for documented noncitizens, access to some parts of the labor market may be cut off. It is common for some civil-service positions to be restricted to citizens—in Germany, for example, the privileged class of positions covered under the term *Beamten* (officials) is generally restricted in this way. Some public-sector jobs there may be performed by noncitizens, but then the occupants typically do not have the same permanency of tenure, or the same income and privileges, as citizens in these positions.

Since the children of immigrants figure prominently among youth, their chances in the labor market are affected by overall levels of youth employment, which vary considerably among OECD countries (DiPrete et al. 2006; Quintini, Martin, and Martin 2007). Where the labor market for young people is tight, as it has been over a substantial period of time in some continental European countries with highly regulated labor markets—France and Germany, for example—native employers may prefer to reserve positions insofar as they can for young natives. In other words, members of the second generation, especially when their ethnic origin is apparent and they belong to stigmatized groups, may suffer discrimination. Roxane Silberman addresses this possibility in chapter 14, which examines the ethnic penalties and difficulties encountered by the second generation in the French labor market. While Silberman finds a great deal of educational mobility when the second generation is compared to its immigrant parents, she also finds an "ethnic penalty," particularly for Maghrebins (North Africans), that makes them less likely to be hired at every level of educational qualification. This ethnic penalty is evident in the private sector but does not apply to civil-service jobs, which suggests active discrimination by French employers. This comports with survey data of the second generation in which Maghrebins report that they perceive themselves as victims of discrimination. Silberman concludes that some of the pessimistic predictions of the segmented-assimilation model developed in the United States do apply to some groups in France, where a pattern of durable inferiorization characterizes young people and produces the conditions that ignited the 2005 riots across the country.

In chapter 6, Rosita Fibbi, Mathias Lerch, and Philippe Wanner also suggest the potential importance of discrimination. This chapter considers the full range of labor-migrant groups in Switzerland; some of these groups hail from nearby, "culturally close" countries such as France and Italy, whereas others originate in more distant countries such as Turkey. The authors find complex patterns of educational attainment and employment by country of origin, generational position, gender, and other factors, but several findings stand out. One is that length of residence, both of the individual's family and of the group itself, affects socioeconomic position, but in general the children of immigrants do not do as well as the native Swiss of the same age. When it comes to educational attainment, which in a common Swiss view accounts for second-generation disadvantage in the labor market, the culturally close groups do not necessarily outperform the culturally distant ones, despite prevailing stereotypes. In the labor market, the children of all the immigrant groups suffer from a higher risk of unemployment compared to native Swiss, even when they hold Swiss citizenship. But unemployment hits the second generation from the culturally distant groups especially hard, and this finding makes plausible the notion of discrimination.

A common argument holds that, because of discrimination in the mainstream labor market, the second generation may benefit from any control over economic niches exercised by members of their ethnic group. The extent of these benefits of immigrant-origin social capital has proven very hard to measure. Some niches arise from a group's entrepreneurial activities. One case, close to an ideal one, is that of the Cubans of Miami, who have established firms that dominate a number of economic sectors in the South Florida economy (Portes and Stepick 1994). These firms employ many Cubans; however, the degree of benefit to the second generation, as opposed to the immigrant one, is unclear. In any event, very few immigrant groups come close to the Cuban case, and most immigrant enterprise involves small businesses with few employees and even fewer who are well paid.

The children of immigrants may also have favored access to jobs that are effectively controlled by coethnics, frequently older relatives, who are already employed. This phenomenon has been frequently described for the immigrant generation: in the United States, many employers of low-wage immigrants prefer to hire individuals who are sponsored by their current employees than to open positions to all comers (Waldinger and Lichter 2003). The extent to which a similar phenomenon holds for the second generation is unknown; but given the degree of ethnic clustering by economic sectors in local labor markets, it seems likely to happen to some extent (Waldinger 1996).

Limiting the impact of immigrant-group social capital, however, is the fact that, as a rule, the second generation strives to avoid immigrant jobs. In chapter 11, Philip Kasinitz, Noriko Matsumoto, and Aviva Zeltzer-Zubida use survey data from the New York Second Generation Study to examine the occupation, industry, and income outcomes of young adults whose parents were immigrants from the Dominican Republic; the Anglophone West Indies; the South American countries of Colombia, Ecuador, and Peru; China; and Russia. They find that all these groups, with the partial exception of Dominican men, are quickly moving into the mainstream economy and away from immigrants' concentrations in ethnic niches. They also find that this move makes sense economically, as the incomes of those who do remain in ethnic jobs and firms are much lower than of those who move into more mainstream occupations and industries. These second-generation groups look more like other New Yorkers their age than they do like their immigrant parents, suggesting that a model of straight-line assimilation fits the experience of the second generation in New York better than does a model of continued reliance on an ethnic economy.

Chapter 8, by Frank Kalter, is one of several here that suggest the equivocal role of immigrant-group social capital in western Europe. The motivating question is, what explains the disadvantages of second-generation Turks in the German labor market? The lower occupational placement of other second-generation groups in Germany, such as Italians and Spaniards, is explained once their educational qualifications are taken into account, but this is not true of Turks. The temptation is to explain this ethnic disadvantage by discrimination, but Kalter examines other possibilities also. Using data from the German Socio-Economic Panel (GSEOP), he finds that the disadvantage is associated with having mainly or exclusively Turkish friends. Although the relatively low social assimilation of second-generation Turks directly explains their labor-market disadvantages, the hypothesis that the low assimilation in turn is explained by discrimination cannot be ruled out.

In any event, the research demonstrates that the possession of ethnic social capital is not an advantage for the Turkish group.

That ethnic social capital has potential downsides also emerges as a conclusion from Karen Phalet and Anthony Heath's chapter 7, on second-generation Turks in Belgium. The authors compare the Turkish group to Belgian natives and to Italians and Moroccans, two other important second-generation populations. Compared to natives, all the second-generation groups appear disadvantaged, but the Italians are least so and the Turks are most, whether disadvantage is measured by attaining some postsecondary education, finding employment, or entering the salariat. The results for self-employment are not clear-cut, however. An analysis of regional differences in opportunity indicates, somewhat surprisingly, that second-generation Turks are best off in the Brussels region. The authors observe in their conclusion that the Turks appear to have invested to an unusual degree in ethnic social capital, but it has brought them little or no advantage in the Belgian labor market.

Despite the existence of ethnic economic enclaves and occupational niches, then, the best opportunities for the great majority of the second generation probably lie in the mainstream labor market, and accessing these opportunities generally requires appropriate educational credentials, preferably involving some degree of postsecondary training. Postsecondary training should not be equated solely with university education, for the evidence in some of the chapters of this volume suggests that postsecondary vocational tracks, including the apprenticeships for which Germany is well known, produce good outcomes for some groups, especially the second generations from labor immigrations. As the chapters in this book demonstrate, the upwardly aspiring second-generation members of such groups as Turks in Europe and Mexicans in the United States are unlikely to derive much benefit from coethnic concentrations in the labor market, because in general these footholds are in modest jobs. This statement of the problem brings us back to challenging questions about how the second generation fares in the educational system.

Local Contexts

By definition, international migration involves moves across national boundaries. But immigrants live their lives in local neighborhoods, cities, and other places with their own institutional arrangements, amenities, and cultures. These can have an enormous influence on young people, and they can also vary a great deal within any given country. In the United States, the early theories developed to understand immigrant assimilation developed from studies of specific cities. The Chicago school of sociology took as one of its main subjects the immigrant experience in that city. With the publication in 1918 of *The Polish Peasant in Europe and America*, by William I. Thomas and Florian Znaniecki, a new urban-focused agenda for sociology was set. The influence of these early sociologists is seen in the extensive research that stressed the role of the city and spatial dynamics in the experience of European immigrants to the United States (Lieberson 1963, 1980).

This research tradition has continued into the current era, exemplified in the studies of established gateway regions such as Los Angeles and New York (Kasinitz et al. 2008). In chapter 10, by comparing such gateways in Canada and the United States, Jeffrey Reitz and Ye Zhang make a strong case that local contexts are critical for assessing the experience of the second generation. They contrast the educational attainments of second-generation Chinese and blacks with the attainments of both the parental immigrant generation and native-born whites. Their overall optimistic assessment is that the economic disadvantages of the parental generation have not prevented substantial educational mobility for the second generation. But they also show that national-level comparisons overestimate the relative educational advantages and mobility for the second generation. This is because immigrants and the second generation are concentrated in global cities—cities that have experienced a great deal of immigration but also cities where natives tend to have higher educational attainments than natives in the nation as a whole. Reitz and Zhang find that although both Chinese and blacks in the two countries show higher educational mobility across generations than do the native-born, when their attainments are examined within the urban context, their relative educational attainments—compared to the native population— are not as high. They argue that rather than assimilating into a broad "native mainstream," the second generation is assimilating into an urban context— one with relatively high levels of income and educational polarization and with high levels of native-born educational attainment.

Recent demographic shifts in the United States mean that studies of the established gateway regions no longer capture the complete picture of the immigrant experience. Although the majority of immigrants still settle in these regions, since the 1990s appreciable numbers have settled in the South and rural Midwest, in places that have had little recent experience with immigration. A small but growing body of social-scientific literature examines the immigrant experience in these new gateways (Massey, Durand, and Malone 2002; Singer 2004; Zúñiga and Hernández-León 2005).

A key difference between new gateways and more established ones lies in the institutional arrangements that influence the immigrant experience. Established gateways have numerous institutions set up to aid immigrants, including legal-aid bureaus, health clinics, social clubs, and bilingual services. Previous waves of immigrants have necessitated the establishment of these institutions, and immigrants who arrive today continue to benefit from them. For instance, ethnographies conducted for the New York Second Generation Study found that West Indian workers have stepped easily into a union founded by Jewish immigrants and recently run by African Americans (Foerster 2004). Ecuadoran, Peruvian, Colombian, and Dominican immigrants and their children have taken advantage of educational programs originally devised for New York City's Puerto Rican population (Trillo 2004). And the city's large Russian-immigrant community has benefited greatly from the organizations founded by the Jewish immigrants who arrived in New York a century earlier (Zeltzer-Zubida 2004). Indeed, Kasinitz et al. (2008) argue that the legacy of the civil rights movement and of New York City's history as an immigrant-absorbing community have significantly and positively affected the ability of current immigrants almost immediately to feel included and to consider themselves New Yorkers. New gateways, in contrast, may lack the institutional arrangements such as bilingual services designed to serve the immigrant population, precisely because there has been no need for such arrangements until recently. The same is true for suburbs, which have become an important location of immigrant settlement (Alba, Logan, and Stults 2000).

The local context is very important for second-generation outcomes. Cities, suburbs, and rural areas all vary in the size of the immigrant populations, the numbers of coethnics the second generation grows up with, local policies toward immigrants, and the availability of public facilities such as libraries, good schools, language programs, and sports programs (Kasinitz et al. 2008). They also differ importantly in the other minorities they contain, an issue that is addressed by Nancy Foner in chapter 12, comparing second-generation Afro-Caribbeans in London and New York. This comparison invokes an issue that is also raised by Reitz and Zhang: the role of a large African-descent native population in shaping the experience of black immigrants. Reitz and Zhang find no support for a segmented-assimilation claim that the presence of African Americans in the United States poses a particular liability for black immigrants in the United States that they do not face in Canada. Foner explores this question in depth by contrasting the experience of second-generation Afro-Caribbeans in London and New York. She argues that the large African American population in New York, along with the high levels of racial segregation in the city, especially when contrasted with the high levels of racial integration in London, lead to a very important contextual difference in the very meaning of assimilation. The presence of a large black population in New York makes becoming American both easier for second-generation Afro-Caribbeans and more problematic. It is easier because being American and being black make for an easy identity to access and understand—the two identities are historically fused in the experience of African Americans. Yet to become African American is also to inherit the costs (as well as the post-civil-rights benefits) of racial distance and inequality. In Britain, the easy friendships, intermarriages, and close connections between the second generation and whites do not necessarily translate into an easy way to be both British and black—an English or British identity is often seen as exclusive to whites.

Local context is also quite variable in Europe, as a number of scholars have argued (Ireland 1994; Body-Gendrot and Martinello 2000; Crul and Vermeulen 2003). This can be because of different labor markets, concentrations of coethnics, or what Ireland (1994) calls different "caring strategies" that vary in how much they emphasize individuals versus groups or in their degrees of inclusiveness. Because the vast majority of immigrants to western Europe settle in cities, research on immigrants and the second generation has had an urban focus there, much as it has in the United States. In chapter 7, Karen Phalet and Anthony Heath examine differences in education and occupation among the Turkish second generation in the urban area of Brussels and outlying areas in both the French-speaking and Dutch-speaking regions of Belgium. They find that the Turkish second generation is doing best in the metropolitan area of Brussels, not in the outlying areas. The major study of the second generation in Europe—the TIES study (Integration of the European Second Generation)—is city based and takes advantage of both national variation and variation between cities in the same national context, yet there is still much work to do to investigate the role of local context in second-generation outcomes.

In both North America and western Europe, our knowledge of second-generation outcomes depends heavily on national-level census and survey data. Yet, in the United States, the three most in-depth investigations of the children of immigrants—the Children of Immigrants Longitudinal Study, the New York Second Generation Study, and the Los Angeles IMMLA study—are all city based, exploring the outcomes of children of immigrants in Miami, San Diego, New York, and Los Angeles (e.g., Portes and Rumbaut

2001; Kasinitz et al. 2008). Chapter 11, by Kasinitz, Matsumoto, and Zeltzer-Zubida, and chapter 2, by Brown, Bean, Leach, and Rumbaut, use some of these data. However, we lack equivalent data for the new areas of reception. The most ambitious study of the second generation in Europe, TIES, is based in fifteen cities in eight countries (Paris and Strasburg in France, Berlin and Frankfurt in Germany, Madrid and Barcelona in Spain, Vienna and Linz in Austria, Amsterdam and Rotterdam in the Netherlands, Brussels and Antwerp in Belgium, Zurich and Basel in Switzerland, and Stockholm in Sweden) (Crul and Schneider 2007). The findings from this study are just starting to appear.

Conclusion

The complex picture of the integration of the second generation in Europe and the United States that emerges from studies of the second generation does not point to an easy answer to the question of how best to integrate the children of immigrants. There is no country that is an unqualified success story, and yet the fears of widespread second-generation decline that motivated a number of studies in the United States in the 1990s are also not supported by this careful research. Instead, what emerges is a number of important factors that can improve the odds for the second generation and a number of areas that require further research.

The children of labor migrants and refugees, whose parents have low levels of education and other human capital, are at greatest risk across a number of these societies. Institutional arrangements that prevent citizenship rights for parents and children clearly have negative effects that last into adulthood, as Brown et al. and Fibbi et al. make clear in their chapters.

Educational systems that sort children early and that are more rigidly tracked, with fewer second chances, would also seem to disadvantage young people from immigrant backgrounds. Discrimination is present in a variety of national contexts, and while theories coming out of the United States relate that discrimination to the long racial history of that country, European studies show that discrimination does not need that history to become entrenched.

Yet the focus on the major impediments to integration that the second generation faces should not blind us to the social mobility that many of these young people have experienced, especially if we measure this mobility against the starting point of their parents' positions. Across all these case studies we see generational progress for the children of immigrants, a finding that immigrants themselves often use to judge whether they made the right decision in immigrating.

We have assembled this volume in order to encourage more of a comparative approach to second-generation incorporation, an approach that, at a minimum, allows the researchers operating within one society to see whether incorporation is more successful somewhere else and to theorize why that might be the case. Several of the chapters in this volume, grouped in the final section, demonstrate the power of the conclusions that can be reached when cross-national comparisons are closely calibrated. Chapters 12 and 13, by Nancy Foner and Maurice Crul, reveal what can be achieved when the same, or very similar, groups are compared in different contexts. The strength of such comparisons does not derive, of course, simply from the happenstance that the same group immigrates to different countries: the comparison must also be guided by a sufficiently precise focus if it is to arrive at solid conclusions—for example, the presence or absence of a disadvantaged native minority to serve as a proximal host for an immigrant group (Foner) or the structure of the educational system and its linkage to the labor market (Crul). But rigorous comparison may even be possible when there is no group common to multiple contexts. Chapter 14, by Roxane Silberman, illustrates an alternative mode of comparison—namely, when a theoretical model developed in one context (segmented assimilation) can be compared in detail to the processes and their outcomes that are observed in another context. Silberman's analysis shows how the model can illuminate otherwise puzzling divergences between Maghrebins and other second-generation populations in France and how the model itself can be refined by the comparison, which can help to identify those features of it that are specific to the national context where it originated and thus to suggest ways of making it more general.

We believe that systematic cross-national research on these issues is the best way to make progress in developing theories and models to explain the patterns of immigrant and second-generation integration. These comparisons are often difficult because of data-comparability problems and definitional differences across countries. Yet the promise for social scientists to understand this complex phenomenon means that it is worth the considerable effort involved. We will judge this volume to be successful if it inspires more students of immigration to look beyond their home societies in search of a deeper understanding of the forces that shape the integration of the children of immigrants.

I

Starting Points

2

Legalization and Naturalization Trajectories among Mexican Immigrants and Their Implications for the Second Generation

Susan K. Brown, Frank D. Bean, Mark A. Leach, and Rubén G. Rumbaut

Discussions over the past four decades about reforming immigration law in the United States seem inevitably to swing to the issue of migration from Mexico. No other national group provides more immigrants to the United States, both legal and unauthorized. As of 2008, Mexican immigrants numbered 12.8 million, or about 32 percent of all immigrants (Pew Hispanic Center 2009). In 2008, 13.7 percent of all the people granted the status of legal permanent residency (LPR) were Mexican (Office of Immigration Statistics 2008). Starting in 2005, annual inflows of unauthorized Mexicans began to fall, and the total unauthorized population from Mexico has leveled off at roughly about 7 million (Passel and Cohn 2008). Moreover, even as the public discourse in recent decades about unauthorized immigration from Mexico has grown more polemical and heated (Chavez 2008), many analysts and policymakers have repeatedly argued that laws and policies to control such migration must precede any other changes in legal immigration policy (U.S. Commission on Immigration Reform 1994).

At the same time, other analysts question whether Mexican immigrants show the potential for social and economic integration. Most of them possess neither much money nor education; despite their work orientation (Van Hook and Bean 2009), pessimistic observers conclude that their chances of joining the American mainstream are dim (Camarota 2001; Hanson 2003). However, such inferences often depend on the assumption that the children of Mexican immigrants, and maybe their children's children, will face similar socioeconomic disadvantages and may actually prefer to sustain a separate culture (see Bean, Brown, and Rumbaut 2006; Chavez 2008). But because persons of Mexican descent may change across generations, an adequate assessment of Mexican incorporation must examine the outcomes not only of the immigrants themselves but also of the second generation. This chapter focuses on how shifts in the legal status of Mexican immigrant parents, both mothers and fathers, relate to their children's acquisition of human capital, occupation, and earnings. The parents' trajectories hint at the speed with which different segments of the Mexican immigrant group may join the economic mainstream and show how pathways to legalization and citizenship (or their absence) may enhance (or delay) progress among their children.

The data for this assessment come from a research project that focused on the children of immigrants in metropolitan Los Angeles. More than any other U.S. city, metropolitan Los Angeles has been a receiving center for Mexicans for generations (Grebler, Moore, and Guzmán 1970). In addition to its sheer size—17.8 million people as of 2008—it is one of the two major immigrant gateways in the United States. Nearly a third of Los Angeles's population is foreign-born, and nearly two-thirds of this group comes from Latin America (U.S. Bureau of the Census 2006a). It is now home to nearly 6 million persons of Mexican origin. Moreover, it has long been the major urban destination of *unauthorized* Mexican entrants (Bean, Passel, and Edmonston 1990). Consequently, California was the state in which the most people legalized their migration status when given the chance through the 1986 Immigration Reform and Control Act (IRCA) (González Baker 1997). Los Angeles is thus the best place in the country to study how changes in the legal and citizenship status of Mexican migrants affect their children.

How Legalization and Citizenship Foster Incorporation

Unquestionably, immigrants benefit from becoming legal permanent residents. Legalization entitles immigrants to a "green card," the document required for legal employment, and provides access to greater legal protection, financial services, and travel. Indirectly, legalization can help ensure stable working conditions and accumulation of the kind of job experience that boosts wages and provides entrée to work through means other than social contacts (Aguilera and Massey 2003; Massey 1987). As a consequence, legal immigrants are likely to be subjected to much less exploitation in the labor market than the unauthorized are. Gaining legal status thus represents a crucial marker for immigrant incorporation. By extension, it should also matter for the well-being of the children of immigrants.

While the benefits of naturalization also are numerous, so, too, are the requirements for citizenship. In the United States, LPRs who wish to naturalize must be adults and must be U.S. residents for at least five years. They must demonstrate their ability to speak, read, and write English; their knowledge of U.S. government and history; and their good character (felons are ineligible). They must pay a fee to naturalize. Those who do naturalize tend to become invested in the U.S. economy (e.g., through home ownership or self-employment) and tend to be less likely to emigrate, because their countries of origin are far away, poor, or largely illiterate (Barkan and Khokhlov 1980; Beijbom 1971; Bernard 1936; Jasso and Rosenzweig 1986; Yang 1994). Those who naturalize are more likely to be parents and to be women (Jasso and Rosenzweig 1986; Liang 1994; Yang 1994).

Two complementary views about the foundations of citizenship highlight its benefits. In one perspective, citizenship is viewed primarily in political-economic terms (Ong 1999), with an emphasis on citizens being eligible to vote and hold certain restricted jobs (Aleinikoff 2001). Those who become citizens can expect to participate in elections, to pursue new job possibilities, and to become eligible to sponsor relatives for immigration or to apply for greater public assistance. In return, they are assumed to embrace largely uniform national identifications (Aleinikoff 2003; Schuck 1998). The other perspective emphasizes multiple kinds of citizenship and often transnationalist forces that might eventually dim the relevance of single-nation citizenship altogether (e.g., Bauböck 1994; Bloemraad 2006; Carens 1987; Feldblum 2000; Jacobson 1996; Soysal 1994). Such approaches also note the growth of dual citizenship (Basch, Glick Schiller, and Szanton Blanc 1994; Gilbertson and Singer 2003; Ong 1999; Portes, Guarnizo, and Landolt 1999) and emphasize social and contextual, material and symbolic benefits of naturalization (Liang 1994; Morawska 2001, 2003; Van Hook, Brown, and Bean 2006). Bloemraad (2004, 2006) and Van Hook, Brown, and Bean (2006) note that the tangible and intangible support provided to newcomers from social, institutional, and state sources helps to shape immigrant contexts of reception (Portes and Rumbaut 2001; Reitz 2003) and influences how welcome immigrants feel at arrival, how much settlement help they receive, and how much assistance they can draw on when learning the skills required for naturalization (e.g., knowledge of civics and English).

Parents' legalization and naturalization may increase their children's economic well-being both directly and indirectly. A positive direct effect could occur for those foreign-born minor children who gained legal status when their parents did. Conversely, parents who remain unauthorized would not have provided their immigrant children the means to become authorized. For the 1.5 generation (those coming to the United States at or before age fourteen) and the native-born children of immigrants, a portion of the differences we observe in our research between those whose parents legalized and those whose parents did not in all likelihood derives from the handicaps facing 1.5-generation children who stay unauthorized when they become adults. Future research is needed to determine the magnitude of this effect. But indirect effects are also likely. Lack of legal status constrains parents' occupational and earnings opportunities. The stratification literature has documented repeatedly the benefits of greater parental income and higher occupational status on children's education (see Breen and Jonsson 2005 for a review). Thus, regardless of the children's nativity, we would expect adults whose parents had legalized and naturalized to enjoy higher economic well-being on account of this factor alone.

As a result, we predict that when immigrant parents become legal permanent residents and naturalized citizens, this will generate improvements in the life situations of their children, including likely enhancements in human-capital attainment and economic well-being. And both parents' experiences should matter for mobility (Beller 2009; Kalmijn 1994), although mother's versus father's status may carry different implications for children's outcomes. Because the migration process varies by gender (Harzig 2006; Hondagneu-Sotelo 1994), particularly for laborers from Mexico, mothers and fathers often have different reasons for migrating and differential opportunities for legalizing their status. Solo male migrants who legalize can apply for spouses to come from Mexico, so that some wives may enter the United States legally even though their husbands were initially unauthorized. Also, wives who enter without authorization may have more trouble gathering the paperwork often necessary for legalization, such as employment records or utility or rental receipts that show continuous residence, especially if the women work in domestic labor or move into households where the records are kept only in the man's name (González Baker 1997). Such considerations suggest that the father's legal status and citizenship may have a greater effect than the mother's status on the acquisition of human capital in the second generation. Alternatively, given the greater involvement of mothers in child socialization (Matthews 1987)—especially Mexican immigrant mothers, whose sex-role attitudes may often be traditional (Ortiz and Cooney 1985)—the mother's status may matter more. Because we have no theoretical basis for predicting which of these kinds of influence might predominate, we treat this matter as an empirical question.

Data and Approach

The data we examine come from a telephone survey called the Immigration and Intergenerational Mobility in Metropolitan Los Angeles (IIMMLA) study, which was supported by a grant from the Russell Sage Foundation (Rumbaut et al. 2004). Conducted in 2004, the research targeted the young-adult children of immigrants from large immigrant groups in Los Angeles and obtained information from 4,780 persons ages twenty to forty who had at least one immigrant parent. Because of the centrality of the Mexican-origin group to the immigrant experience in Los Angeles, the sample was designed to be a random probability sample of all Mexican-origin persons (whatever their generational status) residing in households with telephones in the greater five-county metropolitan region. The size of the Mexican sample of the 1.5 and second generations (children of immigrants who were either born in the United States or came by age fifteen) was 935, of whom not quite 10 percent reported one parent from Mexico and one from either Guatemala or El Salvador. The survey obtained information on parents' migration status, both at the time of their entry into the United States and at the time of the IIMMLA interview. We also collected data on whether the parents had naturalized.

Because respondents may have had only one immigrant parent, it is important to note that the generational status of the parents may differ. In a few cases, mothers were foreign-born but fathers were native-born, or vice versa, meaning that one parent could not have experienced legalization or naturalization. Because respondents with one native-born parent nonetheless constitute a meaningful comparison group, we include them here in a separate category; they provide a useful benchmark for children's economic attainment. We thus examine six nativity/migration status/naturalization trajectories for the mothers and fathers of the IIMMLA 1.5- and second-generation respondents of Mexican origin. These trajectories, applied separately to fathers and mothers, are (1) *Native-Born*: parent is native-born; (2) *Authorized/Citizen*: parent is authorized at entry and later naturalized; (3) *Authorized/Authorized*: parent is authorized at entry and not naturalized by the time of the interview; (4) *Unauthorized/Citizen*: parent is unauthorized at entry and naturalized by the time of the interview; (5) *Unauthorized/Authorized*: parent is unauthorized at entry, obtained legal permanent residency, but is not naturalized at the time of the interview; and (6) *Unauthorized/Unauthorized*: parent is unauthorized at both entry and time of the interview.

Findings

Before examining how pathways to legalization and citizenship among unauthorized immigrants influence children's outcomes, we note first that calculating the proportion of respondents whose parents came as unauthorized entrants depends on the number of parents who in fact were immigrants. Roughly 10 percent of the fathers and the mothers were born in the United States and thus could *not* have been immigrants, although their children qualify as 1.5 or second generation because of the immigrant status of the other parent. In addition, 119 fathers and 81 mothers remained in the home country, a group constituting 12.7 percent of the fathers and 8.7 percent of the mothers in the sample (see table 2.1). We omit both these groups in calculating fractions of 1.5- and second-generation persons with unauthorized fathers and mothers. But what about the sixty fathers and nine mothers whose status was unknown (because the respondent either did not know that parent or that parent's migration status at entry)? These parents could in fact have migrated to the United States. In recognition of this uncertainty, we calculate two percentages of persons with unauthorized parents—one assuming that these parents were unauthorized and the second assuming they were not. We also calculate these percentages a third way, namely, by *not* including this group of sixty fathers and nine mothers at all. The three resulting sets of percentages are shown in the first six rows of table 2.2. They reveal that a little less than half of the 1.5- and second-generation respondents' fathers came to the United States as unauthorized migrants (about 46 percent in the case of the middle estimate), meaning also that slightly more than half came as legal entrants. Among the mothers, the percentage who came as unauthorized migrants is nearly as high as for the fathers (roughly 43 percent). These estimates are reasonably close to previous ones for the fraction of unauthorized entrants from Mexico eventually settling in California during the '50s, '60s and '70s (Bean, Passel, and Edmonston 1990).

By the time of the IIMMLA interviews, most of the unauthorized fathers had become legalized permanent residents. Specifically, only about 5 to 14 percent of the fathers remained unauthorized. Among mothers, about 5 to 6 percent remained unauthorized. If we assume the level of the middle estimate for the percentage that legalized, this would mean that nearly nine of every ten parents who were unauthorized entrants had attained legal status by 2004. Overall, it would mean that about nineteen of every twenty *known* entrants were either legal or had attained legal permanent resident status by the time of the interview. This very high percentage of legal fathers and

TABLE 2.1

Entry Status and Citizenship Trajectories Among Fathers and Mothers of 1.5 and 2nd Generation Respondents of Mexican Origin

	All		Those with foreign-born fathers		Those with foreign-born fathers and known migration status		Those with foreign-born fathers who may have migrated to United States		Those whose foreign-born fathers were known to have migrated	
	N	%	N	%	N	%	N	%	N	%
					Distribution by father's status					
Status unknown[a]	60	6.4	60	7.1	--	--	60	8.3	--	--
Never lived in United States	119	12.7	119	14.1	119	15.2	--	--	--	--
Not foreign-born	93	9.9	--	--	--	--	--	--	--	--
Authorized / naturalized	239	25.6	239	28.4	239	30.6	239	33.1	239	36.0
Authorized /authorized	118	12.6	118	14.0	118	15.1	118	16.3	118	17.8
Unauthorized / naturalized	152	16.3	152	18.1	152	19.4	152	21.0	152	22.9
Unauthorized / authorized	114	12.2	114	13.5	114	14.6	114	15.8	114	17.2
Unauthorized / unauthorized	40	4.3	40	4.8	40	5.1	40	5.5	40	6.0
Total for Fathers	935	100	842	100	782	100	723	100	663	100
					Distribution by mother's status					
Status unknown[a]	9	1.0	9	1.1	--	--	9	1.2	--	--
Never lived in United States	81	8.7	81	9.7	81	9.8	--	--	--	--
Not foreign-born	98	10.5	--	--	--	--	--	--	--	--
Authorized / naturalized	300	32.1	300	35.8	300	36.2	300	39.7	300	40.2
Authorized / authorized	128	13.7	128	15.3	128	15.5	128	16.9	128	17.1
Unauthorized / naturalized	138	14.8	138	16.5	138	16.7	138	18.3	138	18.5
Unauthorized / authorized	142	15.2	142	17.0	142	17.1	142	18.8	142	19.0
Unauthorized / unauthorized	39	4.2	39	4.7	39	4.7	39	5.2	39	5.2
Total for mothers	935	100	837	100	828	100	756	100	747	100

a. Did not know parent or parent's status

TABLE 2.2

Migration Status at Entry and Interview Among Parents of 1.5 and 2nd Generation Respondents of Mexican Origin

	Fathers %	Mothers %
	50.6 [a]	43.4[a]
Percent Entering Unauthorized	42.3[b]	42.2[b]
	46.2[c]	42.7[c]
	13.8[a]	6.3[a]
Percent Unauthorized at Interview	5.5[b]	5.2[b]
	6.0[c]	5.2[c]
Percent Legalizing of Entrants with Known Status	94.0	94.8
Percent Naturalizing of Known Legal Entrants	66.9	70.1
Percent Naturalizing of Known Unauthorized Entrants	49.7	43.3
Percent Naturalizing of All Known Eligible	62.8	61.9

a. Assumes those parents with unknown status were all unauthorized.
b. Assumes those parents with unknown status were all authorized.
c. Only for parents with known entry status.

TABLE 2.3

Indicators of Economic and Social Attainment by Fathers' and Mothers' Legal Statuses at Entry and Time of Interview, 1.5 and 2nd Generation Mexican-Origin Respondents

	Fathers' statuses	Mothers' statuses
RESPONDENTS' EDUCATION		
Percent with less than high school diploma		
Not foreign-born	11.8	15.3
Authorized at entry	13.2	14.0
Unauthorized / authorized	16.9	15.0
Unauthorized / unauthorized	22.5	35.9
Status unknown	26.7	11.1
Never lived in United States	37.0	49.4
Percent with bachelor's degree or higher		
Not foreign-born	19.4	8.2
Authorized at entry	16.2	19.2
Unauthorized / authorized	17.3	15.7
Unauthorized / unauthorized	10.0	0.0
Status unknown	8.3	0.0
Never lived in United States	8.4	8.6
Average years of education		
Not foreign-born	13.5	12.7
Authorized at entry	13.2	13.4
Unauthorized / authorized	13.2	13.2
Unauthorized / unauthorized	13.0	11.4
Status unknown	12.4	13.0
Never lived in United States	11.8	10.9

TABLE 2.3 (CONTINUED)

	Fathers' statuses	Mothers' statuses
Percent of respondents preferring to speak English at home		
Not foreign-born	71.0	80.6
Authorized at entry	65.5	62.9
Unauthorized / authorized	50.8	46.1
Unauthorized / unauthorized	45.0	28.2
Status unknown	41.7	66.7
Never lived in United States	32.8	28.4
Respondents' average occupational socioeconomic prestige		
Not foreign-born	40.4	42.4
Authorized at entry	42.3	41.9
Unauthorized / authorized	41.3	41.4
Unauthorized / unauthorized	38.5	34.0
Status unknown	39.6	42.6
Never lived in United States	38.8	36.9
Respondents' average annual personal income		
Not foreign-born	$23,194	$25,847
Authorized at entry	23,847	23,466
Unauthorized / authorized	22,105	20,014
Unauthorized / unauthorized	16,988	14,218
Status unknown	19,567	16,056
Never lived in United States	17,395	19,685

mothers among the children of Mexican immigrants in Los Angeles testifies to the legalization pathways provided by the 1986 Immigration Reform and Control Act (IRCA) (Bean, Vernez, and Keely 1989), as well as to the legislation's effectiveness and the successful implementation of the law's legalization provisions (González Baker 1990).

Given the widely used provisions for legalization in IRCA, how does legalization among immigrant parents relate to the human-capital attainments of their young-adult children? Table 2.3 shows that those respondents whose fathers legalized are about 25 percent *less* likely to drop out of high school (16.9 percent versus 22.5 percent) and about 70 percent *more* likely to graduate from college. Similarly, they are nearly 13 percent more likely to prefer speaking English at home, they work in jobs with about 7 percent higher occupational prestige,[1] and they report earnings that are about 30 percent higher than those whose fathers did not legalize. Thus, in general, having a father who both had the opportunity to legalize and did so appears to confer appreciable economic benefits on the 1.5- and second-generation children of Mexican immigrants who entered the country with an unauthorized status. Because the legalization and citizenship trajectories involve combinations of transition points, we consider the entire set of trajectories together in conducting tests for statistical significance. All results are statistically significant.

The results for mothers are generally similar, if not more pronounced. When the mother remains unauthorized, her children acquire less human capital than when the father remains unauthorized. Almost 36 percent of those with mothers who remained unauthorized never received a high-school diploma, and none received a college degree. The occupational prestige of respondents' jobs is about one-eighth lower when their mothers remained unauthorized than when fathers did, and their annual income is more than twenty-five hundred dollars lower. Only 28 percent of respondents whose mothers remained unauthorized prefer to speak English at home, compared with 45 percent of those whose fathers remained unauthorized. This finding tends to support the socialization perspective, that the offspring of the minority of mothers who do not legalize their status have inherited some of the disadvantages carried by their mothers and that mothers' role in the socialization of children may have even more effect than fathers'.

Do additional benefits accrue from naturalizing, either among those whose fathers and mothers entered legally or among those whose fathers and mothers were unauthorized entrants who legalized and also went on to become naturalized citizens? Of the former group, more than two-thirds (66.9 percent of fathers and 70.1 percent of mothers) had naturalized by the time of the interview (table 2.2). Of the parents known to be unauthorized entrants, about half of the fathers (49.7 percent) and slightly less than half of the mothers (43.3 percent) had naturalized. Thus, by some twenty to thirty-five years after most of our respondents' fathers and mothers came to the country, about three-fifths of the mothers and fathers had become citizens, including many who started out as unauthorized entrants. Again, it is worth noting that most of these parents qualified for legalization and citizenship by virtue of the legalization programs of IRCA, which created two major pathways to legalization for unauthorized migrants in the country at that time (Bean, Vernez, and Keely 1989). Most of the parents migrated to the United States during an era when almost all of them would have been eligible for one or the other program. Although we did not obtain data on whether our respondents' parents in fact became legal through IRCA's programs, about three-fourths of the unauthorized Mexican immigrants estimated to be in the country during the 1980s legalized as a result of IRCA (Bean, Passel, and Edmonston 1990; Massey, Durand, and Malone 2002).

Examining the experiences of the children of immigrants in the Los Angeles sample thus provides a useful illustration of what might occur among unauthorized Mexican immigrants and their children if new legalization programs and pathways to citizenship are adopted. The IIMMLA data indicate that the legalization and citizenship trajectories of those coming illegally are importantly related to children's outcomes (table 2.4). These patterns hold up even when we control for the effects of parents' education and respondents' age, both of which could affect the outcomes. Thus, we note that when parents who were initially unauthorized *changed* their legal status, and particularly when they also became naturalized citizens, this pathway is related to a substantially reduced likelihood of educational failure among their children. For example, 57 percent *fewer* such children (those whose fathers entered unauthorized but went on to legalize and then eventually to naturalize) failed to finish high school than in the case of children whose fathers stayed unauthorized (13.7 percent versus 31.5 percent for those whose fathers remained unauthorized; see table 2.4). In the case of finishing college, the children of unauthorized fathers who eventually naturalized graduated from college at twice the rate of children whose fathers remained unauthorized (19.5 percent for the former versus 9.8 percent for the latter). The gaps are even wider for the children of mothers who changed status versus those who did not.

To be sure, the number of children going on to college in these cases is not inordinately high. Nonetheless, migration status and citizenship trajectories clearly matter, as indicated by the fact that sizable premiums attach to occupational prestige, income, and the tendency to speak English among the children of parents who took advantage of the opportunity to legalize and naturalize, compared to those who remained unauthorized. For example, the premium that obtains in the case of mothers is almost 13 percent for occupational prestige, about 25 percent for income, and about 45 percent for speaking English (table 2.4). To be more specific in the case of income, those whose fathers entered as unauthorized migrants but then went on to legalize (most probably as a result of IRCA, as noted earlier), as well as to become naturalized citizens, reported an adjusted average annual income of $23,564 in 2004. Those who had fathers, however, who entered illegally but then *stayed* unauthorized (i.e., were still unauthorized at the time of the IIMMLA interview in 2004) reported adjusted annual incomes that averaged only $17,244. In other words, the former group made $6,320 more than the latter, or 37 percent *higher* annual incomes, a considerable income premium for legalization and naturalization. The premium for those whose mothers legalized and naturalized versus those whose mothers remained unauthorized is only slightly less, $4,510, or 25 percent.

TABLE 2.4

Indicators of Economic and Social Attainment by Fathers' and Mothers' Legal Statuses at Entry and Time of Interview, With Adjustments, 1.5 and 2nd Generation Mexican-Origin Respondents

	Fathers' status		Mothers' status	
	Unadjusted	Adjusted[1]	Unadjusted	Adjusted[1]
RESPONDENTS' EDUCATION				
Percent with less than high school diploma				
Not foreign-born	11.8	14.4	15.3	15.3
Authorized / naturalized	10.9	12.9	11.3	13.2
Authorized / authorized	17.8	17.5	20.3	19.2
Unauthorized/ naturalized	14.5	13.7	11.6	10.6
Unauthorized / authorized	20.2	17.7	18.3	13.3
Unauthorized / unauthorized	22.5	31.5	35.9	42.5
Status unknown	26.7	--	11.1	--
Never lived in United States	37.0	--	49.4	--
Percent with bachelor's degree or higher				
Not foreign-born	19.4	15.6	8.2	4.4
Authorized / naturalized	16.7	14.5	22.3	21.3
Authorized / authorized	15.3	16.9	11.7	12.8
Unauthorized/ naturalized	19.1	19.5	20.3	21.4
Unauthorized / authorized	14.9	19.1	11.3	16.3
Unauthorized / unauthorized	10.0	9.8	0.0	5.8
Status unknown	8.3	--	0.0	--
Never lived in United States	8.4	--	8.6	--
Average years of education				
Not foreign-born	13.5	13.3	12.7	12.5
Authorized / naturalized	13.3	13.2	13.7	13.5
Authorized / authorized	13.0	13.1	12.9	13.0
Unauthorized/ naturalized	13.3	13.4	13.5	13.6
Unauthorized / authorized	13.0	13.2	12.9	13.3
Unauthorized / unauthorized	13.0	12.2	11.4	11.3
Status unknown	12.4	--	13.0	--
Never lived in United States	11.8	--	10.9	--
Percent of respondents preferring to speak English at home				
Not foreign-born	71.0	71.1	80.6	92.0
Authorized / naturalized	69.5	69.9	67.0	81.0
Authorized / authorized	57.6	65.5	53.1	70.7
Unauthorized/ naturalized	61.8	72.6	55.1	75.3
Unauthorized / authorized	36.0	50.7	37.3	65.3
Unauthorized / unauthorized	45.0	47.7	28.2	52.0
Status unknown	41.7	--	66.7	--

TABLE 2.4 (CONTINUED)

	Fathers' status		Mothers' status	
	Unadjusted	Adjusted[1]	Unadjusted	Adjusted[1]
Never lived in United States	32.8	--	28.4	--
Respondents' average occupational socioeconomic prestige				
Not foreign-born	40.4	39.3	42.4	40.9
Authorized / naturalized	42.1	41.6	42.5	42.1
Authorized / authorized	42.9	43.3	40.3	40.6
Unauthorized/ naturalized	41.6	41.6	41.7	41.8
Unauthorized / authorized	40.8	41.9	41.2	42.6
Unauthorized / unauthorized	38.5	38.7	34.0	36.9
Status unknown	39.6	--	42.6	--
Never lived in United States	38.8	--	36.9	--
Respondents' average annual personal income				
Not foreign-born	$23,194	$20,501	$25,847	$22,818
Authorized / naturalized	26,151	24,922	25,000	23,754
Authorized / authorized	19,182	20,905	19,871	20,371
Unauthorized/ naturalized	23,638	23,564	21,960	22,627
Unauthorized / authorized	20,061	23,216	18,123	22,439
Unauthorized / unauthorized	16,988	17,244	14,218	18,036
Status unknown	19,567	--	16,056	--
Never lived in United States	17,395	--	19,685	--

1. Controlling for fathers' and mothers' years of schooling and respondents' age.

Discussion and Conclusions

The adult children of those unauthorized Mexican immigrants who were able to change their legal status exhibit better labor-market outcomes than do the children of those immigrants who remained unauthorized. That legalization relates positively to economic well-being provides a basis for anticipating the long-term effects on incorporation of legislative proposals that provide pathways to legalization or citizenship. The research findings here suggest that the kind of legalization possibilities made available by IRCA foster greater educational attainment, English usage, occupational prestige, and incomes on the part of children whose parents initially came to the country unauthorized. Other research, also using the IIMMLA data, on the children of Mexican Immigrants finds that parental legalization and citizenship is related to greater civic engagement, which in turn enhances economic success among immigrants (DeSipio, Bean, and Rumbaut 2005). These effects of parents' migration status hold for both fathers and mothers, and the level of legalization and naturalization among both fathers and mothers is high. If anything, the effect of mothers' status may be slightly more pronounced, particularly for educational attainment.

Even as pathways to legalization and citizenship provide the children of immigrants with a more favorable start in society, the lack of such pathways increases the risk of more children growing up vulnerable to becoming mired in an immigrant underclass. But we emphasize that our results may not indicate that the parents' legalization and citizenship actually *cause* children's higher economic status, although they may, particularly by improving access to economic opportunities available only to legal immigrants or citizens. Instead, the results may derive, at least in part, from processes of selectivity. That is, perhaps more ingenious and industrious parents are also more likely to legalize and obtain citizenship, and those personal qualities partly account for the gains in education and income among their children, rather than legal and citizenship status per se. Even so, legalization and citizenship pathways remain important, because the presence of greater opportunities for legalization, or even the prospect of greater opportunities, is necessary for positive selection to take place (Heckman 1997; Heckman, Smith, and Clements 1997). Such opportunities exist because of public policy. Without the chance to legalize or naturalize, highly motivated people may be less likely to migrate—or they could lose their motivation. Such possibilities contribute to the likelihood that an impoverished, vulnerable, and perhaps alienated underclass of unauthorized migrants may develop in the United States. The enormous response to IRCA's legalization opportunities shows how much the chance to become full members of society matters to immigrants. An important reason was undoubtedly that they perceived that they and their children would gain the opportunity to achieve.

Had a program to enable legalization been unavailable at the time, the parents undoubtedly would not have fared so well in the United States. They would have lived and worked underground to a much greater degree and, in all probability, would have lacked the resources to provide for their children and for their children's education. Without pathways to legalization and citizenship (i.e., in the form of both a welcoming society and opportunities to legalize), they would have had less reason to try as hard as they did (Van Hook, Brown, and Bean 2006). In short, even if selectivity among immigrants partly accounts for who legalizes and naturalizes and for how much the children of immigrants achieve, such mechanisms cannot operate if parents lack the chance to legalize and become citizens. And in fact, as noted earlier, when we control fathers' and mothers' education in regression models predicting children's economic attainment and human-capital outcomes, we find that the premiums associated with legalization and citizenship either do not change or actually increase (adjusted results shown in table 2.4). Migration and citizenship opportunities appear to matter considerably. Thus, pathways to legalization and citizenship for immigrant parents create environments that encourage educational attainment and economic achievement among their children.

NOTES

Some of the research on which the chapter is based was supported by grants from the National Institute of Child Health and Development (RO1-39075) and the Hewlett Foundation. Appreciation is also expressed to the Russell Sage Foundation, which underwrote the collection of data for the Immigration and Intergenerational Mobility in Metropolitan Los Angeles (IIMMLA) study. Infrastructural assistance from the Center for Research on Immigration, Population and Public Policy at the University of California, Irvine, is also gratefully acknowledged.

1. Occupational prestige is based on the Duncan Socioeconomic Index, a widely used measure of occupational status. It is based on the income and educational levels associated with every occupation in 1950.

3

Early Childhood Education Programs

ACCOUNTING FOR LOW ENROLLMENT IN
IMMIGRANT AND MINORITY FAMILIES

Donald J. Hernandez, Nancy A. Denton, and Suzanne Macartney

Research clearly indicates that early childhood education programs can pro-mote school readiness and educational success (Haskins and Rouse 2005; Lynch 2004). Children of immigrant parents with low educational attain-ments and limited English proficiency are especially likely to benefit from such programs (Gormley et al. 2005; Hernandez 2004), but they are less likely to be enrolled than are the children of native parents. This appears to be especially true for the children of Hispanic immigrants. A reason often cited for these lower enrollment rates is a more familistic cultural orientation that leads parents to prefer that their children be cared for at home (or in the homes of relatives), rather than by nonrelatives in a formal educational set-ting (Brandon 2004; Liang, Fuller, and Singer 2000; Uttal 1999).

This explanation, however, ignores alternative possibilities, including the cost of these programs, which may be beyond the economic means of immigrant parents. In addition, the openings in early education programs in neighborhoods where immigrant families reside are often inadequate to accommodate additional demand. Parents with limited educations tend, moreover, to be unaware of how important early education programs are for their children's subsequent school achievements; and they may not realize that such programs are the typical mode of initiation into the education pro-cess for children with highly educated parents. Immigrant parents' limited English proficiency, combined with early education programs' lack of home-language outreach, can also act as a barrier to enrollment.

The reasons for the differences in early education enrollment across immi-grant and native minority groups are poorly understood. In principle, the affordability and accessibility of programs, along with their cultural appro-priateness, appear critical (Shonkoff and Phillips 2000; Takanishi 2004). But past research has not estimated the extent to which enrollment differences result from the values and preferences of parents as compared to the lack of affordable and accessible programs (Takanishi 2004).

In this chapter, we investigate the reasons behind the low early educational enrollment rates for six major immigrant and native groups, using new analyses of Census 2000 data. We begin by estimating early school enrollment rates for these groups and for whites from native families, and we then develop models to assess the relative importance of cultural and socioeconomic/ structural influences in accounting for the enrollment gaps from which the minority groups suffer. By estimating the ranges of the potential influence of these two factors, we are better able to evaluate their relative roles.

School Enrollment, Ages Three to Five

A sizable percentage of children in the United States are enrolled in some form of early education program, one that prepares them for the onset of graded schooling. Overall, about 38 percent of three-year-olds in native-born families are enrolled, compared to 30 percent of children in immigrant families (table 3.1). At age four, enrollment rates rise sharply for both populations—to 63 and 55 percent, respectively—but the gap between them remains consistent.

Table 3.1 shows early school enrollment rates for the six immigrant and native groups that are least likely to be enrolled, as well as for white children from native families.[1] Among the thirty immigrant groups for whom we have calculated estimates (available at www.albany.edu/csda/children), only

TABLE 3.1
School Enrollment

Enrolled in school	Children in Native-Born Families*				Children in Immigrant Families*				
	Total	White	Puerto Rican Islanc-origin**	Mexican	Total	Mexico	Central America	Dominican Republic	Indochina
Age 3	37.9	37.4	31.0	28.3	29.9	17.9	25.2	33.2	24.3
Age 4	63.2	63.0	55.4	52.4	55.3	43.5	51.9	61.3	40.6

Calculated from Census 2000 5 pct microdata (IPUMS) by Hernandez, Denton and Macartney.

 * Children are classified as living in native-born families if they are born in the U.S. to parents who were born in the U.S. Children are classified as living in immigrant families if they are either themselves foreign-born or have at least one foreign-born parent.

** Island-origin Puerto Rican children were born in Puerto Rico or have at least one parent born in Puerto Rico. Though island-origin Puerto Ricans share some characterisitcs with immigrants, they are U.S. citizens and thus must be categorized as native-born.

five, four of them Hispanic, have lower enrollment rates at age three than do native white children (37 percent): these are children with parents from the Dominican Republic (33 percent), Central America (25 percent), Indochina (24 percent), Mexico (18 percent), and Puerto Rico (31 percent).[2] One native-born Hispanic group also has an enrollment rate lower than whites in native-born families: children from Mexican American families (28 percent). All groups experience enrollment increases by age four. Although the enrollment rate for children with immigrant origins from the Dominican Republic (61 percent) is only slightly less than for white children in native-born families (63 percent), the gap remains much larger for the children from the other groups, with the lowest enrollment occurring for the children from immigrant Mexican families (44 percent).

Previous research has found that children in immigrant families are less likely than those in native families to be in preschool education programs (Brandon 2004). Insofar as the five immigrant groups identified as having the lowest enrollment rates amount to 55 percent of children in immigrant families, they account for virtually the entire enrollment gap between immigrant- and native-origin children.[3] The low enrollment rate for children from Mexican American families is a further concern because it demonstrates that, for the largest group in the contemporary immigration stream, the transition to a U.S.-born generation of parents is not sufficient to bring children to parity when it comes to early preparation for school.

Theoretical Background and Key Measures

Children in families with limited incomes are especially likely to benefit from early education, but they also may have less access to such programs because of the costs associated with participation (Gormley et al. 2005; Haskins and Rouse 2005; Hernandez 2004; Lynch 2004; Mezey, Greenberg, and Schumacher 2002). The children in the six groups identified as having particularly low pre-K/nursery-school enrollment rates are also quite likely to be poor, as table 3.2 shows. (Poverty estimates for other groups are available at www.albany.edu/csda/children.) In fact, three of the immigrant groups have child poverty rates of 30 percent or more (compared to just 9 percent for white children in native families): children with Mexican parents (31 percent), Dominican parents (32 percent), and Puerto Rican parents (36 percent).

The lack of economic resources in poor families can prove to be an insurmountable barrier to enrollment in early education programs (Hofferth 1996; Johnson 2005; Leibowitz, Waite, and Witsberger 1988). State or federal

TABLE 3.2
Poverty and Family Circumstances

	Children in Native-Born Families*			Children in Immigrant Families*			
	White	Puerto Rican Island-origin**	Mexican	Mexico	Central America	Dominican Republic	Indochina
Poverty measures							
Official poverty	9.0	36.1	22.6	31.3	22.8	32.4	19.9
Baseline basic budget poverty	11.7	46.7	30.0	46.6	38.9	49.9	29.3
Baseline basic budget poverty plus childcare	26.0	65.3	48.9	69.7	60.3	69.5	46.0
Mother's education							
Less than high school	8.8	35.9	26.1	64.1	52.0	36.9	37.5
High school graduate	25.9	26.9	30.6	20.0	21.8	26.0	23.1
Some College	34.9	27.7	33.2	12.2	18.2	27.2	24.2
Bachelor's degree or higher	30.3	9.5	10.2	3.7	7.9	10.1	15.2
Father's occupation							
Management and related	18.3	8.9	9.9	4.5	7.1	8.2	17.3
Professional and related	18.4	9.1	11.5	2.7	5.9	7.9	41.2
Health Support/ Protective Services	3.8	4.7	5.8	1.1	1.9	3.6	1.0
Service, Other	3.9	13.7	7.1	16.4	16.7	14.6	13.9
Sales	10.8	6.5	9.0	4.6	5.9	11.0	7.3
Office and administrative support	4.7	9.1	8.3	4.4	6.2	8.2	4.8
Farming and forestry	0.7	0.7	1.2	6.5	1.0	0.1	0.2
Construction and production	39.2	47.3	47.4	59.7	55.4	46.4	14.2
Immigration measures							
Mother English fluent	96.6	61.7	87.0	32.2	38.3	37.1	37.4
Child second generation	--	82.2	--	89.0	93.9	93.4	71.2
Parents in U.S. 10+ years	--	14.2	--	41.2	48.5	43.1	31.6
Additional family measures							
Two-parent families	84.9	65.3	64.2	86.5	82.6	66.5	85.8
Sibling ages 0-2	33.0	31.9	34.2	35.4	31.4	26.0	33.7
Sibling ages 3-5	19.0	22.0	21.3	23.4	20.0	17.4	26.0
Grandparent in home	5.9	13.3	19.2	12.5	14.6	17.5	21.0
Mother currently employed	58.1	42.3	54.3	33.1	43.6	40.9	51.7

Calculated from Census 2000 5 pct microdata (IPUMS) by Hernandez, Denton and Macartney.

 * Children are classified as living in native-born families if they are born in the U.S. to parents who were born in the U.S. Children are classified as living in immigrant families if they are either themselves foreign-born or have at least one foreign-born parent.

** Island-origin Puerto Rican children were born in Puerto Rico or have at least one parent born in Puerto Rico.

eligibility requirements for child care, including more costly early education programs, under the Child Care and Development Block Grant (CCDBG) program, the Temporary Assistance for Needy Families (TANF) program, or the Social Services Block Grant (SSBG) program do take economic need into account, but only 14–30 percent of state or federally eligible children received assistance in the early 2000s (Mezey, Greenberg, and Schumacher 2002).

The official poverty rate published by the U.S. Census Bureau is not the best measure of these economic barriers, given its well-known weaknesses (Citro and Michael 1995; DeNavas-Walt, Proctor, and Lee 2005; Hernandez, Denton, and Macartney 2007; Short et al. 1999). In particular, the official measure does not take into account the local cost of living, which includes differences in the cost of housing as well as in early education. Although estimates of the local cost of early education programs are not available, estimates of the local cost of center-based care are available, and we have used them to develop a "Basic Budget Poverty" measure that also takes into account the local costs of housing, food, transportation for work, other necessities, and taxes (Hernandez, Denton, and Macartney 2007). This measure provides a better estimate than the official poverty measure for our purposes because it approximates the actual costs experienced by the families with children. Every group shows increases in poverty according to the Basic Budget indicators, but the rates for children in immigrant Mexican (70 percent), Central American (60 percent), and Dominican (70 percent) families, as well as in island-origin Puerto Rican ones (65 percent), are truly staggering.

A poverty measure provides a narrow window on barriers to enrollment. To provide a more comprehensive assessment of the risks of low enrollment, we use eleven indicators of socioeconomic/structural or cultural influences taken from Census 2000—three measure family socioeconomic status; three, immigrant situation and degree of acculturation; and five, family context.

Socioeconomic Status

In addition to poverty, the most prominent objective indicators of socio-economic status are education and occupation. These two measures clearly correspond with barriers to, resources for, or knowledge about early education for young children. Highly educated parents are likely to know the value of early education programs for children's later educational success and hence to enroll their young children in these programs (Johnson 2005; Leibowitz, Waite, and Witsberger 1988; Lein 1979). Similarly, parents working in higher-status occupations are probably more likely than other parents to be embedded in social networks that serve as a source of information about such programs and of access to them. Moreover, high-status occupations are more likely, on average, to provide "family-friendly" benefits packages that facilitate child care or early education programs for working mothers and fathers. Insofar as parental socioeconomic status has a strong influence on children's educational attainments, it is not surprising that children with higher-status parents are more likely to be enrolled in pre-K/nursery school as a means of ensuring a strong start in the early grades of school.

Immigrant Situation

We use three measures as indicators of immigrant situation and acculturation. English-language fluency has long been employed as a key indicator of cultural integration into American society. The role of language is critical for multiple reasons (Alba and Nee 2003). First, because important aspects of the home culture are embedded in the native language of parents, the reduced use of that language can lead to a weakening of that culture. Second, parents' use of their native language facilitates interaction with peers from their home culture, whereas use of English often engages parents with English speakers embedded in American culture. Thus, to the extent that the Hispanic or Indochinese cultures involve a familistic orientation that is less favorable than American culture to placing young children in early care settings with nonrelatives, an adherence to these preferences may be reflected in the level of parental English fluency (Liang, Fuller, and Singer 2000; Tropp et al. 1995).

Limited English fluency, however, also is an indicator of possible structural barriers to enrollment in early education programs. First, the number of openings located in neighborhoods with many immigrants may be too small to accommodate newcomers (Hill-Scott 2005b). Second, the programs may not reach out to immigrant parents in their home language, thereby restricting access (Matthews and Ewen 2006). Third, immigrant parents may hesitate to enroll their children in programs that are not designed and implemented in a culturally familiar manner, especially if teachers lack a minimal capacity to communicate with children in the home language (Holloway and Fuller 1999; Shonkoff and Phillips 2000). These circumstances may constrain children's enrollment, even when parents recognize the benefits of early education programs.

Thus, parental lack of English fluency may in part indicate a cultural preference for child care within a family setting, but it may also indicate structural barriers to enrollment in early education programs. Unfortunately, it is not possible to know the extent to which this indicator reflects enrollment preferences or enrollment barriers. This is one reason that we calculate lower-bound and upper-bound estimates of the influence of socioeconomic and cultural factors on enrollment gaps.

This ambiguity extends to two other indicators of the immigration context of children: their own generation and the recency of their family's arrival in the United States. The longer immigrant parents live in the United States, the more likely they are to become familiar with and adopt features of the American environment. Children born in the United States are likely to have parents who are more acculturated than are parents of children born elsewhere. Thus, children who are foreign-born or have parents who immigrated recently are likely to have parents who are less knowledgeable about early education programs. In addition, such children may tend to live in neighborhoods with less access to such programs. Thus, children's generation and the recency of their family's arrival to the United States can be indicative of lower acculturation or of structural barriers to enrolling in early education programs.

Family Context

The day-to-day circumstances of families—as determined by household composition and mother's employment—also can affect enrollment, by influencing the need for or access to child care. First, one-parent families usually have greater need for child care because two parents are not available to share the everyday care of children (Hofferth 1996; Johnson 2005; Leibowitz, Waite, and Witsberger 1988). Second, it costs less for families with more than one preschooler to care for children at home, and since the cost of child care decreases as children age, it is especially economical to care for very young children at home (Leibowitz, Waite, and Witsberger 1988). Third, families with resident grandparents may not need to seek out-of-home care (Floge 1985; Leibowitz, Waite, and Witsberger 1988; NICHD Early Child Care Research Network 1997; Presser 1989). Fourth, families with mothers who are not employed may find it less expensive and more convenient to care for preschool children at home (Hofferth 1996; Johnson 2005; Leibowitz, Waite, and Witsberger 1988).

Because these features of family life are influenced, but not completely determined, by underlying socioeconomic circumstances or cultural preferences, household composition and mother's employment can independently influence early school enrollment. Our approach is to assess any additional effect of these indicators after assessing the effects of poverty and parental education and occupation (our socioeconomic/structural indicators) and of the child's generational status and parental English fluency and recency of arrival (our primary cultural indicators).

Descriptive Analyses

Table 3.2 shows the specific measures of socioeconomic status, immigrant situation, and family context that are used in our analysis. Because at least 95 percent of children who live with at least one parent live with a mother, and because there are strong correlations between mother's and father's education and English-language fluency, this study measures these two "parental" variables for mothers only. In addition, the analysis is limited to children with a mother in the home.

In socioeconomic terms, the children from immigrant backgrounds show high levels of disadvantage. Many children in immigrant families have, for instance, mothers with limited educations, though those whose families come from Mexico and Central America are strikingly below mainstream norms in this respect, as the majority of these mothers have not completed secondary school. Patterns for father's education (data not shown) are generally similar to those for mothers. The occupational status of fathers also reveals a general pattern of disadvantage for the children from immigrant backgrounds. Paternal occupation is coded into eight broad categories: (1) management, business, and financial operations, (2) professional, (3) health support and protective services, (4) food preparation and serving, building and grounds cleaning and maintenance, and personal care and service, (5) sales, (6) office and administrative support, (7) farming, fishing, and forestry, and (8) construction, extraction, and maintenance and production, transportation, and material moving. Among the immigrant groups, only the Indochinese are similar to whites in the proportion with fathers in managerial and related occupations (17.3 and 18.3 percent), whereas other groups have roughly one-third to one-half as many fathers in these occupations (4.5 to 9.9 percent). The Indochinese are twice as likely as whites to have fathers in professional and related occupations (41.2 versus 18.4 percent), compared to the much lower figures (2.7 to 11.5 percent) for other groups, and the Indochinese are about one-third as likely as whites to have fathers in construction and production (14.2 versus 39.2 percent), compared to the substantially higher values (46.4 to 59.7 percent) for the other groups. Children in Mexican immigrant families are the only ones with more than 1 percent of fathers engaged in farming and forestry, and overall, half or more of the parents of children in Hispanic immigrant families, including Mexicans, are in construction and production occupations. Mothers were more likely found in office and administrative support occupations (data not shown) rather than in construction and production, which are more common for fathers.

Unsurprisingly, the children in immigrant families are also distinctive on the indicators of immigration and acculturation situation. Of these, the most obviously consequential is the mother's English fluency. Except for Puerto Ricans, the children in immigrant families are unlikely to have a mother who is fluent in English; the percentages range from 32 percent for Mexicans to 38 percent for Central Americans. The children, however, belong overwhelmingly to the second generation, according to its narrow definition (see chapter 1 in this volume); with the exception of children in Indochinese families, and to a lesser extent, those in island-origin Puerto Rican families, the U.S.-born percentage is around 90 percent. For immigrant parents, the situation is quite different—only a minority have been in the United States for ten years or more. Only 14 percent of the island-origin Puerto Rican parents have resided on the mainland for that long; 50–60 percent of parents in other Hispanic immigrant families came within the decade preceding the 2000 Census, as did two-thirds of the Indochinese parents.

Last, we turn to the family composition and employment indicators, which, like English fluency, may reflect cultural orientation, socioeconomic/structural situation, or a combination of both. For example, it might be that groups differ culturally in their tolerance for family arrangements other than two-parent families. At the same time, considerable research suggests that most of the increase in one-parent families during recent decades is a product of constrained socioeconomic circumstances undermining the economic viability of marriage (Hernandez 1993; Wilson 1987). Empirically, children in native white and immigrant Mexican, Central American, and Indochinese families are about equally likely to live with two parents, although the proportions are substantially lower for the native Mexican and island-origin Puerto Rican groups and the immigrant group from the Dominican Republic (table 3.2).

In view of the large differences in fertility and family size across the countries of origin, it is plausible that immigrant groups would differ substantially in their preferences for large numbers of children and hence in the number of young siblings in the home. Empirically, the proportion with siblings aged zero to two lies within the narrow range of 30–35 percent for children in native white families and in five of the six groups whose enrollment gaps are analyzed here (table 3.2). The proportion with siblings aged three to five in the home also falls within a narrow range, 19–23 percent, except for Dominicans and Indochinese. Thus, whatever the differences in fertility or family size preferences, most of these groups are fairly similar in the presence of young siblings in the home. The proportions living with a grandparent in the home differ somewhat more, from 6 percent for the native white group to 13–21 percent for the other groups. It may be that higher propensities to live with grandparents reflect a more familistic cultural orientation and the desire to have grandparents care for young children. But these propensities may also arise from the need to pool limited economic resources (Angel and Tienda 1982).

Mother's employment also varies substantially across groups, attaining its highest rate, 58 percent, among native whites, while the rate is at 52–54 percent for immigrant Indochinese and native Mexicans, 41–44 percent for island-origin Puerto Ricans and immigrant Central Americans and Dominicans, and 33 percent for immigrant Mexicans (table 3.2). Such differences may arise from a cultural preference for mothers not to work and instead to care for children. But mothers' employment also may vary across groups due to differences in educational attainments or access to affordable child care, availability of appropriate jobs or transportation to work, or other socioeconomic or structural factors (Hernandez 1993; Ihlanfeldt and Sjoquist 1998; Oppenheimer 1970, 1997; Presser and Baldwin 1980; Pugh 1998).

Accounting for Enrollment Gaps

To explain the gaps in early school enrollment, we estimate the impact of socioeconomic, immigration-related, and four additional family-context factors—number of parents, numbers of siblings aged zero to two and aged three to five, and presence of grandparents in the home—for children in the five Hispanic groups and in immigrant families from Indochina. Children in native-born non-Hispanic white families serve as the comparison group. Except for the poverty indicator, which measures family income during the prior calendar year (1999), each variable pertains to the census data collection date (April 1, 2000). Because parental education, occupational group, English fluency, years in the United States, and child's immigrant generation are fairly stable indicators and because poverty is measured a year earlier than the others, we view these six variables as causally prior to family composition and mother's employment; hence, their effects are assessed before introducing the family-context variables into the analysis.

As we have noted, differences across groups in family composition and mother's employment may result from cultural influences, socioeconomic/ structural influences, or some combination of both, and we have no way of separating the two empirically. The safest course in drawing conclusions is therefore to view the combined effect of these indicators, in turn, as potentially cultural but then, alternatively, as potentially socioeconomic/structural. The approach developed here, with lower-bound and upper-bound estimates, reflects this idea.

To obtain results, we calculated logistic regression models for each specific collection of independent variables and separately for each group. Next we calculated "predicted probabilities" of enrollment for each group by applying the same "standard" population composition in every case. This standard is defined as children who (1) are U.S.-born and (2) are not poor and (3) live with both parents, who (4) have been in the United States for more than a decade. The mothers (5) have graduated from high school but did not attend college, (6) are English fluent, (7) are employed, and (8) work in food preparation and serving, building and grounds cleaning and maintenance, or personal care and service; the fathers (9) are employed in construction, extraction, maintenance, production, transportation, or material moving. The households (10) contain no sibling ages zero to two, (11) contain no sibling ages three to five, and (12) contain no grandparent. Then we calculate the gap between each minority and native whites in these "predicted probabilities" and compare the "predicted" gap to the actual gap in enrollment rates. Table 3.3 presents the actual and predicted probabilities of school enrollment for these various models.

Drawing Initial Conclusions

Conclusions about socioeconomic/structural influences are initially drawn as follows, using as an example the results for children at age three in immigrant families from Mexico and in native white families. The four socioeconomic indicators—poverty, mother's education, father's occupation, mother's occupation—are the sole independent variables. The predicted probabilities are 0.19 and 0.23 for the immigrant Mexican and native white groups, respectively, for a gap of 0.04. (Actual results are calculated to more decimal places and rounded in text and tables.) The corresponding empirical probabilities are 0.18 and 0.37, for a gap of 0.19 (table 3.3). Thus, the predicted probabilities suggest that these socioeconomic indicators reduce the enrollment gap between the immigrant Mexican and native white groups by 0.15 (calculated as 0.19 − 0.04 = 0.15), or by 80 percent (calculated as (0.15/0.19) × 100 = 80 percent).

TABLE 3.3
Actual and Predicted Probability of School Enrollment for Age 3 and Age 4

| | Baseline | Group Specific Models | | | |
		Model 1	Model 2	Model 3	Model 4
	Actual probabilities	For child not poor[1], mother HS grad, father in construction, mother in service occupation.	For child 2nd generation, mother English fluent, parents in U.S. 10 or more years[+]	For child not poor[1], mother HS grad, father in construction, mother in service occupation and English fluent, child 2nd generation, parents in U.S. 10 or more years[+]	Same as Model 3 plus two-parent family with no siblings ages 0-2 or 3-5, no grandparent in home, mother currently employed.
AT AGE 3					
Children in Native-Born Families					
White	0.37	0.23	0.41	0.26	0.29
P. R. Island origin	0.31	0.31	0.32	0.30	0.32
Mexican	0.28	0.25	0.25	0.22	0.25
Children in Immigrant Families					
Mexico	0.18	0.19	0.24	0.22	0.22
Central America	0.25	0.25	0.29	0.25	0.26
Dominican Rep.	0.33	0.44	0.39	0.51	0.51
Indochina	0.24	0.22	0.24	0.17	0.21
AT AGE 4					
Children in Native-Born Families					
White	0.63	0.51	0.63	0.52	0.55
P. R. Island origin	0.55	0.51	0.60	0.64	0.70
Mexican	0.52	0.48	0.50	0.46	0.49
Children in Immigrant Families					
Mexico	0.44	0.42	0.47	0.42	0.43
Central America	0.52	0.48	0.57	0.50	0.52
Dominican Rep.	0.61	0.52	0.63	0.58	0.61
Indochina	0.49	0.51	0.51	0.48	0.52

1. Poverty measured as Baseline Basic Budget poverty plus child care costs.
+ Children in immigrant families only.
Calculated from Census 2000 5 pct microdata (IPUMS) by Hernandez, Denton and Macartney.

Conclusions about immigration-related influences, based on mother's English fluency, parental duration of residence in the United States, and child's generation, follow a similar, but not identical, logic. Although the socioeconomic/structural indicators are unambiguous, the immigration-related indicators can reflect either cultural or socioeconomic/structural influences. In order to estimate the maximum degree of cultural influence due to the family's immigration context, we first calculate models with the three indicators of this context as the only independent variables. We then calculate predicted probabilities, which are used to estimate the reduction in the actual enrollment gaps separating any two groups.

With children aged three from the immigrant Mexican group used again as the example (table 3.3, Model 2), the results indicate that cultural influences associated with the immigration-related indicators could account for as much as 9 percent of the enrollment gap. This is the "upper bound," which holds only if we are willing to assume that all the effects of mother's fluency, duration of residence in the United States, and child's generation are the result of cultural influences. Insofar as some portion of these effects may result from socioeconomic/structural influences, however, not all of the 9 percent should be attributed to culture. Because the effects could result entirely from socioeconomic influences, the appropriate "lower bound" estimate for cultural influences is always 0 percent.

After estimating the effects of the socioeconomic/structural and immigration-related determinants on early education enrollment, we go on to assess the additional effects of family context by estimating two models. First, we calculate a model including the six socioeconomic and immigration-related indicators to estimate the combined effects of these factors on the enrollment gap for each group compared to the native white group (table 3.3, Model 3). Next, we extend the model by adding the indicators of household composition and mother's employment as independent variables to estimate the combined effect of all the indicators (table 3.3, Model 4). If the estimated reduction in the enrollment gap based on the second, expanded model is greater than that based on the first, then the difference between the two estimates is calculated to measure the effect that family context has in reducing the enrollment gap. Our procedure thus notes only those effects beyond the influences of poverty, mother's education, parental occupations, mother's English fluency, parental duration of residence, and child's generation.

Table 3.4 presents results regarding influences on enrollment gaps separately for each cluster of indicators. It shows estimates of the percentage reduction in the enrollment gap separating specific groups from whites (listed in order from the largest group, the immigrant Mexican group, to the smallest, the Indochinese). In table 3.4, a value of 100 percent is recorded if the independent variables eliminate the entire enrollment gap, that is, if the adjusted enrollment for a particular group is equal to or greater than the equivalent adjusted rate for the native white group. At the opposite extreme,

TABLE 3.4

Percent Reduction in Enrollment Gap Due to Socioeconomic Status and Immigrant Situation, and Additional Reduction Due to Family Composition and Mother's Employment

	SOCIOECONOMIC STATUS Poverty, Mother's Education, Parental Occupations		IMMIGRANT SITUATION Child's Generation, Parental Years in U.S. Mother's English Fluency		FAMILY COMPOSITION & MOTHER'S EMPLOYMENT incl. Parents, Siblings, Grandparents in Home	
Group Specific Models	Age 3	Age 4	Age 3	Age 4	Age 3	Age 4
Mexico, children in immigrant families	80%	53%	0-9%	0-14%	0%	0%
Mexico, children in native-born families	100%	72%	0%	0%	10%	0%
Central America, children in immigrant families	100%	76%	0%	0-39%	0%	0%
Island-origin Puerto-Rican children	100%	100%	0%	0-57%	0%	31%
Dominican Republic, children in immigrant families	100%	100%	0-39%	0-54%	0%	0%
Indochina, children in immigrant families	92%	100%	0%	0-12%	6%	5%

a value of 0 percent is recorded if the effect of the independent variables is to increase, not reduce, the size of the gap separating a particular group from the native white group.

For children aged three, the results suggest that socioeconomic status—measured as poverty status, mother's education, and parental occupation—can account for 80 percent of the enrollment gap for the immigrant Mexican group, 92 percent of the enrollment gap for the Indochinese immigrant group, and the entirety of the gap for the other four groups. Results at age four indicate that the entire enrollment gap can be accounted for by socioeconomic status for children in island-origin Puerto Rican families and in families from the Dominican Republic and Indochina, while about three-fourths of the enrollment gap is attributable to socioeconomic status for children in the Mexican native group and in immigrant families with origins in Central America; one-half of the gap can be accounted for by socioeconomic status among children in immigrant families from Mexico.

The results in table 3.4 indicate that the role of the immigration situation—measured as child's generation, parental years in the United States, and mother's English fluency—is small or negligible at age three for all groups except that from the Dominican Republic, among whom these variables might account for as much as 39 percent of the enrollment gap. The effect of the immigration situation also is small to negligible at age four for children in the immigrant and native-born Mexican groups and the Indochinese group, although it rises to between 39 and 57 percent for three other groups.

Thus, results for three groups, the immigrant and native Mexican groups and the Indochinese group, are consistent in suggesting that the role of the immigration situation is quite limited and that socioeconomic status can account for at least one-half and perhaps all of the enrollment gap. Results for children with parental origins in Central America and Puerto Rico must be viewed, however, as more uncertain. Estimates for both these groups suggest that socioeconomic status can account for most or all of the enrollment gap and that immigration situation can account for none of the gap at age three, while the estimates for age four suggest that the role of culture could be as high 39 percent for Central Americans and 57 percent for Puerto Ricans.

Results are more ambiguous for Dominicans. The results suggest at both ages three and four that socioeconomic status can account for the entire Dominican enrollment gap, which is broadly consistent with the findings for other groups. But they also suggest that as much as 39 percent of the gap at age three and 54 percent of the gap at age four may be accounted for by the immigration situation, although these findings allow for the possibility that the effect of culture is negligible. The unusual situation of the Dominicans may be a consequence of the fact that their enrollment gaps, compared to the native white group, are the smallest of any group in table 3.3, at only four percentage points for age three, and two percentage points for age four. Thus, 39 percent of the age-three gap and 54 percent of the age-four gap amount to reductions of only one to two percentage points.

Once socioeconomic status and immigration situation are taken into account, family composition and mother's employment mostly have little additional effect on enrollment gaps. The estimated reductions are in the low range of 0–10 percent, with one exception: family composition and mother's employment can account for 31 percent of the gap for the Puerto Rican group at age four.

The Big Picture: Socioeconomic/Structural and Cultural Influences

Table 3.5 reports our best estimates of the extent to which socioeconomic/structural and cultural factors can account for enrollment gaps. To arrive at comprehensive upper-bound estimates for socioeconomic/structural influences, we have combined the effects of poverty, mother's education, and parental occupation with those of family context, since the latter may reflect socioeconomic/structural influences, cultural influences, or both. By anal-

TABLE 3.5
Percent Reduction in Enrollment Gap Due to Socioeco-
nomic/Structural Influences and Cultural Influences

	Combined Results			
	Socioeconomic or Structural Influences		Cultural Influences	
	Age 3	Age 4	Age 3	Age 4
Mexico, children in immigrant families	80%	53%	0-9%	0-14%
Mexico, children in native-born families	100%	72%	0-10%	0%
Central America, children in immigrant families	100%	76%	0%	0-39%
Island-origin Puerto-Rican children	100%	100%	0%	0-88%
Dominican Republic, children in immigrant families	100%	100%	0-39%	0-54%
Indochina, children in immigrant families	92-98%	100%	0-6%	0-17%

ogous logic, we have combined the effects of household composition and mother's employment, the indicators of family context, with those of mother's English fluency, duration of residence, and child's generation to obtain more comprehensive upper-bound estimates for cultural influences.

From a quick glance, two points stand out: First, socioeconomic/structural influences trump cultural influences at both ages three and four. Second, cultural influences are more important at age four than at age three. Beyond these basic patterns, results seem potentially inconsistent for the Dominican and island-origin Puerto Rican groups. The estimates suggest that socioeconomic/structural factors can account for 100 percent of the enrollment gaps—and, correlatively, that cultural factors account for none of them—but also that cultural factors might account for 39 percent and 54 percent of the gaps for Dominicans at ages three and four, respectively, and 88 percent of the gap for Puerto Ricans at age four.

Results are more reasonable for the Central American and Indochinese immigrant groups and raise no concerns for the two Mexican groups. The Central American results suggest that socioeconomic/structural factors account for all of the enrollment gap at age three. At age four, the results indicate that socioeconomic/structural factors account for 76 percent of the gap, while the estimate for cultural influences is in the range of 0–39 percent. At the extreme, the sum of the estimates for age four suggests that these factors together might account for more than the entire gap (76 percent + 39 percent = 115 percent). Similarly, for the Indochinese group, the estimates for age four suggest that socioeconomic/structural factors can account for 100 percent of the enrollment gap, while the range for the effect of cultural factors is much lower (0–17 percent). Thus, at the extreme, these factors together might account for more than the entire gap (100 percent + 17 percent = 117 percent). But for neither group does the logic behind these ranges require the conclusion that more than the entire gap is accounted for by these factors. A more reasonable interpretation is that cultural influences account for less than the maximum value suggested by the estimated ranges.

Results for the immigrant and native Mexican groups also suggest that the role of cultural factors in the enrollment gaps is quite small (0–14 percent), while socioeconomic/structural factors can account for 80–100 percent of the gaps at age three and 53–72 percent at age four. Insofar as the effect of socioeconomic/structural factors for these two groups may be somewhat lower at age four than at age three, it is possible that the older children's access to publicly funded pre-K/nursery schools may act to reduce socioeconomic or structural barriers to enrollment for these children; in fact, forty-three states offer some form of pre-K under the auspices of public schools (Barnett et al. 2003).

Discussion and Conclusions

Despite the plausible argument that familistic cultural orientations might lead to lower early school enrollment rates for immigrant and native minority groups, our results (available at www.albany.edu/csda/children) show that these rates at ages three and four are the same as, or higher than, the rates for whites in native families and for four black groups, three Hispanic groups, and four Asian groups, as well as for four of the five predominantly white immigrant groups. In addition, the analysis presented in this chapter for six groups with comparatively low enrollment rates indicates that, for most of them, the likely effect of cultural influences is modest to negligible (table 3.4). Only for children in Dominican families and for four-year-olds in Puerto Rican and Central American families does the upper-bound estimate for cultural influences reach levels near or above the 50 percent mark. In all other cases, estimates of the reduction in the enrollment gap due to cultural influences range between 0 percent and an upper bound of no more than 17 percent.

In sharp contrast, estimated socioeconomic/structural effects are large for all groups. For the immigrant and native Mexican groups, the Central American group, and the Indochinese group, the range spans 53 percent to 100 percent. Socioeconomic/structural factors in principle can account for the entire enrollment gap for the Dominican and Puerto Rican groups, although there is some degree of uncertainty in these results.

The modest and even negligible effects of cultural influences for the Mexicans in particular may come as a surprise, but these estimates are consistent with the strong commitment to early education in contemporary Mexican political culture (OECD 2006). In November 2002, the "Law of Obligatory Pre-schooling" became official in Mexico, requiring the State to provide preschool services for children beginning at age three and requiring the parents to ensure that their children attend preschool. In fact, "this law makes Mexico the only country in the world to make pre-school obligatory as of age 3" (ibid., 13). Obligatory preschooling in Mexico is not viewed as "day care." It is oriented toward "development and learning, and as the name suggests, toward preparation for schooling. . . . Together, pre-school, primary and lower secondary schooling constitute 12 years of obligatory 'basic education'" (ibid., 17). Importantly, "this law sets a schedule for attaining universal enrolment: for . . . age 3 in 2008–9" (ibid., 13). In fact, around the time the law was enacted, Mexico was already spending a larger proportion of its Gross Domestic Product (GDP) on preschool education than the average OECD country (0.5 versus 0.4 percent). "According to the [Mexican] constitution, education, including pre-schooling, should be free. Funding for pre-schools comes primarily from the national budget, with relatively small, but nonetheless important, contributions from state and local governments" (ibid., 25). "Although the constitution stipulates that public education must be free, in almost all public pre-schools, parents are asked to set a fee that they must pay to cover materials and sometimes food. It is also common to ask parents to contribute time to help with the maintenance of the centres" (ibid., 26).

The Mexican commitment to preschool is reflected in enrollment rates. In 2002–2003, 63 percent of children at age four in Mexico were enrolled in preschool, precisely the proportion of white children in native families enrolled in the United States (OECD 2006, 25, and table 3.1). Insofar as preschool is comparatively inexpensive in Mexico compared to the United States, and insofar as poverty is quite high for children in Mexican immigrant families living in the United States, it is not surprising that the proportion enrolled in school for the immigrant Mexican group at age four is substantially lower than is the case for their agemates in Mexico. Prior to the implementation of obligatory preschool in Mexico, the proportion of three-year-olds enrolled there was 21 percent, scarcely more than half the equivalent enrollment rate of 37 percent for whites in native U.S. families but nearly identical to the 19 percent experienced by three-year-olds in Mexican immigrant families living in the United States.

The extraordinary commitment of the Mexican government to early education, the substantial preschool enrollment rates in Mexico even prior to the 2002 law, and the high educational aspirations of immigrants in the United States for their children (Hernandez and Charney 1998; Kao 1999; Rumbaut

1999) are consistent with our estimate that cultural influences account for no more than a small proportion of the enrollment gap separating the immigrant and native Mexican groups from native whites.

Three recent, smaller studies in the United States point in the same direction. California's Proposition 10 is funding the "First 5 LA" program to "create a high-quality preschool experience for every four-year-old child in Los Angeles county whose parents choose to participate" (Hill-Scott 2004, 3). During the planning process, ten focus groups were conducted in Los Angeles County with low- and middle-income Hispanic, African American, Chinese, Korean, and white parents, some of whom did not have children enrolled in preschool. The study found nevertheless that "all groups agreed that four-year-olds would benefit from preschool," that "nearly all respondents felt that preschool was a very important transitional point for their children," and that "there was universal agreement and enthusiasm among all respondents, regardless of income or ethnicity that the state needs to take the initiative to make the preschool/child care system affordable and available to all children" (Hill-Scott 2005a, 11, 13, 24).

Despite the overwhelming preference for preschooling expressed by these parents, a second study by the First 5 LA "Facilities Task Team" found a large unmet need, with a deficiency of more than one thousand seats in each of sixteen zip codes in Los Angeles County. The researchers found across these neighborhoods, which they designated as "hot zones" meriting special attention, that "only 25 percent of four-year olds have access to licensed care" (Hill-Scott 2005b, 6). We have found that, compared to Los Angeles County as a whole, the proportions of adults who speak a language other than English at home (mostly Spanish) are much higher in most of these areas, suggesting that a scarcity of preschool and child-care openings may be especially common in neighborhoods with many non-English speakers (U.S. Bureau of the Census 2006b). Oklahoma, one of six states (along with Florida, Georgia, Massachusetts, New York, and West Virginia) that has established voluntary universal pre-K programs where parents can (but are not required to) enroll their four-year-old children, is the site of the third study, focused on Tulsa. This study finds that Hispanic children in the Tulsa school district account for essentially the same proportion of total enrollment in voluntary, free, high-quality pre-K programs as in kindergarten, which is mandatory for five-year-olds in Oklahoma (Gormley et al. 2005). In other words, Hispanic parents are not hesitant to take advantage of preschool programs when they are available and low in cost.

Results from these three studies, like government-mandated preschool education in Mexico, are consistent with our estimate that cultural influences account for no more than a small part of the enrollment gap for children in immigrant and native Mexican families, while socioeconomic/structural barriers and resources account for the bulk of it. All these findings, taken together, make a strong case against the claim that familistic cultural values can explain the comparatively low early education enrollment rates among children from some immigrant groups. The results in this chapter indicate that, for most groups with lower enrollment rates, socioeconomic influences provide a much better explanation than cultural ones. Other results we have obtained show that most immigrant groups have higher enrollment rates than whites in native families.

This is good news for young children in immigrant families who could benefit greatly from high-quality early education programs, because the results indicate that cultural preferences, which might change only slowly, do not pose a major barrier to enrollment. Instead, it is socioeconomic and structural barriers—such as limited economic resources to pay the cost of early education, limited knowledge about the virtues of early education, or limited local access to programs, especially those that provide early education in a culturally competent fashion—that are the primary impediments to pre-K/nursery school enrollment for children in immigrant families.

Such barriers could be addressed, even eliminated, by appropriate public action. Children in European countries generally have access to early education and child-care arrangements supported by the national government (Kamerman and Kahn 1995; Neuman and Bennett 2001), and they have recently been joined by children in Mexico and selected U.S. states (Barnett et al. 2003; Bogard and Takanishi 2005). As the United States seeks to position itself favorably in the increasingly competitive global economy and to ensure that all our children are able to contribute with their full potential to the well-being of the nation, it would be wise to make investments today in the early education of our children that will repay handsomely during the decades ahead.

NOTES

The authors wish to thank Ruby Takanishi for her wise counsel, William T. Gormley, Deborah A. Phillips, Eugene Garcia, Suzanne Helburn, Bruce Fuller, Linda M. Espinosa, and Karen Hill-Scott for their thought-provoking reactions to an earlier version of this research, Glenn D. Deane and Peter D. Brandon for statistical insights, Hui-Shien Tsao for programming assistance, and Jessica F. Singer for research assistance. The authors also acknowledge and appreciate support from the William and Flora Hewlett Foundation, the Foundation for Child Development, the National Institute of Child Health and Human Development (5 R03 HD 043827-02), and the Center for Social and Demographic Analysis at the University at Albany (5 R24-HD 04494301A1). The authors alone are responsible for the content and any errors of fact or interpretation. The Census 2000 data file used in this research was prepared by Ruggles et al. (2004).

1. Enrollment rates are calculated based on the Census 2000 question "What grade or level (of regular school) was this person attending?" with "Nursery school, preschool" as one of the response categories. Results presented and analyzed here for children age three pertain to nursery school and preschool. Results for children age four include reported enrollment in kindergarten, because, even though the age cut-off for enrollment in kindergarten in every state precludes enrollment by children who are age four as of the April 1 census date, some parents apparently misreport as enrolled in kindergarten their four-year-olds who actually are enrolled in pre-K, Head Start, or other early education programs.

2. Persons born in Puerto Rico are U.S. citizens. However, insofar as Spanish is commonly spoken in Puerto Rico, persons migrating from Puerto Rico to one of the fifty states may have experiences in many ways similar to immigrants from Spanish-speaking countries regarding their cultural integration. For this reason two variables are calculated and analyzed for persons from Puerto Rico in a fashion analogous to those with immigrant origins. The variable "parents in United States ten or more years" is calculated according to the date when the parents arrived in the United States from Puerto Rico. Similarly, for purposes of this research, children are classified as "first generation" if they were born in Puerto Rico and as "second generation" if they were born in the United States but have at least one parent born in Puerto Rico.

3. Children born in Puerto Rico or with at least one parent born in Puerto Rico are included in this estimate as children in immigrant families.

II

Major Case Studies

The Mexican American Second
Generation in Census 2000

EDUCATION AND EARNINGS

Joel Perlmann

I began working on this chapter at the time I was also engaged in the research for my 2005 book, *Italians Then, Mexicans Now: Immigrant Origins and Second-Generation Progress, 1890–2000.* The substantive evidence that I developed then related to crucial claims of segmented-assimilation theory about negative outcomes for children of contemporary immigrants. This evidence, mainly from Census 2000, concerns indicators of downward assimilation into an underclass and levels of second-generation earnings. Since my book appeared, Alejandro Portes and his coauthors have responded at some length to the evidence and arguments (Portes 2006; Portes, Fernandez-Kelly, and Haller 2005; Portes and Fernandez-Kelly 2008; Portes, Fernandez-Kelly, and Haller 2009). I have therefore decided it would be most useful to reshape the chapter so that it could focus as clearly as possible on my application of evidence to segmented-assimilation theory. I also add an entirely new section, an assessment of the state of the debate in light of the responses to the book.

High-School Dropout and Other Young-Adult Risks:
Mexicans and Blacks Today

I begin by highlighting the serious gaps between Mexican American and native white educational attainments today and then explore whether these gaps are best understood as part of a general pattern of socially risky behavior that is associated, as the segmented-assimilation literature argues, with a subculture of poor, disaffected racial minorities in the United States. In order to make the case that this way of viewing Mexican American schooling does *not* appear to be correct, I compare various subgroups of Mexican Americans with U.S.-born blacks—both for educational attainment and for these socially risky behaviors by young adults. The risky behaviors include teen pregnancy, single motherhood, low labor-force attachment, male institutionalization, and missing (possibly dead) men. I argue that the rates for these behaviors among American-born blacks are distinctively high. By contrast, Mexican American rates of high-school dropout are alarmingly high, much higher than black rates, but involvement in these other socially risky behaviors is far less common among Mexican Americans than among blacks. Consequently we do *not* need an explanation for Mexican American educational patterns that places Mexican educational patterns in the context of a wider complex of socially risky behaviors, growing out of a disaffected racial minority's perspective on their world. Instead, we need, and can find, other explanatory frameworks for the distinctive Mexican American educational patterns.

In order to set the discussion in as wide a frame as possible, I present evidence on several subgroups of Mexican American young adults, defined by generation (see table 4.1). I distinguish conceptually among three groups of the Mexican-born in Census 2000: *immigrants,* those who arrived at age six or later; the *1.56* group, brought between their third and sixth birthdays, an intermediate group; and the *1.53* group, who arrived before their third birth-

TABLE 4.1
Ethnic classifications used in this study for Census 2000 data

Groups	Definitions
Mexican-origin groups	
Mexican immigrants	Mexican-born, first arriving in the U.S. at age 6 or older
Mexican 1.56 group	Mexican-born, first arrived in the U. S. at ages 3, 4 or 5
Mexican 1.53 group	Mexican-born, first brought to the U.S. at ages 0-2
U.S.-born of Mexican origins	U.S.-born of Mexican origins (reported in Census ancestry or Hispanic question); 2nd or higher generation -- CPS data indicates that about 65% are 3rd-generation or higher -- included, but not distinguishable:
	i) the unmixed ('true') 2nd generation
	ii) the mixed 2nd generation
	iii) 3rd or later generation
Non-Mexican-origin groups	
native whites	U.S.-born; white is only reported race; no Mexican origins
native blacks	U. S.-born; black racial origins reported; no Mexican origins
All others	-- all individuals not included in any of the categories above

Note: Group definitions are based on the 2000 census questions on respondent's country of birth, age, year of immigration, Hispanic origin, ancestry and race. The census allowed respondents to report more than one racial origin.

day. Because Census 2000 did not include a question on parental birthplaces, the 1.53 group is as close a proxy as we can find for the true second generation (those born in the United States to Mexican-born parents).[1]

I also present results for the U.S.-born of Mexican origin. Unfortunately, this group cannot be subdivided in Census 2000. Yet we know it includes three subgroups of quite different origins: the unmixed ("true") second generation (two foreign-born parents), the mixed second generation (one foreign-born parent and one U.S.-born parent), and the third-or-later generation (two U.S.-born parents). We learn from the Current Population Survey (CPS), which does allow us to break out these three groups, that five-eighths of the U.S.-born of Mexican origins are in fact in the third-or-later generation; among the rest, the unmixed second generation is somewhat more prevalent than the mixed second generation (Perlmann 2005, 145). For comparison purposes, I also present each measure for U.S.-born whites and U.S.-born blacks (without Mexican ancestry).

High-School Dropout Rates

The children of Mexican immigrants drop out of high school at very high rates, and this pattern is very important for later wage earning (fig. 4.1). By way of a benchmark, consider that in 2000, 9 percent of native white young men and close to twice that rate of native black men (16 percent) left school without a high-school diploma. For the 1.53 group of Mexican American men, the rate was 33 percent—twice the rate for black men. The situation is slightly muted among young adult women, but only slightly.[2]

The "true" (unmixed) Mexican second generation probably enjoys somewhat higher high-school graduation rates than does the 1.53 group proxy. Nevertheless, this consideration is but a small source for optimism; the CPS data sets, in which we can identify the "true" group, shows quite similar dropout rates for the same cohorts. Among men, for example, the CPS figures are the following: native whites, 7 percent; native blacks, 10 percent; and Mexican second generation, 23 percent. A reasonable guess is that at least one in four of the "true" Mexican second-generation men in the census sample did not complete high school. The rates for the U.S.-born of Mexican origin fall about midway between the rates for blacks and those for the Mexican 1.53 group.

For those who manage to finish high school, blacks and Mexicans in the 1.53 group do not differ much in their further attainments (fig. 4.2). The striking difference among high-school graduates is between native whites on the one hand and both the Mexican 1.53 group and blacks on the other; however,

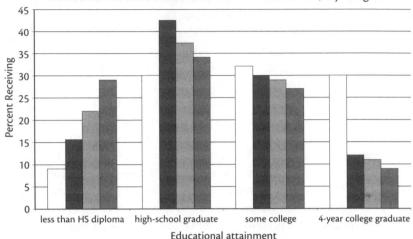

FIGURE 4.1A

Educational attainment in 2000: men 25–34, by origin

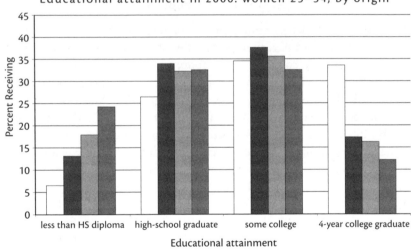

FIGURE 4.1B

Educational attainment in 2000: women 25–34, by origin

☐ U.S.-born white

■ U.S.-born black

▨ U.S.-born reporting Mexican origin

■ Mexican 1.53 group (For group definitions see table 4.1)

Source: IPUMS datasets for 2000 census and 1998–2001 CPS datasets (for adjustment to census data described below).

Note: Based on adjusted educational attainments. Unadjusted figures would reveal higher rates of high-school dropout for the Mexican 1.53 group. See text and Appendix C.

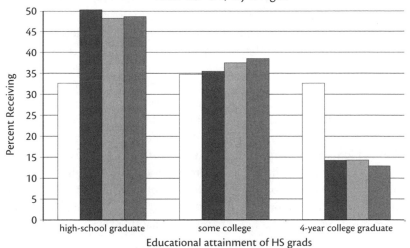

FIGURE 4.2A

Educational attainment of *high-school graduates* in 2000: men 25–34, by origin

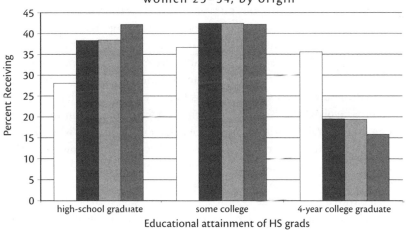

FIGURE 4.2B

Educational attainment of *high-school graduates* in 2000: women 25–34, by origin

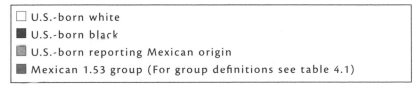

☐ U.S.-born white

■ U.S.-born black

▨ U.S.-born reporting Mexican origin

▨ Mexican 1.53 group (For group definitions see table 4.1)

Source & note: See figure 4.1

the striking difference in high-school dropouts is between the Mexican 1.53 group on the one hand and both blacks and native whites on the other.

If more Mexican Americans graduated from high school, some of that additional number would also surely continue on through college. However, it is important to remember that most young people today—including nearly two-thirds of native-born whites—do not complete a four-year college. Moreover, for all the importance of collegiate education, simply completing high school does matter in America. Quite apart from what greater mastery of literacy means for political participation in a republic, secondary-school completion matters in the job market. Some people might argue that the payoffs to high-school completion may be important to native whites but not to Mexican Americans; the Mexican American dropouts might be making choices about the education they need for the job market on the basis of an awareness of discriminatory hiring patterns or of the jobs available to them through ethnic networks. Suffice it to say here that there is a very wide range of jobs for which a high-school diploma still helps.

Dropout Rates in the Context of Other Social Behavior

Elevated high-school dropout rates are a serious warning sign that upward mobility in future years may well be restricted for a group. For this reason, the Mexican American dropout rates should recall the warnings of the segmented-assimilation hypothesis: that an important part of the contemporary second generation will assimilate downward, into an inner-city minority subculture, in which dropouts are prevalent. But this hypothesis assumes that more than schooling is involved, that high rates of high-school noncompletion are one indicator among several of a wider complex of behaviors that reveal what amounts to a prevalent cultural pattern driving those behaviors. The following sections therefore focus on other risky social behavior in a group near the bottom. These social behaviors are more prevalent among blacks than whites and are especially associated with inner-city black ghettos. The comparison with blacks should not be taken to imply that these behaviors are as prevalent among all black Americans as they are among blacks in inner-city ghettos; obviously they are not, and indeed, "relatively prevalent" does not mean that even a majority of inner-city residents are characterized by most of these behaviors. But because the inner-city black poor are an important minority among all American blacks, the risk factors do show up much more commonly in the native black population as a whole than in the native white population (Jencks 1992; Stier and Tienda 2001; Wilson 1987). How commonly do they show up among Mexican Americans?

Teen Pregnancy and Single Motherhood

Because of the interest in young people of high-school graduation age, I concentrate on women aged fifteen to nineteen and twenty to twenty-four in Census 2000. Throughout American society, the proportion of children born out of wedlock and the proportion being raised by women without a spouse present are high by historical standards—high in white America and far higher in black America. Moreover, these patterns of childrearing have serious effects on the economic well-being of mothers and children. Such effects may be muted or erased entirely among upper-middle-class women, but young women in less-favored circumstances with a child are especially prone to drop out of high school or college and have a hard time arranging and paying for daycare (which might permit school attendance or work). So the prevalence of teen motherhood, and of young adult women raising children alone, is an important measure of potential economic hardship for the women involved as well as for their children.

Teen mothers are relatively rare in all groups; indeed, even among women in their early twenties, a majority in every group are not yet mothers. Still, teen motherhood is more common among blacks than among whites—in relative terms, several times more common, although in actual percentages, only a few points higher (table 4.2). The proportion is higher among Mexican Americans too, but three-fourths of *these* teen mothers are married, whereas almost none of the black teen mothers are. Among women in their early twenties, 36 percent of blacks and 37 percent of Mexicans in the 1.53 group are raising children; but the odds of raising those children without a spouse present are almost nine times as high among blacks as they are in the Mexican group.

Labor-Force Attachment

I classify the men of each group first by whether they are employed full-time and, if not, by whether they are in school and, if not, by whether they are working part-time (table 4.3a). This classification scheme is crude, but it has the advantage of highlighting the full-time workers and those not working (or in school) at all. It reveals that notably more native whites than blacks are full-time workers (54 percent versus 39 percent) and that notably higher proportions of native blacks than whites are neither in school nor working even part-time (28 percent versus 11 percent). By contrast, Mexican Americans are *more* likely to be working full-time than either whites or blacks (63 percent), and the proportion neither at school nor working is about the same as among native whites (12 percent). The distinctive Mexican American feature is the low proportion in school.

TABLE 4.2
Group differences in the prevalence of young mothers, single or with spouse, in 2000

| Age | Group | % mothers | | % not mothers | Total (%) |
		no spouse present	spouse present		
	Mexicans				
	Immigrants	3	9	88	100
	1.56 group	2	3	94	100
	1.53 group	4	4	92	100
15-19	U.S.-born	4	3	92	100
	non-Mexicans				
	NW	2	1	97	100
	NBlk	7	0	93	100
	Mexicans				
	Immigrants	6	34	59	100
	1.56 group	9	31	59	100
	1.53 group	12	25	64	100
20-24	U.S.-born	15	19	67	100
	non-Mexicans				
	NW	8	14	78	100
	NBlk	29	7	64	100

Source: IPUMS dataset, 2000 census.
Note: Immigrants = Mexican-born, arrived at age 6 or older.

I classified women's work status in the same way as men's but distinguished mothers among all women without work (table 4.3b). Generally, of course, fewer women work full-time than men; the exception is blacks, among whom about the same proportion in each sex work full-time. This pattern is the flip side of the relatively low proportion of black men working full-time and the relatively low rate of married black women. By contrast, what most distinguishes women in the Mexican 1.53 group, like men, is a notably lower proportion in school.[3]

Institutionalized and Missing Men

Among all groups, some young people are institutionalized, typically not by choice, most notably in prisons. In every group, the proportion of young men who are institutionalized vastly exceeds that of women; indeed, the percentage of women who are institutionalized rounds to 0 percent in every group except blacks, and it rounds to only 1 percent for black women (table 4.4a). Among young men, typically 1–2 percent are institutionalized. However, 8 percent of U.S.-born of Mexican origin and 13 percent of native blacks are in institutions.

TABLE 4.3A
Work status among young men, 20-24 years of age in 2000

			Percentage in each work status		
			—Not working full time—		
				—Not in school—	Total:
Group	Working full time	In school	Working part time	Not working	work status
Mexicans					
Immigrants	55	5	23	16	100
1.56 group	53	12	23	12	100
1.53 group	53	17	19	11	100
U.S.-born	48	20	21	11	100
non-Mexicans					
NW	48	28	18	6	100
NBlk	32	22	25	21	100

TABLE 4.3B
Work status among young women, 20-24 years of age

			Percentage in each work status			
			—Not working full time—			
				—Not in school—		
					—Not working—	Total:
Group	Working full time	In school	Working part time	mother	other	work status
Mexicans						
Immigrants	23	9	21	24	24	100
1.56 group	34	17	23	14	12	100
1.53 group	32	17	26	12	13	100
U.S.-born	34	25	24	9	8	100
non-Mexicans						
NW	36	33	22	5	5	100
NBlk	32	27	25	7	9	100

Source: IPUMS dataset, census 2000.

As usual, because the census does not specify parental birthplace, we cannot isolate the second generation from the third-or-later generation among those U.S.-born of Mexican origin. Other evidence, however, strongly suggests that the proportion institutionalized in the second generation must be much lower than 8 percent. Specifically, in both the 1.53 and 1.56 groups of Mexican Americans, only 1 percent are institutionalized. It seems most unlikely that the "true" second generation could have an 8 percent rate while the 1.53 group has a 1 percent rate—such a contrast would be far greater than found on any measure on which I have been able to compare them (Perlmann 2005, 142–156).

Clearly the 8 percent institutionalization rate among U.S.-born Mexican Americans deserves a closer look with better data. Nevertheless, from Census 2000 we certainly cannot conclude that the second-generation Mexican American men are falling prey to the high rates of institutionalization that typify young black men.

Moreover, there are sound reasons for predicting that the later-generation Mexican Americans whose families immigrated in an earlier period of American history might well fare poorly on some social outcomes compared to the Mexican second generation of today. The history of Mexican Americans in the Southwest, where the group was highly concentrated until recently, shares elements of social, legal, and educational discrimination with the history of blacks in the South. As such, those earlier Mexican American arrivals and their descendants faced conditions that cannot be compared to conditions of Europeans in the North at the time or to those of the Mexican American second generation today. School discrimination, for example, was incomparably more institutionalized and hence systematic against Mexican American children in earlier periods (Cortes 1980, 709; Grebler, Moore, and Guzmán 1970, 155–158; Olneck and Lazerson 1980, 313–314).[4] Comparable conditions simply do not exist any longer. To ignore all this is to ignore the intersection of generational standing and historical development: the Mexican second generation born 1921–1930 grew up in very different conditions than the Mexican second generation born 1971–1980.[5] Again, none of this means that there has been an end to discrimination; but differences in force and scope do matter immensely.

Institutionalization removes a certain fraction of men from the productive sector and reflects earlier harsh social conditions. But in the case of American black men, there is grim data suggesting that other men have also been removed, possibly by early death. The male-to-female sex ratio is a good indicator of this phenomenon; among blacks in the noninstitutionalized population, the ratio stands at 0.78. Among all blacks in this age range—institutionalized as well as not institutionalized—the sex ratio still amounts to only 0.88; in every other group it equals or exceeds 1.00. To put it differently, for black men, only slightly over three-quarters appear to be active in free society, because of institutionalization or other factors. Nothing remotely like this proportion is to be found in the other groups.

Table 4.4b shows the development of this pattern across the age range fifteen to thirty-four and compares it to the vastly more muted patterns among the U.S.-born of Mexican ancestry. It is possible that black male underenu-

TABLE 4.4A

The institutionalized population by ethnicity and birth cohort, Census 2000

	The 1966-75 birth cohort (25-34 in 2000)			
	% institutionalized		male/female ratio	
	male	female	non-instn. pop.	all
Mexicans				
Immigrants	1	0	1.36	1.36
1.56 group	1	0	1.03	1.04
1.53 group	1	0	1.02	1.03
U.S.-born	8	0	0.96	1.04
non-Mexicans				
NW	2	0	0.99	1.01
NBlk	13	1	0.78	0.88

TABLE 4.4B

A closer look at two groups of males, 15-34: blacks and U.S.-born with Mexican ancestry

		male/female ratio	
	% institutionalized	non-instn. pop.	all
blacks			
25-34	13	0.78	0.88
20-24	13	0.84	0.95
15-19	5	0.98	1.03
U.S.- born with Mexican ancestry			
25-34	8	0.96	1.04
20-24	5	1.03	1.09
15-19	3	1.04	1.07

Source: IPUMS dataset, 2000 census.

meration in the census—rather than black male early death—is creating some or all of this pattern. One must still appreciate, I think, that such a distinctively large population could not be found—despite intensive efforts by the Census Bureau—suggesting that many black men may also be lost to the economic mainstream of the community, even if the worst-case hypothesis is incorrect.

Blacks and whites differ on high-school completion, young unwed motherhood, male and female labor-force attachment, institutionalization, and sex ratios. In each case the difference is consistent with the presence of a youth culture of a disaffected inner-city racial minority. However, the Mexican 1.53

group is much less involved than blacks in all these risky behaviors—except for high-school dropout, for which the Mexican 1.53 group is much *more* at risk than native-born blacks. In a word, the Mexican 1.53 school patterns seem distinctive, unlike those of blacks, and not part of a complex of "underclass" behaviors.

In the light of the material reviewed, the educational behavior of the Mexican 1.53 group can be said to be consistent with an early turn to work for men and perhaps to homemaking for women. Indeed, these patterns seems strikingly reminiscent of earlier second generations, more like the behavior of the Italian or Polish second generation of 1940 than like the patterns of young-adult blacks in 2000. In those earlier second-generation groups, the young men in particular were more likely to leave school before native whites did in the cities of the Northeast and Midwest; and the women were more likely either to stay at home (even when single) or to work than to remain in school as long as native white women did. But whether it is still possible in the American job structure of the twenty-first century to obtain decent economic returns from the school-work-family patterns of 1940 Italians and Poles is another matter.

Earnings

Men's Earnings

I concentrate here especially on total personal *earned* income, that is, principally wages but supplemented by other earnings, for example, from self-employment. Except where stated otherwise, the sample is restricted to those who worked at least forty weeks during the preceding year and thirty-five hours per week. Table 4.5 presents the evidence on the young adult men—members of the 1.53 group and adult immigrants. In addition, the table includes information on the cohort most likely to include the fathers of the 1.53 group men, namely, Mexican immigrants who were born thirty years before that young-adult cohort and who reported arriving in the United States in 1970 or earlier.[6]

The group of likely immigrant fathers were earning 57 percent of what native white men of the same age earned, and the younger group of immigrant men were earning an almost identical 60 percent (table 4.5, column b). Against this background, the 1.53 group was faring much better, earning 79 percent of what the average native white earned. They had, in other words, made up about half the gap in a generation. Results for the unmixed second generation in 1998–2001 CPS data (not shown) are virtually identical.

TABLE 4.5
Weekly earnings of young men (25-34) working full time in 2000:
selected ethnic and racial groups

	weekly earnings (mean)	proportion of native white earnings		
		no controls	controls for: age + place of residence	
				+ education
selected groups	a	b	c	d
55-64 years of age				
Native whites	879			
Mexican immigrants (30+ yrs. resident in U.S.)	504	0.57	0.51	
25-34 years of age				
Native whites	662			
Mexican immigrants	399	0.60	0.57	0.75
Mexican 1.53 group	520	0.79	0.75	0.87
U.S.-born of Mexican origin	524	0.79	0.77	0.86
Native blacks	515	0.78	0.77	0.83

Source: IPUMS dataset for census 2000.

Note: Total earned income regressed on control variables: age (individual years; continuous var.), place of residence (region, metro status, Texas, California, Texas metro area, California metro area), education (LT high school, grades 9-11, grade 12 [no diploma], high school graduate, some college, college graduate, post-BA) ethnicity (as shown+ other)

The average young member of the 1.53 group is earning more than the immigrant three decades his senior, $520 compared to $504 per week (table 4.5, column a). To my mind, this evidence indicates considerable advance by the group. In particular, the means suggest that on average group members find midlevel jobs that pay better than those their parents' generation took—even as fewer than one in ten of this 1.53 group completed college.

Clearly the Mexican 1.53 individuals are a very long way from parity with native whites. Nevertheless, their situation may feel to them like more than standing still, more than facing work that only an immigrant would accept. Still, the mean dollar figures of both the older and younger generations are very close, implying that there are also a great many young men in the 1.53 group who are earning less than their immigrant fathers are earning. And many young workers may wonder how much they can expect to advance on the basis of their low-manual work. That is, the rough equality with older workers is only good news if the workers who are now young can expect their own wages to rise appreciably in future decades.

Earnings of the U.S.-born of Mexican origin average almost exactly the same amount as earnings in the Mexican 1.53 group (table 4.5, columns a, b, and c); I do not think this outcome can be taken to be an indication that generational improvement will stop in the second generation. Rather, it is an indication that the earlier second generations were not reaching the levels of well-being that the contemporary second generation is reaching; consequently, the children of today's second generation will start from a higher point than did the children of the earlier second-generation Mexicans.

The most striking evidence that the glass may be half empty emerges in the comparison with native-born blacks. The Mexican 1.53 group is earning just about the same amount, on average, as the native-born black population (table 4.5, columns a and b). Moreover, the Mexican 1.53 group members are more concentrated in high-earning areas than native-born blacks are; and so when we control for place of residence, the outcomes show a slight shift in favor of blacks (table 4.5, column c). Making these comparisons, it is hard to avoid thinking about the European second generations of the past; their attainments far exceeded those of blacks their own age (Perlmann 1988, 2005). Part of the difference, of course, is that blacks themselves are faring better today compared to native whites than blacks did in 1940–1960. In any case, taking account of contemporary concern for the black-white divide in American economic well-being, we can hardly be sanguine that another huge native-born, nonwhite group is earning at the levels of native-born blacks.

Nevertheless, this comparison is imperfect, and a wider context tends to favor Mexican Americans somewhat more. The wider context comes from taking into account the fact that these earnings are calculated for full-time workers only. And the proportion working full-time varies considerably across the groups, as we have seen. Native whites are most likely to be working full-time (81 percent), followed by the 1.53 group (74 percent) and the U.S.-born of Mexican origin (70 percent); among native-born black men the figure is low (59 percent). At the other extreme, 6 percent of native white men, 10–12 percent of men in the two Mexican groups, and 20 percent of native black men reported no earnings at all in Census 2000. So while the average black and Mexican 1.53 men who work full-time earn about the same amount, roughly five members of the 1.53 group work full-time for every four native-born blacks. A fuller analysis must involve women's and family incomes, but at least among the men, these data clearly reveal meaningful net advantages for the 1.53 group compared to native-born blacks.

Education and Earnings

I control for education by including dummy variables for almost every educational level that the census allowed respondents to select. Thus, educational differences found in the census are allowed to explain as much of the variance in earnings as possible (in particular, the analysis assumes no linearity in the association between educational levels and earnings).

About half the difference in earnings between the Mexican 1.53 group and native whites is due to the impact of schooling; when schooling is taken into account, the 1.53 group members earn 87 percent of the native white mean earnings—compared to 75 percent, when education is ignored (table 4.5 columns c and d). The role of education differs only slightly for the U.S.-born of Mexican origin; but education does explain about twice as much of the Mexican differences from native whites as it does of the black differences.

Big payoffs from schooling, we are always told, come from an advanced education—specifically a four-year college degree. But it is important to insist here on the importance of what is happening at the lower branching point, high-school graduation. The very high rate at which the Mexican 1.53 group, and especially its men, drop out of high school has serious economic implications. We saw that 8 percent of native white men failed to complete high school, whereas about a quarter of the men in the "true" Mexican second generation failed to do so; and college-completion rates for men in the Mexican 1.53 group who have finished high school are also far lower than the equivalent rates for native whites. In short, for the Mexican 1.53 group, there are two distinct forms of educational vulnerability involved in low college completion: low high-school completion rates and low persistence in college through four more years by high-school completers. By contrast, only the second form of vulnerability has an important impact on white-black educational attainment differences.

How much improvement in Mexican 1.53 earnings might we reasonably expect if either of these levels of vulnerability were eliminated? We have already seen that even if *all* educational differences between native whites and the Mexican 1.53 group were eliminated, only *half* of the ethnic earnings gap would disappear. But it is still important to explore what impact is created by the Mexican American failure to complete particular levels of schooling at the rates that native whites do. Affecting high-school graduation rates implies a different set of societal (and indeed familial) policies than affecting educational persistence among high-school graduates. I want to insist on the point that the vulnerability at the lower level, failure to complete high school, has crucial implications.

Elsewhere (Perlmann 2005, 107–109), I have shown that a rise in the high-school graduation rate of Mexican Americans to the level of native whites would produce a larger impact on their earnings than would the equivalent rise in the college-graduation rate of their high-school graduates without any improvement in their rate of completing high school. More high-school graduates would of course translate into more college graduates, since the (lower) rate of college completion by Mexican Americans would apply to a large base.

The point is not that graduating from high school is nearly as reward-ing as graduating from college; of course college graduation produces the far greater payoff. And of course too I am not arguing against efforts to boost the rate of Mexican American college attendance. The point is rather that despite the much higher returns from college compared to high-school completion, the lower—but not negligible—returns from high-school graduation mat-ter for the individual. Moreover, there are a great many Mexican 1.53 group members who are not passing the lower branch point; consequently, when our perspective shifts from the individual to the ethnic group, the results of changes at the lower branch point can be as great or greater for this group than a quite radical change at the higher branch point.

Many Mexican American young men may believe that their job pros-pects will not be much served by finishing high school. They may believe that whatever is true in the mainstream, the sectors of the economy in which *they* will find their best jobs, as a result of ethnic contacts or discrimination, for example, do not reward a high-school diploma very highly. Such sugges-tions amount to a hypothesis that the returns from a high-school degree for Mexican Americans will be lower than for other groups. But the hypothesis is not borne out by the Mexican 1.53 group in Census 2000; higher-order interaction terms for ethnicity, schooling, and earnings are not statistically significant. A particularly vivid demonstration can be found among the young people in the metro areas of California, where more of the Mexican 1.53 group are concentrated than in the metro areas of any other state. For this regional sample, I regressed earnings on specific levels of education for each group separately, native whites and Mexican 1.53 group members. At the very lowest levels, returns (or lack thereof) cannot be compared because less than 1 percent of native whites (but 11 percent of the Mexicans) dropped out before completing tenth grade. However, returns can be meaningfully com-pared at each of seven higher levels of educational attainment. None of those levels shows returns differing between native whites and the Mexican group in a statistically significant way. Mexican American youths may or may not judge the value of secondary schooling to be low for them; but if they do make that judgment, they are, on average, wrong. If social scientists make it, they are wrong too.

Gendered Patterns and Family Structure: The Mexican Second Generation and Native Blacks Reconsidered

The gendered dynamics of the workplace are well known from countless observations: an occupational structure highly segregated by gender, three young men working full-time for every two young women, and those men earning a dollar and a quarter for every dollar earned by those women. It is within this broader pattern that we can explore some additional ethnic and racial differences that are no less striking.

When the comparison is across groups, Mexican 1.53 group men and women fare about the same compared to native whites of the same sex: in 2000, the ethnic wage ratio was 0.75 for men and 0.77 for women (for blacks it was 0.77 and 0.84, respectively). Education accounts for twelve points of the twenty-five-percentage-point ethnic gap among the men and fifteen points of the twenty-three-percentage-point ethnic gap among the women (and roughly the same amounts, respectively, in the black-white earnings gaps). The residual (unexplained) earnings gaps from native whites are thus about 13 percent of native white wages for Mexican 1.53 group men and 8 percent for women (for blacks, about 17 percent for men and 8 percent for women).

Nevertheless, Mexican-black earnings differences among full-time work-ers, whether for men or for women, can take us only so far. We have already seen in the preceding section how substantially smaller proportions of black compared to Mexican 1.53 group men are working full-time, and substan-tially greater proportions of black men are not working at all. The higher proportion of black women working will counterbalance these losses to some extent, but it will not erase them because women earn on average so much less than men. Finally, we must consider the uniquely high proportions of black young men who are either institutionalized or missing (and possibly dead). If we think not of individual earners but rather of the total earnings stream coming into the families of an ethnic group, then all these factors are relevant. Here I focus on *total family income* and include all young-adult families in which an adult woman was present. In 2000, the Mexican 1.53 group families had 80 percent as much income as native white families; the black families had only 57 percent as much. This finding highlights what appear to be economic consequences of the risk factors discussed earlier, which are more common among blacks than in the Mexican 1.53 group.

These comparisons of Mexican American and black earnings should be seen as an attempt to contribute to the literature situating the new labor migrants in the context of black social patterns on the one hand and of our image of European immigrant upward mobility on the other. Of course, I have not attempted here to compare Mexican and European immigrants (but see Perlmann 2005) but only to highlight differences between Mexican American and black social patterns. To the extent that the segmented-assimilation argument can be read as a challenge to the notion that—on average—the Mexican pattern of upward mobility will parallel that of earlier Europeans and as an assertion that it will instead parallel inner-city black social patterns, this chapter can be read as a caution against accepting such a conjecture. It does not follow, however, that Mexican American patterns will parallel those of the European immigrant past—if by that we mean mostly the speed of upward mobility of the Italians and Slavs of the last great wave of immigration (see Bean and Stevens 2003). A prosaic path between segmented-assimilation theory and the application of European upward-mobility patterns to the Mexicans of today is to suggest that upward mobility is occurring for the Mexicans but probably more slowly than it did for the European groups of the last great immigration wave, and the attainment of parity with the offspring of today's native whites may take a generation longer, on average, than it did for those Europeans.

The Preceding Evidence in Discussions, 2005–2009

It was the initial formulation of segmented-assimilation theory elaborated by Portes and Zhou in 1992 and 1993 that made us all sit up and take notice. Since then, the theory has been much elaborated, and the emphases have shifted.[7] Still, its largest claim was already stated in the first iteration (Portes and Zhou 1993, 82):

> The question is into what sector of American society a particular immigrant group assimilates. . . . We observe today several distinct forms of adaptation. One of them replicates the time-honored portrayal of growing acculturation and parallel integration into the white middle-class; a second leads straight in the opposite direction to permanent poverty and assimilation into the underclass; still a third associates rapid economic advancement with deliberate preservation of the immigrant community's

values and tight solidarity. This pattern of segmented assimilation immediately raises the question of what makes some immigrant groups become susceptible to the downward route and what resources allow others to avoid this course. In the ultimate analysis, the same general process helps explain both outcomes.

As the last sentence hints, not only the largest claim but also the basic line of explanation was laid out in this first iteration: various factors in the social context will matter greatly to outcomes—especially American racial hostility to nonwhites, the geographic proximity of second-generation members to adversarial minority youth cultures, and the "absence of mobility ladders."

Moreover, although not stated explicitly in the quoted passage, the prediction of downward assimilation pertains principally to children of labor migrants. This becomes fully clear in the later diagramming of the theory, in which typologies of immigrant human capital, modes of incorporation, and "social contexts" are shown together (e.g., Portes, Fernandez-Kelly, and Haller 2009, 1082). Nevertheless, the emphasis on the children of labor migrants was at least implicit in the earliest formulations of the theory, in connection with the discussion of the transformation of the economic context facing the second generation: "A rapid process of national deindustrialization and global industrial re-structuring . . . has left entrants to the American labor force confronting a widening gap between the minimally paid menial jobs that immigrants commonly accept and the high-tech and professional occupations requiring college degrees that native elites occupy" (Portes and Zhou 1993, 76). This historical change has led to "the evaporation of occupational ladders for intergenerational mobility," and "the new hourglass economy, created by economic restructuring, means that children of immigrants must cross a narrow bottleneck to occupations requiring advanced training" (ibid., 83–85). These transformations obviously matter vastly more to the children of immigrants arriving without high-school diplomas than for those whose parents are medical personnel, engineers, or entrepreneurs bringing assets.

Indeed, if our interest is limited to the groups in which the labor migrants predominate, such as Mexicans, we can imagine a stripped-down version of segmented-assimilation theory that would give primacy of place to economic origins and outcomes. It would show how labor migrants get on with relatively low human capital in a transformed American economy. In such a theory all the other sources of behavioral outcomes would be relegated to a more minor status: threats of adversarial youth culture and even the role of race, at least for immigrants who are not classified as black in the American racial system. Likewise, the countervailing resources captured in discussions of modes of incorporation, and especially in discussions of coethnic community cultural institutions, could find a minor place in such a presentation. Such a stripped-down version of segmented-assimilation theory is very like the perspective of economist George Borjas (1994), who worries about the implications of admitting into the American economy so many immigrants with relatively low human capital.[8]

This worry ties into a crucial later revision of the negative predictions of segmented-assimilation theory. Specifically, in place of the outcomes of "permanent poverty and assimilation into the underclass," the authors now predict both "downward assimilation into deviant lifestyles" and a new, less extreme outcome, "stagnation into subordinate menial working class jobs" (Portes, Fernandez-Kelly, and Haller 2009, 1080). I could have helped my readers by alerting them at the beginning of this chapter to the revised formulation of the theory. Nevertheless, as a test of the downward prediction, the earlier sections of this chapter remain relevant.

We need to look more closely at this new second prediction of "stagnation into subordinate menial working class" jobs. The revised theory provides no sustained discussion. The new prediction, I think, makes its first appearance in *Legacies,* by Alejandro Portes and Rubén Rumbaut (2001, 282–284)—as "failure to attain middle class occupations" leading to "marginal working class communities" in the third and later generation. These phrases come from the diagram of outcomes; but the accompanying text is minimal:

> Other groups fail to move upward in the second generation, the children having educational credentials and occupational opportunities no better than their parents. . . . There is no empirical evidence at present to expect that groups confined to the working class or that have moved downward into the native underclass would miraculously rise during the third generation to alter their collective status. There is on the other hand strong evidence on the intergenerational transmission of both privilege and disadvantage. (Ibid., 283; see also Portes and Rumbaut 2005, 263–265)

In the past, too, immigrants' children did not attain really extensive educations, but they moved ahead into better jobs anyway, often within the working class. Consequently, in order to test the prediction of "stagnation" in our own time, the theory must deal carefully with distinctions among workers who have not yet moved upward so very far; it does not provide that kind of operationalization. Shifts in working-class jobs may seem like "lateral" rather than "upward" mobility to those who hold the really attractive jobs in America, but that is not the appropriate criterion.

The theory is much more detailed in laying out subjective measures about adolescents—measures of their self-identity or other aspects of cultural orientation. This emphasis no doubt reflects the early focus of the research on children under eighteen years of age. Yet even now, as the researchers devise measures for early postschool life, they are focusing on a "Downward Assimilation Index" (Portes, Fernandez-Kelly, and Haller 2009, 1088). We need at least a comparable degree of care devoted to a "stagnation index" if we are to take seriously the claim of negative outcomes for the majority of the labor migrants' children.

Another way to approach second-generation economic outcomes is to focus on earnings instead of (or in addition to) occupations. This is what I did earlier in this chapter. True, earnings do not tell us whether "subordinate menial working class" jobs are at issue for both fathers and sons. But they do tell us whether the sons are being better rewarded than the fathers. It stands to reason that if they are, then they regard their own labor-market situation as an intergenerational improvement and that employers must be regarding their skills as more attractive than their fathers'. The earlier evidence reveals just such improvements. In my book I also drew out comparisons with the past, suggesting that today's Mexicans are probably moving ahead more slowly than did second generations in the past but that they are nonetheless moving ahead, that at least so far the changes in the economy have not been so great as to suggest that the descendants of labor migrants will not eventually join the mainstream. I followed the formulation of Bean and Stevens (2003) in suggesting that this painful process may well take four or five generations rather than three or four, as it did for the descendants of the labor migrants of the last great immigration wave.

At the risk of repetition, this formulation can be restated to address directly the predictions of segmented-assimilation theory. I found that the average outcome for the Mexican second generation was a modest improvement over their fathers' earnings (modest in the eyes of elites certainly). Moreover, socially risky behaviors, a measure of downward assimilation, show up among this second generation at rates decidedly lower than in black America. From such findings I saw no reason to conclude that future improvement would cease. Rather, slow upward movement toward social and economic parity with the descendants of the European immigrants of earlier centuries seemed plausible.

Now Portes and his coauthors believe that with such conclusions I (together with other critics they discuss) ended up supporting their own predictions:[9] "Ultimately results of these studies turn out to be generally compatible with the segmented assimilation model and to support its principal tenets. . . . In the end the vigorous initial critique of the segmented assimilation model by these authors turns out to be quibbles at the margin" (Portes, Fernandez-Kelly, and Haller 2009, 1083).

No; rather, we need to ask just how much difference really remains today between the "revised segmented-assimilation theory" and classical assimilation theory. The former predicts downward assimilation only for a minority and "stagnation" for the majority of labor migrants' children. But the discussion of "stagnation" has so far been too vague to allow for the difference between that term and modest improvement. The result is that in the revised theory as it stands today, the two negative outcomes predicted for the children of labor migrants simply do not distinguish that theory very clearly from what the authors call the classical theory of assimilation. Any sophisticated formulation of the classical theory does not involve "rosy" predictions (Portes, Fernandez-Kelly, and Haller 2009, 1078), but it does predict eventual socioeconomic parity of labor migrants' descendants with the mainstream. Again, the classical theory never argued that parity would be attained in two generations or that the process from immigration to parity was easy and pleasant.

So what does in fact remain novel in "revised segmented-assimilation theory"? Portes, Fernandez-Kelly, and Haller at one point in their 2009 article seem to be struggling with this question themselves. They first note precisely the revision of the negative prediction that I have been stressing—that "downward assimilation into underclass-like conditions is just *one* possible outcome of the process and that an alternative, indeed more common, result among the offspring of disadvantaged labor immigrants is stagnation into the working class" (1083). Nevertheless, they proceed to ignore the latter prediction in their claims for the theory's novel contributions, focusing only on downward assimilation:

> The segmented assimilation model predicts two basic things: first, that downward assimilation, as indexed by the above series of outcomes [i.e., "school abandonment, unemployment, teenage childbearing, and arrest and incarceration"], exists and affects a sizeable number of second-generation youths; second, that incidents of downward or, for that matter, upward assimilation are not random but are patterned by the set of exogenous causal determinants identified by the model. (1083–1084)

This is not the place to enter into an evaluation of the second "basic thing." Suffice it to say that no one should fail to appreciate the effort to systematize the factors that make up the dynamics of immigration; we only need compare the thin typology in Gordon (1964) and the elaborate model of revised segmented-assimilation theory to admire and be grateful for the sustained advances in this effort. And we need not agree with the choice or emphasis on every element in the model to appreciate the contribution.[10] Nevertheless, to return to where I started, I believe that the theory received such wide attention far more because of the first of the two basic things mentioned in this passage than because of the second; certainly this is how I got interested in studying more about contemporary immigration.

Bound up with the predictions of negative outcomes is the assumption that the prevalence of such outcomes and especially of downward assimilation is greater in the current than in earlier immigrations. At times it seems Portes and his coauthors recognize how complicated it would be to document the historical argument.[11] And yet their claim for the uniqueness of the present moment seems impossible to articulate without inviting explicit historical comparisons. The extent of downward assimilation in the past would be worth some scholarly attention. Consider, for example, the Polish and Italian second generation in the 1930s; how large a decline into crime and skid row and bootlegging among them would we have to find in order to argue that the prevalence of downward assimilation in the revised segmented-assimilation model is less novel than one might have supposed?[12]

In sum, I think the claims that segmented-assimilation theory depicts a more negative view of outcomes than do other views of assimilation has already been curtailed in the revised theory, and they may well need to be curtailed still more. Even so, long-term advances will still be provided by the theory's systematization and specificity, and these cannot help but serve also those of us who will disagree with some of those specifics.

In closing, it is useful also to respond to two critiques that Portes and his colleagues raise about the evidence developed earlier; these involve important issues of interpretation.

1. TEEN PREGNANCY. Young Mexican 1.53 group women, like young black women, have high rates of childbearing in their late teens or early twenties; but the Mexican mothers are typically married, whereas the black mothers are not (see earlier in this chapter). Portes and his colleagues are not interested in the marital status of the mothers: for them, early childbirth is the criterion for underclass behavior, whether in marriage or not (Portes 2006,

501; Portes, Fernandez-Kelly, and Haller 2009, 1083). Yet surely even if one asserts that view, teen pregnancy outside marriage is much worse for economic outcomes. I doubt most people would think of childbearing at a young age within marriage as underclass behavior. Portes refers to those marriages as "flimsy," presumably anticipating such a response (Portes 2006, 501). But are they really flimsy? No evidence is mentioned. In any case even if the marriages were shown to be flimsy, surely they are not as flimsy as the commitments among the young unmarried couples?

There is another issue raised by young childbearing in the Mexican second generation, namely, the source of the pattern. Portes and his colleagues apparently assume that this is socially risky behavior picked up from the American inner-city culture. An alternative possibility is that the pattern of young marriage was also common among the Mexican immigrant mothers, including those who had married in Mexico. Such a pattern would count as an example of a retained cultural legacy. This possibility should be appreciated in the context of what segmented-assimilation theory has to say about the value of retaining such legacies as a buffer against downward assimilation. In the case of young marriage we would be confronting an example of a cultural preservation working, according to Portes and his colleagues, as a negative behavior. I do not want to belabor the point, especially since I do not view early childbearing within marriage as an example of downward assimilation. Nevertheless, the larger point here is that more attention should probably be paid to possible negative as well as positive implications of preserving immigrant cultural legacies. Since there is something organic about such a legacy, it will not be so easy for the policy analyst prescribing preservation to pick and choose among its elements.

2. DISTINGUISHING OLDER AND NEWER MEXICAN-ORIGIN POPULATIONS. In general, I found much higher levels of socially risky behavior indicative of "an underclass" among blacks than among the Mexican 1.53 group. On the other hand I noted earlier that among the Mexican American men of later generations, one measure—rate of institutionalization—reached 8 percent. This is not as high a rate as among blacks (13 percent), but it is far higher than the rate found among the Mexican second generation or among native whites. Portes thinks that I am equivocating in treating the evidence from this group of later-generation Mexican Americans as different from the evidence on the second generation (Portes 2006, 501). I could ask in rejoinder, what then explains the absence of elevated rates among the second-generation Mexicans? But the more important point is that I offer a clear explana-

tion for why the trajectory of the present second generation should not be confused with that of the later-generation Mexican Americans: discrimination against Mexican immigrants in the earlier period was much greater than it is today. My critics do not relate to this explanation; perhaps the reason is that in the book I presented it in an earlier chapter and only allude briefly to it in the discussion of underclass behaviors. In any case, in this chapter, I repeat the explanation.[13]

NOTES

1. For an assessment of the adequacy of this proxy, see Perlmann 2005, 142–156.

2. For a discussion of a peculiarity of the high-school completion data in Census 2000 and its relevance to the ethnic data, see Perlmann 2005, 156–161.

3. Among Mexican *immigrants,* a high proportion of young women are found at home even if they do not have a child (24 percent of them); this stay-at-home pattern, despite the low income of the group, probably reflects a more traditional view of women's roles than is prevalent among the American-born.

4. Perlmann 2005, 60–67, presents some discussion of this systematic discrimination.

5. In addition, the subjectivity of the Hispanic-origin question could influence the measure of outcomes. It is at least plausible that the more assimilated and better educated are more likely not to list Mexican origins. On this point, see also Alba and Islam (2009). For further discussion of third-generation behavior, see also Perlmann (2005, 60–64), Alba and Nee (2003, ch. 6) and Bean and Stevens (2003, 130–142).

6. For a fuller discussion of methods, including controls for geographic residence and educational attainment, see Perlmann 2005, chap. 4.

7. Portes, Fernandez-Kelly, and Haller (2009, 1078–1079) date stages in the elaboration of the theory and cite the major publications.

8. In an influential essay, Borjas had also estimated the wages of immigrants from different countries of origin in 1910 (Borjas 1994). Christopher Jencks later used Borjas's historical research to estimate immigrant-to-native-white wage ratios for that year; he then compared those ratios to similarly computed wage ratios today and found the ratios today much more unequal than those of 1910 (Jencks 2001, 2002). Implicit in Jencks's work is the suggestion that this comparison of immigrant-to-native-white wage ratios over time can serve as a simple way to measure the effect of long-term economic change on the prospects for economic improvement among immigrants and their descendants. These are changes about which segmented-assimilation theorists (and many others issuing warnings) only spoke in vague terms. My own study is heavily indebted to Jencks's suggestion; however, using more recently developed evidence on 1910 wages, I have concluded that the historical change in immigrant prospects is far more muted than Jencks believes (Perlmann 2005, esp. chap. 2 and 126–142).

9. Simple misreadings may also contribute to this view. In three different papers the following sentence is cited to show that my findings are in line with the predictions of segmented assimilation theory: "Mexican American dropout rates should bring to mind the warnings of the segmented assimilation hypothesis: that an important part of the

contemporary second generation will assimilate downwards" (Perlmann 2005, 82–83). See Portes 2006, 500; Portes and Fernandez-Kelly 2008; Portes, Fernandez-Kelly, and Haller 2009, 1083. Yet the next sentence in my text reads, "But this hypothesis assumes that more than schooling is involved: that high drop-out rates are one indicator among several of a wider complex of behaviors." And these other indicators do not show an underclass cultural complex at work. The relevant paragraph appears in the first section of this chapter, on high-school dropout rates.

10. The hesitations and cautions raised in Perlmann and Waldinger (1997), Waldinger and Perlmann (1998), and Perlmann (2000) remain relevant; most have not been mentioned here because they are not directly relevant to the text.

11. "Transformations of the American political economy render the comparison of labor migrants at the beginning and end of the twentieth century difficult to sustain. . . . The more appropriate contemporary comparison is between labor and professional migrants" (Portes 2006, 502). For many purposes the latter is indeed an appropriate comparison, but it can hardly make the case for novel *historical* outcomes.

12. An even stronger case could probably be made about the Irish second generation in 1850–1875.

13. The critics also cite evidence on arrests drawn from interview data from the Children of Immigrants Longitudinal Study (CILS) in which ethnic trends differ from those in the census data on institutionalization. I see no reason to privilege their interview data on arrests in two cities over the census evidence on institutionalization.

5

Downward Assimilation and Mexican Americans

AN EXAMINATION OF INTERGENERATIONAL ADVANCE AND STAGNATION IN EDUCATIONAL ATTAINMENT

Richard Alba, Dalia Abdel-Hady, Tariqul Islam, and Karen Marotz

An influential perspective on contemporary immigration and the U.S.-born generations issuing from it originates with the theory of segmented assimilation (Portes and Zhou 1993; see also Gans 1992). It sees the descendants of today's immigrants as at risk of what has been called "downward assimilation": a failure to advance beyond the humble status of the immigrant generation, which is then transformed into a negative self-evaluation because of a change in frame of reference, from that of the origin society to that of the receiving one. Downward assimilation is held to be associated with continuing racism in the United States and is therefore a particular risk for those who appear to be nonwhite by U.S. standards. It presumably "locks" the individuals who experience it into a racialized minority status, implying systematic and persisting disadvantage.

Mexican Americans appear to be prime candidates for downward assimilation. Indeed, the seminal article by Alejandro Portes and Min Zhou (1993) noted studies of Mexican Americans in the school system that found the emergence of oppositional norms, that is, a rejection of the conventional values of school achievement among U.S.-born Mexican students but not among immigrant ones (see Matute-Bianchi 1991). A possible explanation lies in the two groups' different reference points: U.S.-born Mexican Americans evaluate their limited school prospects by the standards of the larger society and reject a system that appears to be rejecting them. Consistent with these ideas are the findings of apparent stagnation in the educational attainment of Mexican Americans between the second and third generations (Bean et al. 1994; Wojtkiewicz and Donato 1995). As a consequence, numerous analysts of the Mexican American situation have been led to pessimistic conclusions about the ultimate place of the group in U.S. society (e.g., Lopez and Stanton-Salazar 2001; Telles and Ortiz 2008).

Other analysts have noted that the very long history of Mexican immigration to the United States, which goes back more than a century, threatens the validity of the conclusions about intergenerational stagnation, since these are typically based on cross-sectional data analyses (Perlmann 2003; Smith 2003). Another confounding factor is the pre-civil-rights-era institutional discrimination from which Mexican Americans suffered, since it impeded the educational mobility of earlier U.S.-born generations. These complexities cannot be unraveled with cross-sectional data of different generational groups. Instead, they require true intergenerational data, as have been gathered by Telles and Ortiz (2008) on the basis of a 1965 survey of Mexican Americans in Los Angeles and San Antonio. Their data reveal substantial mobility by children in comparison with their parents and a narrowing of the gap separating cohorts of Mexican Americans from mainstream educational norms (Telles and Ortiz 2008, 111).

In this chapter, we approach the same problem with national data that allow us to compare parents and children: we examine the educational attainments of Mexican Americans in several different data sets, including the General Social Survey (GSS), the National Longitudinal Study of Youth (NLSY) of 1979, and the National Education Longitudinal Study (NELS) of 1988. The GSS data enable us to gain an overview of generational differences across a broad span of historical time (i.e., birth cohorts), while the NLSY and NELS data allow us to focus on specific recent birth cohorts (1957–1964 in the case of the NLSY and 1972–1975 in that of NELS). The picture we gain is consistent across all three: "downward" assimilation, as evidenced by intergenerational stagnation in education, is uncommon in both the second and the third generations of Mexican Americans. In general, the young members of each generation make a substantial advance beyond the educational attainments of their parents; this intergenerational differential, which averages more than two years even in the third generation, is substantially greater than that found among non-Hispanic whites. Paradoxically, however, even in the recent cohorts of the third generation, the educational attainment of Mexican Americans does not show signs of catching up with that of whites.

Background Considerations

A great deal of research confirms the educational disadvantage of Mexican Americans, but as yet we do not have a satisfactory explanation of it (see, e.g., Attinasi 1989; Garcia 2001; Hirschman 2001; Kao and Tienda 1995; Lopez and Stanton-Salazar 2001; Portes and Rumbaut 2001; Suárez-Orozco and Suárez-Orozco 1995; Velez 1989; Warren 1996). Part of the difficulty lies in the diversity of perspectives employed by the researchers, who have pointed to a wide range of potential explanatory factors, from the social-psychological to the human-capital and linguistic characteristics of Mexican American families, to the racism and discrimination built into the American social system (on the last, see also Bonilla-Silva 2003; Omi and Winant 1994; Telles and Ortiz 2008).

One point seems incontestable, however. In order to evaluate the degree of educational disadvantage suffered by Mexican Americans, one must take their socioeconomic origins into account, especially the educational attainment of their parents (Warren 1996). Mexican immigrants arrive with low levels of formal schooling compared to the general American population. It would be improbable therefore for second-generation Mexican Americans to match the average educational attainments of the U.S.-born in general, and even the third generation generally begins at a lower starting point than the average American. This is all the more the case given the institutional discrimination of the pre-civil-rights era that blocked much intergenerational advance during a good part of the twentieth century. For instance, the analysis by Grebler, Moore, and Guzmán (1970) shows very low levels of education among Texas-born Mexican Americans as of 1960. Moreover, because of the long period over which Mexican immigration extends, there is a heightened risk with cross-sectional comparisons of confounding historical variations in the characteristics of immigration streams with intergenerational differences. Put another way, we cannot assume in the Mexican case that the characteristics of the second generation resemble those of the parents of the third, when we compare these groups at the same moment in time.

For these reasons, it is imperative to conduct research with data sets that contain information about the socioeconomic characteristics of parents. This consideration suggests two strategies: one is to analyze census data by focusing on the educational trajectories of individuals young enough to live with their parents; the other is to analyze special surveys, such as the NELS, that collect information about children and their parents. The former has the disadvantage that it constrains the analysis to ages when the educational records of individuals are still incomplete; the latter, that the samples of Mexican Americans tend to be small and specific to particular regions or birth cohorts. In this chapter, we attempt to overcome the latter difficulty by combining analyses from several different data sets, including the 2000 Census Public Use Sample and the General Social Survey, as well as the NLSY and the NELS.

Data Sources

The General Social Survey is a nationally representative survey of the English-speaking population of the United States, conducted biannually (Davis, Smith, and Marsden 2001). The GSS includes extensive data on the socioeconomic origins of respondents, including the educational attainments of parents. It permits a full identification of generational status, including the separation of the fourth from the third generations. The distinction could be important if there are substantial differences in life chances between the descendants of those Mexicans who became Americans by conquest, at the end of the 1846–1848 war, and the Mexican Americans descended from immigrants. Any differences are potentially visible only if we can separate the fourth (and later) generations, that is, individuals with U.S.-born grandparents, from the third generation, which is mostly descended from early-twentieth-century immigrants.

The General Social Survey has been fielded since 1972, and this collection of data over a long period of time allows us to examine Mexican Americans born in the United States in the early part of the twentieth century, as well as those born after midcentury. One other feature of the GSS is that it collects ancestry data, rather than ethnic-identity information. In principle, then, our analysis includes individuals who have Mexican and some other ethnic ancestry. Our analysis, based on individuals who were twenty-five or older when they were surveyed and who are classifiable in generational terms, includes 554 U.S.-born individuals with Mexican ancestry. Only a very small number, 17, have ethnically mixed ancestry.

The National Longitudinal Survey of Youth (NLSY) of 1979 was designed for the investigation of the labor-market experiences of American youth, aged fourteen to twenty-one in 1979. Since it is a longitudinal survey, the data from subsequent waves allow us to ascertain the completed educational attainment of respondents. The NLSY of 1979 was composed of several different samples: in addition to a strictly representative sample, oversamples of blacks, Hispanics, the poor, and the military were collected. For this analysis, we make use of the representative sample, along with the oversample of

Hispanics. Respondents to the NLSY also can name more than one origin. We include in the analysis anyone who cites Mexican origins regardless of what other ethnic origins are also indicated. From the nativity data collected by the survey, we are able to classify Mexican Americans into the second or the third and later generation; that is, the distinction between the third and fourth generations cannot be implemented here. All in all, we can analyze 906 second- and third-generation Mexican Americans.

The National Education Longitudinal Study (NELS) of 1988 is a nationally representative sample of the eighth graders of 1988, a portion of whom have been followed in subsequent waves. Ethnic data were gathered based on students' responses to a question that asked them to choose the category that best describes their background; so mixed ancestry is not identifiable. As in the NLSY, the nativity data permit us only to divide the U.S.-born between the second and the third and later generations. From these data, we are able to analyze the educational attainments of 707 Mexican Americans.

In all the data sets, we also analyze third- and later-generation Anglos, that is, non-Hispanic whites, as a comparison group. For the NLSY and NELS, which involve recent birth cohorts, we additionally compare educational distributions to those found for U.S.-born Mexican and Anglo Americans in the 2000 Census (as calculated from the 5 percent Public Use Microdata sample).

Analysis of GSS Data

Table 5.1, derived from the General Social Survey, presents the educational attainment of Mexican Americans by gender and generation, with a comparable distribution for later-generation non-Hispanic whites. The most basic pattern in the table is the continued disadvantage of Mexicans compared to Anglos. At the lower end of the educational distribution, Mexicans of all generations display substantially higher rates of failure to graduate from high school than non-Hispanic whites do. In the third generation, for example, the Mexican American dropout rate varies between a quarter for women and nearly 40 percent for men, compared to less than 20 percent among third- and later-generation Anglos (i e , non-Hispanic whites). Mexican Americans of the fourth and later generations also have not caught up to Anglos, though the patterns in this group are hard to interpret because it mixes the later-generation descendants of immigrants and the descendants of Mexicans indigenous to territory conquered by the United States, whose families, frequently settled in heavily Mexican American communities in Texas and the

TABLE 5.1

The educational attainments of Mexican Americans and Anglos, by gender and generation

	less than hs	hs grad	some coll	coll grad	N
MEXICANS					
second generation					
male	39.6	28.1	20.8	11.5	96
female	39.8	28.8	22.9	8.5	118
third generation					
male	38.0	17.7	24.1	20.3	79
female	24.8	33.6	31.0	10.6	113
fourth generation					
male	25.6	23.3	37.2	14.0	43
female	24.3	38.6	25.7	11.4	70
third & fourth generations combined					
male	35.8	20.4	26.3	17.5	137
female	26.9	34.3	28.4	10.4	201
ANGLOS					
third & fourth generations combined					
male	17.8	31.8	23.9	26.5	9389
female	18.6	37.3	23.4	20.7	11971

Source: General Social Surveys, 1972-2002.

Southwest, may have suffered an enduring institutional discrimination more severe than that faced by immigrants and their descendants (Gonzalez 1990).

Disparities of not quite the same magnitude also appear for education beyond high school. In the third generation, for instance, slightly more than 40 percent of Mexican American men and women have attended college, compared to 50 percent of Anglo males but only 44 percent of Anglo females. The inequality appears larger for college graduation, especially among women: the Anglo rate is twice the Mexican American one in the third and fourth generations.

Yet there also appear to be modest generational improvements for Mexican Americans between the second and later generations. Overall, going to college is about ten percentage points less likely for the second generation than for the third and fourth generations. High-school dropout rates are about 40 percent for both men and women in the second generation, and they clearly fall off for later-generation women. The case for men is ambiguous because of the still high dropout rate in the third generation, though this appears to moderate in the fourth.

TABLE 5.2
Average years of education in the contemporary and parents' generations

	mean own education	mean father's education	pct. missing	mean mother's education	pct. missing
MEXICANS					
second generation					
male	11.3	5.6	30.2	5.7	14.6
female	11.0	4.8	37.0	6.4	22.7
third generation					
male	11.9	8.7	25.3	8.0	20.6
female	12.2	8.9	19.5	8.8	6.2
fourth generation					
male	12.6	8.6	25.6	8.5	16.3
female	12.2	9.2	26.8	8.1	11.3
ANGLOS					
third+ generation					
male	13.2	10.9	21.1	11.3	13.3
female	12.9	10.7	24.8	11.0	13.7

Source: General Social Surveys, 1972-2002.

While the data do suggest improvements across the generations, they are nevertheless consistent with the notion of little intergenerational mobility. However, one must always be wary in cross-sectional data of taking an earlier generation to be representative of the parents of a later one. It is preferable to compare the educational status of a contemporary generational group directly to that of its parents, something that we do in table 5.2. This makes clear that there is no intergenerational stagnation in the achievements of Mexican Americans. In fact, their advance over the meager educations of their parents is substantially greater than is the case among Anglos, and this advance is evident from the second through the fourth generations.

What stands out is the low educational attainment of Mexican American parents, whatever their generational position. Table 5.2 reports education in terms of mean years of schooling, and the parents of the second generation, most of whom have immigrated from Mexico, report very low levels of education, which do not exceed the sixth grade on average. This accords with what is generally known about the educational levels of Mexican immigrants. However, even the U.S.-born parents of the members of the third and fourth generations do not attain average levels that indicate any more than a year of high school (eight to nine years). Even more remarkably, there is no change between the parents of the third and fourth generations (and there is also little difference between mothers and fathers). By contrast, the parents of third- and later-generation Anglos reveal levels of education that are two years higher on average (ten to eleven years).

Compared to Mexican Americans' low parental starting point, their educational attainment is, in every generation, several years above that of their parents. The biggest difference, on the order of five to six years, occurs in the second generation and is a consequence of immigration into a society with mandatory schooling well into the teenage years. Even in the third and fourth generations, the advance remains large: three to four years. The advance among Anglos is noticeably smaller, about two years. Thus, these data indicate that most Mexican Americans have no reason to view their socioeconomic position as equivalent to that of their parents, at least if educational attainment is the standard. For the most part, they have good reason to view themselves as having moved ahead.

There is one note of uncertainty in the table: namely, the high rates of missing data for parents' education. However, it appears unlikely that more complete data would challenge the patterns described here. For one thing, the extent of missing data is fairly similar among Mexican Americans and non-Hispanic whites. For another, it seems probable that data are most likely to be missing when children and parents have low levels of education. Thus, more complete data are likely to leave unchallenged the unusual level of intergenerational advance among Mexican Americans.

The regression analyses in table 5.3 give additional insight into how this combination of apparent stagnation between the second and later generations and clear advance beyond the status of the parents may come about. The table is constructed by generation among Mexican Americans and provides a comparable analysis for Anglos. While the regression analyses among the different generations of Mexican Americans exhibit important similarities to that for Anglos, there are also some striking differences.

Among the similarities is the substantial role played by parental education in providing a base for the educational attainment of the children. In the equation for Anglos, the coefficients for both father's and mother's educations are significant and substantial; indeed, they are similar in magnitude. In the equations for Mexican Americans, paternal education is a predictor of child's education, and the magnitude of its effect is very close to that among Anglos. More variable, however, is the role of mother's education. Although it is significant for the second generation and for the combined third and fourth generations, only in the former does the size of its effect approach that among whites. Further, individuals who do not know their parents' educa-

TABLE 5.3

Regressions analyses of years of education by generation, for Mexican Americans and Anglos (i.e., non-Hispanic whites)

	MEXICANS				ANGLOS
	second generation	third generation	fourth generation	third & fourth	third & fourth
father's ed	0.232 ***	0.200 **	0.181 **	0.190 ***	0.193 ***
mother's ed	0.197 **	0.100	0.061	0.096 *	0.249 ***
father's ed missing	-1.362 **	-0.723	-0.888	-0.713 *	-0.225 ***
mother's ed missing	-1.459 *	-1.447 *	-0.468	-1.184 **	-0.530 ***
# sibs	-0.115	-0.040	-0.117	-0.105 *	-0.171 ***
male	0.307	0.569	0.666	0.576	0.162 ***
born 50's	-0.911	0.140	0.246	0.132	0.220 ***
born 40's	-1.009	0.824	0.461	0.518	0.617 ***
born 30's	-1.485 *	-1.101	-0.234	-1.304 *	0.460 ***
born earlier	-2.763 ***	-3.634 ***	-3.251 ***	-3.415 ***	-0.039
nonwht	0.357	-0.268	-0.117	-0.262	n/a
constant	11.177	10.073	11.242	10.652	8.880
R-sq.	0.339	0.349	0.388	0.379	0.350
N	212	191	113	337	21329

Source: General Social Surveys, 1972-2002.

tions are disadvantaged, which suggests that less educated individuals tend to be less informed about the educations of their parents. Perhaps some of these individuals come from families in which the parental level of education was very low, even irregular.

Overall, then, Mexican Americans appear to draw somewhat less of an educational "bounce" from the education of their parents, but this is, as we have already seen, rather low to start with. Other coefficients give some insight into why even U.S.-born Mexican parents may have had low educational attainment. In particular, Mexican Americans of cohorts born before 1940, some of whom would have been in school as late as the 1950s, appear to be substantially disadvantaged by comparison with those born later. The handicap was particularly severe for those born before 1930, who lose more than three years of educational attainment by comparison with individuals in the omitted category, born after the 1950s. No similar pattern of shift across birth cohorts is visible among whites (once parental educational attainment is controlled). Thus, it suggests a substantial institutional or other discrimination against Mexican American students during the first half of the twentieth century, at least.

However, the equations also show signs of a Mexican American catch-up in education, consistent with their greater advance beyond the educational level of their parents. The constants in the Mexican American equations are consistently larger than the Anglo ones: the differences are on the order of 1.2–2.4 years. This differential implies that, even with the larger effect of maternal education among Anglos factored in, Mexican Americans often attain greater education than Anglos with the same parental starting point. This statement holds, to be sure, for those born around midcentury or later, not those born earlier; and the Mexican American "advantage" is most evident when parents have limited educations. When parents have completed high school, however, then the predicted education of later-generation Mexican Americans would be little different from that of Anglos.

This analysis suggests that the Mexican-Anglo differential might be shrinking over time because it is, to some extent at least, a function of the limited educations of Mexican American parents, and this in turn is probably tied to the high barriers to their education in the first half of the twentieth century. This tentative conclusion suggests that we can follow up by analysis of educational differences in recent birth cohorts. In the second half of the chapter, we pursue this idea with an analysis of Mexican American educational attainment in the NLSY 1979 data, which includes individuals born in the 1957–1964 period, and in the NELS 1988 data, which contains individuals born in 1972–1975.

Analysis of NLSY and NELS Data

Table 5.4 presents educational distributions for Mexican Americans, by generation and gender, from the NLSY and NELS data, which represent cohorts that are, very roughly, a decade apart. As a mainstream standard, the equivalent distribution is presented for third- and later-generation Anglos. As a check on the representativeness of the data, similar distributions have been generated for the same birth cohorts from 2000 Census data; because of the limitations of the census, however, they can only be created for second- and later-generation Mexicans and Anglos.

The detailed findings from the two data sets are somewhat different, though the broad conclusions are similar. We begin with the earlier cohort: a comparison of the NLSY data to those of the census shows that, for both Mexicans and Anglos, the survey data underrepresent the extremes of the educational distribution. For instance, among U.S.-born Mexican Ameri-

104 | ALBA, ABDEL-HADY, ISLAM, AND MAROTZ

TABLE 5.4

The educational attainments of Mexican Americans and Anglos, by gender and generation, in NLSY and NELS data

	NLSY					NELS				
	Less than hs	Hs grad	Some coll	Coll grad	N	Less than hs	Hs grad	Some coll	Coll grad	N
MEXICANS										
Second generation										
male	28.0	34.4	24.2	13.4	163	17.8	27.3	45.8	9.1	156
female	16.9	36.5	33.1	13.5	156	22.1	26.4	36.7	14.7	211
Third+ generation										
male	22.7	47.1	22.7	7.5	245	7.3	27.0	54.2	11.3	164
female	18.5	44.1	26.9	10.5	303	10.6	30.3	46.0	13.2	182
ANGLOS										
Third+ generation										
male	10.0	41.2	21.5	27.3	1546	5.6	25.5	35.9	33.0	3318
female	7.2	40.6	24.2	27.9	1456	5.3	25.8	32.9	36.0	3621
2000 CENSUS DATA (1957–1964 COHORT)						**2000 CENSUS DATA (1972–1975 COHORT)**				
U.S.-born Mexicans										
male	27.1	30.4	29.9	12.6	23392	27.5	31.4	30.4	10.8	15150
female	22.9	29.9	33.7	13.5	24371	21.8	27.9	35.4	14.8	14868
U.S.-born Anglos										
male	11.1	31.0	29.2	27.9	721337	11.1	27.9	33.1	27.9	226808
female	8.2	28.9	34.6	28.3	734599	8.5	23.0	34.8	33.8	229584

Note: All percentages are from weighted results; Ns report unweighted numbers of cases.

can males (i.e., with the second and third generations combined), the NLSY shows 33 percent to have attended college, while the census fixes the figure at more than 40 percent. There is also a discrepancy in the percentages who did not complete high school. Bearing in mind that the NLSY is not a wholly accurate representation of Mexican American educational attainment, one arrives nevertheless at two overall conclusions from the survey. First, there is no sign of an improvement in the educational attainment of the third and later generations compared to the second; if anything, there could be a fall-off in college attendance. Second, the Mexican American group lags substantially behind non-Hispanic whites, both in high-school completion and in college graduation. The college-graduation rates of Anglo men and women are roughly double those of their Mexican American counterparts, in both the NLSY data and the census.

In the case of the NELS data, a comparison to the census again reveals nontrivial discrepancies in the educational distributions for Mexican Americans. This time, the survey data appear to overrepresent college attendance, especially in the group that has not completed a college degree. Once again, high-school dropouts are underrepresented in the survey. (Smaller discrepancies are apparent in the Anglo group.) Nevertheless, the NELS data suggest that in very recent cohorts there could be some educational improvement between the second and third generations. That is, the high-school dropout rate is lower in the third than in the second generation, and the college-attendance rate is higher. However, even if this appearance of an upward intergenerational trajectory is real, it seems overshadowed by two other patterns, especially clear in the census data. First, there is no change in the overall educational distribution of U.S.-born Mexican Americans between the NLSY cohort (born 1957–1964) and the NELS one (1972–1975); the census data show them to be virtually identical. Second, there has been a modest upgrading in the educational attainment of Anglos between the two cohorts. This is especially noticeable for Anglo women, a third of whom have earned the baccalaureate degree; the percentage of Anglo men attending college has also increased. The advantages of Anglos over Mexican Americans appear to have grown.

Does this stagnation, visible in cross-sectional comparisons, translate into stagnation in the educational attainments of children compared to their parents? The answer, portrayed in the comparisons in table 5.5, is no. In the more recent cohorts of the NLSY and the NELS data sets, the advance from parents to children is not as large on average as it is in the GSS data, but it is still substantial. It continues to be very large for the children of immigrants

TABLE 5.5
Average years of education in the contemporary and parents' generations, NLSY and NELS data

| | NLSY | | | | |
	Mean own educ	Mean pa's educ.	Pct. Miss.	Mean ma's educ.	Pct. Miss.
MEXICANS					
Second generation					
male	12.1	6.6	25.7	6.9	17.2
female	12.5	6.3	20.3	6.1	4.9
Third+ generation					
male	12.0	9.7	13.5	9.1	7.0
female	12.2	9.5	13.3	9.4	5.5
ANGLOS					
Third+ generation					
male	13.3	12.6	5.9	12.2	4.6
female	13.4	12.5	6.6	12.1	3.4
	NELS				
	Mean own educ	Mean pa's educ.	Pct. Miss.	Mean ma's educ.	Pct. Miss.
MEXICANS					
Second generation					
male	12.8	8.1	0.7	9.1	0.0
female	12.7	6.7	2.5	8.6	5.4
Third+ generation					
male	13.2	10.7	1.2	11.0	0.0
female	13.0	10.2	0.0	11.4	0.0
ANGLOS					
Third+ generation					
male	13.8	12.3	0.2	12.8	0.1
female	13.9	12.0	0.4	12.8	0.1

because Mexican immigrants have low educational levels by the standard of the U.S. population in general. So the real question is how the educational attainments of the third and later generations compare to those of their U.S.-born parents. In the NLSY, the average advance is on the order of two and half years, compared to about one year among Anglos. In the NELS data, the advance is a bit lower, especially if we use the average education of mothers as the standard of comparison. For Mexicans, the advance then ranges from 1.6 years (females) to 2.2 years (males), while for Anglos it remains at approximately one year.

Conclusion

Broadly construed, our findings carry both positive and negative implications for Mexican American socioeconomic incorporation, as glimpsed through the educational attainments of U.S.-born generations. On the positive side is our conclusion that downward assimilation cannot be regarded as a mass phenomenon among the members of the second and third generations. Stagnation between parental and child generations obviously may occur, but it is not a widespread experience. Instead, Mexican Americans experience unusually high improvements in educational attainment when compared to their parents, and this is true even in the third and later generations, whose parents have been born in the United States. The stagnation that appears in cross-sectional comparisons of generational groupings is misleading, in part because of a familiar problem in such comparisons: namely, an earlier generation cannot be regarded as the parents of a later one (see Farley and Alba 2002; Smith 2003). This is compounded in the Mexican case by the long history of Mexican immigration, which extends from the late nineteenth century to today, and by severe pre-civil-rights-era institutional discrimination.

On the negative side, however, we find no convincing sign of convergence in the educational attainments of later-generation Mexican Americans and Anglos; if anything, the gap may be growing because of improvements in the educational attainments of recent cohorts of non-Hispanic whites. As revealed by census data, the high-school dropout rates of second- and third-generation Mexican Americans continue to be more than twice as high as those of their Anglo counterparts, and the discrepancy in college attendance and graduation rates has grown somewhat. A hint of possible improvement is given by the lower high-school dropout rates for third- and later-generation Mexican Americans in the NELS data, but the sample is too small and too deviant from census educational distributions for us to construe this hint as a clear indicator.

There is a paradox in these results, one that calls out for finer analysis in order to resolve it. Each generation of Mexican Americans makes a greater advance beyond the education of their parents than do their Anglo peers and yet fails to close the educational gap. How can this be possible? Does this pattern not imply either that the Mexican American intergenerational advance will soon slow, at least in the third and later generations, whose parents are all U.S.-born, or that the Anglo-Mexican gap will begin to close?

We think an assessment between these two possibilities is still very hard given the limitations of the data we possess about Mexican Americans (cf.

Telles and Ortiz 2008). In addition, the observable patterns point in both directions. On the one hand, the schools that educate the largest numbers of Mexican Americans have not improved; they may have even grown worse. In California, for example, Proposition 13, enacted in 1978 to limit property taxes, appears to have contributed to an overall decline in the quality of public education there, which especially affects the schools attended by socially disadvantaged groups (Gibson et al. 2009). The school inequalities that affect Mexican Americans have been part of the pattern of "racialization" that Telles and Ortiz (2008) conclude applies to the group.

On the other hand, the existing data about Mexican Americans may understate the actual educational attainments of Mexican-descent individuals. This occurs because of selective departures from the group, that is, individuals who no longer describe themselves as Hispanic and/or Mexican, principally because of intermarriage. Two statistical findings raise this possibility. One is the weakness of Mexican identity among those individuals who have grown up as the children of intermarriages (Telles and Ortiz 2008, 281). The other is the evidence of leakage out of the census's "Mexican" category over time (Alba and Islam 2009). That is, if one compares birth cohorts of U.S.-born Mexican Americans across U.S. censuses, they decline in size to an extent that cannot be explained by the losses associated with mortality. The only explanation is that, in later censuses, some individuals who were previously members of the Mexican category have opted out and now place themselves in a different category of origin. The data behind these two findings also indicate that individuals of mixed ancestry, the ones most likely to opt out, tend to have higher educational attainment than other Mexican Americans. Their departure, then, may account for some of the persistence in the relatively low levels of educational attainment of those who unambiguously identify as Mexican American or Chicano.

NOTES

The research reported here was supported by grants from the National Science Foundation and Russell Sage Foundation. A fellowship at the Radcliffe Institute of Advanced Study, Harvard University, enabled the senior author to complete the writing of the chapter.

6

School Qualifications of Children of Immigrant Descent in Switzerland

Rosita Fibbi, Mathias Lerch, and Philippe Wanner

With foreigners (1.5 million in 2000) amounting to 20 percent of Switzerland's resident population, the country has one of the highest noncitizen percentages in Europe, significantly more than Germany (8.9 percent in 2001), Austria (9.4 percent), France (5.6 percent), and Italy (2.2 percent). This high proportion is partly due to Switzerland's relatively restrictive naturalization law, which does not automatically grant Swiss nationality to children born of immigrants on Swiss territory.

Switzerland has also become a true immigration country due to the high flow of immigrants in the 1990s, as 23 percent of the population has been born abroad. Moreover, the most recent census revealed that in 2000, if immigrants' offspring are counted, the population of recent immigrant origins— some 2.4 million adults and children, one-third of whom are Swiss born— rises to one-third of all Swiss residents. One out of four noncitizens belongs to the second or third generation, and one in ten citizens (530,000) acquired a Swiss passport during his or her lifetime. The increase in the Swiss-citizen population in 2002 is due exclusively to naturalizations. Most naturalized persons retained their previous nationality, making them double nationals.

The census of 2000 paints a picture of a progressive diversification of the migrant population over the past two decades. The traditional low-skilled labor migrants recruited from southern Europe to work in Switzerland on a temporary basis (a "guestworker" system) have been progressively replaced by workers from the Balkans. In recent years, moreover, an explicit preference has been given to high-skilled workers. During the 1990s, a large number of entrants (twenty-five thousand on average per year) came under conditions defined by the asylum law. They arrived mostly from war-torn areas and were granted special short-term authorizations with a limited access to the labor market. Family reunification accounts for two out of five entrants and has increased the proportion of migrant women. Of women aged fourteen to thirty-two—a crucial age for family rearing and workforce participation—28 percent are foreigners. This shift from migration governed by market needs to migration governed by legally anchored rights (e.g., family reunification, asylum) has run parallel to a diversification of countries of origin. Labor migrants and their dependents have come mainly from EU countries, whereas new migrants and asylum seekers, by definition, have come from non-EU countries. To summarize, a major diversification of the migrant population has taken place over the past fifteen years in terms of age, gender, geographical and cultural origin, and immigrant status (Wanner and Fibbi 2002).

The geographical terms *close* and *distant* have been used to legitimize differentiation of admission policy according to a migrant's country of origin: the argument of cultural proximity was mobilized to justify the easing of admission of EU citizens, whereas that of cultural distance was invoked on behalf of a restrictive policy toward nationals of other countries.[1] Although the cultural argument is not new in Swiss migration history, the divide between EU and non-EU country nationals was institutionalized in immigration policy only at the beginning of the 1990s.[2] The dichotomy between wanted and unwanted immigration has now spilled over from admission policy into both the integration debate and policy (Wicker 2003).

Immigration Context and Theoretical Background

The notion of "cultural distance" as a cornerstone of Swiss migration policy owes its legitimization to the academic world (Mahnig and Piguet 2003). One of the most highly regarded scholars in the field of migration, Hans-Joachim Hoffmann-Nowotny (1992), used the concept in a normative way in an official report on the future of immigration in Switzerland; and his interpretation largely was left unchallenged. As a consequence of the major changes in Swiss policies during the 1990s, this supposed "cultural" divide has become a legal one. On one side are labor immigrants who have privileged admission and residence rights as EU citizens. On the other side are non-EU groups composed of labor immigrants and asylum seekers who have restricted access to the labor market and suffer from unstable residency status.

Today, although the line of argument has been abandoned because of its racist overtones (CFR 1996), the divide it justified continues to shape the perceptions of immigrants in integration matters, paralleling the distinction between old (Italian and Spaniards) and new migration flows (Portuguese

TABLE 6.1

Labor migration flows to Switzerland and their geographical and historical coordinates

	Labour migration flow	
National origin	Old 1945-1979	New 1980-2000
EU - European Union	Italians Spaniards	Portuguese
Non- European Union		Turks Citizens of the successor States of Yugoslavia

from the European Union as well as Turks and former Yugoslavs from outside the European Union) (see table 6.1).

In fact, perceptions of immigrant groups are framed by these institutional changes and the arguments that support them. An opinion poll has confirmed that a distinction clearly exists in the minds of the Swiss that mimics the same administrative categories imposed by Swiss authorities. The Swiss separate foreign residents into two groups: those whose presence is largely accepted (Italians, Spaniards, Portuguese, French, and Germans) and those whose presence is strongly contested. Citizens from less-developed countries outside the European Union and foreigners from war-torn regions, such as Turks and Serbs, fall into the latter category (Nef, Herrmann, and Martinovits 1997). The most recent opinion poll confirms this phenomenon (Raymann 2003).

This spillover from admission to integration policy concerns also the children of immigrants: it suggests a sharp difference between the "old" second generation, who successfully integrated into Swiss society, and the "new" second generation, whose perspectives are not as promising. This new second generation is perceived as being less likely to reach the mainstream than those from previous immigrant flows. This distinction may seem to mirror the related American debate to a certain extent, but the arguments behind it are fundamentally different.

The U.S. debate (Gans 1992; Rumbaut and Portes 2001; Waldinger and Feliciano 2004) focuses on the evolution of the labor market and the context of reception that immigrants and their children face. In Switzerland, obstacles to integration are primarily ascribed to the specific cultural and, indeed, religious background of recent inflows. Such explanations are consistent with an endogenous understanding of the "assimilation" process, which, as pointed out by Alba and Nee (1997), conveys an ahistorical perception of the intergroup dynamics.

In the Swiss debate, culture has become the deterministic factor for differentiation. Cultural and social phenomena are naturalized and thus take on an essentialist connotation. Categories such as nations and ethnic groups are viewed in a culturally static and natural way. The conflict between groups is spoken of in terms of conflict between cultures. Cultural difference has become a catch phrase in the public arena and is often used in debates on the integration of immigrants, under the influence of strong political entrepreneurs (Skenderovic and D'Amato 2008).

In Switzerland, the second generation is made up of both newly arrived groups and previous second-generation labor migrants from the 1960s—Italians and Spaniards. The geopolitical and economic context has changed drastically for the two flows, as have migration policies, in particular the introduction of facilitated migration for EU citizens. However, differences between old and new flows are interpreted as a consequence of specific cultural and religious differences between the groups. Little attention is paid to the fact that today's "good" old immigrants were considered impossible to assimilate only twenty years ago (Virot 2006). Nor is sufficient attention given to the fact that today's comparisons are made between established groups, on the one hand, in which the majority is native-born, and on the other hand, outsider groups, in which the majority are foreign-born. The historical dimension is completely ignored, and, as a consequence, differences within groups are essentialized.[3]

Census data allow us to challenge some aspects of these explanations for differences among migrant groups. These data allow us to distinguish between native-born and foreign-born residents, thus eliminating a powerful bias in overall intergroup comparisons. We can take into account the social background of migrants and their migration history, as the census data allow us to identify the origin group beyond the nationality screen. Whatever citizenship they possess (only the local one, only the origin one, or both origin and local citizenship), they can be included in the same (national) origin group. Usually naturalized people become invisible as migrants, since they are registered as Swiss in official statistics, a fact that distorts the general perception of changes within the origin group. Finally, census data enable us to discuss differences between boys and girls along the path to integration, a somewhat neglected topic in the second-generation literature. This is even more crucial given that the gender gap is one of the key criteria on which the degree of cultural proximity among groups is judged, with gender equality representing, by definition, cultural proximity.

This chapter addresses the argument that the gap between Swiss and immigrant groups' cultures is an unbridgeable one, especially for non-EU groups. Attention is given to the changes within groups (defined by their national origin) between the foreign-born 1.5 generation and the native-born second generation. School attainment of men and women in all immigrant groups is examined, with special attention to differences between boys and girls on various indicators of structural integration. This chapter also tests previous survey findings on second-generation immigrants in Switzerland on a far more broad and comprehensive basis.

Previous Findings on the Second Generation and Research Questions

The main findings of sociological research on the second generation in Switzerland guide our research questions. Foreign children pursue significantly fewer qualifying school tracks during and after compulsory school (Borkowsky 1991; Hutmacher 1987; Lischer 2002; Lischer, Röthlisberger, and Schmid 1997). School statistical data are often based on dichotomized categories: Swiss versus foreigners. Moreover, such comparisons do not include any data on social background. This supports the widespread belief that foreigners suffer from chronic learning difficulties at school.

However, data also reveal evidence of remarkable intergenerational mobility in school attainment between first- and second-generation youth with a migratory background (W. Haug 1995). This has been interpreted as a sign of progressive future convergence between migrant and local groups. The hypothesis of a linear progression toward general patterns of school attainment is indeed supported by the observation of systematic improvement in school attainment between the 1.5 and the second generation within the various nationality groups: Italians, Spaniards, and Turks (Fibbi et al. 2003; Hämmig 2000). A survey on adult second-generation Italians and Spaniards confirmed the convergent trend of these young people in Switzerland. By focusing on children of immigrants (and not on nationality) and controlling for social background, this survey revealed not only a relatively high rate of school success for this group but also, in some cases, their superior school qualifications compared to Swiss children from similar family backgrounds (Bolzman, Fibbi, and Vial 2003). By demonstrating the potential of naturalized children to perform at school, the study also indirectly revealed to what extent the naturalization process in Switzerland is selective. Initially, these findings were considered to be overly optimistic because they were an outright contradiction of widespread perceptions of immigrant children's low performance at school.

To summarize, data on school achievement may appear contradictory. On the one hand, foreigners consistently perform less well than the Swiss at school, but on the other hand, there are clear signs of improvement over time in some origin groups. This lends weight to the popular hypothesis that immigrants are increasingly differentiating on the basis of the cultural background of their origin group and especially its degree of "cultural closeness" to the Swiss context. So our first research questions are the following: Does school performance improve over generations (1.5 versus second generation)? Is improvement present in both old as well as in new immigrant groups? How can differences among groups be explained?

Instead of one school system, Switzerland has twenty-six different systems, reflecting the number of cantons (member states) in the Confederation. Thus, the ensuing question is the following: Does improvement in school performance occur only in specific urban settings, where surveys were conducted, or does it occur throughout the whole country?

The differential integration path of boys and girls is being given increasing attention (Boos-Nünning and Karakasoglu 2004), after decades of neglect in migration studies (Gabaccia 1994; Kelson and De Laet 1999; Morokvasic 1984). The issue of differences between immigrant boys and girls in educational achievement and investment in education is one of the cornerstones of the integration path. One empirical study in the 1980s showed that migrant girls (all of Italian origin at that time) had higher failure rates at school than boys did. The authors did not explain these differences by invoking traditional gender roles discouraging educational investment in girls. They pointed out instead the tendency for parents to leave their daughters behind in the country of origin, since girls were supposed to be easier than boys for grandparents to take care of. Delayed family reunification in the host country hampered girls' academic progress (Cassée, Gurny, and Hauser 1981). Later studies, however, show that migrant girls from Italy and Spain generally fare better than their masculine counterparts at school (Bolzman, Fibbi, and Vial 2003; Fibbi and De Rham 1988). These diachronic observations may support the hypothesis of convergence toward local standards in gender equality.

Thus, this chapter explores the gender gap in school performance: Do patterns of boys' versus girls' secondary-school tracks vary from one origin group to another? Do women reach similar or higher levels in education than men do, as some researchers have observed elsewhere (Hassini 1996; Tribalat 1995), or do they lag behind, a fact generally attributed to their own or their parents' assumption of traditional gender roles (Kasinitz et al. 2008)? To what extent do women with a migratory background suffer from inegalitarian gender standards in school performance, even though Switzerland is supposed to enshrine gender equality?

Finally, naturalization procedures are somewhat peculiar in Switzerland.[4] The main feature is that there is no *jus soli,* that is, automatic acquisition of Swiss citizenship when a child is born in Switzerland. Therefore naturalization procedures and requirements for the second generation differ only slightly from those for the first generation. Moreover, the fulfillment of all requirements does not entitle the candidate to be naturalized; the final decision is made by a political or administrative body. One of the major consequences of this system is the divergence between the juridical status of nationals and foreigners and the life experience of migration, which is best expressed by the opposition native-born versus foreign-born. In Switzerland, there are consequently three main configurations of cases associated with migration: (a) foreign-born foreigners who are first-generation migrants; (b) foreign-born nationals who are either naturalized first-generation migrants or nationals by birth, born abroad; (c) native-born foreigners who are the nonnaturalized offspring of immigrants. This last configuration, hardly known in countries which practice the *jus soli* principle, was the most common condition of the second generation in Switzerland in 2000.

Previous studies have show that the naturalization process can be extremely selective (Achermann and Gass 2003). Is naturalization selective to the same extent for all origin groups? Is this selectivity visible in secondary-school track choices?

The rest of this section provides a general outline of the specific census database we used for our analyses as well as some general information on the demographic characteristics of second-generation youth. The next section presents and discusses school attainment, with a focus on the indicators of structural integration most used in the literature (Crul and Vermeulen 2003), namely, dropout rate and tertiary education.

Second Generation and Origin Group

The introduction of new questions in the census—nationality at birth ("Swiss" or "foreigner") and year of naturalization—allows us to retrace the integration process beyond nationality criteria. Nationality-based definitions tend to hinder a true representation of the process of integration. This chapter deals exclusively with "origin groups," which are identified in the following way:

- People who hold the nationality of their country of origin
- Naturalized people whose first nationality (nationality at birth or parents' nationality) or place of birth is their own country of origin[5]

TABLE 6.2

Youth aged between 15 and 24 by origin, birth place, length of stay, and residence permit

	Resident population	DE	FR	IT	SP	PT	TR	YAL	Y.SC	Y.CH	BA	MK	HR	Other origins
Place of birth/ Length of residence														
Foreign-born, > 5 years in CH	13.9	30.8	28.6	18.7	31.2	65.9	43.7	67.7	60.1	65.1	75.6	69.9	59.5	36.6
Swiss born	79.1	26.8	31.3	75.2	60.0	10.4	40.0	5.7	19.8	17.6	13.4	7.0	34.0	21.7
Legal Status														
Long residence permits	-	38.6	32.4	72.9	82.7	72.7	54.2	61.2	54.3	52.7	54.2	61.1	58.6	20.0
Swiss citizens	76.0	18.4	26.9	21.4	10.1	3.1	16.7	2.9	13.2	11.4	10.0	5.0	20.0	28.0
N	852225	10279	8221	41846	12804	21152	18885	20005	10377	10265	8689	12726	7654	61088
% total	100.0	1.2	1.0	4.9	1.5	2.5	2.2	2.3	1.2	1.2	1.0	1.5	0.9	7.2

Source: Federal Population Census 2000; SFSO

CH= Swiss; DE= Germans; FR= French; IT= Italians; SP= Spaniards; PT= Portuguese; TR= Turks; Y.AL= Albanian-speaking Yugoslavs; Y.SC= Serbo-Croat-speaking Yugoslavs; Y.CH= Yugoslavs who speak a regional-Swiss-language; BA= Bosnians; MK= Macedonians; HR= Croatians.

We differentiate among young people of migrant origin in the fifteen to twenty-four age bracket[6] according to their place of birth:

- Native-born youth, who correspond to the demographic notion of the second generation and who are not, properly speaking, immigrants.
- Foreign-born youth with more than five years of residence in the country. The lack of information concerning age of arrival in our data prevents us from rigorously delimiting the 1.5 generation. We consider the group "foreign-born with more than five years of residence" a proxy for the 1.5 generation. These young people most likely came into the country as family members of an adult who had been granted the right to reside in Switzerland. It is, however, not possible to know whether they attended a Swiss school.
- Foreign-born youth with less than five years of residence, who most probably were not socialized in Switzerland and may have come to Switzerland not as dependents (family reunification) but rather as adults. They are not included in our analyses since they did not go through the Swiss school system and are therefore best considered as first-generation immigrants.

Youth with a Migratory Background: A Quantitative Profile

Youth aged between fifteen and twenty-four with a migratory background represent almost a third of the resident population. Table 6.2 summarizes the main demographic features of this population. Italians represent the largest group (4.9 percent), followed by Yugoslavs (4.7 percent). However, if we group all former Yugoslav migrants together, the Balkan group is the largest (8.1 percent). Italians and Spaniards constitute the most stable groups with regard to residence because they were part of the first migration wave of 1950 and 1960, whereas the other groups immigrated later. Representing 40 percent of native-born youth, Turks are a stable group with regard to residence, which contrasts sharply with Albanian-speaking Yugoslavs and Macedonians, who make up less than 10 percent of native-born youth.

In the absence of an automatic mechanism granting citizenship to migrants, naturalization rates differ quite markedly from group to group, ranging from 27 percent for the French to 3 percent for Albanian-speaking Yugoslavs.

School Qualifications

How do youth of different origin groups perform at school? Table 6.3 gives an initial description of the situation of the various national-origin groups.

TABLE 6.3
School attainment of native-born and foreign-born young people, men and women, aged 23-24, according to origin

	Less than compulsory schooling	Compulsory schooling	Secondary education	Completed education at tertiary level	Ongoing tertiary education
Residents	2.1	15.7	55.0	7.9	19.3
Swiss	0.6	8.5	61.3	7.1	22.5
Germans	0.6	10.4	44.6	11.7	32.6
French	1.2	12.7	34.3	33.0	18.9
Italians	1.8	17.8	60.2	6.6	13.7
Spaniards	1.6	22.2	53.5	8.5	14.2
Portuguese	7.9	51.2	35.0	3.0	3.0
Turks	9.6	42.3	38.0	4.3	5.9
Albanian-speaking Yugoslavs	14.4	59.6	22.4	2.2	1.4
Serb-Croatian-speaking Yugoslavs	7.2	43.6	41.5	3.5	4.1
Swiss language-speaking Yugoslavs	9.6	52.4	30.6	3.7	3.7
Bosnians	8.0	41.5	43.8	3.0	3.6
Macedonians	12.1	55.4	27.3	3.3	1.9
Croatians	2.8	24.7	57.8	4.5	10.2
Other origin	4.6	27.7	32.7	17.6	17.4

Source: Own calculations using Federal Population Census 2000, SFSO

The percentage of youth who drop out of school—who do not complete compulsory schooling—is below 2 percent among Swiss aged twenty-three or twenty-four,[7] as it is among their peers from former migration flows. However, this rate is four to seven times higher for groups from Turkey and the former Yugoslavia. Other indicators point in the same direction. One person out of five from a previous immigrant flow achieves at most compulsory schooling, whereas on average, this is the modal outcome for young people from Turkey, Portugal, and many groups from the former Yugoslavia. At the other end of the table, those enrolled in tertiary education represent fewer than 10 percent in groups from Turkey, Portugal, and the former Yugoslavia (Croatia excepted), and the percentage is at least double for those from the previous migration flows.

These data may at first sight seem to support the argument of a dichotomy of "culturally close" and "culturally distant" countries of origin. Still, the opposition between culturally close (i.e., immigrant groups from EU countries) and culturally distant (i.e., immigrant groups from non-EU countries) groups does not withstand closer scrutiny. It is true that the old immigrant groups from Italy and Spain display school performances somewhat similar to those of the Swiss-born nationals and that the new groups from Turkey and the former Yugoslavia perform significantly worse than the Swiss-born nationals; however, the Portuguese, although regarded as "culturally close," display education performance similar to the other more recent immigrant groups. Moreover, the different groups under the common label of the former Yugoslavia display a wide variety of profiles. The Croatians' performance is closer to those of the old migration flows of Italians and Spaniards, whereas the Macedonians and, above all, the Albanian-speaking Yugoslavs face serious difficulties in school. Finally, immigration from France and Germany—traditional migration flows which are regaining momentum—show distinctive features, with educational scores way above those of the Swiss. The cultural-geographic terminology is simplistic and even misleading in interpreting patterns of success and failure at school.

The Impact of Family Educational Background, Place of Birth, Naturalization, and Gender

We now analyze school outcomes of the various immigrant groups on a bivariate basis, testing the impact of family educational background, place of birth, naturalization, and gender. We first focus on failure, defined as the proportion of people not having completed compulsory schooling,[8] an almost universal credential for young adults in Switzerland.

High proportions of dropouts can be better understood as mirroring the levels of parental educational background[9] (table 6.4) and—to a large extent—the educational development of their respective regions of origin. Young people with poor school performances in general tend to come from groups with the lowest family educational background. Those groups for which the percentage of youth not completing compulsory schooling exceeds 7 percent are exactly the groups for which the proportion of parents who did not complete compulsory school is above 9 percent.

Italian and Spanish parents do not differ dramatically from new labor migration flows in their human capital. Yet the proportion of their children who did not achieve compulsory school is quite limited in comparison with that of the offspring of those new flows. This fact points at the crucial role of length of residence in Switzerland for children of immigrants.

As indicated by table 6.5, regarding school failure among youth aged twenty-three and twenty-four with a migratory background, native-born

TABLE 6.4
Level of education of parents who live with their children aged 20-24, according to origin country*

	Less than compulsory schooling	Compulsory schooling	Secondary education	Tertiary education
Residents	3.9	18.6	53.5	24.1
Swiss	0.7	10.7	60.7	27.9
Germans	0.2	4.8	46.3	48.8
French	1.0	9.1	43.4	46.5
Italians	13.6	42.7	37.0	6.7
Spaniards	15.2	43.4	34.0	7.4
Portuguese	12.7	51.9	30.8	4.6
Turks	21.2	46.9	26.7	5.3
Albanian-speaking Yugoslavs	17.7	53.2	24.5	4.6
Serb-Croatian-speaking Yugoslavs	9.9	44.3	38.0	7.8
Swiss language-speaking Yugoslavs	9.4	45.6	36.1	8.9
Bosnians	10.6	36.3	45.8	7.2
Macedonians	13.9	50.9	30.1	5.1
Croatians	7.5	30.1	53.1	9.3
Other origin	6.1	17.3	39.3	37.3

Source: Own calculations using Federal Population Census 2000, SFSO
* Relating parents' human capital and children' graduation is only possible with our data if we consider cohabitation. Therefore only parents living with children are taken into account. The median age of the resident population aged 15 to 24 years who no longer live with their parents is 23 for girls and 24 for boys.

youth (column 1) are significantly less exposed to the risk of becoming school dropouts than are foreign-born youth, thus confirming the well-established relationship between residence stability and school performance. Hence, the differences between the performances in this respect of the children of Italians and Spaniards can be partially attributed to their consolidated residence status.

Foreign-born children with a longer period of residence in Switzerland (five years or more, column 2) fare less well than native-born youth but better than residents who have lived less than five years in Switzerland (column 3), who, therefore, might not have attended Swiss schools at all. This means that the differences in education attainment observed between the groups of origin (first column of table 6.3) are due, to a large extent, to marked dissimilarities in the length of residence, place of schooling, and acculturative exposure to Swiss society.

Naturalized people are the category least affected by school failure; the contrast with nonnaturalized people is very sharp, with the latter showing

TABLE 6.5

Proportion, of youth aged 23 and 24 not having completed compulsory schooling, according to national origin, place of birth/ length of residence, nationality and gender

	Native-born	Foreign-born > 5 yrs	Foreign-born <5 yrs	Naturalized	Non-naturalized	RATIO women/men** in general	RATIO women/men** among native-born
Residents	0.7	1.6	7.1	-	-	1.1	0.8
Swiss	0.6	0.6	2.2	-	-	0.9	0.7
Germans	0.4	0.9	0.4	0.9	0.6	1.6	2.5
French	0.0	0.8	1.5	1.1	1.2	1.0	n.a.
Italians	1.1	1.5	5.1	0.5	2.2	0.8	1.1
Spaniards	1.1	1.4	3.2	0.3	1.7	0.9	1.2
Portuguese	5.9	6.3	11.6	3.3	8.0	1.0	0.8
Turks	3.6	8.1	15.9	1.9	11.3	1.4	0.9
Albanian-speaking Yugoslavs	30.0	13.7	16.1	2.6	14.6	1.3	0.7
Serb-Croatian-speaking Yugoslavs	2.6	7.1	7.6	0.4	8.0	1.1	0.6
Swiss language-speaking Yugoslavs	5.3	8.7	12.6	1.3	11.1	1.3	1.6
Bosnians	2.2	7.5	11.0	0.7	8.8	1.0	n.a.
Macedonians	7.7	10.8	16.5	1.9	12.7	1.5	0.8
Croatians	2.1	2.6	4.8	1.5	3.3	0.8	1.5
Other	0.8	2.6	6.6	0.8	6.3	1.1	0.5

Source: Own calculations using Federal Population Census 2000, SFSO

* Proportion of women who dropped out of school in relation to the proportion of men who chose the same secondary school track

six times as many dropouts among Turks and twenty times as many among Serbo-Croatian-speaking Yugoslavs. However, even among the naturalized group, the dropout rate is slightly higher than among Swiss.[10] This finding confirms previous survey results (Bolzman, Fibbi, and Vial 2003) that the Swiss individualized naturalization procedures (see § 1.2) operate in a quite selective way.

The cultural-distance argument places a special emphasis on inequality between men and women, with the idea that culturally distant groups are characterized by larger gaps between genders than are found in culturally close groups—the in-group being the paragon of equality. The question we want to examine, then, is how women perform in school compared to men. School failure concerns—on average—more women than men among youth from Turkey and the Balkans, with the notable exception of Bosnians and Croatians. On the contrary, among older migration groups, dropout rates are higher for men than for women. Although among foreign-born youth,[11] school failure affects more women than men, among native-born the picture changes sharply: in this case, the girls' dropout rate is lower than the boys' in all groups of Muslim tradition, the groups under scrutiny when it comes to gender gap and cultural distance. Moreover, the native-born women in well-established groups such as Germans, Italians, and Spaniards perform less well than their brothers do. These findings indicate that women's higher school failure cannot be attributed to ethnic cultural features but instead appears to be influenced by the situation in the home country and by the migration status in Switzerland.

The analysis of the influence of various factors on educational failure shows very large differences within each origin group according to family educational background, place of birth/length of stay, naturalization status, and gender. Those differences question radically the assumption of fixed and culturally bound origin groups; they appear to be rather a cumulative artifact of many life experiences and circumstances.

Let us now turn to school success: it is expressed as the proportion of persons aged twenty-three and twenty-four who have a tertiary degree or who were enrolled in a tertiary course on census day.[12] Table 6.6 gives an inverted picture of intergroup disparities when compared to table 6.5. Here again, three groups can be distinguished. French and Germans fare extremely well in their educational achievement, much better than the Swiss average. Old immigration groups, as well as the new Croatians and Turks, converge to some extent toward the Swiss average, whereas all other groups lag significantly behind.

TABLE 6.6

Proportion of youth aged 23 and 24 in terms of tertiary education: graduates plus enrolled students, according to origin, place of birth, nationality, and gender

	Total	Native-born	Naturalized	Ratio* among Native-born
Residents	27.2	29.2	-	0.71
Swiss	29.6	29.5	-	0.67
Germans	44.3	46.0	44.5	0.83
French	51.9	46.1	46.1	0.91
Italians	20.3	21.5	33.3	0.83
Spaniards	22.7	26.6	45.0	0.77
Portuguese	6.0	16.4	30.9	0.83
Turks	10.2	14.5	22.4	0.67
Albanian-speaking Yugoslavs	3.6	0.0	11.8	n.a.
Serb-Croatian-speaking Yugoslavs	7.6	21.0	26.4	1.00
Swiss-language-speaking Yugoslavs	7.4	21.6	28.5	0.91
Bosnians	6.6	8.7	18.0	n.a.
Macedonians	5.2	6.2	18.2	n.a.
Croatians	14.7	23.8	29.8	0.77
Other	35.0	40.7	39.4	0.91

Source: Own calculations using Federal Population Census 2000, SFSO
* Proportion of women with tertiary education in relation to proportion of men with the same school record

Length of stay in the immigration country is a variable affecting high educational performance, just as it was for dropout rates: consequently, the native-born (column 2) perform better than the 1.5 generation and recently immigrated youth. Similarly, naturalized youth (column 3) are more likely to attend tertiary education (Fibbi, Lerch, and Wanner 2005). Census data confirm that naturalization continues to be selective (applicants are twice as likely to be selected if they are tertiary graduates), as was observed in previous studies for Italians and Spaniards. This selective process is even more pronounced in non-EU groups. In official statistics, however, highly qualified naturalized persons appear, of course, as Swiss. This reinforces the image of the origin groups as poor performers and further devalues the public's opinion of these groups.[13]

Men are more likely to hold tertiary qualifications than women are, both in general and among native-born youth with a migratory background (1.4 times higher on average). Serbo-Croatian-speaking Yugoslavs, Swiss-regional-language-speaking Yugoslavs, French, Italians, Portuguese, Germans, and Croatians display a gender gap lower than average, whereas in all other groups, gender gaps are wider. The highest gender gaps among native-born persons holding tertiary degrees are to be found among Turks—and among Swiss. In other words, the Turkish gender imbalance is converging to the prevailing gender imbalance among Swiss in higher education.[14]

The gender gap among naturalized youth with tertiary education is substantially similar to that observed for the whole second generation. The only exceptions are the Portuguese and Yugoslav groups, in which the gender ratio is even more imbalanced in favor of men than in the gender ratio for the native-born. Naturalization seems to be more selective for women than for men in those recently immigrated groups.

In summary, within new immigrant groups, native-born women run lower risks than men of dropping out of school. This means that they seize and take advantage of the opportunities they are given of obtaining school qualifications. However, women in all groups, both immigrant and native Swiss, do not push their educational careers as far as men do, so that women are less likely than men to qualify for tertiary-level education—both native-born and foreign-born women, women of foreign origin or Swiss by birth. All in all, gender imbalance appears to be an open issue in Switzerland, not only in immigrant groups but also in the native Swiss population.

Intergenerational Mobility

Table 6.4 showed that the majority of migrant parents completed compulsory schooling at most. Thus, this level of educational qualification is a good benchmark for measuring the progress of these children on the educational ladder. We consider as upwardly mobile those children of immigrants whose level of education goes beyond the level of their parents, that is, the completion of compulsory school. We restrict the analysis to native-born children of immigrants, who—as already shown—stand better chances of higher school performance.

In almost all migration groups the majority of native-born children of immigrants experience upward mobility, as is well documented in the relevant literature. Offspring of traditional labor-immigration groups of the 1960s show high mobility rates (more than 80 percent of them hold at least a secondary-school diploma). This is a higher rate than that observed in the corresponding Swiss population of similar educational background (78 percent). A majority of Portuguese, Albanian-speaking Yugoslavs, and Swiss-language-speaking Yugoslavs are also experiencing mobility, although at a lower rate than the Swiss by birth.

However, three groups experience great difficulty in keeping up with their parents' level of education: Turks, Serbo-Croatian-speaking Yugoslavs, and

TABLE 6.7

Level of attained or ongoing education of native-born youth aged 20 to 24, whose parents have completed compulsory schooling at best, according to origin

	Uncompleted compulsory school	Compulsory school	Intergenerational Mobility		
			Total	Secondary education	Tertiary education
All	0.9	20.4	78.7	67.6	11.1
Swiss	-	22.5	77.5	57.5	20.0
Germans	1.1	27.6	71.2	49.4	21.8
French	0.6	15.4	84.0	67.5	16.5
Italians	0.4	13.3	86.3	58.7	27.6
Spaniards	-	34.0	66.0	44.4	21.6
Portuguese	1.3	35.7	63.0	54.9	8.1
Turks	5.3	61.7	33.0	30.9	2.1
Albanian-speaking Yugoslavs	1.5	32.8	65.7	57.6	8.1
Serb-Croatian-speaking Yugoslavs	3.9	58.9	37.2	31.0	6.2
Swiss-language-speaking Yugoslavs	1.9	25.5	72.6	66.0	6.6
Bosnians	7.7	63.7	28.6	27.5	1.1
Macedonians	0.5	17.5	82.0	71.2	10.8
Croatians	0.4	21.9	77.7	58.4	19.3
Others	0.9	20.4	78.7	67.6	11.1

Source: Own calculations using Federal Population Census 2000, SFSO

Bosnians. Within these groups there is also a trend toward downward mobility, which may be the result of a disruptive migratory experience for all three groups.

Factors Explaining School Success

In addition to descriptive data, we test the independent impact of a number of variables on school success—defined as having reached tertiary education—among children of immigrants aged twenty to twenty-four who are living with their parents.[15] We limit our presentation here to the analysis of native-born youth and focus on the gender issue, by running separate models for men and women, in order to discuss the gender dimension in school attainment. A binary logistic regression model has been specified to predict the logged odds of school success in considering the following variables:

- Social background, expressed by the highest educational level reached by one of the parents (incomplete compulsory schooling, complete compulsory schooling, vocational training, other postcompulsory education, and so on). The literature on social reproduction and social mobility, which stresses the key importance of this variable, is too vast to be cited here. It is expected that parents' human capital, together with completed schooling in Switzerland, will largely explain the differences in school achievement of the offspring, thus reducing the intergroup disparities to a minimum.

- Acquired characteristics of the young person, namely, language skills. We want to test the impact of language shift (Fishman 1964; Pease-Alvarez 2002) for youth of migrant background, as this is usually an issue in the literature on assimilation. We test the impact of different forms of bilingualism by taking into account situations in which bilingualism parallels proficiency in the local language, as well as situations in which bilingualism goes along with poor proficiency in the local language (LL). We make reference to the LP (the main language in which the person feels most proficient), the LM (language of the mother), and the LL (local language spoken by at least 20 percent of the inhabitants of the region where the person is living). We thus take special account of bilingual municipalities in Switzerland when assessing LL.

- Comparative research on integration processes has focused attention on the importance of contextual factors in deciding school success (Crul and Vermeulen 2003; Portes and Rumbaut 2001; Reitz 1998). We have dealt with these factors by using two variables. The first variable is the cantonal school system, grouped into three categories:[16] *Selective* cantonal school systems are those in which less than 25 percent of students in the canton aged nineteen are enrolled in or have completed the top academic track of upper secondary school. *Open* systems are those in which the percentage of young people in the top academic track is at least as high as the third quartile. The remaining systems are classified as *normal.* The second variable is the type of settlement in which the student lives. We distinguish centers of agglomeration/inner cities, suburban municipalities, and rural municipalities to test the hypothesis that inner-city living has a negative impact on educational performance, as suggested by the literature on the new second generation.

Table 6.8 gives the independent impacts of each variable, "all other things being equal," on the logged odds of success for children of immigrants born in Switzerland. Results are presented in the form of odds ratios (see table note). As expected, parents' educational level has a significant influence on their children's access to tertiary education. Children whose parents only attended a few years of compulsory schooling or barely completed this level

TABLE 6.8

Odds ratios for the probability of enrolment in or completion of tertiary level education for men and women aged 20–24, born in Switzerland and living with their parents

	Total Second Generation		Men		Women	
Origin						
Swiss	1.00		1.00		1.00	
Germans	1.56	***	1.57	***	1.56	***
French	1.93	***	1.76	***	2.07	***
Italians	0.87	***	0.92	*	0.82	***
Spaniards	1.31	***	1.21	*	1.42	***
Portuguese	0.94		0.88		1.02	
Turks	0.50	***	0.54	***	0.45	***
Albanian-speaking Yugoslavs	0.16	***	0.17	**	0.16	*
Serb-Croatian-speaking Yugoslavs	0.60	***	0.65	*	0.54	**
Swiss-language-speaking Yugoslavs	0.55	***	0.54	*	0.59	*
Bosnians	0.37	***	0.30	**	0.47	*
Macedonians	0.23	***	0.19	*	0.31	*
Croatians	0.68	***	0.68	*	0.67	*
Other	1.39	***	1.34	***	1.41	***
*Language skills**						
LP = LM = LL	1.00		1.00		1.00	
LP =LL, LM not LL	1.48	***	1.26	***	1.88	***
LP = LM not LL	1.14	**	1.11		1.16	*
Other	1.40	***	1.10		2.45	***
Gender						
Men	1.00					
Women	0.68	***				
Highest level of schooling of parents						
None	0.54	***	0.56	***	0.50	***
secondary I	0.77	***	0.71	***	0.86	***
Apprenticeship	1.00		1.00		1.00	
other sec II, tertiary	3.36	***	3.04	***	3.87	***
Type of settlement						
centre of agglomeration,	1.11	***	1.07	**	1.16	***
other municipality in agglomeration	1.00		1.00		1.00	
Rural	0.75	***	0.76	***	0.71	***
*Cantonal school system***						
Selective	0.91	***	0.98		0.78	***
Normal	1.00		1.00		1.00	
Open	1.66	***	1.48	***	1.96	***

* p < 0.05; ** p < 0.001; *** p < 0.0001

Source: Own calculation using Federal Population Census 2000, SFSO

* Language skills: LP = main language (the most proficient language); LM = language spoken by the mother (if unknown, by the father); LL = local language, spoken by at least 20% of the inhabitants of the municipality where the person lives.

Note: the odds ratios correspond to the estimated relative risk of reaching tertiary level, for a given profile, with respect to the reference group (defined by 1.00). A lower (or higher) value than unity represents, after controlling for other socioeconomic differentials, a lower (or higher) probability of reaching tertiary level education with respect to the benchmark variable. The p-values indicate the statistical significance of the results.

of education are at a disadvantage, in comparison with those whose parents completed at least an apprenticeship, our benchmark value.[17] The higher the parents' level of education, the more likely their children are to reach tertiary studies. The second notable finding is that parents' educational resources have a stronger influence on their daughters' performance than on their sons' performance. This seems to run counter to the conclusion that "female educational attainment is somewhat less sharply differentiated by socio-economic background," which is interpreted as a glass-ceiling effect (Smyth 2001).

Language skills play a significant role in school advancement. Evidence supports the hypothesis that all forms of bilingualism enhance the likelihood of continuing with tertiary education, even when the local language is not a student's most proficient language.[18]

Contextual factors also influence school performance. An open school system significantly enhances the likelihood of a student's graduating from secondary school in the optimal academic track. We tested the difference between language regions in Switzerland (German, French, and Italian), but it did not prove to be as influential a factor as expected. The reason may be that the variation is essentially absorbed by the school system, given that open systems are mainly to be found in the French and Italian areas of the country. As a matter of fact, the PISA study, on the geographical distribution of different types of school systems and their impact on school performances, presents similar findings (Zahner Rossier et al. 2004).

A further contextual factor in school performance is habitat. Rural contexts appear to be a handicap in accessing tertiary education, since tertiary facilities are not generally available outside the bigger cities.[19] Living in centers of agglomeration also makes it less likely for children to access tertiary education, as predicted by the "new second-generation" hypothesis.

Let us now consider the variability in school performance of native-born youth, according to origin group.[20] Three origin groups (French, German, and Spanish) are more likely to attend tertiary education than the Swiss by birth. In these groups, women perform better than men, compared to the benchmark population, both male and female. All other groups are less likely to qualify for tertiary-level studies. The ranking of the various origin groups corresponds to the length of time these groups have been present in Switzerland. However, the notable exception of Italians contradicts the argument that school performance can be explained by the dichotomy between culturally close and culturally distant groups.

Women are at a significant disadvantage in comparison to men with regard to access to tertiary education: table 6.6 suggests that this is the case for Swiss and immigrant-origin youth alike. Let us consider if women stand better chances than their male counterparts to reach tertiary education or, in other words, how this gender gap varies according to origin group. French and Spanish women, just as Macedonian, Bosnian, and Swiss-regional-language-speaking Yugoslav women, stand better chances than their male counterparts to reach tertiary education when compared to the Swiss. In many cases the chances for men and women are quite similar, whereas Italian and Turkish women are confronted with a large gap in their chance of attending tertiary education.

If our analysis is insufficient to point to the reasons for these origin-group patterns, it is clear that the width of the gender gap does not coincide with the dichotomy between culturally close and culturally distant groups. A prime example is the gap among Bosnians and Macedonians, who belong to the newest groups that are often considered culturally distant because of the sizable Muslim component in those flows: the gender gap in tertiary education attendance among these groups is in favor of women, while this is not the case for Italians, a culturally close group.

Conclusions

We have examined whether Switzerland is confronted with a "new second generation": is there a second generation originating from countries outside the European Union whose integration path—analyzed through their school career—significantly differs from the one assessed for the old second generation, originating from Italy, Spain, and other EU countries? Furthermore, can their respective integration paths be attributed to culturally close versus distant origin, insofar as this dimension can be captured by the gender gap in educational attainment? We have demonstrated that this is clearly not the case.

We found that improvement in school performance from the 1.5 generation to the native-born youth with migratory background is a general feature affecting all groups. It affects the whole country, although urban areas constitute a favorable environment for mobility. Moreover, good school performance, although limited, is not reserved to groups originating from "culturally close" countries. When family social background and language practices are controlled for, patterns of school success do not support the divide between EU and non-EU countries. Native-born youth of all immigrant origins are less likely to pursue higher education than are their Swiss counterparts, with the exception of Germans, French, and Spaniards. Among more recent immigrant flows, the norm is for the children to reproduce their parents' low level of education. This disturbing observation was also confirmed when family background and length of residence were controlled for.

Naturalization is generally a highly selective process for all groups, as it is strongly associated with higher school performance. This general tendency is even more pronounced among recent immigrant groups, both from the European Union and from outside it. Naturalized youth from the various groups generally outperform the Swiss by birth at school, irrespective of their country of origin. Naturalized women from all old immigrant flows and some new immigrant groups tend to outperform their Swiss counterparts in pursuing tertiary education.

Finally, the school performance of native-born women is less polarized than that of native-born men. Women tend to be less liable to school failure than men in the most recent immigrant groups, even if most women in new immigrant groups are less likely to reach tertiary education than their Swiss counterparts.

Static comparisons do not take into account what has been shown to be the critical impact of length of residence in the immigration country on school performance, and moreover, the differences observed among groups do not systematically tally with the geocultural cleavage. Finally, gender inequality in school achievement is indeed a reality but is equally shared by immigrant groups and native Swiss youth.

Our findings challenge the argument that integration as expressed by school performance for the second generation aligns with a fixed dichotomy between "culturally close" and "culturally distant" migrant groups. On the contrary, we argue in favor of a dynamic understanding of cultural change in structurally different contexts, in which individuals' length of residence, their original group's presence in the host country, and the type of opportunities offered to the group play a decisive role in shaping integration paths. We have thus shown evidence for the hypothesis that contextual factors affect integration, and these contextual factors may vary historically, a research perspective that needs further development.

NOTES

The research on which the paper is based is supported by a grant from the Swiss National Science Foundation, credit no. 4052-40-69033: Transition into Adulthood of Young People of Immigrant Descent: Intergenerational Dynamics and Social Outcomes.

1. This "cultural argument" has accompanied Swiss admission policy since the 1960s, although the countries belonging to the close and distant categories have changed

over the course of time. In the early 1960s, the Federal Council (the Swiss government) explained its unwillingness to sign an immigration convention with Portugal (as it had done with Italy and Spain) by alluding to the "too big gap between their way of living, their political, social and religious conceptions" (Cerutti 2005, 133). The cultural argument was mobilized once again to support the differentiation between a liberal admission regime for EU nationals and a very restrictive one for so-called Third Country Nationals (TCN), a divide that runs parallel to the distinction between old (Italian and Spaniards) and new second generations (Turks and former Yugoslavs).

2. In 1991, the Federal Council specified entry criteria in its immigrant recruitment policy. It regulated immigrants' ease of access to Switzerland implicitly according to the degree of cultural proximity between Switzerland and the country of origin. EU and European Free Trade Association (EFTA) countries were distinguished as belonging to the first group of countries, with the closest cultural proximity; recruitment from these countries was unlimited. A second group included the United States and Canada, countries from which recruitment was possible although restricted. The remaining countries were classified as the "third circle," from which labor recruitment was no longer permitted. This system was abandoned in 1998 for various reasons, including the fact that this type of the classification was contested for its strongly racist overtones. Today there is a two-track admission system. The first track is for EU citizens with "free movement of labor" in accordance with the Swiss-EU bilateral agreements. The second track is for all other countries, a policy which gives preference to only those deemed to be highly skilled.

3. In much the same vein, school statistics contribute to shaping an image of internally homogeneous immigrant groups on the basis of national origin and neglect to take other relevant variations within the groups into account, such as, for example, social origin and place of birth.

4. Based on the Naturalization Act of 1952, still in force, a foreigner obtains Swiss nationality subsequent to his or her own efforts to apply for it. It is a personal decision and is not initiated by the authorities. Those who have lived in Switzerland for at least twelve years (years between ages ten and twenty count double) may file an application if they can prove they are suitable candidates for naturalization, by showing, for example, familiarity with Swiss customs, support for democracy, linguistic skills, and a stable financial situation. The procedure for naturalization consists of three levels (municipal, cantonal, and federal), and conditions for eligibility vary from one canton or municipality to an other. Citizenship at the municipal level implies cantonal citizenship, which, in turn, is an entitlement to Swiss citizenship. The decision-making body on naturalization can be either the cantonal/municipal government or the legislative body. In some towns, applications for naturalization used to be submitted to a local vote. In this case, a public vote may have prevented a candidate from obtaining Swiss citizenship, even though he or she had successfully completed the administrative requirements. A new naturalization law entered into force in 2009, and communal votes on naturalizations are no longer possible.

5. Since the census provides no systematic data on previous nationality, this information is an estimate based on other data. For details, see Fibbi, Lerch, and Wanner (2005). Further work needs to be done to determine the nationality of youth from the former Yugoslavia and the identification of naturalized persons. Nationals from countries formed after the implosion of the former Yugoslavia (Bosnia, Croatia, and Macedonia) are identified by their nationality at birth. The distinction among the various groups from

the Federal Republic of Yugoslavia was made according to the main language spoken. They are therefore divided into Albanian speaking and Serbo-Croatian speaking. Some young people, however, claim that their main language is one of the four official languages in Switzerland. A group of Swiss-regional-language-speaking Yugoslavs was therefore created.

6. All the analyses pertain to this age group. Nevertheless, at times we have restricted comments to subgroups when appropriate.

7. We use educational outcomes for the age bracket twenty-three and twenty-four in order to distinguish between compulsory school education and tertiary education and to avoid expressing probabilities on a population that is still enrolled in school.

8. By "dropout," we mean people who left during the period of compulsory schooling without having completed it, that is, with no "final diploma," as well as people who were expelled from school before reaching the minimum age of voluntary dropout, fifteen. However, the latter situation is rare.

9. Since socio-demographic characteristics of the parents are only available for those young people living still in their original family household, this analysis could only be carried out on youth living with their parents.

10. Social origin is not controlled in these descriptive data.

11. Recently immigrated groups naturally have a higher percentage of foreign-born children.

12. Census data do not allow us to take into account people who enrolled in tertiary education without completing it, nor do they identify those who are presently enrolled but may not complete tertiary education.

13. Similar distorting effects of selective naturalization mechanisms have been identified in Germany, where there was also no *jus soli* until 2000 (Salentin and Wilkening 2003).

14. The imbalance favoring men in tertiary education is more pronounced in the Swiss population than in foreign ones in all age groups and notably for the younger age brackets, such as twenty to twenty-nine (Bühler and Heye 2005). Moreover, in a recent comparative study on the gender gap in OECD countries and some emerging economies, Switzerland was attributed an overall score of 3.97 out of 7 on a scale to measure women's empowerment in society. A low score indicates a better empowerment framework than a higher score (Lopes-Claros and Zahidi 2005).

15. This restriction is not too limiting since the proportion of young people aged twenty to twenty-four who are enrolled in tertiary education and living with their parents represents around two-thirds of the total in most immigrant groups.

16. Grouping the school systems of the twenty-six cantons proves useful in pointing out the impact of the respective educational institutions.

17. Census 2000 showed that the majority of parents (43 percent) aged between forty and fifty have an apprentice qualification.

18. The fourth modality of the variable is when the LP (principal language) is different from the LL (local language) and also different from the LM (maternal language), e.g., a migrant speaking Turkish at home (LM), having gone to school in the French-speaking part of the country (here French is his LP as language of instruction), but residing in the German-speaking part (hence different from LP and LM). This is the situation for a tiny number of people, so it cannot be properly interpreted.

19. This finding may be a consequence of our selection of young people living with their parents in order to control for parents' educational background.

20. We tested separate models for the 1.5 and second generation. Even though foreign-born nationals are less likely to undertake tertiary education than the native-born, the likelihood within groups is basically the same.

7

Ethnic Community, Urban Economy, and Second-Generation Attainment

TURKISH DISADVANTAGE IN BELGIUM

Karen Phalet and Anthony Heath

Across Western Europe the children of the post-1965 migrants are leaving school and entering the labor market in increasing numbers (W. Haug 2002). How this "new second generation" makes the transition from school to work is crucial for the success of migrant integration in European societies.[1] Our empirical vantage point on this wider question is an investigation of the socioeconomic attainment of the Turkish second generation in Brussels, Belgium. Not only is the Turkish case an interesting puzzle politically—Turkish migration is a key issue in ongoing negotiations and recurrent public debates over Turkey's accession to the European Union (Erzan and Kirisci 2006)—but it is also a conceptual puzzle. Turkish migrants, who typically combine low human capital with high social capital, pose a challenge to the prevailing understandings of intergenerational integration (Alba and Nee 2003; Esser 2004). Using Belgian census data, we estimate the socioeconomic disadvantage of the Turkish second generation relative to native-origin young adults, in terms of their qualifications and destinations in the labor market. We also compare the relative disadvantage of the Turkish second generation to that of the children of other migrant workers in Brussels. This comparison of ethnic community contexts with similarly low aggregate levels of human capital, but varying in ethnic social capital, allows us to explore the role of social capital in protecting the next generation against socioeconomic exclusion. We also examine the socioeconomic disadvantage of the Turkish second generation across local receiving contexts, comparing the urban area of Brussels with its northern (i.e., the Dutch-speaking region of Flanders) and southern (i.e., the French-speaking region of Wallonia) peripheries.

The Turkish second generation shows a pattern of disadvantage across Europe. The analyses for this chapter were part of a major cross-national study of ethnic minorities in Western labor markets, which estimated so-called ethnic penalties on labor-market outcomes for the second generation, including Turkish minority samples in Germany, Austria, the Netherlands, France, and Belgium (Heath and Cheung 2007). Using optimally represen-tative national data sources and standardized model specifications across countries, this research consistently documents significant and often dra-matic Turkish disadvantage. Across countries, the Turkish second generation is less able to avoid unemployment (except for local-born Turks in Austria) and is less able to access higher occupations than are native-origin youth of the same age and with similar educational qualifications.

In line with these cross-national findings, and across the French- and Dutch-speaking regions of Belgium, we find that second-generation Turks are much less likely than native-origin young adults to stay on beyond com-pulsory education, to avoid unemployment, and to access the salariat. More-over, they are at the bottom of the ethnic-stratification heap in comparison with their Italian and Moroccan counterparts. These ethnic differences sug-gest a possible downside to high ethnic social capital in combination with human capital below a critical level (Esser 2004). Lastly, and in spite of con-siderable relative disadvantage, we find that Turks in Brussels have lower unemployment rates—and higher self-employment rates—than Turks living and working in the periphery. This last finding seems to run counter to the idea that the new urban economy increases the risk of downward mobility (Zhou 1999). In the following sections, we build on the segmented-assimi-lation literature to explore the role of ethnic communities in the new urban economy. In particular, our findings qualify prevalent notions of ethnicity as a resource and the metropolis[2] as a mobility trap for the second generation. In the conclusion we briefly discuss implications for the comparative study of second-generation attainment in the United States and Europe.

Segmented Assimilation in Europe

In the wake of the riots in the French suburbs in November 2005 involving second-generation youth, international news headlines were all asking the rhetorical question, has the integration of the second generation in Europe failed? Pessimists found their worst fears confirmed by the segmented-assim-ilation literature on the second generation in the United States, although the framework cannot be applied without qualification to European migration contexts (Crul and Vermeulen 2003; Esser 2004). For a start, comparativists have pointed out that segmented assimilation in U.S. cities is embedded in a history of antagonistic race relations (Reitz 1998). In spite of a well-documented (post)colonial European history of racial violence, contemporary relationships between migrants and European hosts have been less exclusively structured by racial antagonism. Racial boundaries are not the only and, in many cases, not even the most important element in the construction of migrant and minority identities in European societies (Lamont 2000; Wimmer 2004). Thus, Alba (2005) argues that in Europe religious boundaries function in much the same way as racial boundaries in the United States. Like race in the United States, in Europe religion marks the children of Muslim migrants as the "others," excluding them from the nation. Alba argues this case for Germany and France, and Modood (2005a) develops a similar line of argument with respect to Muslim minorities in the United Kingdom. Alternatively, Brubaker (1992) stresses the importance of citizenship rather than ethnicity or race per se and sees it as the prime exclusionary device in European nation-states. By excluding nonnationals and especially non-EU nationals from full citizenship, states institute various degrees of civic inequality between different categories of the population (Brubaker 1989). In the sense that religion is implied in conceptions of citizenship and national belonging (Alba 2005), religious and civic boundaries tend to overlap. Last but not least, there is converging evidence that parental class origins are to a large extent decisive for the life chances of the second generation (Heath, Rothon, and Kilpi 2008). In the Turkish case, religious and civic boundaries, separating this majority-Muslim migrant group from their historically Christian European hosts, coincide with the class disadvantage that affects the life chances of all children of migrant workers.

Segmented assimilation should be further qualified because it theorizes the consequences of postindustrial changes in the urban economies of the United States. The divisive nature of race in U.S. cities, in particular, derives in part from the social pathologies of urban poverty. Over the years, there has been a well-documented trend toward increased socioeconomic inequality in the United States (Zhou 1999), along with the increasing concentration of poverty in the inner cities, where many children of migrant workers grow up (Massey 1985). In continental European welfare states, it has been argued, postindustrial changes follow institutional paths that differ considerably from the new economy of the United States (Esping-Andersen 1999). Most important, and in spite of gradual and partial welfare reforms, relatively inclusive social-security systems in Europe take the edge off urban poverty. Therefore, the notion of an ethnically diverse "rainbow underclass" of urban poor, as the class destination of downwardly mobile children of migrants, has no direct equivalent in European cities. While effectively protecting insiders in the regular labor market from socioeconomic exploitation, however, the highly regulated labor markets on the European continent have been criticized for relegating significant portions of the workforce to enduring unemployment or economic inactivity (Kogan and Schubert 2003). As former guest workers in a shrinking industrial sector, Turkish migrants were disproportionately affected by the postindustrial transition in Belgium, as it appears from relatively high rates of long-term unemployment and economic inactivity. Moreover, Turkish households in Brussels show the highest degree of ethnic segregation in comparison with other ethnic groups (Eggerickx, Kesteloot, and Poulain 1999).

Ethnic Social Capital

A key issue in the segmented-assimilation literature is the role of social capital in shielding the second generation from downward mobility. In the notion of social capital, ethnicity is conceived of as a resource rather than a hindrance (Modood 2004). Economic sociologists define social capital as "the capacity of individuals to command scarce resources by virtue of their membership of networks or larger social structures" (Portes 1995b, 12). Thus, Portes's (1987) exemplary case of the Cuban enclave in Miami combines dense ethnic networks with entrepreneurial know-how. The payoff of dense ethnic ties is less clear, however, in the case of migrant workers in the northwest of Europe, whose children grow up in ethnic communities with very limited human capital. Looking beyond resources, the emphasis is on the relational processes that generate social capital within close-knit migrant families and communities (Bankston and Zhou 2002). Case studies of successful ethnic communities, such as Zhou and Bankston's (1998) signature study of the second-generation Vietnamese in the United States, show that migrant parents typically share high aspirations to achieve upward mobility and that their children develop their own ambitions in tune with their parents' values. In addition, migrant parents usually exert fairly strict behavioral control over their children, in order to ensure sustained effort in an urban school context that often fails to encourage academic achievement. In accordance with Coleman's (1988) conception of social capital, which emphasizes dense associations, norms of reciprocity, and enforceable trust, research on second-generation school achievement associates high degrees of intergenerational closure (when parents know the parents of their children's friends) with shared norms and with the effective enforcement of norm-congruent behavior in migrant families (for a review, see Rothon 2005). Although most research on the second generation is concerned with school achievement, studies of ethnic business development have identified similar dimensions of ethnic social capital, including high levels of aspiration in migrant families and close ties to coethnics, as predictors of economic success (Sanders and Nee 1996; Waldinger, Aldrich, and Ward 1990).

Alternatively, a predominant class-based approach to second-generation attainment in European migration research has associated socioeconomic disadvantage with the lack of relevant resources in migrant families and communities (Modood 2004). This literature suggests that the investment in ethnic social capital may come at the cost of restricted access to relevant resources outside the ethnic community, with dense ethnic networks functioning as a mobility trap for the next generation (Esser 2004). Conceptually, notions of social and cultural capital within a class-oriented approach of intergenerational mobility can be traced back to Bourdieu (Bourdieu and Passeron 1977). Like Coleman, Bourdieu distinguishes different forms of capital in addition to socioeconomic capital. However, since Bourdieu's *explanandum* is the preservation of class advantage, his theory focuses on the mobilization of superior resources by middle- and upper-class families. In particular, cultural capital refers to the cultural preferences of the dominant classes, such as familiarity with literature or beaux arts, which are passed on from parents to children and which are typically rewarded at school (DiMaggio 1982). To the extent that working-class families lack these resources, their children are less likely to stay on and succeed in higher education. By comparison, migrant families' access to cultural capital seems even further restricted because of linguistic barriers and/or ethnic segregation. Thus, the second generation would lack affinity with the cultural tastes and practices of the local dominant classes, which facilitate access to high qualifications and the corresponding high-end jobs.

This Bourdieusian approach has been criticized for denying cultural diversity in repertoires of evaluation and, more generally, for overlooking the impact of the mobilization from below of the social and cultural resources of subordinate groups in society (Lamont and Lareau 1990; Modood 2004). On the positive side, Bourdieu's analysis highlights the wider societal context in which specific forms of social and cultural capital are valued and connected with socioeconomic gain. Along similar lines, the social-capital literature has exposed the limits of a bonding type of social capital à la Coleman, which is typically generated by strong ties with family or coethnics. In addition, bridging and linking types of social capital (cf. Putnam 2000) would be required to connect migrant families with nonmigrants and those in decision-making positions. In Granovetter's words, the attainment of the second generation may depend crucially on "the strength of weak ties" which cut across ethnic and class boundaries (Granovetter 1973).

To sum up, we distinguish intergenerational investment in ethnic social capital from investments in the kinds of social and cultural capital that are most valued by the dominant classes in the host society. From the perspective of segmented assimilation, ethnic social capital, in the sense of strong family and community ties supporting shared values and enabling behavioral control, seems crucial for sustained intergenerational investment in the presence of strong countervailing forces. From a class-based analysis of intergenerational attainment, however, there may be a downside to ethnic social capital when it is disconnected from the forms of capital that are typically rewarded in school and in the labor market.

Urban Economy

The segmented-assimilation literature has generally portrayed the American metropolis as a less-than-welcoming receiving context, where urban poverty and racial segregation in disadvantaged neighborhoods conspire to drag the new second generation down into a permanently excluded urban underclass (Zhou 1999). Accordingly, this literature considers the metropolis as the relevant unit of analysis for research on the new second generation. In the absence of direct empirical comparisons of the economic standing of the second generation within and outside metropolitan areas, it is commonly assumed that the second generation is more at risk in metropolitan areas. More generally, Sassen's (1991) theory of global cities has stressed socioeconomic polarization between the highly qualified and superaffluent elites at the top end of the urban labor market and the permanently excluded at the bottom. Others have emphasized skills polarization, or the tendency of expanding urban economies to attract more people with university degrees *and* more people with less than secondary education (Reitz 1998). Since the second generation, for the most part, makes the transition from school to work in the same urban areas where their parents first settled, urban systems can tip the balance in favor of generational progress or decline. The segmented-assimilation literature highlights the mechanisms of ethnic exclusion at the bottom end of urban labor markets. In addition, the skills polarization that characterizes the urban workforce implies more fierce competition for high-end jobs. It seems, then, that urban economies are a most hazardous environment for the second generation in search of employment in well-paid jobs.

From a competing economic center-periphery perspective, however, both the scale of urban economies and their relative permeability to newcomers, including youth, women, and migrants, may work to the advantage of the second generation (Favell, Feldbaum, and Smith 2006). Accordingly, Reitz (1998) observes most generational progress among ethnic minorities in Canadian and U.S. cities. Moreover, the global dimension of urban economies may dilute the impact of national labor-market regulations, which tend to install rigid boundaries between insiders in the labor market and outsiders (Esping-Andersen 1999). In summary, to the extent that urban economies are more open to new economic developments and international migration than their national peripheries are, they may actually enhance rather than undermine the attainment of the second generation.

Turks in Brussels: Comparisons across Ethnic and Urban Contexts

With close to one million inhabitants, Brussels attracts by far the largest share of new migrants in Belgium and has the most ethnically diverse population (Jacobs, Phalet, and Swyngedouw 2006). At the time of the 1991 census, which was the last one to provide the necessary information to identify the quasi-complete second generation, one in four inhabitants had a foreign nationality, and it was estimated that roughly one in three was of foreign origin, including Belgian citizens. The largest group of labor migrants from within the European Union is the Italian group in Brussels. Of all inhabitants of migrant origin in Brussels, about one in two has non-European origins. The Moroccans are the largest and the Turks the second-largest group of labor migrants from outside the European Union. Our analysis estimates the extent of ethnic disadvantage with respect to avoidance of unemployment, access to the salariat, and successful self-employment as distinct labor-market outcomes. Taking into account ethnic differences in educational qualifications, different unemployment rates indicate degrees of ethnic exclusion at entry into the labor market. In parallel, the access of the second generation to the salariat indicates their inclusion into the more advantaged segments of the labor market. Self-employment is included here as an alternative measure of labor-market inclusion, since ethnic business is often seen as a way to circumvent ethnic discrimination in regular careers (Sanders and Nee 1996).

Looking beyond the replication of the cross-national finding of Turkish disadvantage, this study has a double comparative design. The first comparison is between ethnic community contexts in Brussels: is the Turkish community a better or worse context for second-generation achievement than Italian and Moroccan communities? In addition, the urban context of Brussels is contrasted with the northern and southern peripheries, that is, Flanders and Wallonia: is the urban area of Brussels a better or worse place for the second generation to get ahead than the national periphery?

Ethnic Communities

As a consequence of postwar labor migration from the Mediterranean basin to the highly economically developed northwest of Europe, Brussels has attracted large numbers of Turkish, Moroccan, and southern European labor migrants and their families (Lesthaeghe 2000). Italians, Moroccans, and Turks are the main ethnic groups with significant local-born offspring. The first generation has in common that they arrived without formal qualifications or relevant work experience. This is because they were mainly recruited from the less developed rural areas of their countries of origin to work in the mines and the heavy industries. However, apart from similarities with respect to the poor qualifications of the first generation, Turkish, Moroccan, and Italian communities constitute different contexts for second-generation achievement. The Italians arrived as part of the early postwar labor migration from southern Europe. It was not until the late 1960s that the recruitment of foreign labor extended to non-European countries in the Mediterranean basin, such as Turkey and Morocco (Lesthaeghe 2000). The new migrants were predominantly nonwhite and non-Christian. Although Italians, Turks, and Moroccans have in common their initial class disadvantage as guest workers, only Turkish and Moroccan disadvantage coincides with overlapping racial, religious, and civic boundaries in European nation-states. Accordingly, there is evidence of pervasive ethnic prejudice and discrimination against Turkish and Moroccan workers (Simon 2004). Also, Turks and Moroccans in Brussels are more concentrated in disadvantaged urban neighborhoods than are Italian households. In short, Italians have most access to valued resources in the host society, due to length of residence and reduced ethnic distance.

Despite the commonalities between Turks and Moroccans in Brussels, they have developed distinct patterns of settlement and community building (Eggerickx et al. 1999; Lesthaeghe 2000). Many local Turkish communities are really transplanted villages, replicating kinship networks across national borders. Even in the urban area of Brussels, the bustling and visibly Turkish streets and neighborhoods are connected with specific villages in Turkey by extended family ties. Cross-border family ties often extend into the next generation through cross-border marriage, joint investment in family business, or family-sponsored home ownership. Typically, local Turkish communities are organized around close links between the family and the workplace (Lesthaeghe 2000). A common Turkish settlement pattern is clustering around ethnic businesses or—in the periphery—the ethnic occupational niches in the old industrial sectors, such as textiles or shipbuilding. Not only do Turkish statistics show record rates of residential segregation and cross-border marriages, but special surveys have documented dense ethnic networks and a vibrant ethnic associational life, as well as high levels of ethnic language retention, ethnic media use, and continued involvement in homeland politics (Erzan and Kirisci 2006; Jacobs and Tillie 2004; Swyngedouw, Phalet, and Deschouwer 1999). In contrast, Moroccan statistics show lower levels of cross-border marriages, much lower levels of ethnic language retention and media use, and a rather weakly developed ethnic associational life (ibid.). Moreover, the urban geography of Moroccan migration and settlement is clearly distinct from the Turkish pattern: Moroccan residential clusters are more often situated in inner-city pockets within urban areas. In the absence of kinship ties or economic anchorage in ethnic niches or business, Moroccan segregation has been attributed primarily to the externally imposed yet self-sustaining mechanisms of socioeconomic exclusion and ethnic discrimination in the housing market (Eggerickx et al. 1999; Lesthaeghe 2000). Last but not least, Turkish migrant families exemplify key aspects of family-based social capital, such as close intergenerational ties, shared norms, and norm enforcement, which have been associated with successful ethnic communities in the United States (Bankston and Zhou 2002). Thus, Turkish migrant parents and their children share strong achievement values and stress intergenerational obligations (Dekovic, Pels, and Model 2006). Moreover, the traditional parenting style of Turkish migrant parents is characterized by restrictive behavioral control and strong conformity pressure (ibid.). Although Moroccan parents exhibit similar patterns of parenting, they seem less effective than Turkish migrants in passing on traditional family values to the next generation. One possible reason for the strong normative consensus in Turkish migrant families is that dense ethnic networks facilitate intergenerational closure. Overall, while lacking in human capital, the Turkish group stands out by its impressive investment in ethnic social capital.

Local Receiving Contexts

The urban region of Brussels shares with its national periphery the same redistributive regime of taxation and welfare, the same immigration and citizenship regime, and very similar school systems and labor-market regulations. In particular, Belgium has extended social and economic rights to nonnational legal residents; since 1984, it has facilitated the acquisition of citizenship for the second generation through a series of legislative changes; it has adopted antidiscrimination legislation and instituted an advisory committee to support its implementation; and it is formally committed to promoting equal opportunities for migrants and minorities as part of national integration policies since 1991. Looking beyond this common framework, however, the regions of Flanders in the north, Wallonia in the south, and Brussels in the center constitute distinct local contexts of reception.

The urban region of Brussels, thanks to its geography in the center of "old Europe," has developed an advanced service economy with a strong international orientation. Thus, Brussels attracts a disproportionately large share of highly qualified expat professionals working in multinational corporations, information technology, finance, journalism, and research and development. Conversely, less-qualified migrant workers in Brussels are overrepresented in menial jobs in construction, cleaning, catering, and other personal services, which make up the lower end of the urban labor market. As Brussels is the accidental place where the world does European politics, it is also home to the legal, administrative, and political elites that are connected to international institutions, such as the European parliament and NATO (Favell 2004). With its complex institutional architecture, the region of Brussels recognizes both national language communities (French and Dutch), and it functions as a triple capital at the regional, national, and EU levels. A long cosmopolitan history of migration and ethnic diversity historically precedes its binational institutions and present international status as triple capital. Up to this day, Brussels attracts large shares of new migrants, refugees, and professional free movers. Finally, ethnic electorates have a strong political voice in Brussels, and representatives of non-EU origin occupy key decision-making positions in the urban and regional government and administration (Jacobs et al. 2006).

Belgium is also characterized by a north-south divide between Flanders (where Dutch is the dominant language) and Wallonia (where French is the dominant language). The northern region of Flanders, with its more advanced and wealthier postindustrial economy, should offer the best socioeconomic opportunities to immigrants and the second generation. By contrast, the southern region of Wallonia, with its declining industrial economy, suffered disproportionately from the restructuring of the labor market. Yet the south of the country experienced an earlier and more diverse intake of migrant labor than the north did. Moreover, migrant settlement in the south has been less ethnically segregated than in the north, where migrant groups are more highly concentrated in inner cities and industrial basins. Last but not least, migrant workers in the south have the relative advantage of strong trade unions and no successful xenophobic parties. In contrast, policymakers in the north have to reckon with a strong and steady anti-immigrant vote, causing tension in interethnic relations between migrants and hosts. In short, the second generation may not be able to take full advantage of the better socioeconomic opportunities in the north of the country because of the relatively high levels of ethnic segregation and exclusionism.

Second-Generation Attainment in the Census

Our data are anonymized records sampled from the 1991 Belgian census. In spite of significant rates of naturalization and acquisition of Belgian nationality already in 1991, the ethnic origin of the second generation could still be identified by combining individuals' current nationality with key information about their country of birth and nationality at birth (Eggerickx et al. 1999). This is no longer the case in the most recent census, in 2001, since local-born children of migrant parents who have acquired citizenship now have Belgian nationality by birth. The main advantage of using the census as a source is that large numbers make it possible to assess the socioeconomic attainment of the second generation by ethnic origin. Moreover, the second generation can be compared with the older first generation of migrant parents, on the one hand, and with the younger generation of native origin, that is, young adults whose parents were both born as Belgians in Belgium, on the other hand. One should bear in mind, however, that the census does not reliably measure the attainment of the first generation, because the census questions on education do not tally with the school systems in the countries of origin. To ensure that migrants are assigned to the correct qualification levels, self-reported foreign qualifications were complemented with information on school-leaving ages. Moreover, for reasons of privacy and political sensitivity, the census does not ask questions about language, religion, ethnic ancestry, or the class origins of migrants. In short, the use of census data is restricted mainly by the lack of reliable information on the premigration background of individual migrants. Since the selection of the first generation, with regard to their human and cultural capital prior to migration, influences second-generation attainment, ethnic differences in attainment should be interpreted with due caution.

Specifically, migrant groups were sampled by taking one of every two people of Italian, Moroccan, or Turkish origin at random from the census. Whereas all three migrant groups were sampled in the urban area of Brussels, only the Turkish group was also sampled outside Brussels, in Flanders and Wallonia. Each migrant group consists of a first generation of migrants proper and a second generation of migrant offspring. Across migrant groups, the second generation was defined as either those who were born in Belgium as Italians, Moroccans, or Turks or those who arrived as children before the age of seven, which indicates the start of compulsory schooling in Belgium. Since almost the entire Turkish and Moroccan second generation was still under the age of thirty-six at the time of the census in 1991, for reasons of comparability, the analysis was restricted to second-generation Turks, Moroccans, and Italians in the age range of eighteen to thirty-five. Note that local-born Italian adults include a small yet unidentified percentage of the third generation, that is, the grandchildren of the first Italian guest workers who arrived before World War II and who did not return. Finally, with a view to assessing socioeconomic attainment, a further selection was made of those members of the second generation who had left school and joined the workforce. One should bear in mind that those with higher qualifications are underrepresented among the youngest cohorts within the workforce. The first generation was defined as those who were born in Italy, Morocco, or Turkey with foreign nationality and who arrived in Belgium at a later age, most often as young adults. Because the second generation is the focus of this study, only the older first generation of Italians, Moroccans, or Turks— that is, the potential parents of the second generation—are included in the analysis. As a proxy for the generation of migrant parents at the aggregate level, we took the theoretical age of the parents of the second generation. If one accepts a minimum age difference of fifteen years between parent and child, the older first generation should be at least thirty-three. Since we are assessing socioeconomic attainment across generations, a further selection was made of those older migrants who were still in the workforce. For our purposes, then, the ages of the relevant first generation ranged from thirty-three to fifty.

The attainment of the second generation was compared with that of a charter population whose parents had no migration background. The charter population was represented by a random sample of one in ten people who were born with Belgian nationality. Native-origin comparison groups were sampled within the urban area of Brussels and outside Brussels, in Flanders and Wallonia. To enhance comparability with the second generation, native-origin young adults were sampled within the age range of the second generation, that is, from eighteen to thirty-five. Only young adults who were economically active were included in the analyses. It should be noted that migrants in Belgium are more often economically inactive than nonmigrants (Phalet 2007). The main reasons for this are higher staying-on rates at school, higher incidence of early retirement, and the more traditional gender roles in migrant families. Hence, ethnic differences in unemployment rates will almost certainly underestimate the true extent of ethnic exclusion in the labor market. Another caveat concerns the regional distribution of migrant and nonmigrant groups between the urban center and the periphery. It is important to remember that migrants are less likely to move or to commute long distances to their workplace than nonmigrants are. Thus, the second generation in Brussels is compared with a charter population that includes those who have recently moved to the city but excludes the commuters from the periphery. Hence, our estimates of ethnic disadvantage in Brussels may not reflect the full extent of socioeconomic disadvantage. Lastly, since women's lives run a different course than those of men, we carried out separate analyses of socioeconomic attainment for women and men. This also helps to identify whether imported gender inequalities from Turkey and Morocco, in particular, have been reduced through intergenerational integration.

To assess the socioeconomic attainment of the second generation, the children of Turkish, Moroccan, and Italian migrants were distinguished from the older generations of Turkish, Moroccan, and Italian migrants and were compared with young adults of native origin as the charter population. To begin with, ethnic differences in educational qualifications were analyzed. For comparative purposes, people were assigned to four educational categories, which are derived from Shavit and Müller's (1998) cross-national coding schema. These categories are tertiary qualifications, including university degrees; higher-secondary qualifications; lower-secondary schooling; and primary schooling or none. Next, the analysis turns to the labor-market performance of the second generation: Are they finding jobs? Who gets the better jobs? And who is in business? The unemployed were defined as those who are currently without paid work and are looking for work (the standard International Labour Organization definition). To assess the occupational attainment of those who are in paid work, we specified broad occupational classes by combining EGP categories (a class schema developed by and named after Erikson, Goldthorpe, and Portocarero; see Erikson and Goldthorpe 1992). Following Heath and Cheung (2007), higher occupations were defined as the relatively well-paid, secure, and prestigious jobs of the salariat, that is, the professional, managerial, and administrative elites (i.e., EGP I and II). The salariat was contrasted with a broad reference category, which groups together all routine nonmanual, skilled manual, and semi- or unskilled manual occupations (i.e., EGP III, V, VI, and VII). Finally, there was a separate category for self-employment, which corresponds to the so-called petty bourgeoisie, or the small proprietors and artisans with or without employees, in the EGP class schema (i.e., EGP IV).

The descriptive analyses report ethnic differences in socioeconomic attainment. These differences are informative about the pattern of ethnic stratification. Yet the descriptive analyses may be misleading since ethnic differences in attainment are influenced not only by ethnic origin but also by other factors such as education. For instance, the second generation may be underrepresented in professional and managerial occupations because they lack the required higher qualifications, or alternatively, they may be underrepresented in spite of their high qualifications. Net ethnic differences, taking into account a person's qualifications, will be significant only in the latter case. To estimate net ethnic differences in socioeconomic attainment, then, binomial and multinomial logistic regressions were conducted for men and women, including qualifications and marital status as predictors in addition to ethnic origin and generation. Educational qualifications were included as the main measure of human capital (Heath and Cheung 2007). Furthermore, we controlled for marital status (i.e., being married, widowed, or divorced, with being single as a reference category), since unmarried women and married men are more likely to be employed or self-employed. Comparison groups were matched in terms of the age range of the second generation and that of their potential parents. Overall, the effects of age, qualifications, and marital status on the labor-market outcomes of men and women in our models were always in the expected direction. Hence, the remainder of this chapter presents and discusses only our findings with regard to ethnic and regional disparities.

The Second Generation in Brussels: Turkish Disadvantage

Is there an ethnic gap between the educational and occupational attainment of the second generation and that of the charter population in Brussels? And

TABLE 7.1A
Percentages of the workforce who completed secondary and tertiary education: Ethnic-origin groups and generations in Brussels

	% Secondary Men	% Tertiary Men	Active men N	% Secondary Women	% Tertiary Women	Active women N
Turkish origin						
second generation (18-35)	31	4	487	29	7	425
first generation (33-50)	11	10	716	8	3	390
Moroccan origin						
second generation (18-35)	33	10	1,481	33	14	1,275
first generation (33-50)	14	11	278	12	6	930
Italian origin						
second generation (18-35)	33	15	1,292	37	21	1,162
first generation (33-50)	12	14	1,227	15	10	782
Native origin						
all (18-35)	30	33	4,444	30	42	4,738

how does the Turkish second generation differ from its Italian and Moroccan counterparts? Marginal distributions give a first impression of the pattern of ethnic differences in attainment across generations and gender. In the next section, net ethnic differences give a more precise estimate of ethnic disadvantage.

In Table 7.1a the percentages per group of the second generation who have completed higher-secondary or tertiary education are shown. It can be seen that the Turkish second generation, in particular, is on a par with the charter population up to the level of higher-secondary education. However, Turkish men and women are, respectively, eight and six times less likely than the charter population to continue their education beyond secondary level. This is because the majority of Turkish pupils follow vocational tracks, rather than the academic track that prepares students for university. Interestingly, the striking gender differences seen in the schooling levels of older Turkish migrants have all but disappeared in the second generation. In fact, gender inequality is reversed at the tertiary level, where Turkish second-generation women are more successful than Turkish men.

Across ethnic groups, the second generation in general is less qualified than young adults of native origin. Whereas the majority of native-origin Belgians completed secondary education or higher, about one in two Italians and Moroccans and nearly two in three Turks did not complete secondary education. Because Turkish, Moroccan, and Italian guest workers were usu-

TABLE 7.1B
Percentages unemployed, employed in the salariat and self-
employed: Ethnic-origin groups and generations in Brussels

	% Unemployed	Active total (100%)	% Salariat (EGP I-II)	Employed total (100%)	% Self-employed (EGP IV)
MEN					
Turkish origin					
second generation (18-35)	36	518	11	333	4
first generation (33-50)	30	834	11	582	7
Moroccan origin					
second generation (18-35)	42	1,552	14	902	2
first generation (33-50)	32	3,151	10	2,152	4
Italian origin					
second generation (18-35)	19	1,330	25	1,078	2
first generation (33-50)	17	1,324	24	1,100	7
Native origin					
all (18-35)	12	4,571	44	4,079	3
WOMEN					
Turkish origin					
second generation (18-35)	47	442	8	234	3
first generation (33-50)	49	471	7	241	4
Moroccan origin					
second generation (18-35)	47	1,325	20	709	1
first generation (33-50)	51	1,080	11	527	1
Italian origin					
second generation (18-35)	26	1,194	26	889	2
first generation (33-50)	31	841	21	584	3
Native origin					
all (18-35)	16	4,852	46	4,058	1

ally recruited from the rural and less educated segments of the source countries, there are hardly any ethnic differences in the levels of education of the
first generation. In the second generation, however, educational attainment
levels tend to diverge between ethnic groups. The Italian second generation
comes closest to parity with young adults of the charter population, while
the Turkish second generation evinces the lowest levels of education.

In table 7.1b the employment status of second-generation Turks, Moroccans, and Italians in Brussels is shown, as well as that of the older migrants
and the charter population. Ethnic differences in unemployment rates indicate the degree of ethnic exclusion from the labor market. Across ethnic
groups, we see the same overall pattern of gross ethnic disadvantage, which
largely persists into the second generation. There is higher unemployment
among second-generation men than among first-generation migrants, but
the inverse is true for women: unemployment is rather lower among second-
generation women. This means that the gender gap in employment levels is

smaller in the second generation. The loss of employment that affects second-generation men coincides with economic restructuring: whereas their parents were typically employed in unskilled manual work, the second generation entered the labor market at a time when the industrial sector was already going into decline. In addition, unemployment seems more likely in some ethnic groups than in others. While the Moroccan second generation is most likely to be unemployed, Italians are far less likely to become unemployed than either Moroccans or Turks, and the members of the charter population are the least likely to be out of work. Specifically, the Turkish second generation is three times more likely to be unemployed than people of native origin of the same age.

The degree of socioeconomic inclusion was assessed by the level of access to the salariat among the second generation, the first generation, and the charter population. Table 7.1b shows the percentages of the employed per group with professional, administrative, and managerial occupations. As can be seen from the table, these percentages are extremely low among the second generation, the second-generation Turks in particular. Comparing across ethnic groups, we find that the percentages of the second generation in the salariat range from less than one in ten up to one in four. Turkish second-generation men and women are at the bottom of the ethnic hierarchy, being four and six times less likely, respectively, than young men and women of native origin to enter the salariat. At the other end of the scale, the Italian second generation has a clear competitive advantage over both Turks and Moroccans. Interestingly, most progress is seen for Moroccan women of the second generation, who are outperforming Moroccan men.

Another way to assess the socioeconomic inclusion of the second generation is to look at the number of people in self-employment. In the formal labor market, which is reported in the census, self-employment is a rather marginal phenomenon (see table 7.1b). Only about 3 percent and 1 percent of the men and women of native origin are entrepreneurs. In keeping with the theory that ethnic businesses develop as a way to circumvent discrimination by Belgian employers (Sanders and Nee 1996), Turks in Brussels are more likely to be self-employed than the charter population. This is less clear, however, for Italians and Moroccans. Since the second generation is on average still fairly young, the figures are less informative about generational trends in ethnic entrepreneurship.

Table 7.2a shows the results of multinomial logistic regressions predicting the odds of attaining tertiary education rather than secondary or less. Ethnic differences in education confirm the ethnic disadvantage of the second gen-

TABLE 7.2A
Multinomial logistic regressions of educational attainment in Brussels: Parameter estimates of ethnic differences (contrasts with secondary qualifications, standard errors in parentheses)

	Tertiary Men	No complete sec Men	Tertiary Women	No complete sec Women
Constant/Intercept	.10 (.04)	.22 (.04)	.35 (.04)	-.08 (.04) ns
Ethnic origin:				
Turkish second	-2.23 (.25)	.52 (.11)	-1.79 (.21)	.88 (.12)
Turkish first	ns	1.79 (.13)	-1.30 (.34)	2.50 (.19)
Moroccan second	-1.34 (.10)	.33 (.07)	-1.18 (,.10)	.53 (.07)
Moroccan first	-.33 (.08)	1.43 (.07)	-1.10 (.17)	2.03 (.11)
Italian second	-.90 (.10)	.24 (.07)	-.94 (.09)	.21 (.08)
Italian first	ns	1.57 (.10)	-.74 (.15)	1.67 (.11)
Native origin	0	0	0	0
Chi-square (D.F.)	2,229 (12)		1,747 (12)	
N	12,427		9,702	

eration in Brussels, both at secondary and tertiary levels. Comparing across ethnic groups, we find the greatest educational disadvantage in the Turkish second generation: not only are they least likely to stay on in tertiary education, but they are also most likely to drop out before completing secondary education. We conclude that educational disadvantage persists in the second generation. It must be remembered that the analysis underestimates the future attainment of the second generation, since it does not include those who are still studying.

After leaving school, how well does the second generation in Brussels succeed in avoiding unemployment and in securing access to better jobs or starting their own businesses? In Table 7.2b the results of binomial logistic regressions are shown. The regressions predict the odds of being unemployed rather than employed, of being employed in higher occupations rather than otherwise employed, and of being self-employed rather than being employed in the regular labor market. The net effects of ethnic origin in Model 2 indicate what is left of gross ethnic disadvantage in Model 1, when group differences in relevant characteristics such as education and family situation are taken into account. For men and women alike, significant positive effects of ethnic origin on unemployment risks in Model 1 confirm gross ethnic disadvantage: second-generation Turks, Moroccans, and Italians in Brussels are more often excluded from employment than are young adults of native origin. Although the extent of ethnic disadvantage is generally reduced in

TABLE 7.2B

Binomial logistic regressions of occupational attainment in Brussels: Parameter estimates of gross (Model 1) and net ethnic differences (Model 2)

	Unemployed vs. employed Model 1	Unemployed vs. employed Model 2	Salariat vs. empl other Model 1	Salariat vs. empl other Model 2	Self-empl vs. empl Model 1	Self-empl vs. empl Model 2
MEN						
Constant	**-2.07 (.05)**	**-1.79 (.07)**	-.23 (.03)	**-.73 (.06)**	**-3.61 (.10)**	**-3.39 (.15)**
Ethnic origin:						
Turkish second	**1.48 (.11)**	**1.36 (.11)**	**-1.91 (.19)**	**-1.22 (.20)**	ns	ns
Turkish first	**1.24 (.09)**	**1.43 (.11)**	**-1.84 (.15)**	**-1.44 (.17)**	**1.05 (.20)**	**1.12 (.22)**
Moroccan second	**1.71 (.07)**	**1.39 (.07)**	**-1.58 (.10)**	**-1.22 (.12)**	ns	ns
Moroccan first	**1.25 (.06)**	**1.46 (.08)**	**-1.84 (.08)**	**-1.52 (.10)**	ns	ns
Italian second	**.60 (.09)**	**.41 (.09)**	**-.88 (.08)**	**-.52 (.09)**	ns	ns
Italian first	**.45 (.09)**	**.57 (.10)**	**-.92 (.08)**	*-.33 (.10)*	**1.00 (.16)**	**1.04 (.18)**
Native origin	0	0	0	0	0	0
Chi-square (D.F.)	831 (6)	1,420 (11)	1,045 (6)	3,479 (11)	60 (6)	78 (11)
Chi-square diff.		589 (5) *		2,434 (5) *		18 (5)
N	12,427	12,427	9,647	9,647	9,647	9,647
WOMEN						
Constant	**-1.65 (.04)**	**-1.49 (.06)**	-.18 (.03)	**-.93 (.07)**	**-4.47 (.15)**	**-3.75 (.22)**
Ethnic origin:						
Turkish second	**1.51 (.11)**	**1.11 (.11)**	**-2.27 (.25)**	**-1.40 (.27)**	.86 (.44)	ns
Turkish first	**1.52 (.11)**	**.91 (.11)**	**-2.30 (.26)**	-80 (.30)	**1.38 (.37)**	**1.16 (.41)**
Moroccan second	**1.47 (.07)**	**1.19 (.07)**	**-1.20 (.10)**	**-.73 (.12)**	ns	ns
Moroccan first	**1.67(.08)**	**1.13 (.09)**	**-1.76 (.14)**	**-.48 (.17)**	ns	ns
Italian second	**.55 (.08)**	**.32 (.08)**	**-.88 (.08)**	**-.48 (.10)**	ns	ns
Italian first	**.83 (.09)**	**.33 (.10)**	**-1.20 (.11)**	-ns	**1.04 (.29)**	.83 (.32)
Native origin	0	0	0	0	0	0
Chi-square (D.F.)	892 (6)	1,357 (11)	647 (6)	2,534 (11)	25 (6)	59 (11)
Chi-square diff.		465 (5) *		1,887 (5) *		34 (5)
N	9,702	9,702	6,975	6,975	6,975	6,975

Note: Significance levels: bold print indicates p < ,0001; italicized print p < ,001; normal print p < ,01; levels of p > ,01 are reported as non-significant (ns).
* Compared to Model 1

Model 2, net ethnic differences are significant and large in all groups except for Italian women. Thus, it seems that young adults of the second generation are more likely to be unemployed than are young adults of native origin with the same qualifications and family situation. Again, ethnic disadvantage persists across generations. In addition, migrant groups differ in the size of net ethnic differences. The Italian second generation seems the least likely to be unemployed, and Moroccan second-generation men are most likely to be out of work. Yet ethnic differences between second-generation Turks and Moroccans are negligible.

Turning to occupational attainment, significant negative effects of ethnic origin on occupational class in Model 1 indicate gross ethnic disadvantage.

The greatest gross disadvantage is found for the Turkish second generation in comparison with the charter population in Brussels, and the least disadvantage is found for Italians. As expected, highly qualified men and women are far more likely to be in the salariat than are those with lower qualifications. Accordingly, when education is included in Model 2, net ethnic penalties are reduced. They are still significant and large, however. In other words, the second generation is less likely to enter the salariat than are young adults of native origin with similar qualifications.

Lastly, we estimated gross and net ethnic differences in self-employment. In view of the low levels of self-employment in Brussels overall, the estimates for migrant women in particular may not be reliable. Although the older first generation of Turkish and Italian migrants is most often self-employed, net ethnic differences are not significant in the second generation. The significant positive effect of ethnic origin suggests a strategy among Turkish migrants to escape ethnic discrimination in the labor market through business development. Yet it is too early to say whether this strategy is transmitted to the second generation. In addition, being educated beyond secondary level is related to a lower likelihood of being self-employed. Possibly, some human capital is required for successful business development, but regular occupational careers become more attractive with higher levels of education. This pattern ties in with an interpretation of Turkish entrepreneurship in Brussels as an ethnic investment strategy that does not require prolonged educational investment.

Second-Generation Turks across Regions: Urban Advantage

Does the relative educational and occupational attainment of second-generation Turks differ according to local receiving contexts? Are Turks in the urban area of Brussels doing better or worse than those in the rest of the country? To examine regional differences in ethnic disadvantage, the attainment of the Turkish second generation is compared with that of older Turkish migrants and young adults of native origin in Brussels, Flanders, and Wallonia. Marginal distributions give a first impression of gross ethnic disadvantage in relation to local contexts. To estimate net ethnic disadvantage in the urban region of Brussels and in the rest of Belgium, we used logistic regressions. In addition to the main effects of Turkish origin, qualifications, and region on attainment levels, we tested the interaction effect of Turkish origin with region. A significant interaction effect on attainment indicates that second-generation Turks incur different ethnic penalties in Brussels and in Flanders and Wallonia. Because of the very small proportions of employed

TABLE 7.3A

Percentages of the workforce who have completed secondary and tertiary education: The educational attainment of Turkish- and native-origin groups across regions

	% Secondary Men	% Tertiary Men	Active men (100%)	% Secondary Women	% Tertiary Women	Active women (100%)
Turkish second (18-35)						
Brussels	31	4	487	29	7	425
north	43	2	957	46	2	720
south	32	5	491	40	5	325
Turkish first (33-50)						
Brussels	11	10	716	8	3	390
north	11	7	1,028	7	3	257
south	13	11	600	10	5	127
Native origin (18-35)						
Brussels	30	33	4,444	30	42	4,738
north	41	23	57,877	42	29	53,301
south	35	19	25,013	36	28	22,921

Turkish women in the periphery, we had to restrict the regional comparison of occupational attainment to men only. High levels of female economic inactivity outside Brussels are related to more traditional gender roles in Turkish families, along with a lack of the kinds of jobs, such as housekeeping, that are open to low-skilled migrant women.

Table 7.3a shows the qualification levels of Turkish- and native-origin comparison groups in Brussels, Flanders, and Wallonia. Of the charter population in Brussels, less have completed secondary education, although there are more who have tertiary education than in the rest of the country. This pattern is in line with the common finding of educational polarization in expanding urban economies. As for the first generation of Turkish migrants, they have similarly low qualifications across regions. Disadvantage persists over generations, so that the second generation has less access to higher education than do young adults of native origin in the same region.

There are also regional differences, however. The educational polarization seen in the charter population is echoed in the Turkish second generation in Brussels. Thus, they have the highest risk of dropping out without secondary qualifications, in comparison with the Turks in the rest of the country. Conversely, in Brussels and in the south of the country, the Turkish second generation is about twice as likely to obtain tertiary qualifications as in Flanders. The relative advantage of Turks in Brussels could be explained in part by the closer proximity of universities and more demand for highly qualified professionals. Since second-generation achievement in Brussels follows a general trend toward educational polarization in urban economies, significant and large ethnic disparities with native-origin competitors in the local workforce remain. Furthermore, more frequent early selection and downward reorientation into vocational tracks in Flemish schools (rather than having students repeat the year in the same track) might help to explain why so few Turks in Flanders have tertiary qualifications, in spite of higher completion rates at the secondary level. Indeed, the Turkish second generation in Flanders is over ten times less likely to have tertiary education than are young adults of native origin there.

As a more formal test of regional disparities in educational attainment, the main effects of region in multinomial logistic regression confirm the general trend toward educational polarization in Brussels (see appendix to this chapter). Thus, the urban workforce in Brussels is most likely to have tertiary qualifications *and* to have dropped out of secondary school. Differences in dropout rates between Brussels and Wallonia are not significant. With regard to the Turkish second generation, the main effects of ethnic origin and generation confirm persistent educational disadvantage across regions. Finally, adding the interactions between ethnic origin and region results in a rather marginal improvement in model fit (see appendix). Clearly, general regional discrepancies in educational distributions explain most of the contextual variation in second-generation attainment. In addition, the pattern of interaction effects suggests that ethnic disparities in educational attainment are largest for Turkish second-generation women in Flanders.

In table 7.3b the employment situation of Turkish- and native-origin groups is compared in Brussels and in Flanders and Wallonia. Unemployment levels of the charter population are lowest in the more prosperous Flemish north, and they are higher in Brussels and in the south of the country. In contrast, Turkish migrants and their children in Brussels are more likely to have paid work than are the Turks in Flanders. The relative advantage of Turks in Brussels is evident from the smaller ethnic gap between the unemployment rates of Turkish- and native-origin young adults in Brussels than in the periphery, especially Flanders. Thus, in Brussels, Turkish men are three times as likely to be unemployed as young men of native origin are, whereas in Flanders, Turkish men are seven times as likely to be unemployed. In spite of higher overall levels of unemployment, similar regional differences in the extent of ethnic disadvantage were also found for women. To conclude, while the Turkish second generation suffers very high levels of

TABLE 7.3B
Percentages unemployed, employed in the salariat and self-employed: The occupational attainment of Turkish- and native-origin groups across regions

	% Unemployed	Active total (100%)	% Salariat (EGP I-II)	Employed total (100%)	% Self-employed (EGP IV)
Men					
Turkish second (18-35)					
Brussels	36	518	11	333	4
north	35	990	3	648	2
south	48	499	6	262	2
Turkish first (33-50)					
Brussels	30	834	11	582	7
north	37	1,102	12	698	3
south	35	627	16	406	3
Native origin (18-35)					
Brussels	12	4,571	44	4,047	3
north	5	58,862	28	56,199	5
south	13	25,224	30	21,870	6
Women					
Turkish second (18-35)					
Brussels	47	442	8	234	3
north	74	936	14	195	5
south	76	327	17	98	6
Turkish first (33-50)					
Brussels	49	471	7	241	4
north	71	278	16	82	16
south	60	129	15	52	14
Native origin (18-35)					
Brussels	16	4,852	45	4,058	1
north	15	54,166	32	46,256	3
south	28	23,068	42	16,643	3

ethnic exclusion overall, they are rather less severely penalized in the urban labor market of Brussels than in the periphery, in particular in Flanders.

What does less unequal access to employment in Brussels imply for the occupational attainment of the Turkish second generation? Across regions and generations, Turks are heavily underrepresented in the salariat. At the same time, Turkish second-generation men in Brussels have less restricted access to the salariat than do Turkish men in the rest of the country, and they are also less severely disadvantaged compared to the charter population. Specifically, they are four times less likely to enter the salariat than are young adults of native origin in Brussels; in the south, five times less likely and in the north, nearly ten times less likely. Whereas the main finding is clearly the very restricted access of the second generation to better jobs across regions, regional differences suggest that job opportunities are least uneven in Brussels and most uneven in Flanders.

Ethnic Community, Urban Economy, and Second-Generation Attainment |

Another route to socioeconomic inclusion is self-employment. Interestingly, larger shares of the charter population are self-employed outside than within the urban region of Brussels. Conversely, there are more Turkish men self-employed in Brussels than in the rest of the country. Moreover, the Turkish group in Brussels is more inclined than locals of native origin to start up their own businesses. Importantly, relatively high self-employment rates are passed on to the second generation in Brussels. Across generations, there are twice as many self-employed Turkish men in Brussels as in the rest of Belgium. Although self-employment is very limited overall, the urban area of Brussels again seems to offer the least negative socioeconomic prospects for the second generation.

The comparative advantage of the second generation in Brussels might be due to positive selection, as the urban labor market selectively attracts highly qualified workers or professionals from the periphery and from abroad. Net ethnic disparities involve controls for the differential selection of migrant- and native-origin workers in terms of their educational qualifications. Although we are aware that we do not control for unmeasured factors, net disparities are a more stringent test of contextual variation in second-generation achievement. Since the models replicate the findings on Turkish disadvantage in Brussels, only the main effects of region and the interaction effects of regional context and ethnic origin are discussed (see appendix). Thus, the main effect of region on unemployment rates indicates that, generally, there is a lower chance of being unemployed in Flanders than in Brussels, after controlling for differential qualifications of the local workforce. In addition, ethnic disparities in unemployment risks vary considerably between regions, net of the differential composition of the workforce across regions in terms of human capital. Indeed, model fit is much improved when interactions of ethnic origin with region are included. Apparently, net ethnic disparities in the unemployment risks of the second generation are larger outside Brussels, especially in Flanders. To conclude, less severe ethnic exclusion in Brussels suggests that it is the least uneven place for second-generation Turks to compete for jobs.

In addition, the main effect of region confirms better chances of being in the salariat in Brussels than in the north and south of the country, which cannot be attributed solely to the more positive selection of the urban workforce. However, there is less contextual variation in the size of ethnic penalties in access to the salariat than there is with respect to unemployment. This is evident from the modest contribution of the ethnicity-by-region interactions to the model's overall fit. Net of human capital, ethnic disparities in the occupational attainment of the second generation are similarly large across regions. We conclude that second-generation Turks in Brussels have significantly better chances of entering the salariat *in spite of* similar ethnic penalties across regions. This relative advantage of Turks in Brussels can be attributed to the fact that, generally, the chances of succeeding in higher education *and* of making a career in the salariat are higher in the urban region of Brussels than in the rest of the country. Lastly, the analysis confirms significant ethnic and regional disparities in self-employment rates. The main effects of region indicate that, generally, there is a lower chance of being self-employed in Brussels than in the north or south of the country. Importantly, however, the pattern of significant ethnicity-by-region interactions indicates that regional discrepancies seen in the self-employment rates of the charter population are reversed for Turks. Thus, first- and second-generation Turks in Brussels are more likely to start their own businesses than are those who live outside Brussels. In comparison with the rest of Belgium, then, the urban labor market of Brussels offers distinct opportunities for ethnic self-employment.

Discussion

The Turkish second generation in European cities comes from family backgrounds that are generally weak in human capital. In the case of Turkish migrant families, class disadvantage is aggravated by ethnic segregation, which restricts the participation of the second generation in the cultural practices and social networks of the native middle and upper classes. Moreover, as a majority-Muslim group from outside the European Union, Turkish migrants have to reckon with public hostility and distrust, and they may be formally excluded from EU citizenship. However, the most distinctive feature of the Turkish community is their extraordinary investment in ethnic social capital, as evident from strong family ties, dense coethnic networks, and high degrees of ethnic closure. From the perspective of segmented-assimilation research in the United States, which argues that ethnic social capital can make the difference between generational progress and decline, the Turkish second generation in Brussels seems a critical test case of second-generation attainment in the European context. In line with cross-national evidence of dramatic and persistent Turkish disadvantage (Heath and Cheung 2007), we find that the Turkish second generation in Brussels is very much underrepresented in tertiary education and in better jobs. They are also far less likely than young adults of native origin with similar qualifications to find a job.

Second-generation men in particular are more often unemployed than is their fathers' generation.

Ethnic Social Capital and Its Downside

One important question in the segmented-assimilation literature is the role of ethnic social capital in protecting the second generation against downward mobility. In exemplary cases of successful ethnic enclaves in the United States, ethnic social capital seems confounded with other favorable conditions with regard to human capital and a rather welcoming reception of particular refugee groups in the United States. In the case of labor migrants from outside the European Union, however, the first generation was lacking basic human capital and came from generally devalued ethnic and class backgrounds. We distinguish between investment in ethnic social capital and a distinct kind of investment in the cultural and social capital of dominant groups and institutions, which is entwined with human capital in the host society. The segmented-assimilation literature stresses the prime importance of ethnic social capital in protecting the second generation from downward mobility. In addition, we expect that second-generation achievement will depend crucially on the kinds of resources that are highly valued by the dominant groups and institutions of the host society.

To examine the role of ethnic social capital, as distinct from other forms of capital, we compared the Turkish community in Brussels to the Italian and Moroccan migrant communities. Italian, Moroccan, and Turkish migrant workers have in common low aggregate levels of human capital. Relative to Turkish and Moroccan migrants, who arrived more recently and who are on the far side of racial, religious, and civic boundaries, Italians have more access to the cultural capital of the urban middle classes in Belgium, both in ethnic distance and in real-time exposure. By comparison, the Turkish community stands out by its sustained investment in strong family and coethnic ties. If ethnic social capital matters, the Turkish community should hence provide a less unfavorable context for second-generation achievement than does the Moroccan community, which is on the low end of all types of resources.

As an empirical test, we compared the achievement levels of the second generation across ethnic contexts in Brussels. On the whole, young adults of the second generation in Brussels are much less qualified, much more often excluded from employment, and much less often included in the salariat than are young adults of native origin. Looking beyond overall ethnic disadvantage, there are notable differences between community contexts. Specifically, the Turkish second generation has the lowest numbers in higher education and in the salariat, and they are not more successful than the Moroccan second generation is in avoiding unemployment. In contrast, the Italian second generation is closest to achieving parity with the charter population. The net ethnic disadvantages reflect the same ethnic hierarchy, so that second-generation Turks incur the largest ethnic penalties in the urban labor market and Italians incur the smallest. As expected, the Italian community provides the most favorable context for second-generation achievement. In contrast, the Turkish community provides the least favorable ethnic context. Relative Italian advantage suggests that Turkish and Moroccan attainment may be hampered by the restricted access of the more ethnically marked and segregated groups to highly valued cultural and social capital in the host society. In addition, the finding of Turkish disadvantage seems contrary to expectations from segmented assimilation. Apparently, the high level of ethnic social capital in Turkish families does not effectively support educational investment. Nor does high social capital protect the Turkish second generation from ethnic exclusion in the labor market. Although the relative success of Turkish business development in Brussels does seem to connect ethnic social capital with socioeconomic gains, it is too early to know whether Turkish self-employment can make a real difference for the second generation. To summarize, we have argued that migrant families and communities differ in their investment in relation to distinct types of resources. In addition to human capital, we have distinguished ethnic social capital from the cultural and social capital that is more generally valued in the host society. Ethnic differences in second-generation achievements highlight the limited impact of ethnic social capital if it is disconnected from the social and cultural capital that is valued by dominant groups and institutions in the host society.

Looking for Work in a European City

To assess the specific disadvantage of the second generation in today's urban economies, we compared Turks living and working in the urban center of Brussels with those in the northern and southern peripheries of Brussels. On the one hand, it has been argued that socioeconomic polarization in the new urban economy may undercut the intergenerational mobility of the second generation. On the other hand, an economic center-periphery approach stresses the relative advantages of urban economies in scale, mobility, and diversity, which may offer unique opportunities to the second generation. In spite of persistent ethnic disadvantage across local receiving contexts in Belgium, second-generation attainment varies considerably between regions. These regional disparities are not fully accounted for by the differential selection of the workforce located in and outside the urban area of Brussels. Overall, the pattern of findings suggests that the urban economy of Brussels less severely penalizes the ethnic origins of the second generation than do peripheral labor markets in the north and south of Belgium. Most importantly, and in spite of severe disadvantage overall, the Turkish second generation in Brussels is better able to avoid unemployment than are Turks in the periphery. In the more prosperous Flemish north, where unemployment rates are lowest among young adults of native origin, net ethnic disparities in unemployment levels are largest and ethnic exclusion is most rampant. Furthermore, second-generation Turks in Brussels are more likely to succeed in higher education and to enter the salariat than are those who live outside Brussels. This finding of apparent urban advantage comes with an important qualification: the less restricted access to higher qualifications and occupations of Turks in Brussels is largely offset by the fact that they have to compete with a more highly qualified local workforce of national or European background. Finally, Turks in Brussels are more often self-employed than are most similar members of the charter population, whereas exactly the opposite pattern is found outside Brussels, where they are less often self-employed. The latter finding suggest that a typical Turkish investment strategy, securing employment in ethnic niches or ethnic businesses, may be less ineffective in Brussels than in the north and south of the country, where ethnic networks are more often at an economic dead end, as they are anchored in declining local economies. More generally, our findings are suggestive of the ethnic exclusionism of peripheral labor markets, which has received less research attention due to a one-sided focus on urban areas in second-generation research.

Conclusion

To sum up, this chapter has discussed the attainment of the Turkish second generation in Brussels. Extending segmented-assimilation research to Europe, we have examined the role of ethnic community contexts and their interface with an advanced urban economy. The comparison of second-generation attainment and relative disadvantage across ethnic community contexts has showed that second-generation Turks are at the bottom of the ethnic hierarchy in spite of high ethnic social capital. These findings confirm well-known Turkish disadvantage and question the role of ethnic social capital in supporting the second generation when it is disconnected from the forms of social and cultural capital that are valued by the host society. Moreover, second-generation Turks are more able to avoid socioeconomic exclusion in the urban center of Brussels than outside it. The latter finding qualifies an association of downward assimilation with new urban inequalities in second-generation research in the United States.

It should be acknowledged that the empirical analysis in this chapter is limited by data constraints. Therefore, the findings are mainly illustrative of comparative concepts and strategies, which need to be developed in further comparative research. To begin with, the second generation was identified by nationality at birth, but this categorization method is becoming increasingly problematic. Recent developments in some countries, facilitating naturalization, mean that the European second generation is rapidly becoming statistically invisible. Moreover, regions of settlement are a very rough approximation of local receiving contexts. To get a better grasp of the immediate environment of inner-city neighborhoods and schools, multilevel analysis with more fine-grained spatial units would be required. Similarly, to further develop the comparison of ethnic community contexts, individual- or household-level measures of ethnic social capital would be required. Finally, we sampled the first generation within the theoretical age range of the parents of the second generation. Since we could not link the second generation to their parents at the individual level, however, the analysis does not allow us to give an empirical answer to the key question of second-generation progress or decline. Although the marginal distributions suggest major intergenerational progress in education, they do not evince a similar trend toward progress in the labor market. In view of the evidence of persistent ethnic disadvantage, a major challenge in the near future is to generate optimally representative data on second-generation trajectories in European society.

Appendix

Multinomial logistic regressions of Turkish educational attainment:
Parameter estimates of ethnic and regional differences
(contrasts with full secondary, standard errors in parentheses)

	Tertiary Men	No full sec Men	Tertiary Women	No full sec Women
Constant/Intercept	.10 (.03)	.22 (.04)	.35 (.04)	-.08 (.04) ns
Ethnic origin:				
Turkish 2nd	-2.23 (.25)	.52 (.11)	-1.79 (.21)	.88 (.12)
Turkish first	ns	1.79 (.13)	-1.30 (.34)	2.50 (.19)
Native origin	0	0	0	0
Region:				
north	-.69 (.04)	-.32 (.04)	-.69 (.04)	-.28 (.04)
south	-.71 (.04)	ns	-.61 (.04)	ns
Brussels	0	0	0	0
Origin by region:				
north: Turkish second	ns	ns	-1.25 (.37)	-.36 (.14)
north: Turkish first	ns	ns	ns	-.53 (.16)
north: native	0	0	0	0
south: Turkish second	1.06 (.33)	ns	ns	ns
south: Turkish first	ns	ns	ns	ns
south: native	0	0	0	0
Brussels	0	0	0	0
Chi-square (D.F.)	3,273 (16)		2,678 (16)	
Chi-square diff.	61 (8) *		33 (8) *	
N	91,613		83,204	

Binomial logistic regressions of Turkish occupational attainment:
Parameter estimates of net ethnic disparities across regions

	Unempl vs. employed Men	Unempl vs. employed Women	Salariat vs. empl other Men	Self-empl vs. employed Men
Constant	-2.34 (.09)	-1.50 (.06)	-.34 (.07)	-3.46 (.07)
Ethnic origin:				
Turkish second	1.42 (.11)	1.04 (.11)	-1.21 (.20)	ns
Turkish first	1.50 (.10)	.78 (.11)	-1.50 (.17)	1.01 (.20)
native origin	0	0	0	0
Region:				
north	-.83 (.05)	-.22 (.04)	-.73 (.04)	.54 (.10)
south	.28 (.05)	.60 (.04)	-.43 (.04)	.72 (.10)
Brussels	0	0	0	0
Origin by region:				
north: Turkish second	.94 (.14)	1.47 (.14)	ns	-1.21 (.30)
north: Turkish first	1.09 (.12)	1.19 (.18)	1.09 (.22)	-1.40 (.30)
north: native	0	0	0	0
south: Turkish second	.37 (.15)	.85 (.17)	ns	-1.73 (.59)
south: Turkish first	ns	ns	.91 (.24)	-1.55 (.35)
south: native	0	0	0	0
Brussels	0	0	0	0
Chi-square (D.F.)	8359 (13)	8930 (13)	22,927 (13)	693 (13)
Chi-square diff.	161 (4) *	157 (4) *	33 (4) *	39 (4) *
N	91,613	83,204	83,682	83,682

Note: Significance levels: bold print indicates p < .0001; italicized print p < .001; normal print p < .01; levels of p > .01 are reported as non-significant (ns)
 * Compared to reduced model without origin by region interaction

NOTES

1. The "new second generation" originally referred to the children of post-1965 migrants to the United States, as distinct from early European migrants to the United States. Here the term denotes the children of non-European migrants to the northwest of Europe in the same period, as distinct from earlier migration from central and southern Europe.

2. Since the term *metropolis* refers to distinctly American urban configurations, it does not strictly apply to European cities. As globally connected attractors of migrant workers and professionals in the European migration context, however, world cities such as Brussels are the closest functional equivalent of metropolitan areas in the United States.

8

The Second Generation in the German Labor Market

EXPLAINING THE TURKISH EXCEPTION

Frank Kalter

In recent years a number of large-scale studies have addressed the integration of former labor migrants' children into the German labor market (Granato 2004; Granato and Kalter 2001; Kalter 2005; Kalter and Granato 2002, 2007; Kalter, Granato, and Kristen 2007; Konietzka and Seibert 2003; Seibert and Solga 2005). Despite the use of very different indicators of labor success, the findings are rather consistent and lead to a series of stable common insights. First, although doing noticeably better than the first generation, the second generation is still clearly disadvantaged compared to native-born Germans. This holds true at least for Greeks, Italians, (ex-)Yugoslavs, and Turks, while only second-generation Spaniards seem to have caught up with their German peers in many respects. Second, studies also agree that the second-generation disadvantage in the labor market is mainly due to schooling and vocational training. Upon controlling for formal qualifications, differences to the reference population decrease considerably and are no longer significant for most of the groups in most of the analyses. In other words, so-called ethnic penalties, a term suggested by Heath and Ridge (1983) for disadvantages that are not mediated by educational attainment, seem to play only a minor role in the labor-market integration of the second generation. Third, immigrant youth of Turkish heritage play an exceptional role within this pattern. In all analyses they face considerable and, as a rule, highly significant ethnic penalties. Even if, occasionally, ethnic penalties can also be observed for other groups, these are always, and always by far, overshadowed by the respective figures for the Turks.

In this chapter I want to continue this line of research by more deeply examining the last of these points, the exceptional role of the Turks. More precisely, I ask how their specific disadvantage, even after controlling for education, might be explained. Is there a particular discrimination against Turkish youth in Germany, as many authors tend to assume (Seibert and Solga 2005), or does the particular Turkish penalty result from other processes? Although a number of rival hypotheses have been suggested to account for the ethnic penalties of immigrant youth in the labor market (Kalter et al. 2007; Heath et al. 2008), most data sets do not contain measures that would allow for direct empirical tests. This also holds true for the German Microcensus, which is the data source in all the studies cited earlier. Therefore, I rely here on an alternative data set, the German Socio-Economic Panel Study (GSOEP). The GSOEP contains some helpful indicators for important theoretical concepts, above all country-specific resources, which, besides discrimination, are seen as major potential causes of ethnic penalties. In addition, being a panel study, the GSOEP allows tracking of the early career paths of second-generation immigrants in a longitudinal design. This enables stricter tests of the assumed causal relationships between labor-market success and other factors than would be possible in a mere cross-sectional perspective.

In the next section I start with a brief review of potential mechanisms accounting for ethnic penalties in the labor market and discuss whether their underlying assumptions are met in the case of second-generation Turks in Germany. Afterward, I sketch the data structure and relevant variables of my analyses. I then present the major results: after replicating the three general findings noted earlier, I show that a lack of host-country-specific capital, most notably language proficiency, and the ethnic composition of network structures are critical to explaining the exceptional Turkish case. The latter finding holds also when using longitudinal techniques. Finally, in the concluding section I discuss the major implications of the results for the situation of Turks in Germany and for migration research in general.

Explaining Ethnic Penalties of Turkish Youth in the German Labor Market

To account for variations in ethnic penalties, meaning residual effects of ethnicity net of education, at least four main classes of argument have been proposed (Kalter et al. 2007; Heath et al. 2008). To begin with, ethnic penalties are seen to result from differential treatment, above all from direct and indirect forms of discrimination and social exclusion. In the German case there might be a specific discrimination against Turkish youth in the labor market. Superficially, this hypothesis seems quite plausible, given the fact that many studies have shown that negative stereotypes and social distance on the part of Germans are more pronounced toward Turks than toward any other group of labor migrants (Ganter 2003; Steinbach 2004). Although it is tempting to directly connect these results with the exceptional pattern of second-generation Turks in the labor market, one must bear in mind that there is no automatic relationship between attitudes and behavior—least of all for actors in the labor market. Further, it has been questioned whether the structural conditions fostering discrimination are especially pronounced in the case of the German labor market (Kalter and Granato 2007). For example, comparative research has shown that in Germany the link between educational and vocational qualifications and the labor market is especially close (Müller, Steinman, and Ell 1998). This means, in other terms, that the signaling power of educational qualifications is relatively strong, leaving less room for the occurrence of processes of statistical discrimination based on ascribed characteristics. Thus, before drawing an overhasty conclusion from the aforementioned findings that specific discrimination exists, it seems worth asking what other factors could be responsible for the pronounced Turkish penalties.

A second obvious explanation would be that ethnic penalties arise from skills and abilities that are relevant for an employee's productivity but are not captured by formal qualifications. In other words, unmeasured aspects of human capital may account for ethnic differences, above all aspects that are culturally specific, such as language proficiency or other cultural knowledge. Basically, this argument is the most obvious explanation for why residual effects of ethnicity (controlling for education) may be observed for the first generation (Chiswick 1978, 1991; Friedberg 2000). However, although immigrants' children will probably do much better than their parents with respect to such culturally specific skills, a considerable gap between them and indigenous youth might still exist. And this would be especially reasonable in the case of the Turks: although all labor migrants had to bridge some type of cultural gap on arrival—for example, no knowledge of German, since it is not spoken in any of the six former recruitment countries—there is no doubt that cultural distance is greatest for Turks. Thus, factors related to cultural distance would also be plausible explanations for their exceptional role.

A third possible explanation rests on the notion that one's own human capital is not the only resource relevant to achieving a good labor-market position. Most notably, there might be a direct impact of parental resources on children's success, which is not mediated by children's educational attainment. Parents, for example, might invest money in their children's search for an adequate position or, because of their own socioeconomic position, have better access to job opportunities. Given that the first generation of immigrants, for whatever reasons, occupies lower labor-market positions, this might lead to an ethnic penalty for their children too. Again, this kind of reasoning would apply especially to Turks: among first-generation groups, Turks have the lowest educational and occupational attainment (Granato 2004; Granato and Kalter 2001; Kalter and Granato 2007), and that would reasonably account for the second generation experiencing a specific penalty in the labor market.

Finally, besides using parental resources, young job seekers might also draw on the resources of other persons; that is, they might use their social capital. It is well known in the economic literature that social networks play an important part in the labor market, as many jobs are found with the help of friends and relatives (Granovetter 1995). The theoretical reason for this lies in the fact that for the job seeker, network information on job offers is inexpensive and promises a comparatively high probability of success, while for the firms, referrals by third persons might be important as a comparatively valid and likewise inexpensive screening device (Montgomery 1991, 1408). Therefore, relevant characteristics of a person's network—its size, density, and, most notably, the resources connected to network ties—may make a difference for status attainment beyond a person's human capital (Lin 1999; Portes 1995b, 9).

But why might the characteristics of social networks result in ethnic disadvantages for second-generation immigrants in general and Turks specifically? It is reasonable to assume that the networks of second-generation youth still tend to consist predominantly of coethnic ties. Coethnic ties, however, give access only to the information and resources available within the ethnic community and—given that there is ethnic stratification—might not be as helpful as ties to the indigenous population (Portes and Rumbaut 2001, 48). For example, in a recent U.S.-based study, missing network information turned out to completely explain race disadvantages in hiring processes (Petersen, Saporta, and Seidel 2000). With respect to the German situation, once again, this line of reasoning would indeed be able to account for a specific disadvantage of Turks: they are the largest immigrant group by far and, as a consequence, have more opportunities to build ethnic ties and to engage in ethnic communities. In fact, recent studies find that Turkish youth have considerably more ethnically homogeneous networks than do other second generation groups (Haug 2003, 724). Therefore, a comparatively low level of social assimilation could be a fourth mechanism behind the exceptional role of second-generation Turks in the labor market.

Note, however, that this typical view of "straight-line assimilation" has been challenged, and the reasoning could also be turned upside down. As has been argued, for example, in the concept of segmented assimilation, under specific structural conditions, reliance on ethnic ties and avoidance of social assimilation may even promise a relative advantage (Portes 1995a, 251; Portes and Rumbaut 2001, 44). Most obviously, if discrimination against a certain group is severe, the ethnic community may provide job opportunities that are not accessible within the host country's labor market. In addition, the ethnic community may offer relative economic advantages in the form of self-employment in niches that the mainstream economy does not include (Portes 1995b, 25). A further position—one could call it a pluralist or transnationalist view—argues that it might be especially advantageous for a second-generation immigrant to have *both*: host-country-specific *as well as* ethnic ties. And a similar argument could be made with respect to other culturally specific kinds of capital, for example, language proficiency. The so-called middlemen minorities (Bonacich 1973) would be examples of ethnic groups who profit from their position in between two cultures.

To summarize, there are several plausible hypotheses to explain the exceptional situation of second-generation Turks. Turkish youth are especially disadvantaged not only with respect to prejudices of the indigenous population but also with respect to socioeconomic background, host-country-specific cultural capital, and host-country-specific social capital. As all these factors may reasonably account for labor-market disadvantages, an empirical answer must be sought to the question of which of them turns out to be more or less important. With respect to the fourth of the sketched mechanisms, it is a further empirical question whether ethnically homogeneous social networks work in a negative direction at all and, if so, whether assimilative or mixed networks then promise relatively more success. Analyzing the precise effects of the composition of friendship networks not only contributes to solving the "Turkish puzzle" but also highlights the importance of concepts such as segmented assimilation, pluralism, or transnationalism for the second generation in Germany, thereby contributing to recent discussions in migration research in general.

Data and Variables

The empirical analyses rest on data from the German Socio-Economic Panel Study (GSOEP), a yearly longitudinal survey of private households in Germany conducted since 1984 (see Haisken-DeNew and Frick 2004). Up to 2003, the GSOEP had gathered information on 55,439 persons in total, oversampling nationals of the former recruitment countries.[1] Although the

GSOEP is a sample of households, individual interviews are conducted with each household member once he or she reaches the age of sixteen. In a first step, I select only those individuals (n = 5,179) who had been interviewed at the age of seventeen, in order to follow their career paths. The advantage of this design is that for this specific subgroup there is ample information on family background, and I select only those persons for whom both parents have been interviewed at least once in the GSOEP (n = 4,653). I then restrict my analysis to only three groups: respondents whose parents were both born in Germany, respondents whose parents were both born in Turkey, and respondents whose parents were both born in one of the other four recruitment countries: Italy, ex-Yugoslavia, Spain, or Greece. I drop all persons who were born outside Germany and immigrated at age seven or older. To avoid confounding the analysis with German reunification and its aftermath, I finally select only those persons who had been living in West Germany at the age of seventeen. Using these rules, I end up with 2,931 individuals, 2,150 of whom belong to the German group, 342 to the Turkish, and 439 to the groups of other labor migrants. In total, these individuals reveal information on 21,298 person years, 2,499 of them stemming from Turkish youth and 3,125 from youth with backgrounds from other labor-migrant countries.

The following variables are used in the analyses: The basic dependent variable is a rough measure of *occupational attainment* and contrasts salaried employees (1) with workers (0). It is constructed out of the EGP scheme (Erikson, Goldthorpe, and Portocarero 1979).[2] The choice of this specific indicator of labor-market success makes the analyses directly comparable to those of Granato and Kalter (2001), which are based on the German Microcensus of 1996.[3] Besides *ethnic group membership*—defined as described earlier—in all models I control for *gender* (time-constant), *age, age squared* (time-varying), and I include dummy variables for the *year of the survey*. *Educational qualifications* (time-varying) are captured by the CASMIN scheme, consisting of eight categories (Brauns and Steinmann 1999). Socioeconomic background is measured by *father's years of education* (time-constant), on the one hand, and *father's occupational status* (time-constant) in terms of the ISEI score (Ganzeboom, de Graaf, and Treiman 1992), on the other. If the father's ISEI score is missing, this is indicated by a dummy variable.

In addition to delivering information on socioeconomic background, the GSOEP data have the crucial advantage of containing indicators of culturally specific skills and resources. A central variable for my analyses is the *percentage of best friends who are German*. Six times within the twenty waves of the GSOEP information has been gathered on the (up to) three persons a respondent considers to be his or her best friends. My measure expresses the fraction of these friends having German citizenship. For missing years I impute the last information available. If the respective information is missing at the beginning, I impute the first information available. This measure of social assimilation can also be constructed for the reference group of Germans, but other information is available only for respondents with a migration background. This holds true for the variable *language problems in German,* which is based on a self-reported evaluation of speaking fluency (1 = very good, 5 = very poor). The relevant question is included in the GSOEP at least every two years. Therefore the variable can be built as a time-varying one, imputing the previous value for those years where the information is missing. In a similar manner, a variable for *problems concerning the language of the country of origin* can be constructed. The general design allows me to measure social assimilation and language proficiencies not only for the respondent him- or herself but *also for the father and the mother.* In these cases as well, the variables are treated as being time-varying. When the father or the mother drops out of the panel in a certain year, the last information available is imputed for all subsequent years.

Results

This section analyzes which of the rival, previously offered explanations for the penalty suffered by second-generation Turks turns out to be empirically more important. The next section reports summary statistics of relevant variables, in order to check whether the assumed background conditions of several mechanisms do indeed hold according to the data. The subsequent section moves on to multivariate analyses, allowing me to answer the leading question systematically. To present the major finding in advance: the ethnic composition of friendship networks seems to play the most important part in explaining the specific role of Turks. Building on this result, the final empirical section tests whether this network effect turns out to be indeed a direct and causal one.

Descriptive Statistics

Table 8.1 gives the percentages or means of all variables used in the analyses. Most importantly, the findings show that the second generation is at a considerable disadvantage with respect to access to salaried employee positions, the basic dependent variable: whereas 62 percent of all young Germans in the data set have occupied such a position at least once within the time

TABLE 8.1

Summary statistics of relevant variables

	German	(1)	Turkish	(2)	other labor migrant	Total	n (total)
percentages:					•		
salaried employee[a]	62.2%	*	42.5%		50.0%	57.9%	2038
at least secondary education[b]	66.6%	*	44.3%		46.8%	60.6%	2472
female	48.8%		45.6%		48.7%	48.4%	2931
means[c]							
age	20.2		20.2		20.1	20.2	2931
father's ISEI	47.0	*	31.0		32.3	42.9	2165
father's years of education	12.0	*	9.3		9.1	11.3	2806
percentage best friends German	.97	*	.38	*	.51	.80	2007
father: % best friends German	.98	*	.18	*	.27	.73	1846
mother: % best friends German	.98	*	.15	*	.27	.73	1925
language problems German	–		1.55	*	1.36	1.44	754
language problems country of origin	–		2.09	*	1.97	2.02	754
father: language problems German	–		2.86	*	2.70	2.77	733
mother: language problems German	–		3.33	*	2.83	3.04	746

(1) * = difference between German and Turkish significant on a 5%-level
(2) * = difference between Turkish and 'other labor migrant' significant on a 5%-level
 a an individual is treated as 'yes' if the person was a salaried employee at least once over all years under consideration
 b CASMIN-classification higher than 1a,1b, or 1c; highest value for all years is chosen for each individual
 c for time-varying variables the mean of intra-individual means is reported

span under consideration, this holds true for only 43 percent of Turks and 50 percent of the children of other labor migrants. In addition, the second generation is also clearly disadvantaged with respect to educational attainment. The percentage of those who have at least an upper secondary education (i.e., a credential earned in one of the two higher tracks of the school system) is considerably lower among Turks (44.3 percent) and the children of other labor migrants (46.8 percent) than among Germans (66.6 percent). In the sample, only minor differences between the three groups exist with respect to the composition according to gender and age.[4]

Although these four variables are also contained in many available studies mentioned at the beginning of this chapter, some additional variables relate to possible explanations for the specific ethnic penalty of second-generation Turks. The findings on father's socioeconomic status and years of education indicate that the second generation is indeed underprivileged with respect to familial socioeconomic background, but no specific Turkish disadvantage was found in the GSOEP data. There is, however, a considerable and specific gap for Turks with respect to integration into German networks: on average, the percentage of German friends is only 38 percent for a second-generation Turk, whereas it is 51 percent for a descendant of one of the other former labor migrants. It is interesting to note that a similar difference can also be observed with respect to parents' social integration, the difference being a bit more pronounced for mothers (15 percent versus 27 percent) than for fathers (18 percent versus 27 percent). Turkish youth deviate from the residual second generation also in other culturally specific resources. Their speaking fluency in German is significantly worse than that of the children of other labor migrants, and the same—albeit less pronounced—holds true for their speaking fluency in the language of the country of origin. Again, considerable differences in German-language proficiency already exist for the parents.

Testing Rival Hypotheses on the Exceptional Situation of Turks

To analyze the reasons for the exceptional situation of Turkish youth in the German labor market, several logit models are run using the dichotomous salaried-employee-versus-worker variable, described earlier, as the dependent variable. In a first set of models (table 8.2, models 1–5), data are pooled for all years, and robust standard errors reflecting the clustering of individuals (Rogers 1993; Stata Corporation 2001, 256) are estimated to account for the panel structure of the data. Model 1 shows the gross disadvantages of the second-generation groups, expressed by the log-odds effects of ethnic origin controlling only for gender, age, age squared, and year of the survey. Model 2 then also includes education in terms of the full CASMIN scheme.

Although the analysis rests on a different data set and a somewhat different definition of ethnic origin, models 1 and 2 basically confirm the three major results stemming from former Microcensus analyses, reported in the introduction: there is a distinct gross disadvantage of second-generation Turks in the German labor market. The respective log-odds effect in model 1 is −0.96, indicating that the relative odds to be in a salaried employee position versus a worker position as compared to Germans is $\exp(-0.96) \approx 0.38$. The gross disadvantage for the other labor-migrant groups is much less pronounced, but differences to the reference groups are also highly significant. As can be seen in model 2, this disadvantage is considerably reduced and no longer significant when educational qualifications are controlled. In contrast, the Turkish disadvantage is only reduced, leaving an odds-ratio of $\exp(-0.66) \approx 0.52$, which is still highly significantly different from 1. This illustrates

TABLE 8.2

Log-odds effects (selected coefficients) on salaried employee position (1) vs. worker (0)

	log-odds effects using pooled data (robust standard errors accounting for clustering on ID)				
	(1)	(2)	(3)	(4)	(5)
groups (ref: German)					
- Turkish	-.96*	-.66*	-.54*	-.49*	-.02
	(.19)	(.19)	(.21)	(.21)	(.27)
- other labor migrant	-.39*	-.19	-.07	-.05	.29
	(.15)	(.16)	(.17)	(.18)	(.22)
education in CASMIN categories (ref: 1a)					
- CASMIN 1b		-.38	-.29	-.35	-.37
		(.19)	(.20)	(.21)	(.21)
- CASMIN 1c		-.11	-.04	-.03	-.08
		(.22)	(.23)	(.24)	(.24)
- CASMIN 2b		.67*	.69*	.66*	.60*
		(.20)	(.21)	(.22)	(.22)
- CASMIN 2a		.92*	.98*	.95*	.90*
		(.21)	(.22)	(.23)	(.22)
- CASMIN 2c_gen		1.62*	1.58*	1.55*	1.50*
		(.23)	(.24)	(.25)	(.25)
- CASMIN 2c_voc		2.64*	2.65*	2.64*	2.60*
		(.31)	(.32)	(.33)	(.33)
- CASMIN 3a, 3b		3.59*	3.52*	3.52*	3.47*
		(.42)	(.43)	(.44)	(.44)
father years of education			.02	.03	.02
			(.03)	(.03)	(.03)
father ISEI			.01*	.01	.01*
			(.01)	(.01)	(.01)
father ISEI missing			.41	.43	.47
			(.25)	(.27)	(.27)
% best friends German					.79*
					(.25)
number of persons	2038	1925	1846	1527	1527
person years	11274	10942	10589	9971	9971
Pseudo-R^2	.16	.27	.27	.27	.27

data: GSOEP 20; * = p <.05
in brackets: robust standard errors accounting for clustering on ID
gender, age, age squared and dummy variables for years are also controlled for in all models

and, once again, underscores the exceptional position of Turks among the second generation.

What, now, are the reasons for this ethnic penalty borne by Turks? As stated earlier, one hypothesis assumes that it could result from a different socioeconomic background that impacts labor-market positioning regardless of educational qualification. Therefore in model 3 the father's years of education and the father's socioeconomic status are included as additional independent variables. However, although the latter variable has a significant impact on the odds of attaining a skilled position, it can hardly explain the specific situation of Turks. As compared to model 2, the log-odds effect for Turks is only slightly reduced and still highly significantly different from zero.

But the latter fact changes once we include a measure of social assimilation in the model. Model 5 shows that the percentage of Germans among the three best friends significantly raises odds of attaining a skilled labor-market position, leading to a complete reduction of the disadvantage for Turks. This suggests that a lack of contacts to native-born German peers substantially accounts for their ethnic penalties. As one might assume that this reduction could possibly be due to a selective loss of cases between the two models, model 3 is reestimated only on the basis of those cases also underlying model 5. The results are given in model 4 and reveal that the estimates are nearly the same. So indeed, the conclusion lies near at hand that the structure of friendship networks is a main factor in explaining the specific difficulties of Turks in the German labor market.

Confirming the Effect of Ethnic Network Composition

Although the results seem convincing, one might nevertheless object that the conclusion about the importance of assimilative network contacts may have been drawn too fast, for at least two reasons. First, the correlation between friendship network and occupational attainment could be spurious and the effect therefore biased due to a misspecification of the model. This is the general problem of unobserved heterogeneity. For example, unmeasured aspects of human capital, most notably culturally specific skills such as language proficiency, might be the reason for ethnically endogamous networks, on the one hand, and for lower occupational attainment, on the other. Remember that a lack of culturally specific skills has been proposed as a further potential mechanism to explain the specific ethnic penalties of Turks.

To tackle this problem, I included other indicators for culturally specific skills as independent variables in the model. As these variables are measured only for nonindigenous youth, the analyses must be restricted to second-generation immigrants, now comparing Turks to the group of offspring of all other labor migrants. Models 1 and 2 in table 8.3 reestimate models 3 and 5 in table 8.2 for the subsample of immigrant youth. It is worth noting that one finds roughly the same results as before. A disadvantage of Turks remains, even after controlling for educational qualification (model 1), but it is reduced and becomes insignificant upon controlling for the ethnic structure of the friendship network (model 2). The parameter estimate for the friendship network in model 2, table 8.3, is nearly the same as that in model 5, table 8.2, thus indicating that the German reference group does not dominate the effect strength in the latter model.

Now, in model 3 of table 8.3, two measures of one's own language proficiency (in German and in the language of the country of origin), as well as the father's German-language proficiency and his ethnic network structure, are included in the model to capture culturally specific skills and resources. Not speaking German very well is a further cause of the problems immigrant children face in the labor market and also contributes to explaining the specific difficulties of Turks, since controlling for language proficiency in German leads to a further reduction of the negative effect for Turks. Nevertheless, after controlling for this and for the other three additional variables, the strength of the network effect is only slightly reduced. There is still a significant direct impact of ethnic network structure (log-odds effect: −0.58) independent of these variables.[5]

An interesting by-product of these analyses can be found in model 3 of table 8.4: although language proficiency in German still has a direct impact even in the second generation, language proficiency with respect to the language of the country of origin does not increase the relative labor-market success at all—even when controlling for German-language proficiency. In the context of discussions on transnationalism and multiculturalism, this is an important empirical finding, meaning that there is no positive economic return to bilingualism—the variable "problems with language of country of origin" even shows the "wrong" sign. In the same spirit, one may be interested to know whether ethnically mixed friendship networks—that is, those having *both* German *and* ethnic ties—offer a relative advantage over networks of *only* German ties. This can be done by categorizing the friendship network indicator in model 4. The finding here is basically the same as that in the case of language: compared to a network of only German friends, an ethnically mixed network does not offer any advantage. As expected, a completely ethnically endogenous network, however, leads to a clear relative

TABLE 8.3

Log-odds effects on salaried employee position – immigrants only (selected coefficients)

dependent variable measured at	time t				time t+1
	(1)	(2)	(3)	(4)	(5)
salaried employee at time t					2.70*
					(.24)
other labor migrant	.49*	.34	.25	.27	.07
Ref.: Turkish	(.23)	(.23)	(.23)	(.23)	(.19)
% best friends German		.77*	.58*		.52*
		(.23)	(.24)		(.20)
no German friend				-.57*	
Ref.: all friends German				(.26)	
Germ. and other friends				-.07	
				(.23)	
father years of edu.	.11*	.11	.08	.09	.04
	(.06)	(.06)	(.06)	(.06)	(.05)
father ISEI	.00	.00	.01	.01	-.01
	(.01)	(.01)	(.02)	(.02)	(.01)
father ISEI missing	.19	.22	.27	.27	-.10
	(.46)	(.47)	(.50)	(.50)	(.42)
language probl. German			-.35*	-.34*	-.22
			(.15)	(.15)	(.12)
lang. problems country of origin			.12	.12	-.00
			(.12)	(.12)	(.09)
father: lang. problems German			-.17	-.18	-.07
			(.11)	(.11)	(.09)
father % friends German			.08	.14	.32
			(.25)	(.25)	(.24)
number of persons	533	499	486	486	476
person years	2785	2724	2700	2700	2358
Pseudo-R²	.23	.24	.25	.25	.34

data: GSOEP 20; in brackets: robust standard errors accounting for clustering on ID; * = p <.05
gender, age, age squared, education (full CASMIN), and dummy variables for years are also controlled for in all models

TABLE 8.4

Effects (selected coefficients) on percentage of German friends – immigrants only

dependent variable:	at	
% best friends German	time t (1)	time t+1 (2)
% best friends German at time t		.503* (.032)
other labor migrant Ref.: Turkish	.088* (.029)	.072* (.017)
CASMIN 1b Ref.: 1a	.012 (.045)	.010 (.031)
- CASMIN 1c	.070 (.051)	.030 (.036)
- CASMIN 2b	.072 (.048)	.047 (.035)
- CASMIN 2a	.093 (.057)	.044 (.036)
- CASMIN 2c_gen	.076 (.057)	.023 (.043)
- CASMIN 2c_voc	.053 (.070)	.024 (.048)
- CASMIN 3a, 3b	.174 (.093)	.081 (.046)
father: % of best friends German	.256* (.045)	.032 (.033)
mother: % of best friend German	.161* (.049)	.059 (.032)
language problems German	-.078* (.020)	-.050* (.013)
lang. problems country of origin	.046* (.013)	.039* (.008)
father: language problems German	-.043* (.014)	-.019 (.010)
mother: language problems German	-.017 (.014)	.007 (.009)
salaried employee (ref. worker)	.048 (.027)	.027 (.018)
number of persons	483	473
person years	2723	2444
R^2	.26	.40

data: GSOEP 20; in brackets: robust standard errors accounting for clustering on ID; * = p <.05
gender, age, age squared, and dummy variables for years are also controlled for in both models

disadvantage. Thus, it seems that the subtype of "selective acculturation," as distinguished in the concept of segmented assimilation (Portes and Rumbaut 2001), and ideas on the importance of transnational or pluralistic networks do not receive much support in the case of second-generation labor migrants in Germany.

A second major objection to the conclusion that the ethnic structure of friendship networks matters for labor-market success arises from the general problem of endogeneity, that is, the question about the causal relationship between the two variables involved. In the literature (Esser 1980), social assimilation is often interpreted as being primarily a consequence of structural assimilation rather than a cause thereof. The main mechanism stems from the fact that workplaces constitute important opportunity structures for meeting and forming friendship ties (Feld 1984; Mouw 2003). Therefore, a fifth model (model 5) is estimated, which adds the lagged dependent variable to the model (Wooldridge 2003, 300). More precisely, I define occupational status (salaried employee = 1; worker = 0; else = missing) at time t+1 as the dependent variable, including occupational status at time t (salaried employee = 1; else = 0) plus all other independent variables measured at time t into the model. Model 5 in table 8.3 shows that ethnic network composition has a significant effect (0.52) on occupational status at time t+1 that is independent of occupational status at time t. This finding delivers strong evidence for the thesis that networks really matter, because it goes against the hypothesis that the observed correlation is due only to the influence of occupational status on friendship structure, which is in turn inert. Or, put more simply, of two second-generation immigrants who have the same occupational status at time t (and have the same other covariate pattern), the one with more German friends is more likely to be a salaried employee a year later.[6] Model 5 shows that gender, age, and educational qualifications are also important. All other variables seem to be less important, and the effect of German-language proficiency is significant only at a 10 percent level.

To complete the story, a final analysis addresses the reverse question, that is, whether there is nevertheless an effect in the opposite direction. The results are given in table 8.4, in which the percentage of German friends now serves as the dependent variable and a set of plausible predictor variables includes occupational status. In a model of pooled cross-sections (model 1), the effect of being a salaried employee is positive, as expected, but significant only on a 10 percent level. Likewise, the percentage of German friends tends to rise with the level of education; however, the influence is also very weak. In contrast, other variables are much more important, above all language proficiency and the ethnic composition of the parents' network. The results thus suggest that rather than being a mere consequence of structural assimilation, network structures seem to result from specific cultural skills and traits and the respective transmission processes between generations, thus basically confirming prior research on this topic (Nauck 2001). Note that in this model Turks still have significantly fewer German friends than do the children of other labor-migrant groups, even controlling for all these factors. Following the idea stated earlier, model 2 uses the percentage of German friends at time t+1 as a dependent variable, including as predictors the respective percentage at time t and all other variables from model 1 (measured at time t). When analyzing the problem from this perspective, the effect of occupational status is further reduced. It is, above all, language proficiency that seems to make the difference when it comes to changes in the ethnic composition of the friendship networks.

All in all, therefore, in looking at these kinds of models, the evidence is much stronger that network composition determines occupational position rather than that the influence runs in the opposite direction. Less social assimilation thus really does seem to play an important part in explaining the exceptional role of Turks with respect to structural assimilation, that is, in the labor market.

Summary and Final Remarks

There is no doubt that second-generation labor migrants in Germany have improved their labor-market positions relative to those of their parents. In other words, a marked trend toward economic assimilation over generations can be found. Nevertheless, the descendants of the former labor migrants still face significant disadvantages compared to the indigenous population. In this analysis of the causes of limited structural assimilation, the results strongly support prior findings that it has mainly to do with the difficulties of immigrants' children in the educational system. After controlling for formal qualifications, ethnic penalties are nearly absent in most of the second-generation groups. However, in contrast, Turkish youth still face a specific ethnic penalty.

In my analysis of rival explanations for this exceptional disadvantage, there is strong evidence that existing penalties are related to factors other than labor discrimination in the narrow sense. In addition to the degree of language proficiency in German, the ethnic structure of friendship networks seems crucial for the occupational attainment of the second generation. As a matter of fact, social assimilation is far less developed among Turkish youth than among the children of other groups of labor migrants; and controlling for ethnic network composition, the ethnic penalties of second-generation Turks almost completely disappear. Using the longitudinal character of the data set, I was able to further support the view that the impact of social networks is indeed direct and causal.

These findings immediately give rise to the question of how the missing social assimilation of second-generation youth, especially Turks, can be explained. Although I was able to show that culturally specific skills and their transmission between generations seem to play an important part, additional explanations lie near at hand, among them discrimination. It is important to note that according to my analyses, *labor-market discrimination* does not seem responsible for the specific disadvantage of Turks; however, I do not rule out the possibility that discrimination may occur in relevant processes preceding entry into the labor market. Here, further theoretical elaboration of the exact mechanisms and further empirical research are urgently needed in order to understand the complex processes through which ethnic inequality in Germany is reproduced.

The important role that the ethnic composition of networks plays in understanding the processes of occupational attainment in Germany also challenges traditional views of assimilation as well as newer theoretical concepts and frameworks. One, mostly implicit but sometimes even explicit, assumption of many assimilation theorists is that there is a definite, albeit imperfect, causal order among several dimensions of assimilation. While cognitive assimilation (acculturation) is seen as a necessary precondition of structural assimilation, social assimilation is primarily seen as its consequence. Assuming that immigrants are interested in the benefits of structural assimilation, the idea is that they will sooner or later (in terms of generations and birth cohorts) invest in the cognitive requisites, and social assimilation will then only be a matter of time, as structural assimilation provides the necessary opportunity structures. My results, however, demonstrate that the feedback effects of social assimilation on the "prior" dimensions may be more severe than has long been suggested. This is underpinned by recent parallel research in Germany that has revealed the likewise important effects of social assimilation on the school-choice behavior of immigrant parents (Kristen 2004) and even on their children's success in German soccer (Kalter 2003). Such feedback effects do not imply, however, that there is no baseline trend toward assimilation or that there is even a trend in the opposite direction. Nevertheless, given that effects may be cross-generational and that there are mechanisms of direct intergenerational transmission of social networks (Nauck 2001), the speed of assimilation may be reduced considerably.

On the other hand, the current results clearly indicate that for the second generation in present-day Germany there seems to be no path to economic success other than the routes of the mainstream society. Besides the predominant role of educational qualifications, it is capital specific to the receiving society that accounts for residual disadvantages. In contrast, ethnic capital—that is, capital specific to the country of origin—does not lead to any increase in labor-market success at all, even when controlling for all other assets. Therefore, for the second generation in Germany there does not seem to be any promising third alternative of "selective acculturation" or "pluralism" between straight-line assimilation, on the one hand, and permanent economic disadvantage, on the other.

NOTES

1. As I report summary statistics separately for ethnic groups in the descriptive section and use logistic regression models that deliver unbiased estimates if the sample is exogenously stratified but the models are otherwise correctly specified (Hosmer and Lemeshow 1989, 177), I do not use design weights in my analyses.

2. More precisely, EGP classes I, II, and IIIa+b are recoded to 1, and classes V, VI, and VIIa+b to 0. EGP classes IVa–c are treated as missing values.

3. In the meantime, analyses similar to the ones in this chapter have been conducted using alternative indicators of labor-market success. For example, Kalter (2006) looks at employment versus unemployment and at qualified labor versus nonqualified labor. Results and conclusions are rather similar.

4. The last finding suggests that the average duration of observation of respondents in the panel data is rather similar for all the groups. Note that, in general, the mean for all metric time-varying variables is computed out of individual means over time, without weighting for number of years observed.

5. Given that there is panel information, a more severe test of whether there is indeed a direct effect of networks on occupational attainment could be obtained by estimating a fixed-effects model. As this model accounts for a fixed individual-specific effect, it controls for all unmeasured variables that do not change over time (see Wooldridge 2003, 461). However, as there is little variance in the binary dependent variable, one can run this model with only 110 persons. This leaves the coefficient (0.26) to pure chance to attain significance ($p = .470$). It is worth noting, however, that a somewhat changed dependent variable SKILLED (− 1 for EGP I, II, IIIa+b, V, VI; = 0 for EGP VIIa+b; missing else) leads to a highly significant effect (0.79, $p = .004$) in a fixed-effect model with 147 persons. All in all, my impression, given the available data, is that although the network effect in table 8.2 (model 5) and table 8.3 (model 2) may be positively biased, there seems to be a direct relationship between the ethnic structure of friendship networks and occupational attainment.

6. In addition to the analyses presented here, event-history models were run as an alternative to test the causality direction. They also support the view that networks are a cause of success. For example, in a discrete event-history model analyzing the risk of gaining salaried-employee status there is also a significant positive effect of the network indicator, which reduces the ethnic penalty of Turks considerably. See also Kalter 2006 for similar analyses.

9

Capitals, Ethnic Identity, and Educational Qualifications

Tariq Modood

Savage, Warde, and Devine (2005) argue that if we accept the shift in definition of class as macrorelationships of exploitation to the possession of resources by individual actors—as many sociologists have done—then an argument can be made for the importance of concepts such as cultural capital. They argue, "If social class is a matter of categories of people accumulating similar volumes and types of resources, and investing them in promoting their own and their children's life chances, the metaphor of capital is helpful" (2005, 7). I find helpful this conception of social class as a likelihood of members' achieving certain socioeconomic goals (e.g., sustaining a position in or entering certain kinds of occupations). For the idea of class as life chances means that the definition of a class system depends not just on the existence of a hierarchy of classes but on the probabilities of movement between classes. I also find helpful the metaphorical extension of the idea of capital beyond the financial. Yet I want to argue here that both class and a Bourdieusian concept of cultural capital have certain important limitations, in that neither of them is able to deal sociologically with some contemporary ethnic phenomena in relation to resources, capital, and the likelihood of mobility.

This chapter arises in a context in which, among sociologists, class is seen to be a much more substantial concept than ethnicity is (see, for example, Fenton 1999, 2003), in which the influence of Bourdieu in the sociology of education is immense (Reay 2004) and is believed to be transferable to ethnicity studies (May 1999), and in which the concept of cultural capital is enjoying a currency and an expectancy among those who believe that cultural pursuits have something to contribute to the amelioration of social exclusion. I want to challenge these positions by focusing on a major empirical question: why are nonwhite ethnic minorities in Britain so overrepresented in applications to and among students enrolled in higher education? The fact that they are is so counterintuitive that while British sociologists have developed several lines of inquiry to explain the scholastic underachievement of nonwhites (a phenomenon that has failed to occur, except in pockets), there are no theories to explain the phenomenon that has occurred. Initially, one might expect that this phenomenon might be most amenable to a cultural-capital class analysis, given that it is about the acquisition of credentials for upward mobility in a stratified society, and after all, ethnicity has something to do with "culture." I show that this expectation cannot be fulfilled. Instead, I suggest, a version of or a derivation of the idea of social capital is more promising. The promise can be redeemed by studying some American sociology in which the Bourdieusian distinction between cultural capital, which is acquired through the family, and social capital as benefits mediated through social relations is not maintained; indeed the former is swallowed up within the latter. An older influence on my thinking comes from an approach in British anthropology that was sometimes called "ethnicity as a resource" (e.g., Ballard 1996; Wallman 1979; Werbner 1990a, 1990b), though the interest of these anthropologists was more in employment, especially self-employment.

The chapter is in three parts. First, I make the empirical case about the scale and character of ethnic minority representation in higher education. Second, I refer to some explanations for why this is the case. Finally, I consider whether the concepts of cultural and social capital are of any assistance in organizing and improving some aspects of what I believe are the answers.

Ethnic Minorities in Higher Education

Contrary to the claims of most commentators at the time, when admissions to higher education began to be "ethnically monitored" in 1990, they did not reveal an underrepresentation of ethnic minorities (Modood 1993). Moreover, all minority groups, with the possible exception of the Caribbeans, have increased their share of admissions since then. Ethnic minorities as a whole are much more successful in achieving university entry than their white peers are. There are, however, important differences among and within groups.[1]

Table 9.1 shows that by 2004, nonwhites constituted nearly 18 percent of higher-education places offered to new students, this being almost double their share of the population. However, not all groups approximate to the national advantage established by women, for while all are tending in that direction, women are still a little way behind among some South Asian groups; the most significant gender gap, however, is that Caribbean men continue to be a long way behind their female peers. The 1990s was a period of considerable expan-

TABLE 9.1
Higher Education Entrants (Home (UK) Acceptances only), 2004

		Male – Female %
White	82.3	45 - 55
Black- African	2.7	48 - 52
Black - Caribbean	1.2	35 - 65
Black- Other	0.3	39 - 61
Indian	4.4	50 - 50
Pakistani	2.7	52 - 48
Bangladeshi	0.9	53 - 47
Chinese	1.0	50 – 50
Asian – Other	1.1	53 – 47
Mixed White and Asian	0.8	49 – 51
Mixed White and African	0.3	45 – 55
Mixed White and Caribbean	0.5	41 – 59
Mixed Other	0.8	40 – 60
Other	0.9	44 – 56

Cases where ethnic origin was unknown are excluded.
Source: UCAS http://www.ucas.com/figures/index.html

sion in student places in higher education, and much of it was accounted for by nonwhites. Although this partly reflected demographics, the trend analysis in table 9.2 shows that between 1994 and 1999, at a time when the number of entrants to higher education rose by more than 20 percent, most minority groups increased by 40 to 85 percent (the numbers for black Caribbeans, though, grew by just under 20 percent). At the end of the 1990s the government set itself the target of getting 50 percent of young people into higher education by the age of thirty. Table 9.3 shows the state of play by ethnicity. By the year 2001–2002, the likelihood of whites entering higher education was only 38 percent, and this was not just much lower than that of the ethnic minorities taken together but also lower than every single minority group. Sometimes it was not much lower (e.g., Bangladeshis and black Caribbeans), and sometimes it was nearly half as low (e.g., black Africans and Indians).[2] So we have the extraordinary situation in Britain where white people are far from achieving the government target, but all the minority groups except two have very nearly achieved it or greatly exceed it (Connor et al. 2004, 43, 150).

There are also important differences in the institutions attended and subjects studied by different groups. While some minorities are very well represented in competitive subjects, they are (with the exception of the Chinese) still generally more likely to be in the less prestigious, less well-resourced

TABLE 9.2
Percentages of Home Accepted Applicants to Degree Courses

Ethnic Origin	1994	1995	1996	1997	1998	1999	% change 1994-9
White	85.37	84.27	82.59	81.17	79.64	79.30	12.64
Black Caribbean	0.95	0.97	0.97	0.99	0.95	0.94	19.88
Black African	1.31	1.48	1.55	1.54	1.45	1.51	40.41
Indian	3.23	3.33	3.6	3.67	3.92	4.13	55.01
Pakistani	1.58	1.77	2.00	1.98	2.11	2.17	66.39
Bangladeshi	0.43	0.52	0.57	0.55	0.60	0.66	85.03
Chinese	0.76	0.81	0.88	0.88	0.90	0.94	50.89
Total	228,685	240,710	246,503	276,503	272,340	277,340	

Source: Table 5.2, UCAS Statistical Bulletin on Widening Participation, 2000, p.13

TABLE 9.3
Higher Education Initial Participation Rates (HEIPRs)
For England, ft and pt, 2001-02

Ethnic Group	Male	Female	All
White	34	41	38
All minority ethnic groups	55	58	56
Black Caribbean	36	52	45
Black African	71	75	73
Black Other	56	72	64
Indian	70	72	71
Pakistani	54	44	49
Bangladeshi	43	33	39
Chinese	47	50	49
Asian Other	74	94	83
Mixed ethnic	35	44	40
All (known ethnicity)	37	43	40

Source: Connor et al, 2004

post-1992 universities. This is especially true of Caribbeans (Modood and Acland 1998), who are also more likely to be mature students (Owen et al. 2000; Pathak 2000) (more than half of Caribbean women students are over twenty-five years old) and part-time students (Owen et al. 2000)—all factors which have implications for career prospects. Test scores (A-levels),[3] subject preferences, preference for local institutions, and type of school or college attended are all factors that explain the concentration of ethnic minority groups (again with the exception of the Chinese) in the new universities. Nevertheless, one analysis shows that even accounting for these factors, there is a clear institutional effect (Shiner and Modood 2002). Comparing similarly qualified candidates and controlling for factors such as type of secondary school, gender, and so on, new (post-1992) universities respond more positively than old universities to nonwhite applicants, and within this sector, Chinese, Bangladeshi, and Indian candidates appear to be favored over whites. There is strong evidence, however, that minority candidates face an ethnic penalty when applying to old universities. Institutions within this sector are most likely to select white and, to a lesser extent, Chinese candidates from among a group of similarly qualified applicants.[4] Given the much larger proportion of applications from ethnic minority groups, although ethnic minority applicants may be admitted to old universities in reasonable numbers, they generally have to perform better than do their white peers in order to secure a place. As the type of institution from which you graduate can make a big difference to your career prospects, this bias makes older universities complicit in an institutional discrimination that hinders and slows down the dismantling of ethnic stratification.[5]

Some Possible Causes
Class

For most British sociologists, class is the best explanation of educational outcomes. For example, Goldthorpe's theory of social mobility holds that "individuals of differing class origins will differ in the use they make of available educational opportunities. Those from more advantaged class backgrounds, pursuing strategies from above will exploit such opportunities more fully than will those from less advantaged backgrounds, pursuing strategies from below—and with the backing of superior resources" (Goldthorpe 2003; also Goldthorpe 2000).

Class, however one defines and operationalizes it, is important but may be far from the whole story. Other factors include proximity to good schools or aspects of individual biographies, including the interests and efforts of one's parents. In the case of minorities, there will be factors distinctive to particular minorities or to the condition of being a minority in Britain today, such as racialized exclusion. Some of these distinctive factors will work to reinforce or deepen class effects; others, to lessen them. Or, to put it another way, some of these factors will work to worsen the socioeconomic position of a minority group relative to the rest of society; other factors may have the opposite effect. For example, a study of young people which systematically controlled for social-class attributes found that the likelihood of achieving 5 GCSEs at A*-C (very good test scores, typically achieved at the age of sixteen) for Pakistanis and Indians (analyzed separately) was 10 percent higher than that for their white social-class peers; for black Caribbeans it was 8 percent less (Bradley and Taylor 2004). Ethnic-group membership, then, can mitigate or exacerbate class disadvantage; and this may, of course, change with the circumstances.

Again, while it is generally true that the minority groups with the largest proportions in higher education, especially in pre-1992 universities, have a more middle-class profile than the other minorities do, it is not invariate; Pakistanis have a worse occupational, earnings, and household profile than Caribbeans but a larger proportion in higher education. Moreover, the undiluted class model is no help in explaining why the minorities—all of whom have or until recently had a (much) worse class profile than whites—perform better than whites. This can be seen from table 9.4, which shows university entrants of 2004 by ethnicity and parental social class. It shows that class is a major factor: in nearly every group, the offspring of managers and professionals predominate but not in all cases, notably the Bangladeshis and Pakistanis. Indeed, in most ethnic minority groups, the university entrants are much more likely to be evenly spread across the occupational classes—including those in the "Unknown" category, the majority of whom are likely to be unemployed or in casual work, the informal economy, or hard-to-classify jobs and not merely cases where the information is missing (Ballard 1999). So the significance that the conventional class analysis has in relation to whites seems to be readily extendable to those of part-white parentage but prima facie needs at least to be modified in relation to some minority groups and does not hold at all for Bangladeshis, Pakistanis, and Africans, among whom households headed by a routine, unemployed, or occupation-unknown worker supply the majority of the entrants, nearly three-quarters in the case of Bangladeshis.

To some extent, it can be countered, this finding can be attributed to the fact that the ethnic minority entrants' parental social class and educational capital may have been better than what was suggested by their parents' occupations, for their occupational levels were depressed by migration effects and discrimination in the labor market. Due to this racial discrimination, migrants often suffered a downward social mobility on entry into Britain (Modood et al. 1997, 141–142). The only jobs open to them were often below their qualification levels and below the social-class level they enjoyed before migration. This meant that not only did many minority migrants value education more than their white workmates, but they saw it as part of the process of reversing the initial downward mobility, especially in the lives of their children. Certainly, if we look at the qualification level of the migrants at the time of migration, this argument that migrants' occupational class in Britain

TABLE 9.4
University Entrants by Ethnicity and Parental Social Class, 2004

	White	Black-African	Black-Caribbean	Indian	Pakistani	Bangladeshi	Chinese	Asian-Other	Mixed White and Asian	Mixed White and African	Mixed White and Caribbean	Mixed Other
Managerial and Professional	48	31	32	31	20	13	28	39	56	42	39	47
Intermediate, Supervisory, Technical and Self Employed	23	13	23	23	21	13	20	18	18	19	21	20
Semi-Routine and Routine	14	18	19	23	20	26	29	17	11	15	19	13
Unknown	13	38	26	22	39	47	23	27	15	25	21	20
Total	98	100	100	98	100	99	100	101	100	101	100	100

Source: UCAS.

is not reflective of their true class and hence of their attitudes to education seems to have some plausibility (Modood et al. 1997, 68–69). It is particularly plausible in the case of the African Asians and perhaps also the Indians but less so with other groups. In any case, class analysis by itself, even after taking initial downward mobility into account, is incomplete without acknowledging the economic motivation of migrants, the desire to better themselves and especially the prospects of their children.

Even more fundamentally, if we accept the definition of class in the quotation that opens this chapter—that social class is a matter of categories of people accumulating similar volumes and types of resources and investing them in promoting their own and their children's life chances (Savage, Warde, and Devine 2005, 7)—then, as I expand below, this categorization of people by the possession of similar resources can be a characteristic of ethnicity. That is to say, it can vary across ethnic groups within the same occupational/income classes. Hence, here ethnicity seems to cut across class, possibly even to constitute class in some ways because ethnicity can mean resources.

Racism

Another line of explanation that has prominence in the literature points to the possible role of racism. Racism could, for example, consist of factors influencing how teachers treat different groups, of policies that indirectly discriminate (for example, by placing more pupils from certain ethnic groups in lower sets), and of the general ways in which groups of people in British society are perceived and treated. Each of these can have an effect on the groups in question, who may then react in certain kinds of ways, most notably by being demotivated or confrontational. These reactions may also lead to social stereotyping on the part of educators and university admissions tutors, creating a vicious cycle. This line of explanation seems to work better with blacks than with South Asians. For example, data from local education authorities suggest that at the beginning of schooling, and at the time of the first national tests at age seven, the difference between Caribbeans and whites is relatively slight and is sometimes in favor of Caribbeans. It is South Asian children, often coming from homes in which English, if spoken at home, is a second or third language, who begin their school careers with low averages (this was even more the case when those who are in higher education today would have started schooling). But whereas in secondary school South Asians slowly catch up and, in the case of some groups, overtake whites, the Caribbeans' average steadily drops behind that of the national average (Berthoud et al. 2000, 10; Gillborn and Mirza 2000; NEP 2010; Owen et al. 2000; Richardson and Wood 1999).

Perhaps, then, there is more racism against blacks than against Asians, especially Indians. The evidence, however, points in the other way. For example, the PSI Fourth Survey found that most people in 1994 believed that of all ethnic, racial, and religious hostility, that against South Asians, especially Asian Muslims, is the greatest; this is likely to have increased post-9/11. Indians, clearly a successful group, are not immune from this hostility. The causes of the hostility may lie in perceptions of Pakistanis or (Asian) Muslims, but the effects are visited on South Asians more generally, as turban-wearing Sikh men who have been abused as "Islamic terrorists" could testify. Even within the specific context of schooling, South Asians experience more frequent and more violent racial harassment from other pupils than Caribbeans do (Gillborn 1998; Virdee, Modood, and Newburn 2000). So an appeal to racism by itself may have little explanatory value without considering how a target group reacts to exclusion. Bullying is supposed to put students off schools and academic work; but, as we have seen, Asians make progress, and they have very high staying-on rates beyond the period of compulsory schooling (Modood et al. 1997).

Ethnic Strategies from Below

Perceptions of racism and biases in the labor market may contribute to these high staying-on rates, but when Asians who stay on are questioned, they give positive reasons (especially the desire to go to university) rather than negative reasons (such as the need to avoid unemployment) (Basit 1997; Hagell and Shaw 1996). Even cultures that until recently might have been portrayed as opposed to the higher education and employment of women seem to be producing growing cohorts of highly motivated young women (Ahmad, Modood, and Lissenburgh 2003).

So ethnic minorities in general and South Asians in particular seem to have a strong drive for qualifications. This "motor" cannot be explained by short-term or Britain-only class analysis, though it is partly explained (more in the case of some groups than others) by long-term class analysis, which inquires into premigration class locations. It has to be noted, however, that this type of analysis raises questions of commensurability and fit between what class means in contemporary Britain and what it means in radically different societies and economies. For example, how are Punjabi peasants who own very little individually but through an extended family own a small farm to be compared to hospital porters in London with higher levels of personal consumption and leisure time but little property?

Certainly, one will ultimately need a wider sociological framework, for it would not make sense to answer my question about ethnic minority entry into higher education in a way that does not connect with wider explanations. Racism, cultural adaptation, and deprived neighborhoods are among the features that one cannot ignore. There are indeed various sorts of disadvantage one can stack up, and they offer explanatory assistance if our need is to explain failure. But given that we are explaining a success, all these factors serve only to compound the problem.

So what is the source of this "motor," this ability to drive through large-scale, sociologically corroborated disadvantages? Thinking particularly of South Asians and Chinese, I speculate that the answer might lie in their families and communities, for instance, through the following causal sequence:

- Parents, other significant relatives, and community members share some general but durable ambitions to achieve upward mobility for themselves and especially for their children, and they believe that (higher) education is important in achieving those ambitions and so prioritize the acquisition of (higher) education.

Capitals, Ethnic Identity, and Educational Qualifications | 193

- They are successfully able to convey this view to the children, who to a large degree internalize it; and even when they may not fully share it, they develop ambitions and priorities that are consistent with those of their parents.
  - The parents have enough authority and power over their children, suitably reinforced by significant relatives and other community members, to ensure that the ambition is not ephemeral or fantastic but that the children do whatever is necessary at a particular stage for its progressive realization.

Of course, not all South Asians (even in terms of groups, let alone within groups) are academically successful, but explaining success would be a major theoretical outcome—given the absence of suitable explanatory strategies—and perhaps, though there are political pitfalls here, explaining the successful may help to throw scientific light on the cases of the unsuccessful. Moreover, that may be the basis for an understanding that could assist to reverse the circumstances of the unsuccessful.

My proposed triadic "motor" is consistent with the data presented so far and hopefully can help to explain why socioeconomic disadvantage and racism—indisputably real forces—do not have the effects that sociological research would have predicted. Let me offer a final piece of data that might support the line I am taking. Table 9.4 is from a survey of Year 13 students, in which respondents had to mark statements on a 1–5 scale (5 = strongly applies), and some answers are presented in aggregate form. Besides confirming that ethnic minority respondents in the sample, relative to whites, were more likely to have had few family members who had been to university, it reveals that they nevertheless had received more encouragement from family to go to university. Most counterintuitive of all, they (except black Caribbeans) were more likely to say that it "had always been assumed they would go to higher education." As this counterintuition neatly matches the counterintuition of the fact of ethnic minority overrepresentation in higher education, it is not unreasonable to suppose that the two are linked and that cultural and social capital might play a role.

Cultural and Social Capital
Bourdieu and Cultural Capital

Bourdieu's initial ideas about cultural capital were developed in relation to an inquiry about the nonrandom distribution of educational qualifications, and he speaks about investment strategies employed by different kinds of families (Bourdieu 1997). Moreover, a central point is that there are different forms of capital, so that it is possible for a family to be poor in one form

TABLE 9.5

Factors Affecting Decisions by Potential HE Entrants (Year 13) to Go
on to Higher Education by Ethnic Group (Mean Scores)

Issues affecting decision	Black African	Black Caribbean/other	Pakistani/Bangladeshi	Indian	Chinese/Asian other	All minority groups	White
Few family been to university	2.8	2.9	2.8	3.1	3.0	3.0	2.5
Encouragement from family	4.0	4.0	4.0	4.0	3.8	4.0	3.4
Always assumed would go to HE	4.0	3.2	4.0	4.1	3.9	3.9	3.1
Base N= 100%	94	68	117	166	68	567	217

Scores range from one to five, where one represents 'Does not apply/no effect' to five 'Applies strongly/big effect'.
Source: Connor et al (2004)

and rich in another, which fits the case of socioeconomically disadvantaged Pakistani households having another kind of resource from which they can produce graduates. Highly relevant too is the view that familial norms are not irrelevant to the production of socioeconomic advantages and disadvantages. Moreover, Bourdieu's work offers a theoretical framework for making the links to the wider social structure, power, and ideology.

Yet Bourdieu has very little to say about ethnicity and indeed assumes a cultural homogeneity (at least within classes). Bourdieu is asking about how the dominant class reproduces its domination, whereas explaining minority overrepresentation in higher education requires an explanation of how subordinate groups can achieve upward mobility. His interest is in how those with financial capital can convert it into educational qualifications and then back again. But my starting point is groups with little economic capital, and Bourdieu's framework does not seem to be suitable for examining how such groups can generate social mobility for significant numbers of their members.

Another source of insight is the work of the American anthropologist John Ogbu, who too has tried to create a theoretical framework to connect societywide socioeconomic structures (what he calls "the system") with the different trajectories and dynamics of various minority groups (what he calls "community forces") (Ogbu and Simons 1998). His fundamental distinctions revolve not around capital and class but around different kinds of minorities. He distinguishes between voluntary or immigrant minorities such as, say, Cubans or Koreans in the United States and involuntary or nonmigrant minorities such as blacks, indigenous people, and Mexicans in that country. This is an extremely important and powerful distinction, though it ought not to be treated too dichotomously, for most nonwhite groups in Britain are a legacy of empire, and their movement to Britain needs to be dually characterized as a migration across countries and as a movement internal to a political-economic system. Ogbu shows how the distinction of voluntary/involuntary arises from "the system" (which conquers/enslaves or permits migrants to settle) but has profound consequences for "community forces." For example, it is argued that "voluntary minorities are less conflicted about accommodating to white society, so their role models include people who fully adopt white ways and language," whereas of such persons among involuntary minorities "it is suspected that for them to have succeeded they probably have had to adopt white ways such as speaking standard English, which is seen as giving in to the white oppressor and abandoning their identity" (Ogbu and Simons 1998, 173). As Ogbu develops his theory with primary reference to school performance, it is clear that his cultural-ecological approach, in some ways resembling Bourdieu's ideas of cultural capital and *habitus*,[6] has something relevant to offer to my concerns, as long as the distinction between voluntary and involuntary minorities is not forcefully pressed.

Putnam and Social Capital

Robert Putnam is currently the name most associated with social capital (Putnam 1995, 2000). His interest is in asking about the healthy functioning of contemporary liberal-democratic societies and so, no less than Bourdieu, is some distance from my question about how some specific groups are able to achieve social mobility by means of education. Nevertheless, I do think his work contains ideas useful to my inquiry. For example, his famous distinction between bonding, bridging, and linking social capital is helpful. Bonding social capital describes a distinctive group that bonds together. But the other side of the coin of bonding is that it separates the group from others, unless members of the group at the same time develop bridges to members outside the group. Finally, linking social capital is most relevant to mobility because it links people across classes to those in positions of power or influence (Putnam 1995, 2000). This distinction seems to be prima facie relevant in distinguishing between those South Asian communities who have achieved upward mobility, such as, say, the Gujaratis of Leicester, and those who have not, such as the Pakistanis of Bradford, perhaps because the latter, unlike the former, are strong in bonding capital but lack bridging and linking capital. Of course, I do not mean to suggest—and one has to be careful not to suggest—that communities strong in bonding capital and weak in bridging capital are the sole cause of differential outcomes such as the economic positions of those two communities. For that would ignore how exclusion and segregation in the northern cities and elsewhere have been shaped by white people's preferences as individuals and the decisions of local councilors, not least in relation to public housing. But nevertheless it seems to me to be possible to use Putnam's distinction between forms of social capital without blaming the victim.

Another central contention of Putnam's is that participation in formal, voluntary organizations, regardless of the kind or quality of participation, is itself a decisive measure of all kinds of social goods, from crime free neighborhoods to better personal health and higher personal incomes. I was at first skeptical about the utility of this proposition for my inquiry, but at least one study has found that "the organizational involvement of both parents and children promotes school achievement" (Bankston and Zhou 2002, 311; Zhou and Bankston 1998).

"Ethnicity as Social Capital" Studies in the United States

There are a number of American empirical analyses that apply a concept of social capital to the study of ethnic groups (for a list, see Bankston and Zhou 2002, 289). So far this body of work is not very well known in Britain, if citations are any indication. Broadly speaking, this work seems to be in a stream, but correcting itself empirically as it goes along, derived from James Coleman (e.g., Coleman 1988, 1990; like Bourdieu, Coleman's interest was in explaining unequal scholastic outcomes) and perhaps initially intimated by the economist Glenn Loury in relation to the labor-market position of African Americans (Loury 1977). The empirical studies, while attempting to develop intermediate or grounded theory, do not slavishly follow any particular theorist or all aspects of the work of a useful theorist. For example, they assert the importance of the social in all kinds of ways, whereas Coleman attempted to explain the social in terms of an economic-psychological individualism. Again, Coleman believed that his work endorsed a certain moral conservatism on matters such as the importance of a nonworking mother within a two-parent family for children's development, whereas the later studies on ethnicity give support to a broader range of positions. Moreover,

Alejandro Portes, perhaps one of the first to use the ideas of social capital and network theory in relation to immigrant ethnicity, highlights negative as well as positive outcomes of social capital (Portes 1998).

Bankston and Zhou (2002) too are critical of some of the ways that social capital has been used. They make some important and apposite philosophical points:

> Social capital, a . . . metaphorical construction, does not consist of resources that are held by individuals or by groups but of processes of social interaction leading to constructive outcomes. Therefore, we argue that social capital is not located at any one level of analysis and that it emerges across different levels of analysis. The confusion over the meaning of this term, then, is a consequence of a metaphorical confusion of a substantive quantity (capital) and a process that takes place through stages (embedded, goal-directed relations). Locating and defining social capital is further complicated by the variability, contextuality, and conditionality of the process. Stages of social relations that lead to constructive outcomes for one group of people or in one situation may not lead to constructive outcomes for another group or in another situation. (286).

On their reading of the relevant literature, two particular dimensions of social capital seem to have emerged in research that are particularly relevant to the family: "intergenerational closure" and "norms enforcement" (Bankston and Zhou 2002, 287). The first is a specific case of the general interest, derived from Coleman, in "dense associations" (Coleman 1990), in the belief that the kinds of relationships that lead to nonmonetary exchanges and cooperative behavior involve a high degree of trust and that this is likely to be fostered when individuals see themselves as similar and as sharing the same values, have frequent contact with each other and with each other's contacts, and so on. In the case of families, "intergenerational closure" is achieved when parents know the parents of their children's friends, so that the network of parents and the network of children involve many of the same families. Nevertheless, "intergenerational closure" seems to set the bar too high; continuity of purpose and values across generations may be quite enough. We need to be careful of a general tendency to prefer dense and closed relationships in themselves, for as early as the work of Granovetter (1973), it was clear that for many purposes, such as acquiring information about employment opportunities, positive outcomes are more likely to flow from a set of wide and loose relationships than from "dense" ones. This is one of the advantages of

Putnam's concepts of bridging and linking capital, requiring the analyst to broaden the range of relationships, beyond the obvious ones of bonding, that facilitate valuable social outcomes. Indeed, in at least one empirical analysis, it has been found that the high academic scores of Asian Americans are not due to close parent-child ties, for those ties were absent (Bankston and Zhou 2002, 310). As for "norms enforcement," it is of course critical that if certain goals are dependent on focused effort, then the norms that inform those goals must not only be shared but must be enforced; otherwise they would only be vague aspirations or good intentions.

The kind of ethnic capital I am interested in, then, seems to require three different stages or dimensions: relationships, norms, and norms enforcement—though the kind of relationships, norms, and norms enforcement that will lead to university entry may vary across group, time, and place; indeed, an erstwhile successful strategy may need to be changed as circumstances change. It is not, then, a competition between dense *versus* loose relationships but what might work for a particular group in specific circumstances. What kind and how much of dense and what kind and how much of loose? This, of course, would be highly relevant to current policy debates about segregation, disadvantage, and social cohesion.

To focus, however, on my own question, it does seem to be that this literature suggests an important triad: familial adult-child relationships, transmission of aspirations and attitudes, and norms enforcement. This triad seems to be highly pertinent to my suggestions as to where to find the "motor" of South Asian academic success. This is not at all surprising, for authors such as Zhou and Bankston have focused on groups, such as the Vietnamese, who arrived in the United States poor and without preexisting ethnic community networks to assist them and have achieved outstanding academic performance (Zhou and Bankston 1998). Moreover, the triad should, I believe, offer the opportunity to connect with other and wider social dimensions, for example, identity. People act (or try to act or fail to act) the way they do because it seems to them to be the living of an identity which they believe they have or aspire to have; certain behaviors make sense or do not make sense, become possible or "impossible," easy or difficult, worth making sacrifices for, and so on, if certain identities—such as ethnic or minority identities—are strongly held. The triad may cluster with other beliefs and behaviors that give some South Asians a sense of who they are, their location in the world, and what is expected of them. This can be a fruitful inquiry even if we reject ethnic essentialism (and are careful not to impose too restricted a purview of *which* adult-children relationships are important). For instance if Indians in Britain develop the self-concept that "We as a group are striving and struggling to achieve higher status and prosperity, respectability, in this land where the dice are loaded against us but success is achievable, and you have to play your part," this self-concept should nevertheless be viewed as a contingent, rather than an essential, aspect of being Indian in Britain. The transmission of a normative identity will, I believe, be more important than, say, parental-child "quality-time," talking together about schoolwork or friendships, or any specific skills and knowledge transfer. Indeed, South Asian migrant parents may have little relevant economic-human capital to transmit, but subsequent human-capital acquisition by their children may depend on parent-to-child transmission of norms-laden and goals-directing identities. I believe the motivational power of identity does not necessarily need closed, dense communities and is more at the heart of ethnic minority social/cultural capital than, say, residential concentration, mutual self-help, or community institutions.

If identity is too intangible an example, it is clear that the triad must connect with specific measurable behaviors, for example, making children do academic homework. Moreover, "norms enforcement" cannot just mean discipline; it must extend to also include the provision of resources (such as books and tutors) that enable children to proceed on the appropriate normative path. I believe this is an extremely fruitful line of inquiry; but the first step will have to be the creation of data, for at the moment (because researchers have not asked the appropriate questions) there are no data (by ethnicity) on what periods of academic work—not necessarily just set by the school—are done outside school hours, let alone what proportions of disposable income are spent by households on children's education.

Another way of going beyond the family is by looking at the locales in which the families under study are based and the ways that the neighborhoods contribute to or impede the realization of the families' academic goals. Min Zhou, drawing on her study of Chinatown in New York and elaborating on the role that community organizations play there in assisting upward social mobility, makes a distinction between an ethnic/racial ghetto and enclave (Zhou 1992, 2005). Both are typified by high levels of ethnic-group segregation and an absence of highly paid jobs, but an enclave, unlike a ghetto, is likely to be economically dynamic and aspirant and to allow cross-class relationships, thus enhancing information channels, job opportunities, and models of academic and economic success, all of which reinforce the promise of upward mobility missing in a ghetto. This is a distinction that can be connected with Ogbu's approach as described earlier, as well as Putnam's emphasis on the importance of bridging and linking, in addition to bonding, capitals. It is, therefore, another fruitful distinction to explore, even though the levels of ethnic segregation in Britain are much lower than those in the United States.

Conclusion

In the U.S. literature I have been considering, the Bourdieusian distinction between cultural capital, which is acquired through the family, and social capital as benefits mediated through social relations is not maintained; the former is indistinguishably incorporated within the latter. This suits my purposes too. For if the question is what role ethnic background plays, the family is integral to that background but clearly is not exhausted by it. Hence, perhaps the appropriate term should be "cultural-social capital" or, perhaps, "ethnic capital" (modified from "ethnicity as social capital" in Zhou 2005). This term perhaps runs the risk of reification and suggesting that a certain ethnic group (e.g., Pakistanis) is a static, homogeneous, neatly bounded group—features which I do not mean to imply but to deny, if less radically than in the current social science orthodoxy, and which can be countered in analysis. On the other hand, it has the advantage of highlighting diversity, namely, that the capital in question will vary across ethnic groups, not just in degree but also in kind; it also suggests a certain kind of marginality and exclusion which is not fully explicable in class terms. It has the further advantage that it limits the position that has to be defended: some or all of the uses of "social capital" may be separated out from a particular use that relates to some ethnic groups.

I leave open for another discussion that the concept of cultural capital will resume relevance if we widen the picture and consider why ethnic minorities experience an ethnic penalty in relation to entry into prestigious universities and to the labor-market returns they receive for their university degrees— that is to say, to explain why these groups are not doing even better than they are doing. Let me conclude by considering the suggestion that the reason that the power of established cultural capital does not seem to deter some ethnic minorities from (higher) education is perhaps because they are outside the parameters of "white" cultural capital in its entirety, that, unlike the white working class, they do not really pick up or understand the cues.[7] This view is quite mistaken (though it might have been true at a very early point in the migration process). Leaving aside the perverse implication that ethnic minorities will only start behaving in a disadvantaged way after they are socially included, I suggest that we need to divide "white cultural capital" into at least two parts. First, there is working-class, popular culture, often American-derived, especially in relation to youth culture of Hollywood, soap operas, music, clothes fashion, celebrities, football, pubs, clubs, and bingeing. It is a dominant culture whose cues British African-Caribbeans have not only picked up but in which they have come to be a leading-edge presence, quite remarkable for a group that is less than 2 percent of the population, stigmatized, and economically disadvantaged (Hall 1998; Modood 1999). South Asian parents no doubt have little credibility in this domain and try to limit their children's exposure to it.

Second, there is a middle-class culture, meaning not just "high culture" and leisure pursuits but more importantly including occupations that confer high social status and that tend more toward respectability than celebrity and hedonistic consumption, and entry into which nearly always requires a good university degree. This is the dominant culture that nonwhite ethnic minority parents would like their children to integrate into, as so many other groups have done before, most conspicuously Jews. So it is not a question of missing cues but of a determined effort to avoid one dominant culture and steer toward another. This, of course, still leaves open the question of why in relation to universities many minority ethnic young people fail to think "that's not meant for me" in the way that is supposed to be characteristic of many white working-class young people. I have offered a series of suggestions, ranging from (in the absence of suitable data) my own speculations to critically and syncretically learning from the American literature, which, though much in advance of its British counterpart, will certainly need to be appropriately reworked to answer British questions.

At the moment South Asian university entrants are typically children of migrants; they are "second generation" (Connor et al. 2004). In due course, however, this generation, having lifted itself into the middle class, will produce a generation that will benefit from some of the standard advantages of being born middle class, including the acquisition of cultural capital that assists entry into prestigious universities and professional and managerial jobs. We would then be studying a different phenomenon. My interest in this chapter has been in what kind of capital, if any, can explain the upward educational mobility of predominantly working-class, outsider, ethnic groups. The concept of ethnic capital might help us to understand the counterintuitive findings of high success of members of underprivileged groups. I have shown that their educational progress creates a noteworthy anomaly for current cultural-capital analysis.[8]

NOTES

An earlier version of this chapter appeared as "Capitals, Ethnic Identity, and Educational Qualifications," in *Cultural Trends* 13(2), no. 50 (June 2004): 87–105, and is kindly reproduced here with the permission of the publisher, Taylor and Francis. I am grateful for the support of the Leverhulme Trust for its funding of the Migration and Ethnicity Research Programme at the University of Bristol and University College London. This essay was part of the preliminary and early work within the Programme project Gender, Social Capital and Differential Outcomes; other project members are Claire Dwyer, Gurchathen Sanghera, Bindi Shah, and Suruchi Thapar-Bjorkert. For more details, see http://www.bristol.ac.uk/sociology/leverhulme.

1. For fuller evidential support for this section, see Modood et al. 1997, chapters 3 and 4; Modood 2005b, chapters 3 and 4.

2. This does not consider the "Asian other" category, which includes disparate groups such as Sri Lankans, Vietnamese, and Malaysians. But these groups are relatively small in absolute terms, and so working out the proportion of the age group in higher education is less reliable. The same may apply to the Chinese in table 9.1, for their representation is much lower than all other data has suggested so far (Modood 2005a).

3. A-levels are public examinations typically taken at the end of Year 13 and whose results determine university entry, though at the discretion of each individual university. The higher the score, the greater the likelihood of entry into a prestigious university.

4. The data set in question was reanalyzed recently, with results showing that "bias" against ethnic minorities was confined to law studies for all groups and to Pakistanis in most subjects (see HEFCE 2005). Why the HEFCE analysis differs from Shiner and Modood 2002 has not yet been established but is the subject of a project to be commenced in 2010.

5. It ought to be borne in mind, however, that some ethnic minority groups have a disproportionately large number of their eighteen- to twenty-four-year-olds in higher education and therefore are digging deeper into the natural talent available in that age group. Hence, it is not in itself surprising that a larger proportion of ethnic minority applicants enter institutions that require lower A-level entry scores. For, if we were to compare like with like, the peers of some who enter these universities are whites who are absent from higher education.

6. It has been suggested that even if Bourdieu's concept of cultural capital is not helpful to answering the question that I have posed in this chapter, nevertheless his concepts of *habitus* and *field* could be (May 1999). Such concepts, however, are organized to analyze class divisions. Stripped of that analytical purpose, they become less distinctive. Similar ideas about the importance of preexisting social contexts and ongoing activities are available from other sources. In my case (Modood 1984), I have learned from Wittgenstein's ideas of "language game" and "meaning lies in use" (Wittgenstein 1968), Oakeshott's theories of "mode of experience" (Oakeshott 1933), "tradition," and "practical knowledge" (Oakeshott 1962), and Collingwood on "forms of experience" (Collingwood 1924).

7. I am grateful to Mike Savage for raising this point with me.

8. After writing this chapter, I discovered Laughlo 2000, which, though based on Norwegian data, is closely allied to the argument of this chapter.

III

The Role of Local Context

10

National and Urban Contexts for the Integration of the Second Generation in the United States and Canada

Jeffrey G. Reitz and Ye Zhang

Is the second generation more successfully integrated in some countries than in others? Cross-national comparisons of the success of the second generation suggest countries may differ as contexts for the assimilation of minorities, with some providing better opportunities for economic mobility or social inclusion than others (Crul and Vermeulen 2003). Given that characteristics of host societies shape the reception and integration of immigrants (Reitz 2003), the questions arise whether these effects, and possibly others, carry over to affect the second generation and, if so, how and why. The following analysis provides such a comparison for the United States and Canada and shows that to understand the comparative integration of the second generation in each country, it is important to consider the question of contexts at both national and urban levels.

Immigration is a largely urban phenomenon in the United States and Canada, as in many countries. Previous U.S.-Canada comparative research shows that immigrant settlement occurs in a distinctive group of cities within each country, and the impact of urban areas of settlement is not necessarily the same in each country (Reitz 1998). For example, leading immigration cities in the United States and Canada include New York and Toronto, respectively, both major urban centers but not completely parallel in their impact on immigrant settlement and integration. They and the other key cities must be considered explicitly in cross-national comparisons. Since the children of immigrants reside primarily in the same areas of immigrant settlement as their parents, it is likewise essential for second-generation comparisons to examine processes of integration at the urban level as well as at the national level.

The analysis here focuses on educational attainment as an indicator of integration. It is based on pooled data from Current Population Surveys over the period 1995 to 2003 and the Canadian census Public Use Microdata sample file for 2001. To enhance the relevance of cross-national comparison to identification of context effects, the analysis compares similar origin groups across countries. These include the so-called white second generation of European origin, an Afro-Caribbean second generation, an Asian second generation, and the Chinese-origin subgroup. Mexican and other Latin American immigrant groups are not as important in Canada as in the United States and are not included.

Potential Implications of National Differences for the Second Generation
Equal Treatment of Minorities

At the national level, it is clear that the United States and Canada are similar societies, with many features suggesting comparable treatment of second-generation minorities. Both have long histories as countries of immigration, both express a philosophy of inclusiveness by providing fairly rapid pathways to full citizenship, and both have made symbolic and legislative commitments to equality of opportunity for ethnic and racial minorities.

On the other hand, the two countries have different histories of interethnic relations, marked in the United States by the legacy of mass slavery and racial polarization and in Canada by linguistic conflict and the potential for Quebec succession. These different histories have contemporary relevance. Although racial disparities have not been overcome, the struggle for racial equality in the United States has yielded many institutional protections and resources for racial minorities. In Canada, the policy of "multiculturalism," proclaimed as part of the effort to build national unity, has been warmly embraced as promoting ethnic inclusion and equity. Both developments might affect immigrants and the second generation alike, although the size and direction of any resulting cross-national difference is difficult to predict.

Speculation about "segmented assimilation" for the second generation in the United States (Portes and Zhou 1993) is a related concern. Immigrant groups may assimilate either into the mainstream society or into their own immigrant community, but in a racially segmented society, a third possibility exists: assimilation into an existing racial minority segment. To the extent this happens, the existing patterns of racial inequality could be reproduced among racial minority immigrants, particularly in the second generation. In the United States, significant racial segregation and polarization might be expected to affect the offspring of Afro-Caribbean immigrants. Since Canada lacks a comparable legacy of slavery, Afro-Caribbean immigrants to Canada might be relatively unaffected and have more positive outcomes (Boyd 2003a). For groups such as Chinese or other Asians, existing patterns of race relations are more similar for the United States and Canada; hence, less cross-national difference would be expected. Against this line of speculation stands the counterargument, namely, that the American racial struggle has produced benefits for native-born blacks which could also benefit black immigrants and their offspring, offsetting any negative effects of segmented assimilation (Foner 2003; Nee 2003).

Existing evidence suggests that any U.S.-Canada differences in patterns of racial or ethnic discrimination are small, thereby implying small differences for the minority second generation. Reitz and Breton (1994) show in their work on cross-national differences for racial minority Afro-Caribbean and Asian immigrants that differences in earnings net of measured qualifications such as education and work experience are small. Discrimination field trials show similar results in the two countries. But to date, there has been no direct U.S.-Canada comparison of second-generation minority experiences of racial discrimination or minority integration, and this is one objective of the present analysis.[1]

Unequal Economic Status of Immigrants

In cross-national comparisons, Borjas (1988, 1990, 1999) notes that immigrant earnings for all major immigrant groups are lower in the United States than in Canada and links this to lower relative educational levels for immigrants in the United States. Whereas Borjas points to immigration policies as a possible source of this difference, Reitz (1998) shows that a range of institutional sectors is involved, including labor markets. The most important difference concerns educational institutions; higher native-born educational levels in the United States represent greater obstacles for immigrants from all origin groups, lowering their relative earnings.

Poorer outcomes for Asian, Afro-Caribbean, and other immigrants in the United States suggest more negative outcomes for the second generation, specifically with respect to educational opportunity. First, the greater educational gap for immigrants in the United States could mean that the second generation faces a greater challenge in the degree of intergenerational educational mobility required to achieve equality with the native-born. Second, the relatively lower earnings of immigrants in the United States create the potential for problems for their children. Immigrants who struggle economically and who more frequently live in conditions of poverty will have greater difficulty providing the resources for their children to do well in school and to finance a postsecondary education. Compounding this funding problem are high tuition levels for the best postsecondary institutions and weaker social-welfare protection in the United States.

There is nothing automatic about these effects, however. Social-class differences in educational attainments in the native-born population may or may not apply to the children of immigrants. These class differences are related to economic or financial matters, but only partly so. To some extent, they reflect differences in social aspirations and the social hierarchy of society. Immigrants may or may not assimilate into social-class groupings based on their income level, and their children may or may not follow a particular socially defined pattern based on social-class distinctions in the mainstream society. Unlike the hypothesis of segmented assimilation suggesting that the children of immigrants become oriented toward particular ethnoracial groups within the host society, here the question is whether the second generation assimilates into its native-born social-class counterpart.

In sum, U.S.-Canada differences in the experiences of the second generation may be related to differences in discrimination and equality of opportunity and to differences in overall immigrant inequality. Regarding the former, previous research suggests that differences for the second generation may be small, but for the Afro-Caribbean second generation, segmented assimilation is an issue. Regarding the latter, an important question is how (or if) the greater inequalities affecting the immigrant generation in the United States carry over to affect the second generation.

Implications of Urban Contexts and Immigrant Settlement Patterns

Cross-national differences in the experiences of immigrants in the United States and Canada cannot be understood properly without considering differences in the distinctive urban contexts of immigration. These urban contexts may affect the second generation because of their impact on the immigrant parents or for other reasons.

The concept of "global cities" put forward by Sassen (1988, 1991) suggests that immigrants have a distinctive experience in those cities which play a major role in management of the global economy (especially New York) because of the considerable labor-market polarization these cities exhibit. In Sassen's view, superaffluent elites in global cities create a demand for low-paying personal services, and this attracts immigrants. But evidence from the census (Reitz 1998) suggests that greater inequalities affecting immigrants in

New York arise from a more pervasive skills polarization rather than labor demand in specific occupations. Further, such skills polarization affects not only New York but other high-immigration cities in the United States, regardless of occupational structure or position in the global economy.

There are two aspects to this skills polarization. One is the high level of education of the native-born workers, which reflects advancing "postindustrial" developments in technology, finance, and other high-end services and is characteristic of all urban areas experiencing economic expansion, not just global cities. The other is the attraction of large numbers of immigrants. Again, this occurs not just in global cities but in all economically expanding cities. In the United States, high immigration is associated with lower levels of immigrant education, as Bartel (1989) notes, so patterns of immigrant settlement contribute to educational polarization. The result is more extreme inequalities for minorities in many high-immigration cities in the United States, not just in New York as a global city.

Educational polarization has been less characteristic of Canadian cities, for reasons which relate to the overall pattern of Canadian development and the continuing importance of immigration. More specifically, Canada's immigrants have been recruited as part of a program of nation-building (Reitz 2004). Hence, the proportion of immigrants in Canadian cities is higher than in U.S. cities, and there are fewer immigrants with very low skill levels. As well, they tend to be distributed more uniformly across the major urban areas, both in number and educational level, possibly because settlement policies matter more than family networks in steering settlement location.

As a result, immigrant inequalities have been less pronounced in Canada than in the United States, and they are more uniform across Canadian cities. Put another way, the difference in immigrant inequality in the United States compared to Canada is more extreme when urban contexts are factored into the comparison. In 1980, recent black (Afro-Caribbean) immigrant men in the United States on average earned 54 percent of mainstream earnings, whereas their counterparts in Canada earned 70 percent. Recent black immigrant men in New York, Washington, DC, Los Angeles, and Miami averaged only 48–49 percent of mainstream New York earnings, whereas their Toronto counterparts earned the national average of 70 percent. Similar findings hold for black immigrant women and for Chinese immigrant men and women (Reitz 1998, 62–63).

The second generation may be affected by these urban circumstances if they remain within the cities of immigrant settlement. They may do so for a number of reasons, beyond a general tendency for children to remain near their parents. The ethnic community may be an attraction for the second generation, as it is for the parents. Cities lacking an immigrant community may be seen as less hospitable to minorities with foreign origins and hence less attractive places in which to live or work.

Immigrant cities may or may not be the context for second-generation integration, but to the extent that the second generation remains in immigrant cities, questions raised about the impact of variations in immigrant economic success at the national level can be raised again at the urban level. Higher native-born educational levels in the high-immigration cities such as New York have an important bearing on the context for the second generation. Lower immigrant earnings may create barriers and obstacles, and inter-urban mobility for the second generation may also play a role in determining the overall pattern of integration. These elements all figure in a valid cross-national comparison.

Previous Research on Second-Generation Integration of Minorities within Each Country

The education and labor-market integration of the second generation has been examined within each country separately. Studies in the United States (Farley and Alba 2002; Kasinitz, Mollenkopf, and Waters 2004; Min 2002; Portes 1996; Portes and Rumbaut 2001; Rumbaut and Portes 2001) show very positive results for Asians; positive results for blacks, though somewhat less so; and significant inequality and poverty for Mexicans and a number of other Latin American groups. In Canada, native-born "visible minorities" have attained levels of education comparable to the native-born majority group or higher, in both secondary school and university completion (Davies and Guppy 1998, 136; see also Worswick 2001). While analyses of educational opportunity by Boyd (Boyd 2002; Boyd and Grieco 1998) show positive results in survey data for visible minorities overall, Simmons and Plaza (1998), using 1991 census data, examine university attendance among the second generation in Toronto and find that "young black men in Canada show some disadvantage, though a modest one" (see also Corak 2008).

Although for specific groups, such as Afro-Caribbeans and Asians, these results seem broadly similar, it is difficult to draw precise comparative conclusions. Boyd (2003, 111) states that "contrary to the 'second-generation decline' and segmented 'underclass' assimilation models found in the United States, adult visible minority immigrant offspring in Canada do not have lower educational attainments than their parents or their not-visible-minority counterparts." Yet in the United States, for Caribbean black and Asian groups comparable to those studied by Boyd in Canada, researchers have found a similar lack of support for the segmented-assimilation model. Farley and Alba (2002, 697), for example, conclude that there is "no evidence supporting the segmented assimilation hypothesis," a finding which mirrors what Kasinitz, Mollenkopf, and Waters (2004) find in New York (see also Model 2008, 41–44). A direct cross-national comparison will show more clearly any distinctive disadvantage for the Afro-Caribbean second generation which might be attributable to segmented assimilation in the United States.

Data Sources and Analytic Framework

The cross-national analysis performed here compares a merged file from five Current Population Surveys (CPS) in the United States (1995, 1997, 1999, 2001, and 2003) with the 2001 Canadian census Public Use Microdata file. CPS data have been used previously to study the second generation (Model and Fisher 2002a; Farley and Alba 2002; Rumbaut 2003), and in this analysis, the five independent surveys are used, yielding an overall N of 759,065. The Canadian census for 2001 is the first since 1971 to include a question on parental birthplace, and the microdata file for 2001 has an N of 801,055.

CPS data provide white, black, and Asian racial categories,[2] and the same ethnoracial origin categories can be identified in Canadian census data using a question similar to the "race" question used in the United States, plus a question on ethnic origin. Persons of Hispanic origin, far less prominent in Canada than in the United States, are excluded in both analyses. In both the United States and Canada, the benchmark "mainstream" population includes non-Hispanic whites with two native-born parents; hence, they are of third or higher generations. The second generation is defined as native-born with one or both parents foreign-born.

The analysis identifies a young age cohort, twenty-five to thirty-nine, most of whom have completed their education and begun their working careers. In both countries, most of the children of immigrants of non-European origin are relatively young, so the twenty-five-to-thirty-nine age cohort is the appropriate focus (see Reitz and Somerville 2004). To provide an indication of progress toward equality, this young second-generation group is compared to mainstream whites in the same age group. The young second-generation group is also compared with a group taken to represent the parental generation, namely, immigrants aged fifty and over. This comparison will provide some indication of intergenerational mobility, even though, of course, the older group may have changed in some ways since the time the second generation was growing up. Since the mainstream norm for intergenerational educational mobility is variable across contexts, intergenerational mobility represented by the status of the second generation is compared to a mainstream benchmark.

The selection of origin groups for cross-national comparison is determined in part by available sample sizes in the second generation. The U.S. second-generation sample aged twenty-five to thirty-nine includes 5,050 whites, 324 blacks, and 691 Asians ($N = 6,065$ in all). The Canadian second-generation sample aged twenty-five to thirty-nine includes 24,919 whites, 703 blacks, and 1711 Asians ($N = 27,333$ in all). Our particular interest is in the newer immigrant groups of non-European origin. In both countries, an Afro-Caribbean second generation includes persons of Caribbean and Latin American origin, with a relatively small group of sub-Saharan African origin. The Asian second generation in both countries includes Chinese, Filipinos, South Asians, Koreans, Vietnamese, and other groups. The composition differs somewhat between countries, with Filipinos relatively more numerous in the United States, and Chinese and South Asians more numerous in Canada. The analysis here focuses on the Chinese as the largest Asian second-generation group common to both countries. Significant numbers exist in both samples: 158 in the United States, 819 in Canada. In the U.S. data, Chinese and other specific Asian origins are identified based on parental birthplace. In the Canadian data, Chinese origin is distinguished in the "race" question. The samples for older immigrants aged fifty and over and the mainstream populations are fairly large.[3]

Two educational attainment categories are examined: attainment of some postsecondary education but no bachelor's degree, and attainment of a bachelor's degree or higher, including graduate and professional degrees. These categories appear to be broadly similar in the two countries, but some differences are noteworthy. On the one hand, Americans have university degrees more often than Canadians do. For mainstream white populations in our data, the proportion in the United States with a bachelor's degree or higher is 26.1 percent, compared to 15.9 percent in Canada. On the other hand, Canadians more often have other types of postsecondary education than Americans do. The figures are 36.8 percent in Canada, compared to 26.1 percent in the United States. The proportion with any type of postsecondary education is about the same in each country, just over 50 percent.

Two cross-national differences may be reflected in these data: a greater Canadian emphasis on vocationally oriented postsecondary education and a difference in the institutional labeling. What Americans call "colleges" are more likely to include academic institutions with programs comparable to universities, whereas in Canada, "colleges" are generally vocationally oriented. American colleges which offer bachelor's degrees are quite diverse, and the mix of academic and vocational content in their curricula may vary. But bachelor's degrees in Canada come from "universities," and the larger proportion of Canadians who identify their degree as not in the bachelor's category may or may not reflect a different level of education as compared to Americans who identify their "college" degree as a bachelor's degree.[4]

Findings
National-Level Differences in Second-Generation Education

At the national level, the relative educational performance for second-generation origin groups is quite similar in the United States and Canada. In both countries, educational levels of the younger second generation aged twenty-five to thirty-nine, including white, Afro-Caribbean, and Asian, exceed those of same-aged mainstream whites. Ethnic differences follow roughly the same pattern in each country, with some variations by type of education, as shown in table 10.1 (columns 3 and 4). In both countries, the proportion of the white second generation with bachelor's degrees is roughly 10 percentage points higher than for the same-age white mainstream population (column 4), and the same is true of the proportion with any postsecondary education (column 3). For the Afro-Caribbean second generation in both countries, bachelor's degree attainment is higher than for the mainstream population, although slightly less than for the white second generation. In Canada, the proportion of the Afro-Caribbean second generation with any postsecondary education is about 15 percentage points above the mainstream level and is higher than for the white second generation.

The second generation of Asian origin has even higher levels of education, again in both countries. In the United States, the proportion of the Asian second generation with either bachelor's degrees or any postsecondary education is over 20 percentage points higher than for the U.S. mainstream population. In Canada, the figure is about the same for any postsecondary education and is over 30 percentage points higher for bachelor's degree attainment. Recall that Chinese are relatively more numerous among Asians in Canada and have higher levels of education on average than the other Asians. When we compare Chinese specifically in each country, we find that in the United States, the percentage of the young Chinese second generation with bach-

TABLE 10.1
Post-secondary and Bachelor's Degree Educational Attainment in the
United States and Canada by Generation, Origins and Age

	50 and over			25 to 39		
	Any Post-secondary	Bachelors and higher	(N)	Any Post-secondary	Bachelors and higher	(N)
	(1)	(2)		(3)	(4)	
UNITED STATES						
Native-born White Third Generation and Higher						
	45.6	22.7	(121,576)	60.2	30.3	(100,515)
Immigrant Origins Groups						
	(Immigrant Parental Generation)			(Young Second Generation)		
White	42.4	25.4	(7,613)	71.4	40.4	(5,050)
Afro-Caribbean Black	31.7	16.4	(1,119)	70.4	38.9	(324)
Asian, all origins	48.4	35.4	(3,961)	83.7	55.9	(691)
Chinese	46.8	35.2	(940)	88.6	75.3	(158)
CANADA						
Native-born White Third Generation and Higher						
	39.7	11.1	(126,242)	65.9	18.7	(109,210)
Immigrant Origins Groups						
	(Immigrant Parental Generation)			(Young Second Generation)		
White	45.3	13.3	(44,186)	75.6	27.6	(24,919)
Afro-Caribbean Black	52 1	11.5	(2,480)	80.9	24.6	(703)
Asian, all origins	43.7	20.5	(14,282)	89.1	53.1	(1,711)
Chinese	36.9	16.3	(6,624)	89.5	56.0	(819)

elor's degrees is a spectacular 45.1 percentage points higher than the same-age white mainstream population, and their counterparts in Canada enjoy a 37.3-percentage-point advantage over the mainstream. For all postsecondary education, figures for the Chinese second generation still slightly favor the United States: 28.4 percentage points higher in the United States, compared to 23.6 percentage points higher in Canada.

These results show in a general way that the cross-national differences for particular groups and particular types of education are less striking than the similarities. Precise description of these differences is difficult because of considerable variation in baseline figures cross-nationally and by type of education, and conclusions drawn from percentage differences differ from conclusions drawn from percentage ratios. For example, the proportional difference in bachelor's degree attainment between the Chinese second generation and the mainstream is 45.1 percentage points in the United States and 37.3 percentage points in Canada. The advantage for the Chinese in the United States seems greater, but the Canadian figure employs a lower mainstream standard. Ratios of percentages give a different view. The Chinese-to-mainstream ratio of the proportion with bachelor's degrees in the United States is 2.5; in Canada, 3.0. In terms of ratios, then, the advantage for Chinese looks a bit greater in Canada. Both differences and ratios should be taken into account; what is of interest is the relative likelihood of educational attainment for the second generation compared to the mainstream.[5] This appears to be roughly the same for second-generation whites, Afro-Caribbeans, and Chinese.

Differences in Intergenerational Mobility

These roughly equivalent outcomes for the U.S. and Canadian second generation imply very different relative[6] rates of intergenerational mobility. The different starting points for immigrants of the parental generation in the two countries, described earlier (cf. Borjas 1988; Reitz 1998), provide an essential context for the achievements of their children, although they do not determine them. More lowly beginnings for immigrants from particular origin groups in the United States, with regard to relative education and income and compared to their counterparts in Canada, clearly do not confine or constrain the experiences of their children. In terms of educational outcomes, the children of immigrants to the United States seem to have achieved as much relative to the mainstream as their Canadian counterparts; the educational system functioned as an equalizer. But achieving these outcomes requires higher relative rates of intergenerational mobility for the U.S. second generation.

Higher mobility rates for Afro-Caribbeans in the United States may be indicated by intergenerational change. For older Afro-Caribbean immigrants the data here (table 10.1, columns 1 and 2) show educational levels to be significantly lower than for the older mainstream population. For Afro-Caribbean immigrants in Canada, they are higher, particularly with regard to any type of postsecondary education. In the United States the intergenerational difference in bachelor's degree attainment for the Afro-Caribbean group is 22.5 percentage points, bettering the difference of 7.6 percentage points in the mainstream population by 14.9 points. In Canada the intergenerational difference for Afro-Caribbeans is 13.1 percentages points, bettering the difference of 7.6 percentage points in the mainstream population by only 5.5 points. The intergenerational difference in any postsecondary education is 24.1 percentage points higher in the second generation in the United States, compared to only 2.6 percentage points higher in Canada.

The very highly educated Chinese second generation has achieved much higher rates of educational mobility than has the mainstream population in the United States. However, the data here from recent years show that older Chinese immigrants in the United States are on average actually better educated than the U.S. mainstream (cross-national comparison shows that the extent of intergenerational change is about the same in each country). It appears that both immigrants and their children in the U.S. communities have invested very heavily in postsecondary education.

Three significant findings at the national level set the stage for a focus on urban contexts. First, within each country, evidence of strong educational attainments, and a positive intergenerational change, shows that the economic and other difficulties faced by Afro-Caribbean and Chinese immigrants have not prevented their children from succeeding educationally. Second, the greater economic difficulties that black and Chinese immigrant groups experienced in the United States have not carried over to produce either lower educational attainments for the second generation in that country or lower rates of educational mobility than the native-born, or compared to what is observed in Canada. Quite the contrary, second-generation patterns of educational attainment on average exceed what is typical for the native-born, who are often in more favorable economic circumstances. Third, the expectation that the Afro-Caribbean second generation in the United States might be negatively affected by the racial polarization of the host society—the segmented-assimilation hypothesis—is not supported. Although the black second generation has lower educational attainments than Chinese or other Asians in both countries, a relatively higher proportion have bachelor's degrees in the United States than in Canada. Overall the Afro-Caribbean second generation in the United States achieves greater educational mobility both with respect to bachelor's degrees and with respect to all postsecondary education, than its counterpart in Canada. The comparison favors Canada at lower levels of education, so segmented assimilation might have some relevance.[7]

Urban Contexts for the Second Generation

The second-generation concentration in the immigration cities settled by their parents is quite considerable in both the United States and Canada. Although certain "gateway cities" are important for many or most immigrant groups—New York and Los Angeles in the United States; Toronto, Montreal, and Vancouver in Canada—each origin group has a distinct settlement pattern.

Intergenerational continuity is shown in table 10.2 by comparing the urban residential patterns for generational cohorts by origin group and country. Whites are concentrated in particular cities, minorities much more so. For Afro-Caribbean immigrants in the United States, the concentration in New York is extremely high (38.5 percent), but there are substantial concentrations in Miami, Washington, DC, Boston, Newark, and Fort Lauderdale (4–7 percent in each). These six cities account for 64.4 percent of Afro-Caribbean immigrants. They also account for 45.4 percent of the second generation, implying an intergenerational retention rate of 70.5 percent. For Chinese immigrants, the large concentrations are in New York (16.1 percent) and Los Angeles (17.7 percent), with significant groups in San Francisco (6.9 percent), Honolulu (4.9 percent), Washington, DC (3.5 percent), and Philadelphia (3.3 percent). These six cities account for 52.3 percent of the Chinese immigrants and 44.9 percent of the second generation. Since the retention rate is 85.8 percent, it appears that intergenerational continuity is somewhat greater for Chinese than for Afro-Caribbeans.

Afro-Caribbean immigrants in Canada are heavily concentrated in Toronto, which contains over half (52.1 percent) of all black immigrants in Canada. Most of the others are in Montreal (25.9 percent), which has both French- and English-speaking Caribbean black immigrants. The three main immigration cities contain 80.2 percent of Afro-Caribbean immigrants in Canada and nearly as many—78.8 percent—of the Afro-Caribbean second generation. The retention rate here is huge: 98.2 percent. For Chinese, the largest group is also in Toronto (41.6 percent), and although Vancouver is prominent as a "second city" for Chinese (34.2 percent), there is a significant group in Montreal (5.2 percent). The three cities contain 81.1 percent of Chinese immigrants and 71.9 percent of the Chinese second generation. The retention rate is 88.6 percent.

Intergenerational continuity of residential patterns is to some extent simply a "hometown" effect, whereby all children tend to remain in the city in which they grew up, in a bid to remain close to friends, relatives, and familiar places. However, for immigrant groups additional factors may be at work. The immigrant community is undoubtedly an attraction, as are larger numbers of coethnic persons, who represent social and economic opportunity. There may be a perception that key immigration cities are more receptive to members of one's minority group. Notably, the Afro-Caribbean second generation in the United States seems less tied to immigration cities than their counterparts in Canada do, whereas intergenerational retention rates are about the same for Chinese in the two countries. Because of the large

TABLE 10.2

Settlement Patterns of Immigrant Groups, United States and Canada by Generation, Origins and Age (Percent living in each category of city)

	Age			
	50 and over	(N)	25 to 39	(N)
UNITED STATES				
6 White immigrant cities (32.4% of white immigrants)				
New York (12.0%), Los Angeles (6.8%), Chicago (5.0%), Detroit (3.2%), Boston (3.1%), Nassau-Suffolk (2.3%)				
Native-born White Third Generation and Higher	7.2	(121,576)	8.8	(100,515)
	(Imm. Parental Generation)		(Young Sec. Generation)	
White Immigrant Origins	32.4	(7,613)	22.3	(5,050)
6 Afro-Caribbean Black immigrant cities (64.4% of Afro-Caribbean black immigrants)				
New York (38.5%), Washington (6.5%), Newark (5.2%), Fort Lauderdale (5.1%), Miami (5.0%), Boston (4.1%)				
Native-born White Third Generation and Higher	4.0	(121,576)	4.9	(100,515)
	(Imm. Parental Generation)		(Young Sec. Generation)	
Afro-Caribbean Black Immigrant Origins	64.4	(1,119)	45.4	(324)
6 Chinese immigrant cities (52.3% of Chinese immigrants)				
Los Angeles (17.7%), New York (16.1%), San Francisco (6.9%), Honolulu (4.9%), Washington (3.5%), Philadelphia (3.3%)				
Native-born White Third Generation and Higher	5.4	(121,576)	6.0	(100,515)
	(Imm. Parental Generation)		(Young Sec. Generation)	
Chinese Immigrant Origins	52.3	(940)	44.9	(158)
CANADA				
3 Immigration Cities (68.6% of all immigrants)				
Toronto (40.5%), Montreal (13.3%), Vancouver (14.8%)				
Native-born White Third Generation and Higher	22.8	(126,242)	23.6	(109,210)
White Immigrant Origins	47.3	(44,186)	44.9	(24,919)
Afro-Caribbean Black Immigrant Origins	80.2	(2,480)	78.8	(703)
Chinese Immigrant Origins	81.1	(6,624)	71.9	(892)

Note: Among Afro-Caribbean black immigrants in Canada, Toronto contains 52.1%, Montreal 25.9% and Vancouver 2.2%. Among Chinese immigrants in Canada, Toronto contains 41.6%, Vancouver 34.2% and Montreal 5.2%.

Percentages of immigrants in each city based on populations aged 50 and over.

native-born African American community, the children of black immigrants may feel at home in more U.S. cities, suggesting that the process of residential location for the second generation could be "segmented."

Educational Attainments within Urban Contexts

The educational attainments of the second generation in the urban context do not look as positive as they do in the national context. However, because of greater educational polarization in U.S. immigration cities, the impact of urban context varies cross-nationally. Educational attainments and intergenerational mobility are examined for the Afro-Caribbean and Chinese second-generation populations in table 10.3, parts a and b, respectively. For convenience, the table repeats the basic national analysis in table 10.1 and then shows the breakdown according to urban area.

For the Afro-Caribbean second generation there are two major findings. First, relative to urban contexts of concentration, the educational attainments of the second generation in the two countries are generally lower than appears in the national comparison, somewhat more so in the United States. The actual educational achievements of Afro-Caribbeans in immigration cities are as high as the national average—in the U.S. case somewhat higher— but they pale when measured against the high educational standards in the urban areas in which they live. This is particularly evident in the U.S. immigration cities, where Afro-Caribbean bachelor's degree attainment rates fall short of the mainstream average by 6.5 percentage points, though the rate of postsecondary participation by Afro-Caribbeans matches the standard in those cities. In the Canadian cities, this negative effect of urban context is evident in Toronto, where the bachelor's degree attainment rate for the Afro-Caribbean second generation is a bit lower than in the U.S. immigration cities. In Montreal, however, relative rates are higher. And outside the main immigration cities, the relative education of the Afro-Caribbean second generation is consistently higher in Canada.

The second finding is that intergenerational change in educational levels within the Afro-Caribbean community is quite high and is generally higher in the U.S. immigration cities than in the Canadian. In New York and the other five key cities of their concentration in the United States, the Afro-Caribbean second generation achieved bachelor's degrees at a rate of 49.7 percent, fully 36.7 percentage points higher than the parental generation, and reflecting a rate of intergenerational change over 20 percentage points higher than in the mainstream population. The intergenerational increase in all

TABLE 10.3A
Educational Attainment of the Afro-Caribbean Black Second Generation in the United States and Canada, National and Urban Contexts Compared.

Generation:	Percentage bachelor's degree			Percentage any post-secondary education		
	Older 50+	Younger 25-39	Difference-Mobility	Older 50+	Younger 25-39	Difference-Mobility
UNITED STATES						
National (from Table 1)						
Mainstream white	22.7	30.3	7.5	45.6	60.2	14.6
Afro-Caribbean black	16.4	38.9	22.4	31.7	70.4	38.6
Difference-Inequality	-6.3	8.6		-13.9	10.2	
6 Immigration cities						
Mainstream white	40.9	56.2	15.3	59.6	76.1	16.5
Afro-Caribbean black	13.0	49.7	36.7	28.7	76.2	47.5
(N)	(721)	(147)				
Difference-Inequality	-27.9	-6.5		-30.9	0.1	
Rest of country						
Mainstream white	22.0	28.9	6.9	45.0	59.3	14.3
Afro-Caribbean black	22.6	30.0	7.4	37.2	65.6	28.4
(N)	(398)	(177)				
Difference-Inequality	0.6	1.1		-7.8	6.3	
CANADA						
National (from Table 1)						
Mainstream white	11.1	18.7	7.6	39.7	65.9	26.2
Afro-Caribbean black	11.5	24.6	13.1	52.1	80.9	28.8
Difference-Inequality	0.4	5.9		12.4	15.0	
Toronto						
Mainstream white	20.9	32.3	11.4	51.9	74.2	22.3
Afro-Caribbean black	8.8	23.3	14.5	50.1	81.3	31.2
(N)	(1,321)	(386)				
Difference-Inequality	-12.1	-9.0		1.8	7.1	
Montreal						
Mainstream white	11.9	24.5	12.6	37.3	71.2	33.9
Afro-Caribbean black	12.0	25.2	13.2	44.0	83.5	39.5
(N)	(600)	(139)				
Difference-Inequality	0.1	0.7		6.7	12.3	
Rest of the country						
Mainstream white	10.2	16.6	6.4	39.3	64.3	25.0
Afro-Caribbean black	17.5	27.0	9.5	63.5	78.1	14.6
(N)	(559)	(178)				
Difference-Inequality	7.3	10.4		24.2	13.8	

Note on N's: For mainstream populations all N's are large; for immigrant groups, in national data N's are as in Table 1; in urban data N's for post-secondary and bachelor's degree are the same.

TABLE 10.3B

Educational Attainment of the Chinese Second Generation in the United States and Canada, National and Urban Contexts Compared.

Generation:	Percentage bachelor's degree			Percentage any post-Secondary education		
	Older 50+	Younger 25-39	Difference-Mobility	Older 50+	Younger 25-39	Difference-Mobility
UNITED STATES						
National (from Table 1)						
Mainstream white	22.7	30.3	7.5	45.6	60.2	14.6
Chinese	35.2	75.3	40.1	46.8	88.6	41.8
Difference-Inequality	12.5	45.1		1.2	28.4	
6 Immigration cities						
Mainstream white	37.2	50.1	12.9	59.8	72.9	13.1
Chinese	26.2	78.9	52.7	36.0	85.9	49.9
(N)	(492)	(71)				
Difference-Inequality	-11.0	28.8		-23.8	13.0	
Rest of the country						
Mainstream white	21.9	29	7.1	44.8	59.3	14.5
Chinese	45.1	72.4	27.3	58.7	90.8	32.1
(N)	(448)	(87)				
Difference-Inequality	23.2	43.4		13.9	31.5	
CANADA						
National (from Table 1)						
Mainstream white	11.1	18.7	7.6	39.7	65.9	26.2
Chinese	16.3	56.0	39.7	36.9	89.5	52.6
Difference-Inequality	5.2	37.3		-2.8	23.6	
Toronto						
Mainstream white	20.9	32.3	11.4	51.9	74.3	22.4
Chinese	16.6	65.9	49.3	36.7	91.7	55.0
(N)	(2,712)	(296)				
Difference-Inequality	-4.3	33.6		-20.0	16.5	
Vancouver						
Mainstream white	18.5	24.6	6.1	58.3	73.4	15.1
Chinese	15.7	50.0	34.3	38.3	89.9	51.6
(N)	(2,354)	(296)				
Difference-Inequality	-2.8	25.4		-20.0	16.5	
Rest of the country						
Mainstream white	10.2	17.3	7.1	34.3	64.8	29.4
Chinese	16.8	53.5	36.7	35.4	87.1	51.7
(N)	(1,558)	(271)				
Difference-Inequality	6.6	36.2		0.0	22.3	

Note on N's: For mainstream populations all N's are large; for immigrant groups, in national data N's are as in Table 1; in urban data N's for post-secondary and bachelor's degree are the same.

postsecondary education is also quite high. By contrast, in Toronto the inter-generational educational mobility of the Afro-Caribbean second generation with respect to bachelor's degrees is much lower and only slightly higher than for the native-born. They achieved bachelor's degrees at a rate of 23.3 percent, only 14.5 percent higher than for their parents, reflecting a rate of intergenerational educational mobility only 3 percentage points higher than the mainstream population. A parallel situation exists in Montreal.

Similarly, for the Chinese second generation, there are two major findings. First, educational attainments relative to urban contexts are quite high. However, as in the Afro-Caribbean group, they are lower than in the national comparisons, particularly in the United States. In the Chinese immigration cities in the United States, the second-generation bachelor's degree attainment rate is 28.8 percentage points above the mainstream but 45.1 percentage points above the national average. In Canada, the Chinese second-generation bachelor's degree attainment is 33.6 percentage points above the mainstream in Toronto and 25.4 percentage points above in Vancouver but 37.3 percentage points above in the national data. If overall rates of attainment of any postsecondary education are considered within urban areas, it is found that such rates are in fact extremely high in Toronto and Vancouver and actually exceed mainstream rates a bit more than for their counterparts in U.S. centers of Chinese immigration.

Second, rates of intergenerational educational change for the Chinese second generation are very high at the urban level in both countries. This is somewhat different from what is observed for the Afro-Caribbean group, for which the rate of intergenerational change particularly for bachelor's degree attainment is markedly greater in the U.S. immigration cities. Intergenerational change is substantial for Chinese in both countries and is similarly substantial for bachelor's degree attainment and for all types of postsecondary education. For the Chinese second generation in U.S. immigration cities, bachelor's degree attainment is 52.7 percentage points higher than for the immigrant generation; in Toronto it is 49.3 percentage points higher, and in Vancouver it is 34.3 percentage points higher (these Canadian figures are over lower base points). The intergenerational change figures are comparable or higher for attainment of any postsecondary education.

Conclusions

National-level data suggest that second-generation immigrant minorities, represented here by Afro-Caribbeans and Chinese, integrate equally well in the United States and Canada, based on educational attainment as a key indicator. In both countries, educational attainments among Chinese are high enough to be called spectacular, and Afro-Caribbean attainments are well above national averages for mainstream populations of the same age. The gap between the two groups is about the same in each country, and both achieve considerable upward mobility from their parents' immigrant experience.

These national findings have a number of important implications. For one, the economic difficulties faced by Afro-Caribbean and Chinese immigrants, which exist in both countries but are more pronounced in the United States, have not prevented the second generation from beginning the process of upward mobility. For another, the Afro-Caribbean group does not appear to suffer any greater disadvantage in the United States than in Canada, suggesting that any negative effect of African American poverty and disadvantage on black immigrants and their descendants—the so-called segmented-assimilation effect—is small.

This national comparison is significantly enhanced by taking account of the situation of the second generation within the urban areas in which they most often reside. Afro-Caribbean, Chinese, and other second-generation groups remain heavily concentrated within the "gateway" immigrant cities settled by their parents, and they live their lives within that context.

First, quite clearly since educational levels of the native-born in immigration cities are comparatively high relative to the national standard, particularly in the United States, the competitive position of the second generation within these cities is less favorable than in the context of the national standard. Educational levels for the Chinese second generation remain well above mainstream standards even for the areas in which they reside, but those for the Afro-Caribbean group are lower and in some major cities fall below the mainstream standard. This effect is more pronounced in the United States than in Canada, and although the mainstream population of Toronto is relatively educated compared to the national average, this is less the case in Montreal and Vancouver.

Second, urban educational polarization has been offset by considerable intergenerational mobility, particularly in the U.S. immigration cities. The impact of high education in U.S. immigration cities, compounded by relatively low levels of education for immigrants in those cities, produces lower earnings for immigrants, thereby raising the possibility of disadvantages for the second generation. However, for second-generation Afro-Caribbeans and Chinese, this possibility has not become the reality. Members of these groups not only meet but substantially surpass the rates of intergenerational educational mobility of mainstream native-born whites. In key immigration cities where immigrant educational levels are particularly low compared to the native-born, the rates of intergenerational mobility are particularly high. Essentially, the pattern of educational polarization experienced by the immigrant generation has been eliminated by the second generation. In Canada, where educational levels of native-born whites in major immigration cities are lower, the rates of intergenerational educational mobility, particularly for the black second generation, also are lower. Overall, the educational attainment of the second-generation minorities is strongly influenced by mainstream standards within the urban context, specifically by the local educational standards set by native-born whites and, to a lesser extent, by levels of education or the economic position of the parental immigrant generation.

The fact that interurban and cross-national variations in economic disadvantage within the families of these second-generation populations does not appear to reduce prospects for educational attainment is significant and requires explanation as part of a broader understanding of the processes of immigrant integration. Each city is unique in its capacity to provide educational opportunity to the children of immigrants, including its position in the national economic structure, specific institutional traditions, and other factors. However, attention should focus on the relation between immigrant families and various segments of the native-born population. Even where immigrant educational levels and economic attainments may not be high relative to the mainstream population, most of the second generation have completed at least a secondary education, and many have attained postsecondary educational qualifications as well. The educational characteristics and attitudes to education within immigrant communities may be a factor, to some extent independently of the immigrants' economic or financial situation. Corak (2008) finds that in Canada, the impact of parents' background on the educational attainment of their children is much less for immigrants than for the native-born. Even immigrants who are poor may not integrate well with the native-born poor, choosing instead to adopt their own goals and aspirations. Difficulties of immigrants' experience, translating foreign-acquired education into occupational status and resulting experiences of economic hardship and in some cases poverty within their adopted host society, may not prevent immigrants from identifying with the host society's middle class. As a result, they may encourage their children to aspire to levels of education which are conventional among the middle-class population. Economic difficulty and high educational costs definitely influence the experiences of the second generation, but in a final analysis, they do not determine it. For both the Afro-Caribbean and Chinese second generation, the interurban and cross-national differences are not governed by economic levels in the parental generation. Put otherwise, in their cases, assimilation does not appear ultimately to be segmented by economic strata or social class.

Although many of these immigrant families have been poor, the extent of their poverty is generally less than for many immigrants of Mexican and other Latin American origins in the United States, and this difference has significance for the second generation. The earnings of men in black and Chinese immigrant families are about 70 percent of the native-born average, whereas among Mexicans, the average earnings are in the range of 40–50 percent of the native-born average (Reitz 1998, 62–64). This is a substantial disparity and may mean the difference between an adequate and an inadequate platform for intergenerational mobility. For Mexicans and other Latin Americans, the educational experience of the second generation has been much less positive than for blacks and Asians (Farley and Alba 2002).

Implications for the segmented-assimilation hypothesis are enhanced by the urban-level analysis. We find that rates of educational attainment for the U.S. Afro-Caribbean second generation are highest and involved the greatest intergenerational change, within major immigration cities. This is true in comparison to other areas of the country, where the presence of the African American population is somewhat less than in the major immigration cities,[8] not just to Canada. The contrast with Toronto, where educational standards are lower and yet the Afro-Caribbean second generation does not do relatively better, is particularly striking. The cross-national comparison favors Canada mainly in the areas outside immigration cities. These findings echo those of Model (2008, 44), who notes that West Indian immigrants in the United States have somewhat better outcomes, relative to African Americans, in central cities, commenting that "this is the reverse of the pattern expected by segmentationists."

Comparative study often identifies explanatory issues not evident in studies of a single setting or context. In this case, two issues have been identified. One is the significance for the second generation of integration into social segments in the mainstream society other than ethnic groups (be they majority or minority) and of integration into particular groups based on social-class levels. A second issue is the significance of the persistence of the second generation as residents within major immigration centers and how the decisions of the second generation about urban residence affect their overall integration and status in society.

Overall, the results underscore the significance of the national and urban contexts for the second generation in the two countries. The integration of the second generation must be examined within both contexts, taking into account distinctive characteristics of urban areas and the question of mobility between them. Taken together, they help tell the story of the second generation's integration into society.

NOTES

Helpful comments from Kara Somerville and the editorial assistance of Elizabeth Thompson are acknowledged with thanks.

1. A U.S.-Canada comparison of first- and second-generation immigrants by Aydemir and Sweetman (2008) is based on the same two data sources but is directed at economic issues; nor does it include a focus on specific origin groups or on urban areas of settlement.

2. The 2003 file includes mixed-race categories, White-Asian, Black-Asian, and so on, which are recoded here as "other" and hence excluded. Alternative coding for 2003 does not affect the results.

3. The U.S. mainstream sample is 100,515; for Canada, 109,210. Samples for immigrant populations aged fifty and over are the following: for the United States, 7,613 whites, 1,119 blacks, and 3,961 Asians (including 940 Chinese), a total of 12,693; for Canada, 44,186 whites, 2,480 blacks, and 14,282 Asians (including 6,624 Chinese), a total of 60,948. Samples for the older mainstream population are 121,576 for the United States and 126,242 for Canada.

4. The possibility that the cross-national difference is partly or mostly a question of labeling is reflected in the fact that immigrants in the United States are more likely to describe their postsecondary degree as a bachelor's degree, whereas immigrants in Canada are more likely to describe their postsecondary degree as not at the bachelor's level. This difference seems unrelated to specific question wording.

5. An index of group inequality representing the relative probability of attaining high-status outcomes in each of two groups has been derived by the senior author (Reitz 1977). This index is computed from high-status proportions for each of two groups, and the relative-probability interpretation holds regardless of the absolute value of the proportions. (The index formula is a ratio of logarithms of proportions in low-status positions.) The index helps interpret the difference and ratio measures.

6. During recent decades postsecondary educational expansion has been more rapid in Canada, following earlier periods of more rapid expansion in the United States. As a result, there is greater intergenerational difference in postsecondary education for the mainstream population in Canada compared to the United States.

7. This supposition is also supported by a somewhat higher relative high-school dropout rate for second-generation Afro-Caribbeans in the United States than in Canada.

8. In our data, 15.5 percent of the population in the six black immigration cities are African Americans (third- or higher-generation black), compared to 8.5 percent of the total population in the rest of the country.

11

"I Will *Never* Deliver Chinese Food"

THE CHILDREN OF IMMIGRANTS IN THE NEW YORK METROPOLITAN LABOR FORCE

Philip Kasinitz, Noriko Matsumoto and Aviva Zeltzer-Zubida

Few arenas of second-generation incorporation are more important than the labor force. Yet in the most influential accounts of the children of immigrants the discussion of their work lives is largely speculative (i.e., Gans 1992; Portes and Zhou 1993) or aspirational—that is, based on the educational attainment and occupational ambitions of young people still in their late teens (Portes and Rumbaut 2001). This is because the data behind these discussions largely date from the early 1990s, and it was not until later in that decade that the children of post-1965 immigrants began to enter the American labor force in significant numbers. Now, however, we have the data to begin to understand the role that the new second generation plays in the U.S. economy and to see how the predictions of the earlier models are playing out.

In this chapter we examine the labor-force activity of young adults (ages eighteen to thirty-two) who have grown up in immigrant families, as seen in the Second Generation in Metropolitan New York Study. This study is based on a random telephone survey of approximately four hundred members of the second generation, broadly defined to include immigrants who arrived before age twelve (the so-called 1.5 generation), from each of five of the largest immigrant groups in the area: Dominicans, Anglophone West Indians,[1] Chinese, Russian Jews, and a composite group of Colombians, Peruvians, and Ecuadorans (hereafter "South Americans"), as well as comparably sized samples of native whites and blacks of native parentage and mainland-born Puerto Ricans. Approximately 10 percent of the respondents in each group were reinterviewed in a loosely structured life-history interview lasting two to four hours. The quotations presented here are from these interviews. (For a full descriptions of the sample and the study, see Kasinitz et al. 2008). These data allow us to move beyond hypothetical models to see how the children of immigrants are actually reshaping the labor force.

Immigrants, the Second Generation, and the Economy

The classical assimilation perspective implies that concentrations in particular occupations should be seen most strongly among recent immigrants and should diminish over time as immigrants and their descendants disperse across the labor market (Alba 1998; Alba and Nee 2003; Farley and Alba 2002; Lieberson and Waters 1988). Ethnicity, according to this view, may continue to have psychological salience for the children of immigrants for many generations, but over time it will become less crucial in shaping their labor-market opportunities. Gans's (1992) "second-generation decline" thesis builds on this notion, but with a twist, arguing that having assimilated the American disdain for "immigrant jobs," but also being seen by white Americans as "black" or "Latino," many of the darker-skinned children of immigrants may find themselves unwilling to take the sorts of jobs their parents hold while being unable to get good jobs in the mainstream economy. Other scholars stress the enduring role of ethnicity in economic life across the generations (Glazer and Moynihan 1963; Light and Gold 2000; Model 1993; Portes and Manning 1986; Waldinger 1996; Waldinger and Lichter 2003). They argue that ethnic and racial concentrations in the labor markets are not likely to disappear over time or will do so only very slowly.

The "segmented assimilation" approach (see Portes and Rumbaut 2001; Portes and Zhou 1993) argues that all these outcomes are likely—for different segments of the population. Some of the children of immigrants, particularly those culturally and phenotypically closest to the white majority, will lose their occupational distinctiveness over time. Others will reject their parents' niches but also find themselves rejected by the mainstream and experience "downward assimilation" into an increasingly multiethnic urban "underclass" (see Wilson 1996). Yet others, Portes and his collaborators argue, may seize on the social capital and the economic opportunities in the dense ethnic economies created by their parents' immigrant communities. They may thus achieve upward mobility not by assimilating but rather by acculturating only selectively and partially while staying at some distance from the broader society.

New York throws all these questions into sharp relief. The immigrant communities in which the young people we spoke to grew up were characterized by high levels of labor-force participation. Foreign-born New Yorkers are more likely to be in the labor force than are natives, and almost 16 percent of immigrant-headed households report *three* or more wage earners (as opposed to less than 9 percent of households headed by natives; American Community Survey 2006). Further, in many of these communities it is commonly assumed that ethnicity and economic opportunity are connected. Social science and everyday observation tell us that immigrants and their children are not randomly distributed in New York's local labor force. Rather, they are often concentrated in certain industries or occupations. These ethnic concentrations may be the result of a lack of other options. Yet "ethnic niches," to borrow Roger Waldinger's (1996) term, may also provide access to jobs immigrants might not have otherwise. In some cases "ethnic economies" (see Light and Gold 2000) may be creating jobs and wealth that otherwise would not exist.

Ethnic niches are most visible when they come in the form of self-employment in small businesses. Such businesses are a well-known feature of the urban landscape. New Yorkers often call a particular kind of small fruit-and-vegetable shop a "Korean store," and everyone knows that the term "Greek diner" describes the origins of the owner, not necessarily of the cuisine. However, ethnic concentrations may be equally important among workers in less entrepreneurial arenas and even in the public sector.

In our New York study the immigrant parents of the second-generation respondents were highly, indeed almost stereotypically, concentrated in certain occupations and industries—far more concentrated than immigrants in general. Most of these parents entered the New York labor force in the 1970s and early '80s, and their place in the labor market today is partially a reflection of the economy of New York in those decades. The mothers of our Chinese, Dominican, and South American respondents were heavily concentrated in manufacturing. The fathers of our Chinese respondents were very likely to work in restaurants, and almost a third of the mothers of the West Indian respondents were nurses or nurse's aides.

How do these ethnic niches get started? It is not usually the case that a group simply continues in the line of work it specialized in before migration. Although there often *is* a relationship between ethnic niches and a group's premigration attributes, it is usually indirect. For example, there is little in Korean culture or history that predisposes migrants from South Korea to small-business ownership, and few Korean store owners in New York were self-employed in Korea. However, the fact that the early Korean migrants were largely middle class and came with some capital but usually lacked the English-language skills to resume their old professions may explain their attraction to small business (D. Kim 2004; I. Kim 1982; Min 1996, 2008).

Similarly, many of the parents of our Russian Jewish respondents were once physicians, a common job for Jews in the former Soviet Union. Few were able to meet the licensing requirements to resume medical careers in the United States. However, many made use of their premigration human capital to obtain related, if lower-status, positions as dental hygienists or pharmacists. Although some of the mothers of our West Indian respondents did arrive with nursing degrees from the Caribbean, most obtained their nursing credentials after migrating. West Indians did, however, come with certain attributes that may have facilitated taking advantage of opportunities in health care. They spoke English on arrival, and they had a long tradition of women working outside the home (Kasinitz 1992). These traits may also help explain the large number of West Indian child-care workers in New York, despite the fact that few of these workers had done that sort of work in the Caribbean (Brown 2010; Waters 1999).

It is harder to explain the fact that the mothers of our Dominican, South American, and Chinese respondents worked in garment manufacturing in numbers vastly out of proportion to their share of the population. This, New York's quintessentially immigrant industry, was actually in sharp decline during the years of the immigrants' arrival. The work of Margaret Chin (2005) suggests that part of explanation may be found in the very different ways in which the Chinese and Latino garment industries are organized. The Chinese women generally work in small shops with Chinese owners, often located in or near Chinese neighborhoods. Many of these firms depend on Chinese transnational financial institutions for credit and Chinese employment agencies for workers. This ethnic enclave (see Portes 1987; Portes and Manning 1986) is to some degree autonomous from the ups and downs of the larger economy. Such enclaves may provide jobs and opportunities for capital accumulation for workers who speak no English, mothers caring for small children, and others with few options in the mainstream economy. Yet these opportunities come at a price. Wages in ethnic enclaves are usually lower than in the mainstream economy (Gilbertson 1995; Sanders and Nee 1987). Working conditions are less well regulated, and in the most extreme cases the enclave may tolerate child labor, debt peonage, and organized-crime activity (Kwong 1997). The heavy reliance on ethnic networks by workers in ethnic enclaves can also prove a liability. When the events of 9/11 shut down much of the lower Manhattan garment industry for several months in 2001 and 2002, workers long embedded in locally based ethnic networks discovered the weakness of strong ties. With their networks almost entirely within the enclave, they had difficulty accessing jobs elsewhere (Chin 2005).

By contrast, the Dominican and South American parents in the garment industry generally work for noncoethnics, usually Koreans or Jews. The formation of this ethnic niche had less to do with ethnic ties to employers than with the opportunity structure and the timing of immigration. Even though the garment industry was already in decline when these immigrants entered the New York labor force in the 1970s, the number of available workers in the ethnic groups who had traditionally staffed the industry was declining even faster. Paradoxically this created new opportunities at the entry level of a declining industry (see Waldinger 1996). As a result, for a time, the industry was segmented by age as well as by ethnicity. Middle-aged and older Puerto Ricans worked alongside a handful of even older African Americans, Italians, and Jews who held on to a few of the most highly skilled and supervisory positions. Younger workers in entry-level positions, however, were overwhelmingly recent immigrants from the Dominican Republic and South America. To what extent the children of the Puerto Rican garment workers came to avoid what was seen as "dead-end" immigrant work and to what extent they were pushed out of the industry by this immigrant competition is not entirely clear.

Whatever the combination of factors shaping the labor-market behavior of the first members of the immigrant groups, the social networks among them allowed ethnic niches to grow over time. As the vast majority of legal entrants to the United States come via provisions for family reunification, later immigrants in almost every group generally enter the country with some network connections already established. Over time, by monopolizing information about jobs and the culture of the shop floor, as well as referring new employees and thus saving employers the costs of recruiting and vetting new workers, these kinship and ethnic networks may ensure a degree of "closure" over access to jobs within an industry (Elliott 2001; Kasinitz and Rosenberg 1996; Light and Gold 2000; Mouw 2003).

Despite the huge literature on the role of ethnic economies, the overall effect they have on the labor force and on the immigrants is hard to determine, in part because of the difficulties in linking different levels of data. On the one hand, we have numerous case studies of hiring conditions and workplace dynamics in specific industries and among specific ethnic groups. Yet these rarely add up to an overall picture of the labor market. On the other hand, we have large-scale quantitative studies that give us a broad picture of the role immigrants play in the labor force but tell us little about what is actually going on at the level of hiring and investment decisions. Although the economic sociology of immigration emphasizes the importance of social networks (see Granovetter

1995 Portes 1996), much of the analysis is based on statistical concentrations in particular occupations or industries (Logan, Alba, and McNulty 1994), in which networks are invisible. This empirical literature often assumes that such concentrations are the result of ethnic network hiring—a reasonable assumption but by no means the only possible explanation. Ethnic networks may also create statistically invisible, "hidden niches," in which a group is not overrepresented in an industry (or occupation) as whole but is highly concentrated in some work sites or firms within that industry. Finally, ethnic networks may function at levels of aggregation far below the radar of most quantitative data sources. A group not particularly concentrated in "retailing," for example, may be highly concentrated in newsstands or fruit stores. And for the immigrant, the relevant social network might not be based on national identity but rather on region, religion, or even village of origin. Thus, the relevant ties might not be to fellow Chinese but to the Fujianese, not to people from the former Soviet Union but to Georgian Jews.

The Second Generation Goes to Work

How has the new second generation fared in the labor force? Its members generally do not show the high levels of labor-force participation of their immigrant parents. Indeed, none of the second-generation groups we studied was as likely to be working full-time as were native whites, as table 11.1 shows. The Chinese, Russian Jewish, and West Indian respondents were all less likely to work full-time than were either native African Americans or Puerto Ricans. This is due to the fact that second-generation groups are more likely to still be in school, whereas many of the natives in our sample came to New York postcollege, specifically for employment. All the second-generation groups were more likely to be working part-time than were the native groups—in most cases while also pursuing education.

Perhaps more important, however, is the fact that few second-generation respondents were neither working nor in school full-time. The percentage of Chinese, Russian Jewish, and South American respondents in this category is lower than that of native whites. The percentage of West Indians and Dominicans is higher than that of native whites but considerably lower than that of Puerto Ricans or native African Americans. Indeed, with the exception of Dominicans, the second-generation groups resemble each other more than they do the native minorities on this measure.

How does the second generation enter the labor force? They often start work early, usually before finishing their education, often before the legal

TABLE 11.1
Labor Force Status by Group

	Employed Full-Time	Employed Part-Time	Attending School Full-Time and Not Working	Neither in School Nor Working
Chinese	38.9%	23.2%	28.2%	9.7%
Dominican	50.3%	17.4%	11.8%	20.6%
Russian Jews	41.7%	24.6%	24.8%	8.9%
South American	57.1%	16.7%	15.0%	11.2%
West Indian	47.5%	17.9%	19.2%	15.5%
Native Black	49.3%	12.2%	9.4%	29.1%
Native White	63.4%	14.6%	9.1%	12.9%
Puerto Rican	50.9%	13.8%	10.1%	25.2%

minimum age for most work. Kin and friends most commonly provide initial entry into the labor force, a fact that clearly advantages those whose kin, friends, and ethnic group are well embedded in the labor force. Early entrance into the paid labor force has little effect on adult incomes. In only one of the groups we studied, Dominicans, did having worked in high school have a statistically significant association with higher income as an adult, once age and gender were controlled for, and then only mildly so. In no group did it lower income. Given the number of hours many students were working, it is also interesting that in no group did working while in high school have any statistically significant effect on eventual educational attainment.

Access to jobs while very young was easiest for those whose relatives owned businesses. Some, such as the twenty-three-year-old West Indian whose mother owned a small janitorial service or the twenty-eight-year-old Dominican man whose father owned a gas station, reported how "helping out" in the family business as a teenager made them feel grown up and responsible and how it inspired them to want one day to have their own business, where they can avoid "dealing with bosses and managers." More often, however, working with kin was remembered as a burden and a cause of tension within the family. Even successful family businesses were seen as robbing young people of their independence and childhoods and involving them in family fights and disputes with co-workers long before they felt ready for such adult roles. Less-successful businesses were remembered even more bitterly. One twenty-four-year-old Dominican recalled hating being expected to work in her aunt's perennially struggling restaurant: "I speak English, I should do something better." Or as one twenty-year-old Chinese college student explained,

RESPONDENT: My father, he is always working [in a restaurant]. Never home. My mom works like six days a week, and my dad works six. . . . Don't think he likes it. It is just to make money, pay my tuition, my brother's tuition, pay the bills.

INTERVIEWER: Would you ever work that job?

RESPONDENT: NO! Too much running around. My parents work long, long hours. I want to work nine to five! I guess it's all right for someone with his level of education. For them it's good, but not for me. I would not want to do it.

In many cases, particularly among the Chinese respondents, parents' often stereotypically ethnic small businesses embarrassed their children. Few of the children expressed any interest in taking over these businesses, nor did many parents want them to. Most seemed to share the sentiment of the Chinese restaurateur's son who, when asked if there was a job he would never take, answered, "I will *never* deliver Chinese food."

Even second-generation respondents with very limited job prospects often shared this disdain for the "immigrant jobs" held by their parents. One twenty-four-year-old Dominican woman, who was unemployed when interviewed and whose prospects were limited by an arrest record, noted,

RESPONDENT: My mom, she didn't have papers. So she was working under the table, cleaning, ironing for people. That's like an Hispanic thing, you know? It was a way of getting through rough times.

INTERVIEWER: Would you ever see yourself working that kind of job?

RESPONDENT: I *never* say "never," but . . . I wouldn't want to. Because I was raised here, you know? I speak very good English! So, I don't know. . . .

How did the second generation get their current jobs? Table 11.2 shows how the respondents obtained the job they held at the time of the interview. The data make a strong case for Granovetter's "strength of weak ties" (1983). In every second-generation group, and indeed in every native group, friends were the most common way respondents heard about their current job, far more common than relatives. Indeed, the Chinese and the Russian Jews, the groups with the strongest ethnic economies, were actually the *least* likely to get jobs through kin networks and the most likely to use the formal, bureaucratized route of school-placement programs. Native whites were the most likely to get jobs through former employers and co-workers, although in no group was this method very important. Interestingly, native African

TABLE 11.2
Method of Finding Current Job

	Relative	Friend	Co-worker or previous employer	School placement	Ad	Labor union or state emp. agency	Private emp. agency	Other
Chinese	9.0	32.7	2.9	19.1	15.7	1.2	8.2	11.1
Dominican	16.0	33.9	4.8	9.1	15.6	1.5	3.6	15.5
Russian Jews	8.2	34.3	2.0	15.8	18.7	1.4	4.3	15.3
South American	11.3	40.7	4.0	9.6	16.8	1.8	4.9	10.9
West Indian	11.5	32.5	3.0	13.5	15.9	1.7	7.3	14.6
Native Black	11.9	34.3	1.4	8.6	19.9	4.0	5.2	14.8
Native White	11.6	29.1	6.7	9.7	17.6	1.2	7.8	16.2
Puerto Rican	18.5	31.5	3.4	6.9	14.7	2.9	4.9	17.2

Americans were among the least reliant on social networks and the most likely to have simply answered an ad. They were also the most likely to seek jobs via labor unions and governmental employment agencies, although the numbers in this category were quite small. In general, throughout the interviews, native African Americans were the most wary of informal job-search procedures, the most concerned about office politics and getting along with bosses, and the most comfortable with formal procedures and cut-and-dried business relationships. In general, the group with the greatest, and most justified, fear of discrimination in hiring and of on-the-job racism is the one least likely to put faith in social networks and most likely to see the networking of other groups as unfair, exclusionary, and illegitimate (see also S. Smith 2007). Paradoxically, however, this has not kept African Americans from being among the most ethnically concentrated groups.

Looking at where the second-generation respondents were employed, one is struck by how much more the second-generation groups look like other young adults in the New York labor market then they do like their immigrant parents. About two-thirds of the second-generation groups were working in retail and wholesale trade (which includes restaurants) and business services (which includes many clerical workers). Manufacturing employment, which plays a huge role for the immigrant generation, especially in the Chinese, Dominican, Russian Jewish, and South American groups, was negligible among all the second-generation groups. In general, the second generation is far less concentrated in terms of industry of employment than are their immigrant parents.

In table 11.3 we use an index of dissimilarity to compare the industry distribution of each second-generation group with that of the same-sex parent.

This index measures the evenness with which different groups are distributed across the industries and asks what share would have to be moved to produce a completely even distribution (see Duncan and Duncan 1955). Chinese, Dominican, and South American women were unlikely to work in the same industries as their mothers. Russian Jewish men were likely to leave the niches of their fathers. In all these cases, social capital built up out of connections in given industries seems to be playing little part in the second generation's job choices. Natives were generally far more likely to work in the same industries as their parents. The most notable exception is the case of second-generation Dominican men, whose distribution was quite like that of their fathers. This stands in sharp contrast to the pronounced intergenerational change between second-generation Dominican women and their immigrant mothers. Given the low-paying jobs held by many of the Dominican fathers, this may be a case of second-generation decline (or, more accurately, stagnation). Yet the contrast between men and women in this group adds another dimension to the story, particularly in light of the fact that Dominican women also consistently outpace Dominican men in education (see N. Lopez 2003).

The other group that looks remarkably like its parents is the West Indian one. As this is the group that most resembles African Americans phenotypically, culturally, and residentially, we may be seeing another case of second-generation decline, or at least stasis. However, before seizing on this finding, we should also remember that the English-speaking parents of the West Indian respondents were, in fact, the least segregated by industry from the rest of the labor force.

Second-Generation Earnings

Why does the second generation tend to shun its parents' occupations and ethnic niches? One simple answer is that, more often than not, wages, working conditions, and opportunities for advancement are better in the mainstream economy.

Given the age of our sample, it is not surprising that many respondents in all ethnic groups had relatively modest earnings. Being older is a consistently strong predictor of higher earnings. Across all the groups, women were working an average of about four hours less per week than were men, who averaged around thirty-eight hours per week. Despite the fact that women outperform men at school, they were earning less among all groups except South Americans and Dominicans.

TABLE 11.3
Index of Dissimilarity for Industrial Sector
Comparing groups with same gender parent

	Chinese	Dominican	RJ	SA	WI	NB	NW	PR
Male w/Dad	39.5	18.4	38.5	29.1	17.9	22.5	22.7	22.9
Female w/Mom	50.3	41.3	27.1	46.3	20.6	20.5	19.6	26.7

TABLE 11.4
OLS Regression of Logged Weekly Income: Second-Generation Immigrant and Native Groups (Entire Sample and Those Who Grew Up in New York City), Aged 18-32, New York Metropolitan Area

	Entire Sample		Raised in NYC	
	b	s.e.	b	s.e.
Chinese	.091	.078	.209*	.086
Dominican	-.218***	.049	-.046	.058
Russian Jews	.159	.104	.303**	.111
South American	-.242***	.055	-.109	.064
West Indian	-.209***	.044	-.082	.054
Native Black	-.270***	.034	-.139**	.047
Puerto Rican	-.291***	.036	-.109*	.048
Controls:				
Gender (Female=1)	-.134***	.025	-.110***	.029
Age	.058***	.003	.058***	.004
Intercept	.502		4.867	
Adjusted R^2	.246		.221	
	n=1,443		n=974	

*	$p < .05$
**	$p < .01$
***	$p < .001$

However, as table 11.4 shows, once age and gender are controlled, the earnings of the Chinese and Russian Jewish second-generation respondents who were working full-time are not significantly different from those of native whites. The West Indians, South Americans, and Dominicans all had hourly incomes significantly *less* than those of native whites—but also higher than those of native African Americans and Puerto Ricans (with Dominicans being the closest to the native minority groups). The differences between the black and Latino second-generation groups and native blacks are also significant.

The comparison to native whites is, however, somewhat misleading. Many highly educated native whites come to New York after finishing college, often elite colleges, to start careers. Their presence skews the native white educational and earnings levels upward. Postcollegiate in-migrants constitute about one-third of our native white sample and slightly under 10 percent of the native black sample, but they make up a much lower portion of the second-generation groups and the Puerto Ricans. If we look only at those respondents who spent their high-school years in the New York metropolitan area, the picture changes considerably, as we see in the second set of columns of table 11.4. In this model the Chinese and Russian second-generation respondents earned significantly *more* than native whites. Although the West Indians, Dominicans, and South Americans still earned slightly less, the differences between them and the native whites are no longer significant. Nevertheless, native African Americans and Puerto Ricans continue to earn significantly less than whites do.

Of course, wages tell only part of the story. The jobs the respondents held vary greatly in their potential for long-term advancement. The large concentrations in some groups in retailing and clerical positions are a cause for some concern and suggest that the earnings gap between the groups may widen over time. However, at least so far, there is little evidence of "second-generation decline."[2]

And what of the notion that some second-generation members will avoid downward assimilation by staying closely tied to their parents' ethnic economy? One advantage of the New York second-generation study is that we collected data on the ethnic composition of the workforce and the management in the respondent's particular workplace. This allows us to examine the issue without inferring ideas about the work sites from the ethnic composition of the industries. Examining these data, we see that there is no group in which a majority of individuals were working alongside coethnics. As table 11.5 shows, native blacks were in fact the most segregated on the job, but even among them, only about 40 percent were working in places where most of their co-workers are African Americans, though just over 60 percent said they worked in predominantly *black* (that is African American, Caribbean, or African) work sites. About a quarter of the African Americans reported that their supervisors are also African American. This is particularly striking in light of native blacks' reliance on formal, and theoretically less ethnically biased, job-search methods and their reluctance to resort to social networks. It suggests the continuing high level of racial discrimination operating in the low-wage job market (see Pager 2007).

The Chinese were the second-generation group most likely to work with coethnics. About a third of employed Chinese respondents reported that

TABLE 11.5
Co-ethnic Employment across Second Generation Groups

	Sup&cwr same eth	Cwr same eth	Sup&cwr same race	Cwr same race
Chinese	27.0	32.0	28.8	39.2
Dominicans	6.4	21.0	18.6	53.1
Russian Jews	7.7	22.4	71.3	82.1
South Americans	2.1	9.8	14.2	43.4
West Indians	7.1	24.5	24.5	56.8
Native Blacks	23.0	40.3	27.2	60.0
Native Whites	14.8	23.5	74.7	81.9
Puerto Ricans	14.6	29.1	16.3	47.2

most of their co-workers are Chinese, and 27 percent were working in jobs where both their supervisor and most of their co-workers are Chinese (40 percent reported that most of their co-workers are Asian, suggesting considerable mixing between Koreans, Vietnamese, and Chinese in some workplaces). Although the Hispanic groups were far less likely to work with coethnics in the narrow sense (i.e., South Americans with South Americans, Dominicans with Dominicans), they were more likely to work with fellow Hispanics, although only among Dominicans did a majority work in a predominantly Hispanic work site.

Why does the ethnic economy play such a small role for the second generation? Part of the answer may be that such jobs often do not pay very well. When we compared the weekly earnings of those who were working in jobs surrounded by coethnics with those who were not, the latter situation yielded higher pay for *every* group except, predictably, for native whites. The differences for most groups were relatively small. However, as figure 11.1 shows, among native African Americans and the Chinese, the differences were both statistically significant and theoretically revealing. Native African Americans working in predominantly African American work sites earned the *least* of any group in the sample. By contrast, native African Americans working in racially integrated workplaces earned almost exactly the same as the overall sample median—more than any of the Hispanic groups or the West Indians.

Chinese respondents working in mixed, usually predominantly white, workplaces reported the *highest* earnings of any group—higher than native whites. Chinese in largely Chinese work sites, by contrast, earned well below the overall average, about the same as Puerto Ricans. Some of the Chinese working in coethnic work sites may be young people at their first jobs or, as Zhou (1992) suggests, women caring for small children. Yet the negative

FIGURE 11.1

FIGURE 11.1
Weekly Income by Co-Ethnic Workplace

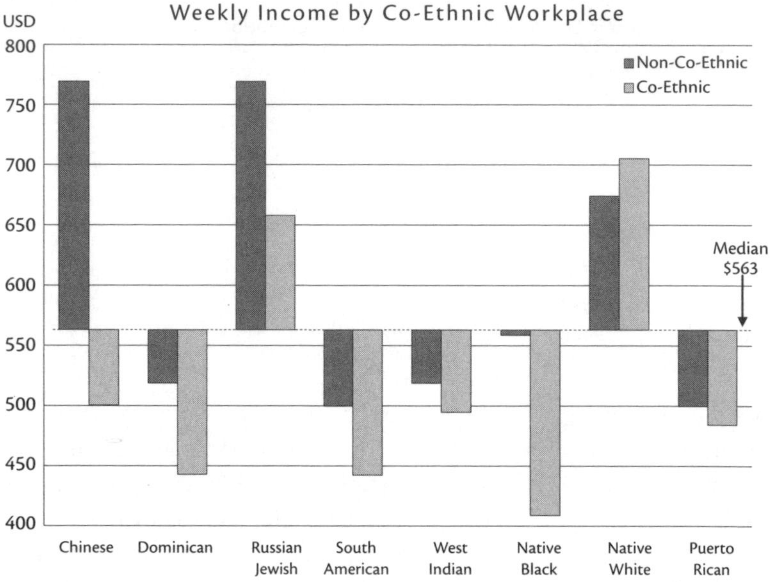

effect of working in coethnic work sites remains significant even after controlling for age and gender.

The negative effect of working in coethnic or coracial work sites is not surprising for native minorities. There has always been good reason to think that workplace segregation is a bad thing for African Americans and Puerto Ricans. The negative finding for members of the second generation is more striking. Many people have pointed to New York's Chinese as an example of a successful immigrant ethnic enclave (Zhou 1992), and Chinese and Russian parents both have high rates of self-employment. Yet the children from these backgrounds have found large payoffs by leaving the ethnic economy and joining the mainstream. (We should note that in a recent revisiting of the ethnic-enclave concept with particular attention to Cubans in Miami, Portes also found enclave employment to be largely a one-generation phenomenon, with the second generation anxious to find opportunities elsewhere; see Portes and Shafer 2007.) Of course, wages are only part of the story. Working conditions and benefits are also better in the mainstream economy. For example, half of the Chinese working in mixed settings reported receiving health insurance from their employer, in contrast to only 28 percent in coethnic workplaces.

Members of the second generation generally have an accurate understanding of where career opportunities lie for them in the New York economy. Finance, for example, was the glamour sector for many young adults in late-1990s New York. As one NYU graduate, the daughter of a Chinatown store owner, put it,

> I always knew I wanted to work for J. P. Morgan. I don't know why. I like the name. I thought, "J. P. Morgan, yeah, that sounds like an institution that has been around for a long time, and it's an old standard of Wall Street. And if I am going to work on Wall Street, I kind of like that name." And I like Goldman Sachs. So I went in, without really researching it. I went to one of those headhunters and told her, "I want to apply for a job at J. P. Morgan."

Asked if her father had ever suggested she take over his relatively successful business, the respondent laughed and commented, "He doesn't hate me that much."

Victoria Malkin's ethnography of retail clerks (2004), conducted for this study, documents the more typical experience of New York's second generation. Malkin did participant observation among retail workers in two Manhattan branches of a regional housewares chain. The largely twenty-something workforce she studied included Dominicans, South Americans, Asians, and West Indians, as well as native blacks, Puerto Ricans, and the occasional white migrant from another part of the United States. Most were high-school graduates, and many had some college or other post-high-school training, although few had four-year degrees. The managers were almost exclusively native whites.

By almost any standard, these were bad jobs. The hourly wages were at best only slightly higher than what might be available in the ethnic economy. Entry-level employees got the legal minimum wage and were given small raises thereafter. The stores were unionized, theoretically entitling full-time employees to health insurance and a modest package of other benefits after they had worked for a set period. Yet almost everyone started as a part-time worker, making them ineligible for union membership or benefits. These "part-time" jobs actually required full-time availability, as the store frequently changed the workers' hours depending on customer demand. These unpredictable schedules wreaked havoc with the workers' attempts to pursue further education or vocational training. During slow periods, full-time employees struggled to get enough hours to maintain full-time status—and keep their benefits. Sometimes they could only do this by working split shifts—working a few hours in the morning then returning at busier times in the late afternoon or evening. Since most lived too far from the stores to return home between shifts, this meant that workers were paid for six or eight hours for what was, in effect, a ten- or twelve-hour day.

The workers soon realized that they had little chance for advancement. At best, they could hope to become supervisors on the shop floor, earning a few dollars an hour over minimum wage. Unlike the practice of the larger department stores of previous decades, managers were generally hired out of college-placement offices, and the stores rarely provided job ladders leading from the shop floor to the executive office. Most workers had few illusions about their prospects with the firm. This was only a job, one of many they would hold in their life. The company made little commitment to them, and they made little commitment to the company.

Yet, even here, most of these workers preferred this job to the blue-collar and ethnic-economy jobs held by their parents. They liked working in the middle of a city and having contact with a wide variety of people. Many had grown up in black, Latino, or Asian neighborhoods and attended overwhelmingly black or Latino public schools, so their co-workers were the most diverse social group they had ever been part of. Their friendship and dating networks expanded accordingly. They learned about different parts of the city and different ways of doing things from each other and came to share an interest in panethnic, youth-oriented popular music and fashion. Unlike ethnic-economy workers, the young clerks had to dress neatly in low-cost, knock-off versions of high-fashion clothes. Although this strained their already tight budgets, they enjoyed it and took full advantage of the sales and changing styles of the stores around them, discount and chic. Few envisioned doing this sort of work for long, but it was also not seen as a ghetto or an enclave—and it was seen as a step up from their parents' parochial lives.

And what of the young people who do work in the ethnic economy? Some scholars suggest that young people would do well to avail themselves of work in these niches when their parents have been successful in them (Bankston and Zhou 2002; Zhou and Logan 1989). Further, some of the young people we spoke to had actually worked in specifically second-generation niches that constitute in effect bridges between the ethnic and mainstream economies. For example, we spoke to one second-generation Dominican man who worked as an insurance agent for largely immigrant-owned Dominican businesses, and several Russian and Chinese second-generation respondents had found lucrative niches as real-estate agents, accountants, and attorneys for largely immigrant clienteles. Some second-generation young people have even sought to build on the transnational side of contemporary immigrant communities, working in the American branches of corporations based in their parents' home country or for American companies doing business there. Yet, although such positions, requiring a knowledge of both the immigrant ethnic economy and the world of mainstream institutions, would seem a natural for the second generation, those who do this sort of work are few and far between. Dae Young Kim's (2006) parallel study of Koreans, for whom the large ethnic economy provides even more opportunities for second-generation professionals, also found fewer young people than expected in these "bridge" positions. And although many Korean Americans did work for Korean multinational corporations for periods, most found they were unable to make careers there. Unused to the hierarchy and sexism of Korean corporate life, young people also found that, to their surprise, they were confronted with glass ceilings because they were regarded as Americans (see D. Kim 2004).

Of the second-generation groups we studied, the Chinese were the most likely to work among coethnics, though not all these firms were in Portes-style ethnic enclaves. Some of the Chinese respondents were working in geographically dispersed Chinese small businesses—for example, suburban Chinese restaurants or small stores in native minority neighborhoods—that resemble the "middleman minority" model more than a true enclave (Bonacich 1973; Min 1996). Others occupied what Zeltzer-Zubida has called "hidden ethnic niches," where Chinese do not predominate in a particular industry (e.g., finance) or even a particular firm but do make up most of the workforce of a particular work site (Zeltzer-Zubida 2004). Yet most of the roughly one-third of our Chinese respondents working with largely Chinese co-workers appear to have been working in what one could reasonably describe as an ethnic enclave. They were in geographically concentrated firms, in which not only were the workers Chinese, but so were the supervisors and owners, as well as many of the suppliers and customers.

In many ways, the situation of these young people resembles that of their parents. They were more likely to be immigrants themselves—a higher share arrived in the United States as young children, as opposed to being born here—as compared to those in other work sites. They were also younger and more likely to be male. Many were finding their first job within the enclave and may eventually move out. They were also less educated than the other Chinese respondents. Indeed, the ethnic economy may be providing a safety net for the least well-educated members of the Chinese second generation, especially those whose education was interrupted by their migration, as well as for those who face other problems getting ahead in the mainstream economy. Second-generation Chinese men in the ethnic economy were more likely to have been arrested than those in the mainstream economy, though the share is still not high—13.8 percent of the men working in coethnic settings, as opposed to 8.7 percent in ethnically mixed sites.

As bad as the ethnic-economy jobs are, the young people who hold them might be significantly worse off if the Chinese ethnic economy did not exist (see D. Kim 2006). Indeed the enclave may account for some of the Chinese success compared to other groups, as it provides opportunities for young people with significant labor-market disadvantages. Members of other groups with similar disadvantages (particularly native African Americans and Puerto Ricans) are often outside the labor market altogether. However, in contrast to what previous theories have implied, the benefits of the ethnic enclave go primarily to the worst-off members of the second generation, not to the upwardly mobile. Although ethnic enclaves and other forms of ethnic economies have clearly been useful for many members of the immigrant generation, our findings offer little support for the idea that the ethnic enclave will be a significant source of upward mobility for their children. For the children of Chinatown, "moving up" generally means "moving out."

Joining the Mainstream, for Better . . . and Worse

The second generation has largely been assimilated into the mainstream economy. The labor-force participation of its members resembles that of other New Yorkers their age, and there is little about their jobs to distinguish them as the children of immigrants. Some groups, of course, tend toward certain occupations and industries, but these tendencies are far less pronounced than among their immigrant parents. Rarely do parents pass jobs or businesses down to their children, and doing so is most common among the least successful. Even the Chinese ethnic enclave functions more like a safety net than a springboard.

The work lives of the second generation also provide little evidence of second-generation decline into an "underclass" marked by persistent poverty and unemployment. The economic fate of the second generation seems tied more closely to the overall economy than it is either to protective ethnic enclaves or to a marginal underclass. This result seems more consistent with Alba and Nee's (2003) guardedly optimistic account of assimilation into a reshaped mainstream than with any notion of downward assimilation. Of course, race continues to matter, and black and Latino second-generation youth do not close the gap with native whites in a single generation. Who ever imagined they would? However, when comparing the children of immigrants to black and Latino natives, even those second-generation groups who face the highest levels of discrimination still outperform members of native minority groups in the labor market.

Why are these results different from those that the segmented-assimilation model would predict? For one thing, the labor market may not be as hour-glass shaped as earlier accounts have suggested (Alba 2008, 2009). Yes, manufacturing has been in marked decline for decades, unionization is decreasing, and many of America's best-paying working-class jobs have disappeared. But the service sector is not without ladders of upward mobility, particularly for those who manage to get at least some post-high-school education. And this may be especially true in cities such as New York, whose diverse economy was never as dependent on manufacturing as was true in many midwestern cities. In addition, New York's history as a gateway for immigrants, its heritage of ethnic diversity, and its many institutions dedicated to immigrant mobility may have made it a particularly welcoming environment for the children of immigrants. It is a tough and competitive town, but one rich in second chances, particularly to obtain educational credentials (Attewell and Lavin 2007).

It should also be noted that much of the empirical work inspired by the segmented-assimilation model is based on the Children of Immigrants Longitudinal Study (CILS). One of this study's great advantages is that it is, in fact, longitudinal, following young people from their early teens into their midtwenties. However, although this is a strength, it also presents a practical problem. The most theoretically influential products of the study (Portes and Rumbaut 2001) were published after only the second wave of CILS interviews—that is, based on data collected when most respondents were still in their late teens, before any significant indication of adult labor-force status was available. This problem is compounded by the fact that the second generation, like many native minority youth, tends to complete education later than native whites do. When the third wave of CILS data did become available (see Portes 2006) support for the downward-assimilation trajectory turned out to be more modest than originally suggested.

There may also be a historical dimension to the contrast in findings. The segmented-assimilation and downward-assimilation scenarios were both originally suggested in the early 1990s—near the end of a long recession. By contrast, our data—and the third wave of the CILS data—were collected between mid-1998 and 2001, near the top of a significant economic expansion. Of course, this raises the question of how our second-generation respondents have fared in the recession of the late 2000s. Only time will tell whether the setbacks they have no doubt suffered will be permanent or, for that matter, whether more of them will fall back on the ethnic-enclave safety net if hard times continue.

Finally, we should remember that assimilation is not the same thing as upward mobility. There are many reasons to be concerned about what the future will hold for the young people we studied. Many were working in relatively low-paid retail and service-sector industries that are heavily reliant on young part-time workers. Although such jobs may impart more skills and work habits than is generally understood, they may not translate into better-paying positions as workers get older. Yet these are problems facing all young working-class New Yorkers, including many native whites. Thus, in contrast to the situation in western Europe, little about the labor-market experience of the second generation in New York seems attributable to the fact that their parents are immigrants. Whereas immigrant niches often shaped their parents lives, it is the mainstream economy that shapes the lives of the second generation.

NOTES

Much of the material in this chapter also appears in Kasinitz, Mollenkopf, Waters, and Holdaway, *Inheriting the City: The Children of Immigrants Come of Age* (Cambridge, MA: Harvard University Press, 2008). Professor Kasinitz is thankful to his collaborators in that effort. Responsibility for the material in this chapter, however, is ours. We also wish to thank Richard Alba, Mary Waters, and the two anonymous reviewers for extremely helpful comments.

1. In this chapter "West Indian" or "West Indies" refers to English-speaking, former British colonies of the Caribbean, which became independent nations between 1962 and 1980.

2. Controlling for education yields almost the same result. Once education is controlled, the differences between West Indians, South Americans, and Dominicans and native whites disappear (Russian Jews and Chinese continue to earn more than native whites). The gap between native whites and native African Americans and Puerto Ricans, however, remains significant.

IV

In Closing

COMPARATIVE STUDIES

12

Black Identities and the Second Generation

AFRO-CARIBBEANS IN BRITAIN AND THE UNITED STATES

Nancy Foner

It is a sociological truism that the place where the children of immigrants grow up and live shapes how they come to see themselves and others. Context matters. This is obvious. What is not obvious, however, is just *how* context matters. Although we may expect to find contrasts among the second generation who live in different countries, we cannot always predict how they will differ. Nor are the structural differences among receiving societies that influence identity formation always immediately apparent. Careful cross-national comparisons allow us to appreciate the complex, sometimes subtle, and often surprising ways that the social, political, and economic milieu of different receiving societies leads to specific responses and experiences among immigrant children in particular groups.

The relationship between the national context and second-generation identities becomes particularly clear when we consider the experiences of black immigrants in Europe and the United States. Within the United States, black immigrants are often viewed as a special case because their African ancestry appears to be an uncrossable boundary and because they and their descendants are unable to avoid being viewed through the prism of race (Alba 2005). Is this situation an example of American exceptionalism and the particular legacy of slavery and segregation in the United States? How does the presence of the African American community—and the place of African Americans in the nation's ethnoracial hierarchy—make the American context special? And are there any parallels in Britain? How, in other words, does the racial context in Britain and the United States matter for the children of immigrants who are defined as "black"? This chapter explores these issues by looking at the Afro-Caribbean second generation in Britain and the United States—in particular, in London and New York City.

It is a commonplace in the social sciences to say that race is a social and cultural construction, but this statement is the beginning of an inquiry rather than the end of it (Fredrickson 1997, 78). A cross-national perspective highlights just how this process of construction takes place—as well as the ramifications for other aspects of the lives of the Afro-Caribbean second generation. Comparative studies, as Reinhard Bendix (1964, 17) has written, "increase the 'visibility' of one structure by comparing it with another." They bring into sharper focus the factors determining racial and ethnic identities that may be taken for granted if the second generation in only a single setting is considered in isolation.

In my earlier writings comparing first-generation Afro-Caribbean immigrants in London and New York, I emphasized the importance of the presence (or absence) of a large disadvantaged native black community for identity formation (Foner 1985, 1998a, 1998b, 2003, 2005). For immigrants from the Anglophone Caribbean, part of the adjustment to life in the United States involves coming to terms with America's culture of race and learning that identification with African Americans is something that, at least on some occasions, they wish to avoid. This dynamic is absent in Britain, where post–World War II immigrants of African ancestry and their descendants are generally thought of as *the* nation's blacks. This has drawbacks for Afro-Caribbeans in London, who cannot profit from alliances with a large native black community or piggyback on gains won by African Americans. At the same time, the racial system in London is less rigid than in New York, where Afro-Caribbeans find themselves more segregated residentially and less likely to intermarry and socialize with whites.

What happens among the second generation, those who were born and raised abroad and who have spent little, if any, time in the Caribbean? Like their immigrant parents, Afro-Caribbean youth are deeply affected by the structure of race relations in Britain and the United States, although, as one might expect, their experiences do not replicate those of the immigrant generation. Once again, what emerges as critical in the New York context is the large native black population—and the place of African Americans in the city's (and nation's) ethnoracial hierarchy—which affects the second generation's identity choices, social relations, and opportunities in a way that is markedly different for their cousins in London. It even influences scholarship about the Afro-Caribbean second generation, which has taken different directions in Britain and the United States. Being black, to put it another way, has a different meaning among the second generation depending on the national context and has different implications for their everyday lives.

A few preliminary comments about population numbers and terminology are necessary. By the beginning of the twenty-first century, both Britain and the United States had substantial Afro-Caribbean populations. In Britain, a massive immigration from the early 1950s to the mid-1960s brought hundreds of thousands of colonial Caribbean migrants to the metropole. In 1951, the Caribbean population in Britain was tiny, only 27,000, almost two-thirds of them immigrants (Peach 1998). Forty years later the black Caribbean population (including the British-born) in Britain had grown to 500,000, and by the time of the 2001 census, the figure was more than 560,000. Over time, the proportion of those born in the Caribbean has steadily declined, which is not surprising given that the cycle of primary immigration from the Caribbean was over by the early 1970s (Peach 1998). Since then, the Afro-Caribbean population has grown through increases in the British-born. By 1991, only a little more than half the British African Caribbean population (265,000) had been born in the Caribbean, and this proportion has continued to fall.

In the United States, the large-scale migration from the Anglophone Caribbean in the post–World War II period was made possible by the 1965 amendments to the Immigration and Nationality Act and has continued apace since then, with no signs of stopping. In 2000, the Jamaican foreign-born population in the United States—Jamaicans are the largest Anglophone Caribbean nationality group there, as in Britain—stood at 513,000; together with immigrants from Trinidad and Tobago, Guyana, Barbados, the Bahamas, Dominica, St. Vincent, and Antigua-Barbuda, the figure was about 1.1 million (Camarota and McArdle 2003). Reliable estimates about the number of the second generation in the United States with parents born in the Anglophone Caribbean are not available, but it seems reasonable to assume that adding them would bring the figure to over 1.5 million.

London and New York are the centers of the Anglophone Caribbean population in their respective countries. Close to 350,000 Afro-Caribbeans (including the British-born) lived in London in 2001, or three-fifths of the national total. In the United States, about half the immigrants from the English-speaking Caribbean counted in the 2000 census resided in New York State, the overwhelming majority in New York City. Taken together, immigrants from the English-speaking Caribbean are now the largest immigrant group in New York City, numbering about half a million. As for the second generation, in 2000, some 317,000 non-Hispanic black native-born New Yorkers had a parent born abroad, presumably most in the Caribbean (Mollenkopf, Olson, and Ross 2001).[1]

Throughout this chapter, I use the term *Afro-Caribbean* to refer to immigrants and their descendants of African ancestry from the Anglophone Caribbean, including the mainland nations of Guyana and Belize. In the U.S. context, this use is somewhat unusual, for the term is frequently used to encompass the sizable number of people of African ancestry with roots in the Hispanic Caribbean and Haiti, whom I do not include here. I have chosen to use Afro-Caribbean as a way to emphasize African ancestry—quite a number of Caribbean immigrants, in particular from Guyana and Trinidad, are of East Indian descent and confront a different set of identity issues—and because in Britain the term *West Indian* is out of favor.

New York: Will the Second Generation Become African American?

Whether in London or New York, second-generation Afro-Caribbeans, like their parents, must cope with living in cities (and societies) where they experience prejudice and discrimination on account of being labeled black. Although the term *black* was widely used in Britain in the 1970s and 1980s to include people of South Asian as well as African and Caribbean origin, in recent years British usage has moved in the American direction to refer to people of African ancestry (see Alexander 1996, 2002; Baumann 1996; Modood et al. 1997; Song 2003; Sudbury 2001; Toulis 1997).

If there has been a terminological coming-together, so to speak, between Britain and the United States in defining *black,* there is still a profound difference related to demographics in the two countries that has critical implications for Afro-Caribbeans, whatever their generation. In Britain, *blacks* may now be primarily evocative of people of African origin (Modood et al. 1997), but they are immigrants or descendants of immigrants from the Caribbean and Africa who arrived in the second half of the twentieth century. In 2001, about 10 percent of London's population was black; 4.8 percent were of Caribbean origin, 5.3 percent of African origin, and 0.8 percent of other origin. In the United States, *black* mainly means African Americans—whose ancestors were brought to the country as slaves many years ago and who represent the bulk of the black population in the nation as a whole as well as in New York City. In 2000, one out of four New Yorkers was non-Hispanic black—about two-fifths of the non-Hispanic black New Yorkers were foreign-born or the children of the foreign-born.[2]

Another important difference needs to be noted: the extraordinary residential segregation of Afro-Caribbean New Yorkers from non-Hispanic whites compared to the situation in London. In 2000, the index of dissimilarity between those of Afro-Caribbean ancestry and non-Hispanic whites in the New York metropolitan area was a remarkable 83 (100 represents total segregation between the two groups) (Logan and Deane 2003; see also Crowder and Tedrow 2001). In London, despite the fairly dense concentration of Afro-Caribbeans in particular areas and particular streets, there is not the same pattern of residential segregation. Ceri Peach's analysis of the 1991 census found that the index of dissimilarity between black Caribbeans and whites at the enumeration district level (the smallest census unit) in London was 54 and at the ward level, 49; the highest proportion that Afro-Caribbeans formed of any ward in London was 30 percent, and even with the addition of black Africans and other blacks, the highest proportion was less than 50 percent (Peach 1998, 2005; see also Glazer 1999). According to another analysis of 1991 census data, over three-quarters of London Afro-Caribbeans lived in areas where whites were the majority population (Johnston, Forrest, and Poulsen 2002).

In this context, in New York City, and indeed in the United States as a whole, a key question—some people would say *the* key question—is whether the children of Afro-Caribbean immigrants will become African American. How they identify themselves therefore takes on special significance. For their Caribbean-born parents, it should be noted, there was no question of becoming African American; the first generation generally had a sense of shared racial group identification with American blacks, but they also had a strong ethnic identity in terms of their country of origin or as West Indian, and they often sought to distinguish themselves from, and avoid the stigma associated with, African Americans, particularly poor African Americans.

In the case of the second generation, Mary Waters has pointed to three possible paths: the assertion of a strong ethnic identity that involves a considerable amount of distancing from American blacks, an immigrant identity stressing national origins and their own or their parents' experiences in the home country, and an American—that is, an African American—identity, in which they choose to be viewed as black American and do not see their ethnic origins as important to their self-image. As Waters notes, these three categories are ideal types that simplify a more complicated reality. Ethnic and racial identities, as is often noted, are situational, fluid, and contextual—and the categories Waters puts forward are not mutually exclusive and frequently overlap (Waters 1999, 2001).

Several studies of the West Indian second generation underline these complexities. The second-generation New Yorkers in Sherri-Ann Butterfield's ethnographic study saw themselves as both black and as West Indian;

whether they emphasized a racial or ethnic identity depended on the circumstances and the audience. Many engaged in code switching, using West Indian accents with their parents and American English with their peers. One respondent said that during her high-school years, when she (like many other second-generation West Indians) felt a strong pressure to conform to being "black American in school," she was "black by day and . . . West Indian by night" (Butterfield 2004, 298). Milton Vickerman (2001b) describes second-generation individuals who shifted back and forth between "American," "black" and "West Indian" in discussing their identity. Nearly all the second-generation individuals he interviewed saw themselves as "partially West Indian"—specifically as "West Indian blacks." Indeed, they were more conscious of race as a life-shaping issue than their parents were because they had grown up in the American, rather than Caribbean, racial system and had only a secondhand understanding of Caribbean culture. At the same time as they became incorporated into the African American community and had a strong sense of shared bonds with African Americans, they saw their West Indian identity and cultural values—they frequently used the term "West Indian" in the interviews—as setting them apart from generalized negative views of blacks (Vickerman 2001b, Waters 1999; see also Bashi Bobb and Clarke 2001).

How members of the second generation in New York City identify themselves is rooted in structural circumstances; those from middle-class backgrounds and from families involved in ethnic organizations and churches were most likely to be strongly ethnic identified (Waters 1994, 2001). Middle-class second-generation Afro-Caribbeans, according to Butterfield, seek to avoid identification with poor and working-class African Americans—as well as with poor and working-class Afro-Caribbeans—as they struggle to maintain a middle-class identity in the face of persistent negative stereotyping of blacks by other New Yorkers. Gender makes a difference in identity formation, too. Second-generation Afro-Caribbean men feel racial exclusion more strongly than women do and thus tend to identify more strongly with African Americans (Waters 2001). Residential patterns are also involved. A West Indian identity, as Butterfield (2004) suggests, is nurtured and reinforced among second-generation New Yorkers when they grow up and, as many continue to do, live in neighborhoods with a critical mass of Afro-Caribbeans.

Identities can affect economic outcomes, and this leads to the segmented-assimilation perspective, which has been influential in second-generation studies in the United States; it predicts divergent outcomes for today's second generation, depending on the human and social capital of immigrant parents, location in urban space, skin color, and the protective capacities of the ethnic community. Among some nationality groups, according to the segmented-assimilation model, the contemporary second generation will move easily into the middle-class white mainstream; others will do well on the basis of networks and resources of their solidary communities; while for others, their ethnicity or race will be a mark of permanent subordination (see Portes and Rumbaut 2001, 2005).

In the segmented-assimilation view, children of immigrants growing up in inner cities in the midst of poor native minorities are at risk of being influenced by the oppositional counterculture said to be widespread among inner-city youth. In the case of second-generation Afro-Caribbeans who strongly assert an ethnic identity, the argument is that this identity, as well as involvement in the ethnic community, can reinforce attitudes and behavior that contribute to success in school and shield them from the negative features of American—and black American—youth culture (Zhou and Bankston 1998). In Waters's study, the young people whom she labels the "American identified" came from poorer families and attended dangerous, substandard, and virtually all-black schools. Their experiences with racial discrimination and their perceptions of blocked social mobility led many to reject their parents' immigrant dream—and to be receptive to the black American peer subculture of their inner-city neighborhoods and schools that emphasizes racial solidarity and opposition to school rules and authorities and had "the effect of leveling [their] aspirations . . . downward" (Waters 1999, 307).

Recent critiques of the segmented-assimilation perspective have challenged these gloomy predictions. One issue is how extensive really *is* an oppositional outlook or ethos among native minority—and immigrant—youth today. Assumptions about the pervasiveness of an oppositional ethos that devalues academic achievement have, to date, mainly been based on a few ethnographic studies in various locations.[3] It has also been argued that the discussion of oppositional culture among the children of immigrants may confuse style for substance: listening to hip-hop music and affecting a "ghetto" presentation of self should not be taken as evidence of joining a subordinated "segment" of society that engages in self-defeating behavior (Kasinitz, Mollenkopf, and Waters 2004, 396). Furthermore, several studies suggest that identification with African Americans often does not lead to downward assimilation. One national study, using pooled Current Population Survey data from 1998 and 2000, indicates that the Afro-Caribbean second generation is doing better than their first-generation parents in educational attainment, occupational achievement, and economic status (Farley and Alba 2002). A New York study of second-generation young adults shows a similar trend: most, including West Indians, did not indicate signs of the second-generation decline that had distressed some analysts in the 1990s (Kasinitz et al. 2008). Finally, in stressing how becoming a native minority can lead to a negative path of assimilation for the second generation, the seg-mented-assimilation model also overlooks the possible benefits—and that identification with African Americans can provide resources that promote upward mobility, a point I return to later.

What is important here is not whether the predictions of the segmented-assimilation model are right or wrong. It is that the perspective reflects, once more, the view that the fate of the Afro-Caribbean second generation is closely tied to becoming incorporated into black America. On this point virtually all scholarly observers agree: given the nature of racial divisions in America, assimilation into black America (including the growing black middle class) is, at least at the current moment, an inevitability for most second-generation Afro-Caribbeans in New York City. This is so even if, at the same time, they embrace cultural elements from their Caribbean heritage (Vickerman 2001b, 255). (Following Richard Alba and Victor Nee [2003, 11], *assimilation,* as I use the term, does not require the disappearance of ethnic-ity or ethnic markers; it refers to the decline of an ethnic distinction as that distinction attenuates in salience and the experiences for which it is relevant diminish in number and contract to fewer domains of life.) What is at issue is the consequences of this incorporation—not that it takes place.

Whatever the second generation's economic outcomes and self-identities, the question remains as to how others will view them. Will they be rec-ognized as Afro-Caribbean or West Indian? As black ethnics? Or as black American? At present, as Vilna Bashi Bobb and Averil Clarke (2001, 233) note, second-generation Afro-Caribbeans "have difficulty marshalling their West Indianness in a society that racializes black people with little regard to ethnicity." Or as Vickerman (2001b, 254) puts it, American society has a powerful tendency to homogenize blacks. Whether these trends will con-tinue largely depends on the future of the color line in America. It may be, as some observers suggest, that New Yorkers will become more sensitive to ethnic distinctions within the black community, particularly if continued mass Caribbean immigration sustains, and probably increases, the propor-tion of Caribbeans in the city's black population. Ongoing replenishment of the Afro-Caribbean immigrant community may not only enhance its vis-ibility and chip away at notions of a monolithic "blackness" but also keep alive an ethnic awareness among the second and third generations in a way that did not happen in the past. Although there was a significant Caribbean migration to New York City in the first few decades of the twentieth century—by 1930, some fifty-five thousand foreign-born blacks lived in the city—from the 1930s to the 1960s, migration from the Caribbean dwindled to a trickle (on early-twentieth-century Afro-Caribbean migration to New York, see Kasinitz 1992; Reid 1969; Watkins-Owens 2001). In contrast, many of today's second and third generations will grow up alongside immigrants of the same age and in communities where sizable numbers retain ties to the home country.

Yet if, as some scholars predict, the United States is moving toward a black/nonblack racial order, then the Afro-Caribbean second—and third—generation will have fewer options. "Because being black," Waters (2001, 213) writes, "involves a racial identity, people with certain somatic features—dark skin, kinky hair, and so on—are defined as blacks by others regardless of their own preferences for identification. . . . For most non-black Americans the image of blacks as poor, unworthy, and dangerous is still very potent, despite the success of many black Americans and the growth of a sizeable black middle class." Without an accent or other clues to immediately telegraph their ethnic status to others, second-generation Afro-Caribbeans, in the words of Kasinitz and his colleagues, are likely to fade to black (Kasinitz, Battle, and Miyares 2001).[4] Those who continue to identify with their ethnic backgrounds are aware that unless they are active in conveying their ethnic identities, they are seen as African Americans and that the status of their black race is all that matters in encounters with whites. The crux of the problem is that being seen as black American, they are subject to the same kind of racial prejudice and exclusion as black Americans are (see Waters 1994, 1999).

Given the role of race in American society, it is not surprising that the scholarly literature puts so much emphasis on the difficulties that come with being classified as black in America—and the lack of ethnic options open to second-generation Afro-Caribbeans. Yet it is important to bear in mind that the presence of a large black community in New York City, and in the United States more generally, has created opportunities for second-generation Afro-Caribbeans that their counterparts in Britain lack.

In the United States, as the authors of the New York second-generation study note, the civil rights movement, "along with the minority advancement in mainstream institutions, has created a legacy of opportunities for new members of old minority groups. The struggle for minority empowerment has established new entry points into mainstream institutions and created many minority-run institutions" (Kasinitz, Mollenkopf, and Waters 2002, 1032). Becoming part of the black community can give second-generation New Yorkers contacts in and entry into institutions dominated and controlled by black Americans—for example, labor unions and political groups—that can facilitate their upward movement. Moreover, there is now a considerable African American middle class; incorporation into the African American middle-class "minority culture of mobility" provides resources for upward mobility, including black professional and fraternal associations and organizations of black students in racially integrated high schools and universities (Foner 2001; Kasinitz 2001; Neckerman, Carter, and Lee 1999).

Nor should we forget that many of the children of black Caribbean immigrants have benefited from affirmative-action programs originally designed to help black American students—programs that have not been used in Britain. A survey of freshmen at twenty-eight selective colleges and universities in the United States found that blacks with immigrant origins were substantially overrepresented among black freshmen. These selective institutions, it should be noted, included one of the nation's historically black colleges—which do not exist in Britain (Massey et al. 2003).

Finally, there are political benefits that result from being part of a large black community in New York City. Second-generation Afro-Caribbeans can, on the one hand, play the ethnic card to appeal to the growing number of Afro-Caribbean voters, but, at the same time, they can unite with African Americans on many issues and elections, thereby exerting influence and gaining positions in the political sphere. Non-Hispanic blacks are the most reliably Democratic of any voting group and are a significant component of the electorate in New York City—in 2000, they constituted about a quarter of the city's voters and one-third of Democratic primary voters (Mollenkopf 1992, 2001). As a result, in recent years many high-ranking elected and appointed officials in the city have been black, and the city had an African American mayor, David Dinkins, in the early 1990s.

Black and British: The Comparison with London

In London, there is no question of the second generation's assimilating into a large native black population. Nor are blacks as segregated from whites as they are in New York City (and in the United States as a whole). Partly for these reasons, the experiences and dilemmas of British-born African Caribbeans are different from those of their cousins in New York City, and the scholarly literature on them has a different emphasis as well. No theoretical model akin to segmented assimilation has gained prominence in Britain, where many scholars write instead of hybridity, creolization, and the emergence of syncretic cultures bringing together white and black. African Caribbean communities, in the words of one social scientist, have been defined as outward looking, moving into mainstream culture, and redefining notions of Britishness (Alexander 2002, 563). (According to a recent study, based on analysis of census data, children of Caribbean migrants in Britain with working-class parents are more likely to move into the professional/managerial class than are their white nonmigrant counterparts, although Caribbeans are also at greater risk of unemployment than are their white British counterparts from similar backgrounds; Platt 2005.) There is no notion of Afro-Caribbean ethnic communities or networks acting as a source of protection from a potentially corrupting native minority culture. Indeed, when reasons have been sought by social workers and others for social problems among Afro-Caribbean youth in Britain—underachieving children, delinquency, or "dysfunctionality"—West Indian homeland culture and institutions, particularly lone-parent households, are often among the factors blamed (see Barn 2001, 215; Goulbourne and Chamberlain 2001, 7).[5]

As for identities, it is often pointed out that African Caribbeans born in London, like those in New York City, are less likely than their parents are to identify themselves, or see their primary identity, in terms of their island origins. Yet encounters with discrimination lead many to express doubts about or feel uncomfortable describing themselves as "British" or "English." To the extent that the Afro-Caribbean New York second generation understand "American" (or "real" American) to mean native white American, something similar is going on across the Atlantic (Kasinitz, Mollenkopf, and Waters 2004). At the same time, many second-generation Afro-Caribbean New Yorkers have trouble or resist thinking of themselves as American because in New York non-Hispanic Americans with visible African ancestry are African Americans. For the London second generation, the difficulty with identifying as British or English has to do with what one sociologist calls the "racist identity riddle"—that blackness and Britishness or Englishness often have been seen as mutually exclusive identities. The second generation in London form their identities, in other words, in a context in which they feel that many whites do not accept them as British or English—as one youth said, they think that "'black English' people do not exist" (Back 1996, 151; see also Gilroy 1993, 27–28, and Modood 2005a, 196).[6] In a recent study, one black man explained, "English people will never see you as English if you've got a black skin, never." Or as another put it, "I was born here, I'm English, but you really can't [describe yourself that way] because, at the end of the day, you are not accepted as being so" (Commission for Racial Equality 2007, 28).

The response of many young people in London has been to focus on their blackness as a basis for identification, with language and music playing a particularly important role. Some resist notions that they are British or, even more, English and emphasize their Caribbean origins and being black: "I don't want to be classified on the British sides" is how one young man in Les Back's study put it (Back 1996, 149; see Goulbourne 2002a, 178).[7] "I know that I am British because that is what it is on my passport," said a second-generation seventeen-year-old, "but I don't feel accepted in England because I'm black, . . . and we're not treated equally here. . . . I know I'm not Jamaican in the sense that I wasn't born out there but I still choose to identify culturally with them" (Reynolds 2006, 1096).

Others see themselves as British yet also stress their black and Caribbean identity. The London youth in Claire Alexander's study felt they could only describe themselves as British if they made further qualifications; they saw themselves as black first, with views of nationhood secondary. "I do see myself as British," said one young woman, whose parents were from the Caribbean. "But I see myself as Black British. There is a difference. You see I've got my identity and culture about being black. It's very important to me; it's foremost than being British" (Alexander 1996, 40, 48).

It is not, as Back (1996, 151–152) argues, that black youth are suffering from a crisis of identity; rather, they are seeking to actively "define what their identities are and what their culture means." Or as Alexander (1996, 199) notes, being black "is at once a demand for inclusion within the bounds of 'British' identity and a celebration of 'hybridity.'" "Well, I am British, I was born in London," said a young woman, "but I am not the same as English people, it's like I'm a different kind of English—a different way. I mean we have different ways of—a different culture. But I am still British" (Back 1996, 145). For most of the second generation, and as Stuart Hall argues for the third generation as well, it is a question of multiple identities—knowing, as Hall (2000, 152) states, that "they come from the Caribbean, . . . that they are Black, . . . that they are British. They want to speak from all three identities. They are not prepared to give up on any of them." Moreover, as Tracey Reynolds (2006, 1097) notes in her study of second- and third-generation young people of Caribbean descent, they highlight or play down different identities—as Caribbean, black, British, Londoners—depending on the time, audience, and space.[8]

For Afro-Caribbeans in London, the process of working out their identities takes place in communities where there is much more mixing with whites than in New York City neighborhoods. Even in London neighborhoods where black young people are a significant, even dominant, presence, there are usually many whites. In black sections of New York City, as one Afro-Caribbean activist in London pointed out, you can walk through and not see a white face, except passing in a car. "But that's not the case in Britain. We see them every day. We move with them every day" (quoted in Cockburn and Ridgeway 1982). Or as Trevor Phillips, now head of the Equality and Human Rights Commission, said, "When I go to New York to visit my sisters, I can, if I so choose, never speak to someone who is not black. Here [in London] that is not possible" (quoted in Worrall 2000, 14). Brixton may be a heavily Afro-Caribbean neighborhood (in South London), but as Henry Louis Gates Jr. (1997) notes, "Americans who imagine Brixton to be analogous to Harlem are always surprised to see how large its white population is." Young people of Afro-Caribbean origin often socialize with white youth in school playgrounds, youth clubs, and street corners, where they come to know each other and may develop close friendships. Ethnographies of working-class areas in South London indicate that black-white friendships are common and unremarkable, and they report cultural borrowing, exchange, and creolization between black and white working-class youth—in speech, modes of dress, and music (see Back 1996; Hewitt 1986). Back argues that the young people living in a South London council estate he studied were creating syncretic cultures that were neither black nor white—what he calls new ethnicities. As one black youth he knew said, "It's like if you are white living in a black area you'll have a little black in you, and if you are black living in a white area you will have a little white in you" (Back 1996, 159).

In New York City neighborhoods, the Afro-Caribbean second generation has little, if any, contact with whites in public schools or local arenas. To the extent that friendships develop between second-generation Afro-Caribbean and white young people, they tend to occur among the middle or upper-middle class who live in more integrated suburban areas or attend magnet schools or, later on, when they enter college or university. Even in these settings, friendship groups and social circles tend to be highly segregated by race. The syncretic or hybrid cultures in the process of creation in New York City that involve Afro-Caribbean young people are developing in the context of interactions with other first- and second-generation immigrant groups and native minorities. American scholars are becoming more sensitive to the dynamic possibilities of these hybrid youth cultures—and the limits of an exclusive focus on assimilation or a view of assimilation that fails to appreciate how the second generation are remaking not only the mainstream but native minority communities as well. Vickerman (2001a, 214) speaks of cross-fertilization between second-generation Afro-Caribbeans and African Americans on the level of popular culture, particularly music. Kasinitz and his colleagues write of how the "city abounds in clubs where African American hip hop has been fused with East Indian and West Indian influences into new musical forms. . . . African American young people dance to Jamaican dance hall and imitate Jamaican patois, even as West Indian youngsters learn African American slang. . . . Whether one looks at the music in dance clubs, the eclectic menus in restaurants, or the inventive use of slang on the streets, one cannot but be impressed by the creative potential that second generation and minority young people are contributing to New York today" (Kasinitz, Mollenkopf, and Waters 2002, 1033–1034).

Finally, there is the role of intermarriage. The ease and frequency of relations with whites in communities in London is reflected in the remarkably high rates of intermarriage—rates that are far higher than in the United States. An analysis of 1990 U.S. and 1991 British census data shows that among native-born West Indians, 40 percent of the men in Britain and 12 percent in the United States had a native white partner; for native-born West Indian women, the figure was 9 percent in the United States and 24 percent in Britain (Model and Fisher 2002b). The Fourth National Survey of Ethnic Minorities (conducted in 1994) found that half of British-born Caribbean men (and a third of women) who were married or cohabiting had a white partner. For two out of five children with a Caribbean mother or father (who were living with both parents), their other parent was white. Thus, in that most intimate arena, the family, many of the second (and third) generation in Britain have grown up with a white parent and, in adulthood, have a white partner. The indications are, moreover, that mixed relationships cut across economic groups (Berthoud 2005, 230). Whereas mixed-race couples still find themselves "stared at even in the most cosmopolitan metropolitan areas" of the United States, in Britain, they "draw virtually no notice in the metropolitan areas where they tend to reside" (Patterson 2005, 98).

Whether the high rates of black-white unions are contributing to the erosion of the color line is a key question. Some scholars go so far as to forecast a complete absorption of the Afro-British population of Caribbean ancestry into the mainstream British population over the course of the next three or so generations, or a "convergence with the majority white society of Britain" (Patterson 2005, 109; Peach 2005, 200). Much depends on the range of options available to the children of mixed unions—and whether the dominant society automatically assigns them the heritage of the parent who belongs to the more stigmatized group or, alternatively, allows them to take on the identity of either parent or a separate biracial identity (Model and Fisher 2002b, 747–748). The jury is still out on this question. Some observers argue that young people of mixed-parentage in Britain are, invariably, viewed as black or nonwhite, whatever their own preferences. Others point out that these young people may assert an identity as mixed race, which is recognized, or at least not challenged, by their peers (Back 1996, 156–157, 242; see also Song 2003, 77–79; Tizard and Phoenix 1993). Interestingly, in 2001, when people were allowed for the first time to describe themselves as being of mixed ethnicity on the British census, 237,000 people in England and Wales said they were Caribbean and white—as against 564,000 who said they were black Caribbean. (To put it another way, in England and Wales, 5.2 percent of the people who indicated that they were "not white" said they were Caribbean and white, and 12.6 percent said they were black and Caribbean.) Since black-white unions are steadily on the rise in Britain, where they constitute a growing sector of British society—and are increasing in the United States as well—how young people of mixed parentage see themselves and are viewed by others is obviously an important topic for research. In the United States another crucial question is on the table: the extent of intermarriage between the children of Afro-Caribbean immigrants and African Americans and the impact for their identities and social relations.

Although London, as an African American journalist living there notes, may be more at ease with integration than New York City is, and mixed-race friendships and couples more common, it is well to remember that London is not yet a postracial city (or Britain a postracial society) (Alibhai-Brown 2000). Racial prejudice and racial inequalities, unfortunately, persist in London, and young people of Caribbean origin continue to encounter racism in numerous contexts.[9] Nevertheless, the lives of the Afro-Caribbean second generation in London, like those of their parents, are much more intimately involved with whites than in New York City—where interactions with African Americans remain of paramount importance.

Conclusion

If there is one lesson to be drawn from this analysis, it is that the national context matters. Although the ethnic options for second-generation Afro-Caribbeans are severely constrained in both London and New York City by their African ancestry, the process of identity formation is not the same in the two places. The crucial difference, as I have shown, is that Afro-Caribbeans in New York City grow up, go to school, and live in a city with a large native-born African American population—and in a society where blacks, as the quintessentially racialized Americans, have a history of special disadvantage as a result of slavery, Jim Crow, and ghettoization. African slavery played a crucial role in the British colonial empire, but slave plantations were across the ocean, far from home. When "the empire struck back" with the postwar immigration to Britain, no large native black community was already in place. As second-generation Afro-Caribbeans have come of age in London, they have found that *British* and *black* have been viewed—and are still often viewed—as mutually exclusive identities; in New York City, *American* and *black* are inextricably linked, so that the Afro-Caribbean second generation find that becoming American means becoming African American. At the same time, second-generation Afro-Caribbeans in London mix and intermingle with whites more easily and more frequently than they do in New York, where outside of work, second-generation Afro-Caribbeans generally move in all- or nearly all-black social worlds.

There may be nothing magical, as Gates has written, about being around white people, but from the point of view of many Americans, the ease of mixing with whites in London is highly desirable (Gates and West 2004, 35). From the British standpoint, the ability to be part of a large black community in New York City often has an appeal. Interestingly, the British sociologist Harry Goulbourne (2002b) (himself of Jamaican origin) has complained of the strong assumption in American scholarship that "race (colour, phenotype) per se endows disadvantage" and that "West Indians are disadvantaged because they share blackness with African Americans." Part of the romance with America among black Britons, as Gates (1997, 202) notes, has to do with a sense that America "has, racially speaking, a critical mass." As I pointed out, Afro-Caribbean New Yorkers have benefited from political initiatives put in place as a result of the gains that African Americans won in the civil rights movement, including affirmative-action programs and policies designed to assist African Americans in gaining access to government employment as well as entry and scholarships to colleges and universities. For aspiring Afro-Caribbean Americans, incorporation into the growing African American middle-class minority culture of mobility has offered strategies for economic advancement.

Clearly, further studies are required to compare and contrast the identities and experiences of the Afro-Caribbean second—and indeed third—generation in London and New York City. One intriguing topic is the role of African American–rooted styles and music, as well as those from the Caribbean, in helping to shape understandings of blackness among the second generation on both sides of the Atlantic (e.g., Reynolds 2006, Warikoo 2007). Another question is how—and to what extent—participation in transnational networks operates to reinforce a sense of Caribbean identity among the second generation. I have mentioned the continued replenishment of the Afro-Caribbean immigrant population in New York City in contrast to London, where the migration has long since ended. Will the continued inflow of immigrants—in combination with sheer proximity to the Caribbean—help keep alive ties to the homeland among the second generation in New York City more than in London? What difference will this make to identities? An additional question concerns Afro-Caribbean relations with the African immigrant—and second-generation—populations, which have grown dramatically in recent years in both London and New York City. What kind of mixing and interactions occur between native-born Afro-Caribbeans and Africans? And what effect do they have on how U.S.- and British-born Afro-Caribbeans define themselves?

The focus in this chapter has been on New York City and London, but of course Afro-Caribbeans have moved to other cities in the United States and Britain, and there is a need to explore whether the ethnoracial identities and relations that have emerged in New York City and London parallel those that have developed beyond the two Afro-Caribbean migrant capitals. And, finally, if our concern is to chart the influence of national context on identities, then we need look beyond Britain and the United States to the process of identity formation among the second generation in France and the Netherlands (in Europe) and Canada (in North America), which also have large second-generation Afro-Caribbean populations. This essay, in short, represents a beginning step in a comparative analysis of the Afro-Caribbean second generation on the two sides of the Atlantic to more fully understand how they come to see themselves, are viewed by others, and, ultimately, are integrated into the societies where they, unlike their immigrant parents, are lifelong members from birth.

NOTES

1. This figure is from the March 2000 Current Population Survey. The 2000 census counted 425,428 immigrants born in Jamaica, Guyana, Trinidad and Tobago, and Barbados in New York City (Lobo and Salvo 2004).

2. In the nation as a whole, Census 2000 counted nearly thirty-three million non-Hispanic blacks, with more than nine out of ten (94 percent) African American (Logan and Deane 2003).

3. For a critique of the oppositional-culture explanation for racial/ethnic differences in school performance, see Downey 2008. Downey points to survey data revealing relatively proschool attitudes among American blacks and emphasizes American blacks' physical and social isolation—which limits their exposure to school-related skills—in accounting for their relatively poor school behaviors and achievement.

4. In this regard, data from the large-scale New York second-generation study show that most of the young-adult West Indians reported working in predominantly black work sites (Kasinitz et al. 2008, 198).

5. Explanations for the high rates of disciplinary action and exclusion from school among Caribbean males also emphasize teacher racism as well as an antischool ideology present in the youth/street culture embraced by many black boys (Modood 2005b, 294–295).

6. As Modood notes, the category *British* is a problematic feature of identification among some white people in Britain as well, especially the young, and has long been resisted by many Irish in Britain and is being eclipsed by *Scottish* in Scotland. He argues that *Englishness* has so far largely been treated by new Britons as a closed ethnicity rather than an open nationality, so that although "many ethnic minorities have come to think of themselves as hyphenated Brits, they have only recently started to think of themselves as English" (2005a, 196). Recent qualitative research conducted by the Commission for Racial Equality (2007, 27) indicates that for most of the black participants in London, Englishness was regarded as an exclusively white identity, whereas Britishness was felt to be more inclusive.

7. In the Fourth National Survey of Ethnic Minorities in Britain, just over a quarter of British-born Caribbeans did not think of themselves as British (Modood et al. 1997, 329).

8. In a recent discussion of "plural Britishness," Modood (2005a, 199) argues that blackness is increasingly experienced less as an oppositional identity than as a way of being British—and that hyphenated identities "that extend what it means to be British" have become accepted by "some, perhaps many, in the wider British public."

9. Back notes that racist practices survive and to some degree militate against the cultural bridges being built by black and white young people. The young people in his study indicated that they mostly encountered racism in educational institutions and from the police (Back 1996, 168–169).

13

How Do Educational Systems Integrate?

INTEGRATION OF SECOND-GENERATION TURKS IN GERMANY, FRANCE, THE NETHERLANDS, AND AUSTRIA

Maurice Crul

Research on the second generation of postwar immigrants is a relatively new phenomenon. Only in the past decade has it become a central focus in the study of immigrant integration. In the United States in particular, a theoretical debate has evolved in which research on the second generation plays a fundamental role. That research began to emerge in the mid-1990s, and one of the first publications was *The New Second Generation*, edited by Portes (1996). The postwar second generation in Europe came of age at roughly the same time as the American one. Examples of early studies in various European countries are Seifert (1992), Crul (1994), Tribalat (1995), Veenman (1996) and Lesthaeghe (1997).

In this chapter I discuss several topics[1] that figure prominently in both the American and European debates.[2] The primary focus of the present chapter, however, is the comparison of integration processes in different countries. More specifically, I compare the integration of second-generation Turks in Germany, France, the Netherlands, and Austria. The importance of the national context has received more attention in European than in American research (Crul and Vermeulen 2003; Doomernik 1998; Eldering and Kloprogge 1989; Fase 1994; Heckmann, Lederer, and Worbs 2001; Mahnig 1998). The American debate largely has been restricted to the United States itself.[3] The emphasis has been on comparing different ethnic groups in the same city or national context. (See the most important studies: Kasinitz, Mollenkopf, and Waters 2002; Kasinitz et al. 2008; Portes 1996; Portes and Rumbaut 2001; Portes and Zhou 1993.) There have been comparatively few studies in which the integration of American children of immigrants is compared with the integration of children of immigrants in other countries. (Exceptions are the studies of Alba 2005; Faist 1995; and Mollenkopf 1999.)

North American researchers, as Reitz (1998, 8–9) argues, have only recently started to give more attention to the importance of the national context in which immigrants and their children try to move forward. The national context has mostly been taken for granted (Alba 2005, 23).

That research in Europe is more cross-national probably has to do with the fact that there are many countries close to each other, which, although economically linked, are structured very differently. It is therefore more obvious to look at the effects of these differences. The countries I focus on in this chapter (Germany, Austria, France, and the Netherlands) are almost all bordering countries. The capitals of the countries are between three hundred and five hundred miles away from each other. Although these distances are small, the Turkish communities take on very different shapes in the different countries. This chapter tries to explain some of these differences.

The Turkish Community in Europe

Turkish labor migration followed comparable patterns everywhere. Beginning with Germany in 1961 and ending with Sweden in 1967, European countries signed official agreements on labor migration with Turkey. Spontaneous migration through relatives and covillagers then also ensued, later even surpassing the scale of official immigration. The peak of labor migration was between 1971 and 1973, years in which more than half a million Turkish workers came to work in western Europe, 90 percent of them recruited by German industry (Özüekren and Kempen 1997, 5). Beginning in 1973, the economic recession following the oil crisis slowed the demand for labor and prompted an official immigration stop in 1974. Unemployment forced many immigrants to return to their home countries, but many men who had remained began sending for their wives and children. Migration took a new upturn in the 1980s and 1990s, when the in-between generation reached marriage age and began choosing spouses from Turkey. The Turkish population in Europe (outside of Turkey) now totals about four million, including naturalized and second-generation Turks. More than 60 percent of them live in Germany.

European industry was in need of low-skilled labor at the time, and indeed the majority of these first-generation Turkish "guest workers" were recruited from the lowest socioeconomic strata in their home countries and had very little education. In the rural areas where most of them grew up, educational opportunities were limited to the primary-school level. Generally speaking, first-generation men had finished primary school only, and most women had just a few years of schooling. Because small-scale subsistence farming was the primary activity in this peasant way of life, school played no particular role. Sending children to school brought no advantage in the struggle for existence; having them help on the farm had a high priority. Another reason that education seemed to hold little promise was the nature of the schooling on offer. Education in Turkey was not primarily geared to conveying knowledge that would aid people in their peasant existence or in breaking away from it. Its main aim was to transmit the Turkish national ideology and promote the cultural integration of the country.[4] The first generation made few advances in the European labor market—in fact, the contrary occurred. Economic crises and industrial restructuring put many Turkish immigrants out of work. Despite this, a substantial group of first-generation men did manage to start their own business or to help their children to do so.

Most second-generation children—those born in the country of immigration or (more broadly) those who arrived before primary school—grew up in unfavorable circumstances. Family income was often very low by European standards, and most families lived in substandard and cramped accommodation. In many neighborhood schools, children from a mix of migrant backgrounds were in the majority.

I have chosen the Turkish group for comparison across countries for obvious reasons. They are the largest immigrant group in Europe, numbering up to four million, and they reside in a large number of European countries. Yet to compare "Turks" in different countries does not necessarily mean one is comparing the "same" group. An adequate comparison must also take account of the internal differences *within* the Turkish immigrant populations, based on characteristics such as ethnicity, first-generation education levels, and religion.

Most Turkish migrants came from small villages in central Turkey or along the Black Sea coast; those from large cities (Istanbul, Izmir, and Ankara) are in the minority. Some districts in central Turkey delivered inordinate numbers of migrants over the years, often dispersed over various European countries. People from the Afyon district, for instance, now reside in Germany, the Netherlands, and France. The socioeconomic backgrounds of Turkish labor migrants of the first generation as a result turn out to be fairly similar in the four receiving countries, with some variations (for example, in Germany; see Worbs 2003).

Labor migrants form the vast majority of the Turkish migrants in Europe. However, there are also significant groups of refugees who fled political persecution in Turkey or the armed conflict between Kurds and Turks. One should be aware that I have chosen the Turkish immigrant group partly because of the sharp contrasts between it and the native populations of the western European countries. Its socioeconomic background is extremely low (unlike the Turkish American population, who are generally better educated; Karpat 1995), and it is a group with a traditional Muslim background. Turkish immigrants are widely considered to be one of the toughest groups to integrate, and they thereby put to the test the wide panoply of European national policies aiming at the integration of newcomers.

School Careers of Second-Generation Turks in Four Countries

In this chapter I compare the educational careers of second-generation Turks in Germany, the Netherlands, France, and Austria. Ideally, educational status would be described by several indicators identical in each country. Unfortunately, not all the pertinent categories of data are known for all countries. Relevant indicators for educational status are school attendance rates, educational performance of school students, highest educational attainments of graduates and dropouts, dropout percentages, and repeater rates. My comparison draws on all the available information. In all four countries, data sets on the second generation are available on a national level. I make use of the microcensus data in Germany and Austria, the SPVA (Social Position and Use of Facilities by Ethnic Minorities Survey) in the Netherlands, and the INSEE (Census and Labor) survey in France. The national data are collected independently from each other, and as a result some differences occur. To start with, researchers use different definitions as to what is considered to be the second generation. In France the definition includes only those born in the country of migration; in the Netherlands and Austria, those who came before the age of six; and in Germany, those who came before the age of seven. In Germany and Austria the surveys exclude those second-generation Turks who are naturalized, whereas in France and the Netherlands they are included. The surveys were also gathered at different moments in time. The INSEE survey is from 1999, the SPVA is from 1998, the microcensus from Germany is from 1995, and the one of Austria is from 1999. I chose the surveys that were most close to each other in time. Sampling methods also varied across these surveys, and this will have had an effect on the outcome. Because of this incomplete evidence, I make comparisons only with great caution and as a rule only describe situations for which differences are clear and substantial.

Differences in Outcomes

The school careers of second-generation Turks exhibit remarkable differences across Europe. The greatest distinctions can be seen in the percentages of young people in vocational tracks—the lowest secondary-school type in all countries. In France and the Netherlands between one-quarter and one-third of the second-generation Turks follow a vocational track, whereas in Germany and Austria the figure is between two-thirds and three-quarters. At the top end of the educational ladder, a considerable group of second-generation Turks (ages eighteen to forty) in France has an academic degree (10 percent), and 21 percent have a diploma (*baccalauréat*) from *lycée* (Simon 2003, 1105). In the Netherlands 5 percent of the second-generation Turks (ages fifteen to thirty-five) who have ended their educational careers have an academic degree (Crul and Doomernik 2003, 1046). Those in higher education are much more numerous. About 23 percent of the eighteen- to twenty-year-old Turks in the Netherlands entered higher education in 2001 (Herwijer 2004, 133). In Germany there are no figures available for those who already obtained an academic degree. Based on my own calculations of the microcensus, 11 percent of the second-generation Turks (ages sixteen to twenty-five) have finished a preparatory track (*Gymnasium*) that gives access to university. That is about half the amount compared to France and the Netherlands. In Austria the situation seems most dramatic. The percentage of second-generation Turks (ages fifteen to thirty-five) who have an academic degree is closer to zero than to 1 percent. Only 4 percent have finished a preparatory track that gives access to higher education (Herzog-Punzensberger 2003, 1133).

National contexts vary widely in the types of opportunities they offer to second-generation Turks. Considering the foregoing one might be tempted to conclude that France and to a lesser extent the Netherlands provide the best institutional contexts for migrants. This is not the whole story, however. A comprehensive assessment also requires knowledge of how children *perform* in vocational or in preparatory tracks. In France, for instance, the Turkish second generation has high rates of children who drop out without a diploma. Almost half (46 percent) of the Turkish second-generation children in the age category eighteen to forty did not get a diploma of either *lycée* or vocational education (Simon 2003, 1105). Of all the Turkish second-generation children in the Netherlands in the age category fifteen to thirty-five, one-fifth (21 percent) leave school without a secondary-school diploma. There are especially high rates of dropout in lower vocational education (Crul and Doomernik 2003, 1051). On the other hand, the percentage of children who leave school without a secondary-school diploma in Germany and Austria is very small (7 percent in the age category sixteen to twenty-five in Germany [Worbs 2003, 1020] and 3 percent in the age category fifteen to thirty-five in Austria [Herzog-Punzensberger 2003, 1135]).

The two most important indicators for school success, school performance, and dropout rates show contradictory outcomes across countries, with France and the Netherlands performing better in terms of moving up to higher school levels and Germany and Austria performing better in terms of dropping out.

Explaining Differences in Outcomes

The differences between the countries are large enough that differences in sampling and use of concepts and definitions alone cannot explain them. A dominant approach to explain differences so far has been to look at national models of integration. Usually three models are distinguished: the model of differential exclusion, the assimilationist model, and the multicultural model (Castles and Miller 1993). The first two are often associated with Germany and France, respectively. The multicultural model is often connected with the Netherlands. The German and the French model represent opposite positions. The German model follows the *jus sanguinis,* or blood, principle; the French model follows the *jus soli* principle (Castles and Miller 1993).[5] National models of integration transmit "national" ideas, norms, and values which shape the interaction (both ideologically and legislatively) with new-comers and their children. The assumption is that this will also have a sub-stantial effect on the socioeconomic position of immigrants and their children (Brubaker 1992; Castles and Miller 1993; Joppke 1999).

On the basis of the outcomes just presented, the idea that a national model of integration has an unequivocal effect on the socioeconomic integration of children of immigrants should be dismissed. There are contradictory outcomes on different educational indicators of integration. We can only tentatively identify what is good and bad in a particular country relative to another. We cannot really single out one country in which the second generation is doing better than in the others. There is not a hierarchy of success. National integration models have an effect on different spheres of integration. They clearly have an effect on naturalization rates and most probably also on the identity formation of the second generation.[6] The educational position of the second generation seems not to be affected in the same unequivocal way by national models of integration (see also Alba 2005, 22, 23). We will have to dig deeper to understand the differences within and across countries.

The differences, on further inspection, can be related to national educational institutional arrangements and the different ways in which the transition to the labor market is formalized between the countries.[7] The factors in the national education systems that explain the differences in the school careers of second-generation Turks include school duration, face-to-face contact hours with teachers, selectivity, amounts of supplementary help and support available to children inside and outside school, and type of schooling (especially apprenticeship tracks). The only feature of the national systems that specifically relates to migrant children is second-language training.

One significant disparity between countries lies in the age at which education begins. In France the majority of Turkish second-generation children start school at the age of two; in Germany and Austria, at age six; and in the Netherlands, at age four. Thus, immigrant children in France have about three to four more years of education in that crucial developmental phase in which they begin learning the majority language. In France very young Turkish children thus find themselves almost every day in situations in which they have to speak French with their peers, and they learn the language in an educational environment.

Striking differences also appear in the number of face-to-face contact hours with teachers during the years of compulsory schooling. Here, once again, these are below average for Turkish pupils in Germany and Austria, especially during the first part of their educational careers. Nine-year-olds in German schools have a total of 661 contact hours, as compared to 1,019 hours in the Netherlands, because children in Germany and Austria attend school only on a half-day basis. Turkish children in Germany thus receive about ten hours less instruction per week than those in the Netherlands. Although children in Germany and Austria are assigned more homework, help with homework is a scant resource in Turkish families. This may be a source of serious disadvantage.

A third distinction, which in combination with the first two can culminate in serious disparities, lies in school selection mechanisms. Germany and Austria both select at the age of ten. In Germany the selection mechanism channels the children into three school levels; and in Austria, into two. Coupled with the late start in education and the below-average contact hours, Turkish second-generation pupils in Germany and Austria are thus given little time to pull themselves out of their disadvantaged starting position. In this respect, Turkish children in Germany and Austria are in the worst possible situation. Selection in the Netherlands occurs two to four years later, and France selects at age fifteen. In Germany and Austria most pupils, because of the early selection, end up in short vocational streams—*Hauptschule*. In the Netherlands a considerable group enters lower vocational education at the age of twelve. The higher selection age in France results in the highest percentages of Turkish children moving into more prestigious streams. As suggested earlier, this has its benefits and drawbacks. Though it may offer more opportunities to Turkish children than they receive in other countries, many of them falter and end up with no diploma at all.

A fourth area in which major differences between countries are evident involves the amount of assistance and support made available to migrant children inside and outside school. All countries have a host of educational priority projects aimed either specifically at migrant youth or more broadly at youth with learning problems. Some programs are national; others are regional or municipal initiatives. Though cross-national comparisons are difficult to make, the most reliable data so far derive from an international study known as PISA 2000 (www.pisa.oecd.org). It questioned fifteen-year-olds about the supplementary assistance and support they received inside and outside school. Although it only distinguishes between youth with migrant backgrounds and native youth, it gives a good indication of the extra support received by Turkish children in each country. It delivers a clear ranking of countries. Migrant children in France, and to a lesser extent in the Netherlands, receive the most support, and Germany performs worst of all. Since basically the same differences between countries apply to native youth, we may simply speak of divergent general education practices in different countries.

Less meaningful for explaining differences between countries, but not altogether insignificant, are the second-language programs. The options and practices of second-language education are many and varied, and there is still considerable debate about the best method for improving proficiency in official national languages. This has yielded a multitude of programs and methods, ranging from transitional bilingual programs to intensive instruction exclusively in the second language. No country appears to have clear-cut guidelines in place for the provision of second-language teaching. Normally it is a part of primary-school curricula, but it may be integrated there into mainstream language programs, given as supplementary instruction to migrant children during school hours, or provided outside of school hours. In comparing countries in relation to language instruction, I focus on two issues: when the countries introduced second-language programs on a substantial scale and how the quality and results of the programs roughly compare. Virtually all countries now have well-established programs. The biggest distinction lies in when they were introduced. France began implementing orientation classes back in the early 1970s. Other countries were much later to start. The Netherlands did not introduce programs on a larger scale until the early 1990s. In Germany some federal states opted for intensive second-language programs, whereas others provided instruction in migrant languages, creating separate classes for the children. Even into the 1990s, however, methods of learning German other than the traditional approaches were still rare. Overall, then, the group I am focusing on here—the second generation above age fifteen who attended primary school in the 1980s or early 1990s—did not profit from special language programs to any reasonable degree. In most countries the programs reached only limited numbers of children, and their quality was questionable. In some cases, as in France, second-generation children born in the country itself were mostly excluded from the programs, because they were thought to have no language problems.

If we view all five of these factors together, it seems no wonder that second-generation Turks in France enter preparatory schools for higher education at higher rates than elsewhere in Europe. Children start to go to school early in France, have more hours of face-to-face instruction, have the most supplementary help and support available inside and outside school, and do not undergo educational selection until a fairly late age. At the other extreme we find Austria and Germany, where children enter school at a relatively late age, are selected only a few years after, have fewer contact hours, and receive less supplementary support.

But how do we explain the high dropout rates in France and the Netherlands compared to the other two countries? In Germany and Austria only a very small percentage of second-generation Turks fail to get a *Hauptschule* diploma (lower secondary vocational education, the lowest track of secondary education) or another secondary education diploma. In France many Turkish second-generation children drop out of the *lycée* without a diploma. The stakes are higher in *lycée*, and as a result those who cannot make it often end up with no meaningful credential at all.

In the Netherlands a considerable group of Turkish second-generation children move into a vocational track at age twelve. Their situation resembles that of second-generation Turkish children in Germany who move into vocational education at age ten. The dropout rate in the Netherlands, however, is much higher. If we compare the situation between the vocational educational tracks in Germany and the Netherlands, a number of things come up which explain the large differences in dropout rates. Dropping out is especially high in the age group of sixteen years and older. By the age of fourteen or fifteen most second-generation Turks in Germany already possess a *Hauptshule* diploma. At the age of sixteen children in the Netherlands are still at school full-time. Even in the lower vocational education track in the Netherlands the period of apprenticeship—which is called *stage*—is limited. Half of the subjects the children get are theoretical subjects; the other half are devoted to the vocation they are trained for.

The vocational educational stream in the Netherlands is considered a marginal stream within the educational system. Lower vocational education (VBO) has often been described as the garbage can of the system. It takes on the children with learning problems and all the children who were unsuccessful in higher streams (often because of behavioral problems), and it also absorbs newly arrived immigrant children (who, of course, have their own specific problems). Pels (2001, 6) has depicted teacher-pupil interaction in a VBO school. She counted about eighty admonitions during one mathematics lesson. Crul (2000, 139) reported on the prisonlike climate and the regular fights that break out in VBO schools, sometimes even between pupils and teachers. The resulting school climate is not very conducive to school performance. Dropout rates in VBO are very high. In contrast, the vocational track (*Hauptschule*) in Germany is the main stream in the German educational system. Many children of native-born parents go through this track. The educational climate in *Hauptschule* is not considered problematic.

The starting position of the first-generation Turks in the four countries was very similar. They mostly came from the countryside and had little to no education. They constituted a very homogeneous group across Europe. The outcome for the second generation, however, is very different. The comparison between the four countries shows the importance of institutional arrangements in education (starting age of compulsory schooling, amount of school contact hours in primary school, school system characteristics, and the importance of early or late selection in secondary education). An institutional approach to immigrant integration in education seems to be better in explaining differences between countries than the approach based on the notion of "national integration models."

Different Scenarios

In France and the Netherlands a sizable number of second-generation Turkish dropouts are seriously at risk of becoming an underclass. Unemployment among this group is extremely high. On top of this they often marry young, with a spouse from Turkey. In general, the educational level of the spouse is also low. In the Netherlands half of the spouses coming from Turkey finished primary school at the most. Because of the cultural and linguistic adaptation process that the imported spouse needs to go through, he or she will not be able to get a job easily (Crul, Pasztor, and Lelie 2008). Sometimes the ethnic niche provides employment but in very bad working conditions. The large group of dropouts and their partners reproduce the low class position of their parents. The only difference is that the unskilled work their parents did has in the meantime disappeared. This group of second-generation young-sters often lives in the same neighborhood as their parents (in the beginning, often with their parents), and their children (the third generation) will grow up in extremely negative circumstances. The household income will be low, and the children will attend the worst schools, often only populated by other children of low-income immigrant parents. If the mother is an imported bride from Turkey, the situation for the children of the third generation will be comparable with children of the second generation. Children will grow up speaking Turkish at home, and their parents will be unable to help them with their homework. Furthermore, the experience of parents who dropped out of school can have a negative influence on how they perceive teachers and schools. This depends on the reason for dropping out, of course. If dropping out was the result of conflicts with teachers, a negative influence is probable. If it was for reasons unrelated to school (for instance, an early marriage), the atti-tude of parents could well be to stimulate their children to continue studying.

At the same time, there is a sizable group of Turkish academics emerg-ing in France and in the Netherlands—that is, sizable compared to Germany and Austria. This group made an immense leap compared to their parents, who most often had only a few years of primary school or were illiterate. They accomplished a goal that more often takes three to four generations. After finishing their academic degrees, they apply for the better-paying jobs. Unemployment among this group is much smaller, especially in the Nether-lands (Crul and Doomernik 2003, 1056; Crul, Pasztor, and Lelie. 2008; Simon 2003, 1152). This group moves out of the neighborhoods of their parents, and their children (the third generation) grow up in middle-class neighborhoods and attend schools which will give them good prospects to succeed. In gen-eral, they marry at a later age; and if these second-generation young adults look for a spouse in the home country, they more often choose a better-edu cated urban partner from Turkey, who will also have problems adapting but not so much as the imported uneducated rural partners. This group of well-educated and highly paid second-generation professionals and their partners form the first elite in their community. They take over the leading positions in cultural and political organizations and mosques. They voice their opinions in the public debate as young politicians, community leaders, stand-up comedians, or columnists (Crul 2000). The polarization within the Turkish communities is echoed in the public debate about integration in the Netherlands. The visibility of the first elite in the media and at the same time the alarming signals of a rising underclass among the second generation fuel the discussion of whether the glass is half full or half empty.

In Germany and Austria there is a totally different trend. Only few second-generation youngsters reach higher education. The Turkish elite, still small as it is, is mostly formed by people who came as refugees or who came later for study reasons.[8] The absence of a sizable second-generation elite is accompanied by the near absence of a second-generation group dropping out of secondary school. The large majority of the Turkish second generation in Germany and Austria ends up being skilled blue-collar workers (Worbs 2003, 1030). This is a step higher in the hierarchy than their parents, who were most often unskilled workers. The wages and the labor conditions for skilled workers in Germany and Austria are among the best in Europe. This means that the majority of the second generation can move into a lower-middle-class position. Housing and school segregation in Germany and Austria is relatively low compared to France and the Netherlands, which means that most children of the third generation will go to ethnically mixed schools (Özüekren and van Kempen 1997).

The comparison between the countries shows that national educational institutional arrangements have a significant effect on how the communities develop and will further develop in the future. The Turkish communities in France and the Netherlands will become more and more heterogeneous. The Turkish second generation in Germany and Austria is and will be more homogeneous. The large majority of the second generation will only slowly move up the social ladder.

It is difficult to tell which of the two scenarios will in the long run bring the best results for the second and third generation: the heterogeneous scenario or the homogeneous scenario. In the heterogeneous scenario it can be assumed that the small upcoming elite can play a crucial role in the emancipation of the group as whole. They can act as spokespersons for the group and make claims to improve the position of the group. The group who is not doing well, however, can also drag the community into a negative spiral. There is evidence that if a group cannot make it to a middle-class position in the second generation, the third generation will run the risk of merging with the native underclass city youth and develop an oppositional stand (Alba and Nee 2003; Portes and Rumbaut 2001).

In the scenario in Germany and Austria there are also both positive and negative trends. Germany and Austria more so than other European countries possess a large industrial sector in which skilled workers can find employment. The second generation can still profit from this sector now, but this option will probably be gone by the time the third generation make their move to the labor market. Like everywhere else in the Western world, the restructuring of the industrial sector is in full swing. The big question is whether the third generation will be able to move up through education. The German and Austrian educational systems are among the most selective in Europe (www.pisa.oecd.org). Prospects to move up through education will therefore not be very favorable for the third generation. If the third generation cannot move up the educational ladder, unemployment will probably hit them hard.

Conclusion

The comparisons I make in this chapter are not comprehensive. The data needed for adequate comparisons are missing in some countries, and research on the second generation is still scant everywhere. Although we need to be cautious in drawing conclusions, I have identified some leads that could be used to build on in future research. I now want to propose some hypotheses to guide that research.

The position of second-generation Turks varies widely among the different countries in Europe. The picture is further complicated by the polarizations within the Turkish group that exist in France and the Netherlands. The debate about integration seems to have had a persistent blind spot for the importance of national institutional arrangements for education and labor-market transition. Although rigorous study is still urgently needed, I believe we can already conclude from the material presented here that the national institutional setting has a considerable impact on the paths of integration that the second-generation Turks are following in the various countries.

Interestingly, the differential outcomes reported here seem to be attributable not to arrangements specifically targeted at migrant youth but more to the generic policies and the resulting institutional arrangements prevailing in each country. A further conclusion, then, which I again draw with some caution, is that the probability of underclass formation may be linked to the opportunities that national, generic institutional arrangements for education and labor-market transition offer to the second generation. This means then that a debate on the differential effectiveness of national institutional arrangements is just as urgently needed as the discussions on distinctions between ethnic groups.

NOTES

This chapter takes the argument further which Hans Vermeulen and Maurice Crul developed for the special issue of *International Migration Review*, "The Future of the Second Generation" (Winter 2003). I would like to thank Hans Vermeulen for his comments on an earlier version of this chapter.

1. For an overview of the most important topics, see Crul and Vermeulen (2003, 2006).

2. For the relevance of the American debate for research in Europe, see Lucassen (2002); Vermeulen (2001).

3. Portes and De Wind (2004, 847) argue that most scholars' disciplinary training is focused on examining migration within a single national context.

4. On the role of education in rural Turkey at the time of mass emigration, see Coenen (2001, 56–73).

5. For a further discussion on models and modes of integration, see Vermeulen (2004).

6. In the EFFNATIS field survey, children of immigrants were compared in Germany, France, and Britain. Children of immigrants in Britain identify more with the country in which they live than in Germany. The same trend could be found in the preservation of the mother tongue by the second generation. Children of immigrants in Germany hold on to their mother tongue longer than in France and Britain. An intervening variable, however, could be that in the three countries different ethnic groups were chosen (Heckmann et al. 2001).

7. Reitz, in his study *The Warmth of Welcome: The Social Causes of Economic Success for Immigrants in Different Nations and Cities* (1998), was one of the first to point to the importance of differences in educational institutional arrangements for the integration of immigrants. Waldinger, in *Strangers at the Gates: New Immigrants in Urban America* (2001), shows how differences in labor-market structures in different cities can explain different paths of integration of immigrant groups.

8. There are, of course, exceptions to this generalization. Young writers, politicians, and artists from the second generation often get wide coverage in the media because of their second-generation status.

14

The Employment of Second Generations in France

THE REPUBLICAN MODEL AND THE NOVEMBER 2005 RIOTS

Roxane Silberman

The November 2005 youth riots in France revealed serious shortcomings in the "Republican model" for the integration of immigrants and their off-spring into French society. The riots marked an escalation in a two-decade history of weekend car burnings and confrontations with the police. Occurring in low-income neighborhoods characterized by unemployment, drug use, crime, and violence, the riots spurred increasing reference to "ghettos," a term long rejected by some researchers (Body-Gendrot 1999), who deny any resemblance of these neighborhoods to the low-income minority areas of the United States. Unsurprisingly, the riots involved many second-generation Maghrebins (who are of North African descent), but black youngsters from the more recent sub-Saharan immigration also participated. Since 2005, troubles have occurred every weekend, generating an estimated thirty to forty thousand burned cars per year. Violent episodes following the death of a youngster during a police intervention (Saint-Dizier in October 2007, Villiers-le-Bel in November 2007, Saint-Étienne in July 2009) regularly make the headlines. Urban violence is no longer restricted to the suburbs and has spread into big cities, with young people rampaging downtown on various occasions such as demonstrations and football matches.

Few people noticed that schools including kindergartens were targeted for pillage and arson during the 2005 riots and more recent episodes—thereby suggesting that adolescent anger is delivering payback for broken promises. This directly challenges the claims of Schnapper[1] (1991) and others about the central role of the school as a springboard for upward mobility and cultural assimilation in their apology for the French model over the "communitarian" U.S. model, with its "ethnic divides." Numerous researchers have stressed that where socioeconomic backgrounds are equal, second-generation youth succeed at least as well as youth with French-born parents (Vallet and Caille 1996).

| 283

Yet this argument proves to be lacking when it comes to outcomes on the labor market. Youth have suffered disproportionately from the chronically high unemployment rates that France has seen for the past two decades, thus undermining confidence in a linear social-integration process. Some second generations have suffered more than others, and there is ample research to demonstrate an ethnic penalty in the labor market (Dayan, Échardour, and Glaude 1996; Richard 1997; Silberman and Fournier 1999, 2006, 2007a; Tribalat 1995). Most observers have linked the volatile situation in the low-income suburbs directly to this penalty. Recent results on educational attainment and youth unemployment highlight particularly the situation of the "Zones urbaines sensibles," those urban enclaves now frequently designated as ghettos where no improvement seems to have happened in the past decade and youth unemployment is rising to unprecedented levels (ONZUS 2009).

A key issue is whether the ethnic unrest is a passing crisis or a chronic phenomenon that invalidates the Republican model and may be the source of durable ethnic frontiers in French society. One has to ask: since the unrest points to segmented processes of social integration consistent with downward assimilation for some minorities, to what extent does the U.S. concept of "segmented assimilation" apply to France (Portes 1995a; Portes and Zhou 1993)?

In this chapter, I try to provide a broad overview of the difficulties facing second generations in the French job market, identifying the mechanisms at play and discussing the pertinence of a model that has been formulated in the U.S. context. France is an important case because (1) the country has seen sustained immigration for over a century, longer than other European countries, (2) its integration model has regularly been contrasted to those of the other main immigration societies, and (3) the French unrest is of deep concern to other European governments with substantial immigrant populations and growing migrant inflows.

In focusing on ethnic penalties in the labor market, I first present an overview of intergenerational changes and then examine the access of young second generations to the French job market. Empirically, I track job-market entry for successive cohorts of school leavers over a period of fifteen years. The results demonstrate persistent barriers and ethnic penalties for some second-generation groups, mostly of ex-colonial origins, and especially those from the Maghreb. I then discuss some of the mechanisms at work—namely, education, social capital, labor-market context, and discrimination—that point to a possible downward-assimilation process for a part of the second generations. This leads to a discussion of the segmented-assimilation model in a more general perspective than the U.S. context provides.

Data

Contrary to a widespread impression, numerous French surveys now allow work on second generations despite ongoing controversies with advocates of the Republican model, who claim that measuring origins might stigmatize French citizens.

In this chapter, I rely on results based on the *2003 Formation Qualification Professionnelle* (FQP 2003) survey by the Institut National de la Statistique et des Études Économiques (INSEE), which gives data on intergenerational changes, and on three longitudinal surveys conducted by the Centre d'Études et de Recherche sur les Qualifications (CÉREQ): Entrée dans la vie active 1989 (EVA 89), Génération 1992 (Gen 92), and Génération 1998 (Gen 98), which together allow me to follow successive cohorts of school leavers.

FQP 2003 is the main French national survey about social mobility and has been conducted at seven- to ten-year intervals since the 1960s. It gives an overview of the social backgrounds of the second generations, as well as a broad yardstick for measuring social mobility between immigrant parents and their second-generation children. I focus here on the 35,065 persons eighteen to fifty-nine years old.

The CÉREQ surveys track the 1992 and 1998 cohorts of school leavers (from all levels) through their first five years on the job market. Sample sizes are 26,359 and 55,345, respectively, and 22,021 for the Gen 98 follow-up survey. When combined with the EVA 89 survey that tracked undereducated school leavers (less than a high-school diploma) over four years, these data yield a picture of job-market entry for youth that spans from 1989 to 2003. High unemployment prevailed throughout this time frame, except for a brief improvement that benefited the 1998 cohort.

I employ the conventional definitions of the first, 1.5, second, 2.5, and third generations. The distinction between the 2.5 and second generations is not always made: the 2.5 includes French-born individuals who have only one foreign-born parent, whereas the second includes those whose parents were both foreign-born. The third, then, includes French-born individuals of French-born parents. For the FQP survey, the sample size does not allow such distinctions among immigrants' children, and I collapse the 2.5 and second generations into one broad category, putting 2 in italics in the tables to identify it. Throughout the chapter, I generally refer to the immigrants' children as the "second generation" in its broadest sense to include the 1.5, second, and 2.5 generations.

Though all the surveys allow me to identify immigrants' children, they do not all contain equivalent information on one crucial point, the citizenship at birth of the parents. This leads to potential difficulties for ex-colonial territories where the European-ancestry population and some natives possessed French citizenship in the preindependence period; in these cases, the second generations of non-European origin cannot be identified on the sole basis of parents' country of birth. This is particularly true for Algeria, an ex-French department, where independence led to the arrival of one million repatriates of European origin, whose children have to be distinguished from those of the Maghrebin immigrants coming before and after independence in 1962 (Alba and Silberman 2002). As the Génération 1992 survey does not include parents' citizenship at birth, I supplement the 1992/1998 tables based solely on the parents' country of birth with more precise information for the 1998 cohort. This statistical uncertainty carries over to second-generation Southeast Asians and sub-Saharans, also from ex-French possessions, because, albeit much less so than for Algerians, they may include the offspring of Europeans, mixed marriages, and non-European beneficiaries of pre- and postcolonial attributions of French citizenship. Such distinctions require a large sample in addition to information about the parents' country of birth and citizenship at birth. I have this information only in the Génération 1998 survey.

Second Generations in a Difficult National Context

I begin by providing a rapid overview of the French context for second generations, focusing on the different ethnic groups, the educational system, and the labor-market context.

Second generations are nothing new to the French job market, given that the first major immigration waves arrived in 1880 and have become permanent components of the national population. This history is distinctive because substantial immigration to western Europe only began in 1945 and even later in southern Europe. On this point, France most resembles the United States. Both countries also grant citizenship by virtue of native birth (*jus soli*) and make naturalization relatively convenient. However, they differ in two respects. First, with the exception of a *populationist* period after World War II, France never promoted immigration as a permanent feature of population policy (Noiriel 1988). Second, contrary to a common view, *jus soli* is more restrictive in France because immigrant offspring born in France only acquire citizenship at age eighteen, thus leaving young people in some uncertainty.

Historians and sociologists long took little interest in these second generations except for some mention of their presence in the French school system as of the 1930s (Mauco 1932). Interest increased during the 1970s for second generations of post-1945 immigrants. Yet the focus remained on school attainments until the end of the 1980s, when the future of second-generation school leavers became an issue. This coincided with higher unemployment and the rise of "SOS Racisme" activism led by second-generation Maghrebin youth, the "*beurs.*"

Ethnic Groups

Today's second generations represent a variety of origins, with a rise in the share of non-Europeans. The south European component from neighboring Italy and Spain shows continuity with pre-1940 immigration, and Portugal joined this group with an immigration in the late 1960s and early 1970s. All three countries are now EU members but joined after their immigration waves to France had peaked. Today, the Portuguese predominate in the younger age groups of the south European second generation, whereas Italians and Spaniards dominate the older ones. Other second generations stem from the Yugoslavs who came in the 1970s and Turks in the 1980s (despite the immigration "ban" in 1974). The Turkish migration is not as important in France as in Germany but deserves attention because it led to the one Muslim population that has no ex-colonial relationship with France. Second-generation Turks are just now entering the job market. The most recent arrivals include Poles and Romanians, with some of the incoming adolescents going straight onto the labor market after completing compulsory schooling in France.

Important and growing second generations originate from postcolonial immigration. France had an extensive colonial empire and the post–World War II decolonizations accelerated migrations toward the ex-mainland. The main groups are from the Maghreb (Algeria, Morocco, and Tunisia), Southeast Asia, and sub-Saharan Africa.

The Maghreb was the most proximate part of the empire, just across the Mediterranean. The first Maghrebin waves date back to 1914–1918, when it was necessary to replace French workers drafted during World War I. The immigration developed during the postwar reconstruction of the 1950s despite national policy aimed at recruiting immigrants other than North Africans. Since Algeria was still legally part of France, entry was unproblematic. The inflows climbed after Morocco, Tunisia, and Algeria achieved statehood between 1956 and 1962, and they surged in the 1970s when established immigrants brought over their dependents. Maghrebins, especially Algerians and Moroccans, formed an important part of the low-qualified migration that filled the mining sector, the metallurgical industry, and other sectors such as the automobile industry until the middle of the 1970s.

Algeria is a special case because it was the only North African colony legally incorporated as a French department, and the independence war was unusually brutal. The outcome triggered the transfer en masse in 1962 to the mainland of one million Algerian-born French citizens (so-called *pieds noirs*), along with the indigenous Algerian "Harkis," who sided with French forces. Separating in data the children of Algerian immigrants, the Maghrebins, from the children of the 1962 repatriates is not straightforward and requires data on parental nationality at birth, which in general was not French for the indigenous Algerians, in contrast to the *pieds noirs*.

The general perception is that the Maghrebins are a problem in French society. Opinion polls from the 1950s forward consistently report that the Maghrebins attract the fiercest hostility (Girard and Stoetzel 1953; Mayer 1994). Moreover, this population appears at risk, despite some success stories,[2] with a significant share of immigrant Algerian and Moroccan parents on early pensions or in long-term unemployment as a result of the French transition to a postindustrial economy after 1973, when unskilled factory jobs became scarce. Algerians and Moroccans also suffer severe housing segregation that relegates them to low-income housing outside major cities. More inclined to open convenience stores, Tunisians may have suffered less unemployment and segregation. Migration from all three countries has brought to France a Muslim population, which is mainly Berber, a minority in the case of Algeria. The relationships with French natives carry different histories. In Algeria, the colonization was more intense. Thousands of people were expelled from their lands, and the memory of the independence war and of violent episodes in Algeria and the mainland is still vivid on both sides, even if the two countries have maintained strong economic ties (because of Algeria's important oil and gas resources). Practically no one of European ancestry remained in Algeria after 1962, but the Evian agreements at independence maintained special rights for native Algerians to come to France until 1973. No other ex-empire country reveals such a mixture of proximity and continuous conflictual relationship.

Sub-Saharan Africa represents another important part of the ex-French empire. Independence has not cut the links with the ex-mainland, and the term *France-Afrique* is still invoked when France intervenes in African affairs. Second-generation sub-Saharans from Cameroon, Ivory Coast,

Mali, and Senegal are a growing component of first-time job seekers and will continue to be so for a number of years. Their parents are mostly unskilled laborers from rural backgrounds who work in the construction and service industries, along with a fair share of artisans and craftsmen; but some were sent by middle- to upper-class parents to France as students to complete their education. Thus, this migration shows bimodal characteristics. Its youth now constitute a substantial share of the nation's nonwhite population, which also includes nonwhite French citizens from the French Caribbean (Antilles Islands) who have been migrating to the mainland in large numbers since the 1970s and securing civil-service jobs in the hospital system. Little comparative analysis is possible on the condition of these domestic migrants (Marie 2002) and that of black African immigrants because of the French reluctance to collect data about race and color. Some people have recently demanded official French acknowledgment of past involvement in slavery,[3] and the color line is now a growing component of the French debate about integration. A part of this African population is Muslim.

Southeast Asian countries are a third major component of the former French empire. Migration to France from "Indochine"—Cambodia, Laos, and Vietnam—started in the mid-1970s in the wake of the U.S. exit from the region. The second generations from these origins come from families of widely varying educational or social backgrounds and of far more diverse social status than the Maghrebins. Over one-third of the parents of pre-1975 Southeast Asian immigrants held middle or upper-level professional occupations, a share that fell off as the number of economic refugees rose (Tribalat 1995). These groups quickly established businesses and ethnic neighborhoods such as the Chinatown of Paris, where they developed communitarian practices rather orthogonal to the French model. Asian immigrants are generally considered successful. This population also brought religious diversity to France.

The FQP 2003 survey shows that second generations as a whole (including the 1.5, second, and 2.5 generations but not the repatriates' children) amount to about 11 percent of French sixteen- to fifty-nine-year-olds (table 14.1). Within this age range, the group distribution is rather different. South European second generations are more concentrated in older ages than are other ethnic groups: 45 percent of Maghrebins and 50 percent of Turks are twenty to twenty-nine years old, against 20 percent for south Europeans. These differences go along with a larger share of French-born individuals or of those from mixed marriages within the south European second generation than within the other groups, although for the non-Europeans the demographic changes are rapid.

TABLE 14.1
French population (aged 18-59), by origin and generation
Percentage of total population (Weighted)

	First generation	Second or later generation	Sample N
Native-born French	-	76.5	27,290
Maghrebin	2.2	2.2	1,287
Repatriate	0.7	3.9	1,568
South European	1.6	4.9	2,299
East European	0.5	0.9	457
Sub-Saharan African	1.3	0.6	569
Near Eastern	0.6	0.3	274
Southeast Asian	0.3	0.4	216
Other	1.4	1.8	1,105
Sample N	2,770	32,295	35,065

Source: FQP Survey 2003. INSEE

French-Educated Second Generations on an Adverse Job Market

Second generations have experienced very different educational opportunities and job-seeking environments. The youngest second generations, now aged eighteen to thirty, enjoyed a more flexible school system with greater access to higher diplomas, the result of a continuous educational reform process since the 1950s. An increase in the minimum school-leaving age led to overhaul of a system once based on strict separation between the academic and vocational curricula at the primary-school level, the consequence of which was to put some children rapidly on the factory floor and to reserve academic diplomas—particularly the *baccalauréat,* the standard secondary diploma—for children from the middle and upper classes, thus setting them up for admission to university. The French school system stresses educational streaming based on parents' aspirations and the school's assessment of a student's academic performance. The standard wisdom is that a vocational education is for underachievers. Most vocational students hail from working-class families, which includes second-generation youth. Yet several educational reforms in the late 1980s and early 1990s gradually pushed the academic/vocational branching point to the end of secondary school and founded new diplomas, vocational and technological *baccalauréats,* which qualify holders for admission to university. The new array of postsecondary vocational "BTS" and "DUT" diplomas rounded out the reform, and the job market welcomed these graduates at a time when liberal-arts students were dropping out in large numbers and/or becoming increasingly unemployable— significant numbers of them second-generation Maghrebins (Beaud 2002).

A final feature of the French school system is the overrepresentation of second-generation Maghrebins and other victims of housing discrimination in certain schools and classrooms. France never adopted busing policies to counteract residential segregation, and its policy of combating social inequalities by limiting parental choice about schools may have in fact enhanced the effects of spatial segregation. Since the 1980s, national education policy allocates some extra funding to schools in socially disadvantaged areas (the number of immigrants in the area is one of the criteria); but the sums are minimal, and this policy of ZEP (*zones d'éducation prioritaire*) has proven relatively inefficacious. France's stress on egalitarian policy, accomplished through reforms to democratize schooling, may not have succeeded better than other systems in dealing with social inequalities at school (Alba and Silberman 2009). This lack of success may reinforce the feeling of injustice for those who do not succeed at school, especially since the Republican model puts the school at the center of the integration process.

These trends are happening in an economy of consistently high unemployment since the mid-1970s, with greater impact on youth than in other EU countries (Goux and Maurin 1998). However, a brief end-of-century upturn in the national economy did see a significant rise in employment, providing more opportunities for jobless youth. Meanwhile, job security for youth continued to decline as contract employment expanded. Throughout this period, the government stimulated youth hiring through payroll tax breaks for the private sector and new contract jobs in the civil service. In March 2005, the conservative political leadership sought to undermine job security even further, precipitating two months of student demonstrations (in which second generations were participants), thus finally leading to renewal of new jobs programs. In this context, lower and intermediary vocational diplomas often prove to be better job qualifications than their academic equivalents, except for master's degrees and doctorates. With the financial and economic crisis of the late 2000s, youth unemployment has dramatically increased, particularly in the segregated suburbs.

Chronic Controversy over Second Generations

For more than twenty years now, second generations have been at the heart of the debate on the so-called Republican model, a unique French model of assimilation seen as diametrically opposed to the German model in one way and to the U.S. model and its "multiculturalism" in another (Schnapper 1991). In a context of high youth unemployment and increasing urban unrest, the model led to a demand for second generations both to "become invisible" and to clearly affirm allegiance to the nation. This began with the 1980s law that undermined *jus soli* by replacing a French-born immigrant child's automatic entitlement to citizenship at age eighteen with a requirement to explicitly claim it. Such a claim supposedly reflected a proactive will to integrate into mainstream French society. That law came and went, but the attempt revealed a change in the way some second generations, particularly the Maghrebins, were viewed in relation to French society. In the late 1990s, public debate targeted Islamic headscarves in the classroom. The upshot was a 2004 law that forbade the wearing of any "ostentatious" religious symbols in schools. In practice, the new law affected almost only Muslim schoolgirls, mainly from Maghrebin and Turkish origins. France was first in Europe in making headscarves controversial. The debate goes beyond the claim for "*laïcité*," as it regularly involves other visible signs of Islam such as mosques with their apparent minarets.

Yet second generations are also increasingly at the heart of the public debate on how best to fight ethnic and racial discrimination. France has long opposed any move that smacks of affirmative action or quota systems on the grounds that they violate the democratic principle of equal treatment. Despite a growing body of ad hoc commissions and official reports on the subject of discrimination, France has also long resisted EU requirements for racial and ethnic indicators. Moreover, the number of lawsuits for discrimination filed in the French courts has remained low, even if recent efforts are noticeable (Commission Nationale Consultative des Droits de l'Homme 2008). Though such ideas as the deletion of names from curriculum vitae and the special admissions program initiated by the elite Institute of Political Studies (*Sciences Po*) to recruit top students from low-income neighborhoods where most second generations live show important changes, France still is resistant to "affirmative action" programs.

Meanwhile, second generations still remain the subject of heated debate over the issue of their identification in census and other national surveys, opposing those who are in favor of identifying second generations through parents' birthplace (Héran 2002; Silberman 2008; Simon 2003, 2004, 2008; Tribalat 1995) with those who see this as a form of racism fraught with risks of stigmatization (Le Bras 1998). De facto, a growing number of surveys since the 1980s have been identifying second generations through information about parents' birthplace and nationality, finally recognized as "objective" by the Constitutional Court (Silberman 2008). Debate recently shifted to a new issue: indicators of ethnic and racial discrimination, which France is loath to adopt despite EU requirements. In May 2009, a new committee, the COMEDD (Comité pour la mesure et l'évaluation de la diversité et des discriminations), was asked by the French government to indicate how "ethnic statistics" could be implemented in order to fight discrimination.

Changes in Education

Because many immigrants came from countries where average education was low, the formal education gap between first and second generations is wide. FQP data show that over one-third of Maghrebin fathers have no schooling. Lower shares of unschooled fathers are found among east Europeans, Portuguese, other south Europeans, sub-Saharans, and Turks. Unsurprisingly, more mothers than fathers are unschooled, with Maghrebin mothers atop the list. At the opposite end, we find that Asians show the greatest proportion of fathers with a tertiary education. In addition, a healthy fraction of sub-Saharan mothers and fathers are well schooled. The higher average education level of this recent immigration wave is consistent with the general trend for recent flows.

Second generations are much more educated than their parents as a rule. The share of the unschooled is tiny and may concern youths entering France in their late teens. The share with only a primary-school education has been falling for both genders, with the mother/daughter education gap being the greater. As a rule, second generations are more numerous in the tertiary level, with Southeast Asian men and women clearly outperforming their parents at the upper tertiary level.

Yet these results only give a broad-brush view of the condition of second generations. Differences between ethnic groups are prominent in the second generation. Asians remain more educated than others. We also see that Portuguese, once known as having a preference for secondary-level vocational tracks, have now surpassed Maghrebin boys at the tertiary level. Second-generation men of Maghrebin origin also seem surpassed by the current first generation, that is, recent immigrants from Maghreb now on the labor market. This is also true for the sub-Saharan second generation.

The Génération 1992/1998 data provide a complementary view on recent trends for the youngest generations. A greater fraction of younger second-generation males now exits secondary and postsecondary vocational and technical programs. The Portuguese have led the way in exploiting the new postsecondary vocational opportunities, in which they outnumber Maghrebins. This is significant because vocational diplomas are better job qualifica-

TABLE 14.2
Highest educational qualification, by ancestry and generation:
Row percentages (weighted)

	Men			Women		
	Primary or none	Tertiary	N	Primary or none	Tertiary	N
Native-born French	24.0 (0.2)	21.0	12,899	22.6 (0.2)	22.6	14,391
First generation						
Maghrebin	63.3 (12.2)	12.3	334	69.7 (26.6)	7.8	313
Repatriate	38.9 (3.1)	20.5	106	30.4 (3.5)	27.0	130
South European	76.3 (3.3)	3.6	277	77.9 (1.7)	7.6	290
East European	34.0 (1.6)	26.5	51	24.8 (1.0)	42.3	93
Sub-Saharan African	32.5 (8.1)	33.0	183	39.9 (14.7)	20.8	221
Near Eastern	48.8 (2.7)	19.9	102	62.6 (11.1)	16.1	80
Southeast Asian	36.7 (2.4)	19.2	48	52.2 (3.4)	7.4	46
Fathers and mothers of the second generation						
Maghrebin	86.9 (35.5)	2.7	279	87.9 (47.8)	2.3	361
Repatriate	46.2 (4.4)	18.5	609	52.6 (6.7)	9.6	723
South European	79.4 (8.5)	2.4	838	84.4 (11.1)	1.5	894
East European	71.8 (4.1)	8.9	142	77.6 (6.1)	3.6	171
Sub-Saharan African	44.9 (8.1)	20.4	64	43.2 (14.8)	12.1	101
Near Eastern	72.3 (11.0)	13.5	42	68.0 (20.1)	10.5	50
Southeast Asian	39.1 (2.9)	27.4	62	54.7 (13.3)	8.3	60
Second generation						
Maghrebin	33.3 (0.0)	11.8	279	30.8 (0.5)	18.0	361
Repatriate	20.6 (0.3)	24.4	609	15.8 (0.0)	30.4	723
South European	30.7 (0.2)	14.2	838	23.5 (0.2)	18.9	894
East European	23.7 (0.0)	22.7	142	35.1 (1.0)	16.6	171
Sub-Saharan African	23.3 (0.0)	25.7	64	22.2 (0.0)	24.2	101
Near Eastern	29.8 (0.0)	24.1	42	28.7 (0.0)	11.6	50
Southeast Asian	12.3 (0.0)	43.1	62	16.7 (0.0)	54.1	60

Note: Figures in brackets give the percentage with no formal schooling.
Source: FQP Survey 2003 INSEE

tions, and, indeed, second-generation south Europeans show lower unemployment rates. They also now access the highest tertiary levels, an inversion of the trend for the Portuguese, long known for wanting their offspring on the job market as early as possible. Maghrebins continue to prefer academic tracks, with relatively high early dropout rates, and to attain low levels of secondary or tertiary achievement. These findings are also in line with qualitative research that notes substantial numbers of early school dropouts in some suburbs where unemployment is very high for the Maghrebin second generation. The Turkish second generation does not reach high education levels at the moment, but this is a more recent group. The sub-Saharans also out-number Maghrebins in vocational diplomas, and a proportion get tertiary-level diplomas. These may be the children of wealthy parents who have sent them to France to get higher education. Second-generation females generally profile similarly.

In sum, all second generations have more education than their parents, but they show wide gaps between one another in terms of ultimate achievement and curricular options, with Maghrebins seeming to perform the worst among the long-established ethnic groups.

Ethnic Penalties in the Labor Market

What do these trends mean on the job market? Undereducation, limited language proficiency, and barriers due to work permits combined to lock first generations into less skilled jobs. Research shows that some ethnic groups suffered more than others and faced an ethnic penalty, that is, a net difference after allowing for education and other factors (Dayan, Échardour, and Glaude 1996). What about their children who have been educated in France? Earning a living is now a crucial issue for second-generation job seekers in a context of chronically high unemployment. I begin by examining intergenerational trends according to occupational category before tracking several cohorts of second generations and their (un)employment histories in the 1990s.

First-/Second-Generation Ethnic Penalties in Occupation

The FQP survey recorded the occupational position of a respondent's parents at the time the respondent left school. The data also allow me to compare second generations to first generations currently in the labor market. The first key observation from table 14.4 is that immigrant fathers are overrepresented among un-/semiskilled manual workers when compared to native French males. We also see the familiar difference between Maghrebins and Portuguese, with south Europeans markedly overrepresented in skilled manual jobs. However, some immigrant groups are well represented in nonmanual labor. Repatriates but also Southeast Asians and sub-Saharans access routine nonmanual work and the salariat category (salaried professionals and managers) more easily, although some African-born Europeans included in this category may explain away the advantage in their case. The bimodal nature of the current sub-Saharan migration is another probable

TABLE 14.3

Changes in educational attainment between the 1992 and 1998 cohorts

Qualification	French-born in France, father and mother also	Father or mother born in North Africa regardless of nationality	Father or mother born non-French in North Africa	Father or mother born in Southern Europe	Father or mother born in Turkey	Father or mother born in Southeast Asia	Father or mother born in sub-Saharan Africa	Father or mother born in Northern Europe or elsewhere in Europe	Father or mother born elsewhere
MEN									
Cohort 1992									
Some secondary school	32.4	50.0		40.0	82.8	28.3	51.2	29.3	34.9
Vocational degree secondary school	21.5	15.4		23.0	12.2	11.2	16.0	14.4	18.9
Baccalaureat	17.5	12.1		19.0	2.6	17.3	11.4	22.4	13.5
Some tertiary	28.6	22.5		18.0	2.5	43.2	21.4	34.0	32.8
n=14445	12075	920		871	85	59	159	146	130
Cohort 1998									
Some secondary school	18.7	39.2	48.0	25.6	57.0	29.2	40.3	17.5	33.2
Vocational degree secondary school	25.1	23.8	25.0	30.2	26.6	12.1	18.4	20.6	21.9
Baccalaureat	23.2	18.1	15.0	19.6	11.8	27.5	21.3	16.5	17.3
Some tertiary	33.0	19.0	12.0	24.7	4.6	31.3	20.0	45.4	27.5
n=25722	20265	2531	1728	1441	269	323	179	256	458
WOMEN									
Cohort 1992									
Some secondary school	27.2	44.9		30.8	88.3	41.6	35.5	16.6	19.5
Vocational degree secondary school	20.0	13.4		21.7	7.1	4.7	8.5	8.6	15.8
Baccalaureat	20.9	18.4		23.4	2.1	22.0	30.6	31.8	15.0
Some tertiary	31.9	23.4		24.1	2.5	31.7	25.4	43.1	49.8
n=11911	10011	752		706	56	55	126	115	90
Cohort 1998									
Some secondary school	14.0	27.1	34.4	14.0	58.1	23.6	21.8	13.5	23.1
Vocational degree secondary school	20.6	20.6	23.2	26.6	21.3	18.6	38.3	11.7	20.2
Baccalaureat	26.5	27.4	24.5	29.4	13.5	26.5	22.0	28.5	25.6
Some tertiary	39.0	25.0	18.0	30.0	7.2	31.4	18.0	46.2	31.2
n=21319	16691	2237	1437	1153	229	257	149	215	388

Source: Génération 1992 and 1998 Surveys CÉREQ

TABLE 14.4
Current occupational class, by ancestry and generation:
Row percentages (Weighted)

	Salariat	Routine non-manual	Petty bourgeoisie	Skilled manual	Semi- and unskilled manual	N
MEN						
Native-born French	30.2	10.1	10.3	37.9	11.4	10,401
Father's occupation of the second generation						
Maghrebin	13.7	3.2	3.4	43.9	35.8	193
Repatriate	41.5	12.7	6.1	30.0	9.8	500
South European	10.8	4.6	14.9	49.5	20.0	701
East European	16.5	6.0	12.1	44.6	20.8	112
Sub-Saharan African	48.5	10.8	3.0	22.2	15.6	48
Near Eastern	13.8	3.7	9.9	38.4	34.2	35
Southeast Asian	50.6	7.0	9.8	26.1	6.6	48
Second generation						
Maghrebin	15.4	9.1	10.4	44.8	20.4	183
Repatriate	42.3	10.5	5.5	31.6	10.2	444
South European	26.8	8.7	10.2	41.4	13.0	698
East European	29.5	8.7	7.2	48.4	6.2	118
Sub-Saharan African	47.1	16.0	5.3	22.8	8.8	37
Near Eastern	24.8	6.2	8.1	29.5	31.5	34
Southeast Asian	52.8	11.5	9.8	21.2	4.7	37
WOMEN						
Native-born French	35.9	30.1	5.2	5.9	22.8	9,554
Mother's occupation of the second generation						
Maghrebin	16.4	23.4	1.6	4.2	54.5	73
Repatriate	36.6	34.5	3.4	3.4	22.1	353
South European	12.2	20.6	6.0	7.4	53.9	382
East European	18.2	17.8	11.4	6.4	46.3	72
Sub-Saharan African	37.0	25.8	2.3	6.0	28.8	60
Second generation						
Maghrebin	23.4	36.2	3.1	4.1	33.2	150
Repatriate	40.8	32.5	5.8	2.0	19.0	452
South European	29.8	31.7	3.9	4.8	29.8	597
East European	37.7	26.2	7.5	3.7	24.9	110
Sub-Saharan African	44.7	31.8	0.0	3.9	19.6	47

Source: FQP 2003 Survey INSEE

factor. The second key point is that Maghrebins (with the exception of the Tunisians, who cannot be isolated in this table) and sub-Saharans are under-represented in small business. This is particularly true in comparison to the Portuguese, with their established niche in the construction industry.

The immigrant/second-generation comparison indicates strong continuity. In most cases, the intergenerational categories bear resemblances, especially for the relatively successful repatriates from the Maghreb, plus Southeast Asians and sub-Saharans. Yet there is substantial change in some cases between immigrant parents and the second generation. All groups show some intergenerational upward mobility. One illustration is that nearly 80 percent of Maghrebin fathers are manual workers, against less than 65 percent for second-generation males, or 70 percent for south European fathers, against less than 55 percent for the second generation. However, the shift into a postindustrial economy accounts for a part of this intergenerational change. A second observation is that although the proportion of the Maghrebin second generations in un-/semiskilled manual work dropped between generations, their progress into salaried professional and managerial jobs seems quite limited.

Intergenerational changes for women have two dimensions. The second generations, especially Muslims, are far more active than their mothers were (Silberman and Fournier 2006) Thus, the comparison may be in part biased. Predictably, women generally gravitate in greater numbers toward services and unskilled jobs. We also see that all mothers except repatriates are over-represented in this lowest occupational category by comparison to their French peers. Repatriates alone are overrepresented in the salariat. Interestingly, all women show low self-employment rates, native Frenchwomen included. Are second generations more present at the top than their mothers were? This is indeed the case for southern Europeans, who are increasing their share of professional and managerial jobs. But even though the share of Maghrebin females in un-/semiskilled manual labor fell from 55 percent in the first generation to 33 percent in the second, the resulting upward shift only goes as far as the routine nonmanual class, in which the share of Maghrebin females has grown sharply.

I now turn to ethnic penalties, that is, net differences from the native French after allowing for age, education, and marital status. These analyses are for working respondents. Table 14.5 shows the results for second generations and current first generations, whereas table 14.6 is for the parents of the second generations. In general, ethnic European groups fare better on the job market than do their non-European peers, and there is little evidence of upward intergenerational mobility. Moreover, the ethnic penalty permeates most occupational categories.

I find no ethnic penalty for second-generation repatriates or southern Europeans when it comes to salaried or routine nonmanual labor or skilled manual labor, which was not the case for their fathers. Southeast Asians perform much like European immigrants: no parameter estimate for either Southeast Asian generation reaches statistical significance. Although the sample size is small, my interpretations match those found in other countries where Southeast Asians have settled.

However, substantial ethnic penalties dog other groups—for example, Maghrebin fathers score a penalty of –1.01 for salaried jobs, against –1.19 in the second generation, and penalties are found for other occupational categories. Likewise, second-generation Turks score –1.42 for salaried jobs, against –2.55 for their fathers. These results broadly show strong intergenerational continuity in the nature and size of the ethnic penalty. But we also see that in the case of the Maghrebins, the second generation, though raised and educated in France, suffers a larger ethnic penalty than does the current first generation (i.e., recent immigrants) in access to the salariat and a similar penalty in access to the routine nonmanual occupations. We do not find such a situation for the other long-settled groups.

Hiring Barriers for Second-Generation School Leavers 1989–2003

These results do not provide a complete overview of the situation of the second generations, as they are facing a situation in which getting a job is quite difficult in an economy with twenty-plus years of high unemployment, especially for youth. Numerous studies see job finding as a critical issue and detect an ethnic penalty in France. Consequently, I now focus on how job searching eased or toughened for successive second-generation cohorts in a time frame marked by the following three features:

1. Aging in some immigration populations, boosting the share of French-born youth or of mixed-marriage offspring, and the arrival of recent migration waves, may change the order in the "queue" entering the labor market. Demographic changes in second generations between the 1992 and 1998 cohorts were important. The two more established groups experienced a sharp rise in mainland-born offspring, with southern Europeans in the lead among mixed-marriage offspring (rising from 36 percent to more than 45 percent), and Maghrebins showing a stable if lower proportion (33

TABLE 14.5
Ethnic penalty for occupational class (multinomial analysis)
Parameter estimates; contrasts with unskilled manual

	Salariat		Routine non-manual		Petty bourgeoisie		Manual supervisor or skilled manual	
MEN								
Intercept	**2.49**	(0.50)	**1.88**	(0.55)	**1.99**	(.56)	**2.57**	(0.43)
Ancestry/Generation								
Native-born French	0		0		0		0	
Maghrebin 1	**-0.96**	(0.32)	**-0.67**	(0.34)	-0.23	(0.31)	-0.33	(0.22)
Repatriate 1	0.67	(0.52)	0.11	(0.63)	0.56	(0.55)	0.31	(0.48)
South European 1	**0.80**	(0.36)	-0.66	(0.51)	**1.23**	(0.36)	**0.90**	(0.28)
East European 1	**-2.87**	(0.67)	-0.89	(0.63)	**-1.89**	(0.82)	-0.73	(0.44)
African 1	**-1.48**	(0.35)	-0.10	(0.33)	**-1.76**	(0.52)	**-0.63**	(0.28)
Near Eastern 1	**-1.65**	(0.48)	**-2.89**	(1.03)	-0.55	(0.41)	**-1.21**	(0.33)
East Asian 1	-0.22	(0.66)	-1.25	(1.11)	-0.18	(0.77)	**0.02**	(0.54)
Maghrebin 2	**-1.19**	(0.34)	**-0.70**	(0.33)	**-0.87**	(0.35)	-0.46	(0.24)
Repatriate 2	0.32	(0.21)	0.02	(0.23)	**-0.72**	(0.28)	-0.19	(0.19)
South European 2	0.07	(0.16)	-0.29	(0.18)	-0.09	(0.17)	0.03	(0.13)
East European 2	0.60	(0.47)	0.67	(0.50)	0.29	(0.53)	**0.94**	(0.42)
African 2	0.38	(0.67)	0.40	(0.67)	-0.78	(0.92)	-0.51	(0.62)
Near Eastern 2	**-1.42**	(0.67)	-1.18	(0.70)	-1.20	(0.72)	**-1.17**	(0.48)
East Asian 2	0.09	(0.85)	0.44	(0.90)	0.13	(0.93)	0.05	(0.81)
Chi-square (D.F.)				5,879.6 (88)				
N				12,756				
WOMEN								
Intercept	**2.11**	(0.42)	**2.21**	(0.37)	-1.19	(.67)	**-0.53**	(0.63)
Ancestry/Generation								
Native-born French	0		0		0		0	
Maghrebin 1	-0.43	(0.36)	-0.35	(0.27)	-0.58	(0.54)	-0.66	(0.49)
Repatriate 1	0.27	(0.23)	-0.12	(0.38)	-0.45	(0.65)	0.32	(0.54)
South European 1	**-0.90**	(0.38)	**-0.60**	(0.24)	**-1.16**	(0.52)	-0.39	(0.37)
East European 1	**-1.83**	(0.46)	**-0.81**	(0.40)	-1.69	(1.04)	**-0.44**	(0.57)
African 1	**-2.64**	(0.39)	**-0.95**	(0.25)	-	-	-1.17	(0.49)
Maghrebin 2	**-1.13**	(0.29)	**-0.63**	(0.22)	-0.60	(0.47)	-0.99	(0.46)
Repatriate 2	-0.24	(0.17)	-0.04	(0.15)	0.22	(0.26)	**-0.99**	(0.35)
South European 2	**-0.43**	(0.14)	**-0.24**	(0.11)	**-0.57**	(0.23)	**-0.40**	(0.20)
East European 2	0.14	(0.31)	-0.12	(0.28)	0.31	(0.40)	-0.27	(0.50)
African 2	-0.22	(0.52)	-0.07	(0.47)	-	-	**-0.20**	(0.81)
Chi-square (D.F.)				5,424.9 (88)				
N				11,551				

Note: Standard errors are given in brackets; emboldened coefficients indicate significance at the .05 level or higher.
Control by marital status, qualification, age/10 and (age/10)**2
Source: FQP 2003 Survey INSEE

TABLE 14.6
Ethnic penalty for fathers' and mothers' occupational class
Parameter estimates; contrasts with unskilled manual

	Salariat		Routine non-manual		Petty bourgeoisie		Manual supervisor or skilled manual	
MEN								
Intercept	**3.23**	(0.23)	**1.54**	(0.25)	**1.61**	(0.24)	**2.14**	(0.23)
Father's ancestry								
Native-born French	0		0		0		0	
Maghrebin	**-1.01**	(0.26)	**-2.03**	(0.42)	**-2.55**	(0.37)	**-0.65**	(0.17)
Repatriate	**0.58**	(0.18)	**0.51**	(0.20)	**-0.88**	(0.23)	0.18	(0.17)
South European	**-0.78**	(0.16)	**-1.011**	(0.20)	**-0.72**	(0.13)	0.04	(0.10)
East European	-0.79	(0.38)	-0.84	(0.43)	**-0.85**	(0.33)	-0.07	(0.25)
African	0.23	(0.54)	0.13	(0.59)	-1.62	(0.82)	-0.48	(0.52)
Near Eastern	**-2.55**	(0.81)	-1.69	(0.77)	**-1.72**	(0.57)	**-1.02**	(0.40)
Southeast Asian	0.62	(0.61)	0.09	(0.72)	-0.32	(0.67)	-0.01	(0.59)
Chi-square (D.F.)				3856.98 (44)				
N				12,274				
WOMEN								
Intercept	**2.80**	(0.17)	**1.90**	(0.18)	-0.49	(0.24)	-0.32	(0.26)
Mother's ancestry								
Native-born French	0		0		0		0	
Maghrebin	**-1.33**	(0.43)	-0.50	(0.29)	**-3.21**	(1.01)	-0.90	(0.60)
Repatriate	0.13	(0.17)	0.28	(0.15)	**-1.45**	(0.31)	-0.32	(0.30)
South European	**-0.99**	(0.19)	**-0.70**	(0.14)	**-1.75**	(0.22)	-0.28	(0.20)
East European	-0.50	(0.37)	-0.79	(0.35)	-0.75	(0.36)	-0.45	(0.53)
African	0.12	(0.38)	-0.20	(0.37)	-2.25	(1.03)	-0.09	(0.56)
Chi-square (D.F.)				3123.26 (44)				
N				8,700				

Note: Standard errors are given in brackets; emboldened coefficients indicate significance at the .05 level or
higher.
Controlled by qualification
Source: FQP 2003 Survey INSEE

percent), against only 3 percent for Turks. Yet during the same period, the proportion of sub-Saharan and Turkish second generations who have been entirely schooled in the French system increased. These groups may now better challenge the others in the queue on the labor market.

2. Educational reforms have greatly facilitated access to secondary school diplomas and higher education, though the benefit to second generations has been uneven.

3. The chronically high youth unemployment rate dipped briefly in the late 1990s; and unemployment fell for all categories in the 1998 cohort group by several percentage points. However, the unemployment rate for Maghrebins remained much worse (about 20 percent for men and 23 percent for women) than for French-ancestry youngsters (7 percent for men and 12 percent for women), reaching critical levels in low-income suburbs, where unemployment rates are typically twice the national average. By contrast, south European second generations, male and female, show rates of unemployment similar to French-ancestry youngsters.

Table 14.7 shows the consistent link between unemployment and ethnic penalty for certain groups. That penalty subsists regardless of the seniority of an immigration wave, better educational opportunities, and upturns in the economy.

Ethnic penalties hit both genders of Maghrebins the hardest. Although cohort comparisons show a mild improvement for the second cohort in the third year on the job market, the Maghrebins' ethnic penalties remain consistent. Their results are the most distinct. Statistical significance becomes low or absent for the negative coefficients found for sub-Saharans in the 1998 cohort. Southeast Asian males show a significant but falling penalty at three years after school exit. Finally, the powerful ethnic penalty hampering the first cohort of Turkish females in their third year on the job market vanishes in the second cohort. No other overall trend stands out.

An initial conclusion is that the high second-generation unemployment rates have fallen, which is consistent with the general trend, but the ethnic penalties subsist for certain groups and remain fully intact for Maghrebins. A second conclusion is that seniority on the labor market—that is, two more years' presence—does not improve the situation in the same way for all youngsters. Table 14.8 shows that the least educated improve their lot unequally. This is particularly true of vocational-school dropouts. Men and women with academic high-school diplomas both see improvement, but the return on vocational high-school diplomas improves only for males, whereas it deteriorates for females. Likewise, seniority improves the lot of postgraduate males but not of their female peers. This reflects the existence of different career paths for males and females.

The impact of seniority also differs between ethnic groups. Particularly noticeable is the large ethnic penalty in the fifth year for Maghrebins in all cohort groups. We also see that this penalty did not erode with seniority for the 1998 cohort, as it did for the 1992 one. For the later cohort, it is as if the ethnic penalty were at rock bottom at the outset due to the better economic context in the first years on the labor market for this cohort. The ethnic penalty shows less continuity with seniority for the other ethnic groups. For Southeast Asian males, negative coefficients gradually fall to nonsignificance. The strong penalty affecting 1992 Turkish females disappears, as it does for sub-Saharan females, although sub-Saharan males in both cohorts show stronger negative coefficients, but these lose significance.

One important point must be stressed. Throughout this period, holders of lower diplomas derived no benefit from a better job market, unlike their peers with intermediate vocational qualifications; Maghrebin youth held diplomas that were both low and academic, thus showing unfavorable characteristics. So let us concentrate now on the categories of low education. I am able to track undereducated youth over a longer period, by comparing undereducated youth in the 1992 and 1998 cohorts with 1989 school leavers for whom we have a specific study (EVA 1989) on those with low levels of education. In this study, ethnic groups are collapsed into EU and non-EU origins; at this date, the Portuguese predominate in the first group and the Maghrebins in the second. I have built similar categories for the 1992 and 1998 cohorts. Table 14.8 shows very clearly that the ethnic penalty for undereducated non-EU youths is on the rise just as the job-qualifying power of lower diplomas continues to fall.

In sum, the observation of a consistent hiring penalty for Maghrebins shows that it remains broadly immune to upturns in the economy. All the relevant coefficients are statistically significant, and this penalty is the most consistent. The penalties for the other ex-colonial groups, sub-Saharans and Southeast Asians, are more variable. Smaller sample sizes for these two populations make interpretation riskier, although the penalty for sub-Saharan males seems the more sustained. Finally, more recent immigrant groups all face hiring penalties, although Turkish males, in large numbers enrolled in vocational programs, seem to escape for the most part, even though a large share hold no diplomas. Turkish females were few but faced a strong penalty in two cases. As a group, Turks seem to behave like Portuguese, but the small sample size makes interpretation hazardous.

TABLE 14.7
Access to employment by cohort, 3 and 5 years after leaving school

	Cohort 1992, 3 years after	Cohort 1992, 5 years after	Cohort 1998, 3 years after	Cohort 1998, 5 years after	Cohorts 1992 and 1998, 3 years after
MEN					
Constant	2,19***	2,19***	2,62***	2,44***	2,26***
Origin (father's or mother's country of birth)					
France	*ref.*	*ref.*	*ref.*	*ref.*	*ref.*
Maghreb	-0,54***	-0,32*	-0,48***	-0,49**	-0,49***
Southern Europe	0,06	0,22	0,15	0,24	0,11
Turkey	0,26	-0,03	0,10	-0,09	0,14
Southeast Asia	-0,72*	0,36	-0,40*	-0,19	-0,45*
Sub-Saharan Africa	-0,32	-0,39	-0,45*	-0,53	-0,38*
Other Europe	0,29	-0,09	-0,33	-0,35	-0,09
Other countries	-0,14	-0,03	-0,4*	-0,19	-0,34*
Qualification					
Some secondary school w/out any degree	-1,44***	-1,79***	-1,80***	-1,72***	-1,64***
Academical track to last year w/out any degree	-0,83***	-0,74***	-1,09***	-1,13***	-0,99***
Vocational track w/out any degree	-0,62***	-0,65***	-0,82***	-0,85***	-0,73***
Vocational degrees (certified)	*ref.*	*ref.*	*ref.*	*ref.*	· *ref.*
Academical Bac and further studies w/out degree.	-0,48**	0,45	-0,27*	-0,05	-0,31**
Technological Bac and furthers studies w/out degree	0,4**	0,56***	0,41***	0,68***	0,41***
Bac + 2	0,58***	0,64***	0,53***	0,54***	0,54***
> Bac + 2	0,43***	0,76***	0,23*	0,64***	0,30***
Generation					
Generation 1	-0,51	-0,99**	-0,44	0,8	-0,47
Generation 1,5	-0,32*	-0,6**	-0,07	-0,33	-0,17
Generation 2	-0,27	-0,36*	-0,27*	-0,53*	-0,27**
Generation 2,5 and 3	*ref.*	*ref.*	*ref.*	*ref.*	*ref.*
Cohorts					
G 98					0,32***
G 92					*ref.*
N	12848	13872	24222	9782	37070

TABLE 14.7 (CONTINUED)

	Cohort 1992, 3 years after	Cohort 1992, 5 years after	Cohort 1998, 3 years after	Cohort 1998, 5 years after	Cohorts 1992 and 1998, 3 years after
WOMEN					
Constant	1,29***	1,28***	1,53***	1,78***	1,31***
Origin (father's or mother's country of birth)					
France	*ref.*	*ref.*	*ref.*	*ref.*	*ref.*
Maghreb	-0,5**	-0,31*	-0,39***	-0,46**	-0,43***
Southern Europe	0,16	0,18	0,08	-0,18	0,12
Turkey	-1,00*	-0,34	-0,07	-0,58	-0,32
Southeast Asia	-0,53	0,14	0,02	-0,33	-0,11
Sub-Saharan Africa	-0,71**	-0,21	-0,28	0,13	-0,47*
Other Europe	-0,19	-0,34	0,23	0,24	0,05
Other countries	-0,66*	-0,26	-0,35*	-0,39	-0,42*
Qualification					
Some secondary school w/out any degree	-1,55***	-1,33***	-1,08***	-1,64***	-1,34***
Academical track to last year w/out any degree	-0,38**	-0,51***	-0,75***	-0,79***	-0,59***
Vocational track w/out any degree	-0,39***	-0,44***	-0,61***	-0,85***	-0,49***
Vocational degrees (certified)	*ref.*	*ref.*	*ref.*	*ref.*	*ref.*
Academical Bac and further studies w/out degree.	0,05	0,65*	0,43***	0,40**	0,35***
Technological Bac and furthers studies w/out degree	0,51***	0,24*	0,74***	0,47***	0,64***
Bac + 2	1,16***	0,82***	1,31***	0,99***	1,25***
> Bac + 2	1,27***	1,17***	0,99***	0,96***	1,08***
Generation					
Generation 1	-0,28	-0,69*	-0,04	0,07	0,19
Generation 1,5	0,24	-0,28	-0,08	-0,27	-0,003
Generation 2	0,02	-0,35*	-0,12	-0,18	-0,06
Generation 2,5 and 3	*ref.*	*ref.*	*ref.*	*ref.*	*ref.*
Cohorts					
G 98					0,21***
G 92					*ref.*
N	10567	10710	18991	7552	29558

Note: Significance thresholds : 0.001***, 0.01 ** and 0.1 *.
Source: Génération 1992 and 1998 CÉREQ

TABLE 14.8
Ethnic penalty in access to employment for low educated (cohorts 1989, 1992, 1998)

	Men			Women		
	Cohort 1989	Cohort 1992	Cohort 1998	Cohort 1989	Cohort 1992	Cohort 1998
Intercept	2.01***	2.19***	2.64***	1.19***	1.29***	1.51***
Ancestry						
French	*Ref.*	*Ref.*	*Ref.*	*Ref.*	*Ref.*	*Ref.*
EU	0.25	0.06	0.1	0.29	0.24	0.09
Non EU	-0.50***	-0.52**	-0.62***	-0.08	-0.55***	-0.28*
Qualification						
Some school	-0.91***	-1.42***	-1.78***	-0.91***	-1.57***	-1.09***
Academic track w/out degree	-0.76***	-0.82***	-1.08***	-0.45*	-0.39***	-0.76***
Vocational track w/out degree	-0.41**	-0.62***	-0.81***	-0.25	-0.39***	-0.62***
Vocational degree CAP-BEP	*Ref.*	*Ref.*	*Ref.*	*Ref.*	*Ref.*	*Ref.*
Generation						
G.1	-0.26	-0.62	0.06	-0.14	-0.38	0.66
G. 1,5	-0.01	-0.08	0.06	-0.46	0.14	0.04
G.2	-0.51**	-0.22	0.15	-0.21	-0.02	-0.04
G. 2,5 et 3	*Ref.*	*Ref.*	*Ref.*	*Ref.*	*Ref.*	*Ref.*
N	7392	6713	10982	4049	4897	5979

Source: EVA 1989, Génération 1992 and 1998 Surveys, CÉREQ

The Mechanisms of Durable Downward Assimilation

Thus, certain groups suffer a robust ethnic penalty that carries over from parent to child or from one second-generation cohort to the next despite better educational opportunities or a more favorable job market, and it shows up over time in individual job histories. Let us concentrate now on some of the underlying mechanisms that may explain this situation and the way they combine to provide a scenario for a durable downward assimilation.

Educational Profiles and Statistical Evidence of Discrimination

Education, of course, is a main issue. Differences in educational attainment explain much of the differences in unemployment and occupational attainment for the different ethnic groups. Yet further effects of lower educational attainments appear. First, the results show that, in the relatively favorable job market of the late 1990s, the lowest diplomas lost ground to intermediate and higher vocational qualifications, and consequently second-generation Maghrebins were placed at a further disadvantage. Then, if we add that Maghrebins with diplomas still suffered the penalty to some extent, we infer that there are grounds for interpreting the ethnic penalty in terms of what economists call "statistical discrimination" (Arrow 1973). In a context of incomplete information, employers rely on the average profile of job candidates at the time of hiring (viewed as negative for Maghrebins). This reasoning suggests a ripple effect that hampers more qualified candidates in the same ethnic group, as seems to be the case. However, we should remember that this assumes classification of individuals into a given category on the basis of socially constructed "visible" traits. This hardly rules out the presence of overtly racist discrimination.

These mechanisms come on top of persistent, negative scholastic profiles, which raise the question of what is happening in the school system and call for a reassessment of the school careers of relatively unemployable ethnic groups. Advocates of the Republican model regularly point to research reporting that, after allowing for social background, immigrant offspring fare just as well as their native French peers do, if not slightly better, in part due to the higher ambitions of immigrant parents (Vallet and Caille 1996). A superficial reading of these results indicates a fairly favorable status for Maghrebin youth, with parents holding high educational ambitions for their children and a preference for academic programs (Brinbaum and Kieffer 2005), backed up by a few stunning success stories (Santelli 2001; Zéroulou 1988). The situation has seemed in the past to be more negative for Portuguese offspring, who frequently opted into low-prestige vocational programs, with their parents' blessings. Yet, coming from undereducated working-class families, Maghrebin youth often leave school with low diplomas earned in academic programs; few reach university. On a tough job market, these diplomas are worth far less than the vocational qualifications held by their Portuguese peers, who often enter the job market through apprenticeships (Silberman and Fournier 1999). This situation has worsened over the past decade: a significant share of Maghrebins are still underqualified despite greater educational opportunities, while their Portuguese and other peers have been exploiting the new educational opportunities to access postsecondary education.

Thus, behind the difficulties of Maghrebin youth, we find educational strategies. Differences in parental experiences probably underpin the differences in aspirations, choice of educational programs, and scholastic achievement: on the one hand, Portuguese parents, most of them skilled workers, encourage their children to enter vocational careers that build gradually, while on the other, Maghrebin parents, who were unskilled workers and often retired or laid off in the 1970s, see their priority as saving their offspring from unskilled manual labor, for which there is no mobility path. The preference of Maghrebin parents for an academic education may be reinforced by their familiarity with the French educational system from the colonial era, though a high proportion has little if any education and cannot help their children at school. Within this context, low scholastic achievement in these offspring is a sensitive matter, as it clashes with aspirations (Silberman and Fournier 1999), and is prone to spark conflict in the classroom (Van Zanten 2001), which triggers early school leaving, minimal returns on the labor market, and, ultimately, the sort of unrest seen in late 2005, in which numerous early school dropouts were involved.

Social Capital and Job-Market Entry

Maghrebin parents' educational strategies may also anticipate their lack of social capital to help their children get a job, as they do not hold good positions on the labor market. The U.S. literature points to the importance of the social capital available to an ethnic group for securing first jobs. Coleman (1988) defines social capital as the number of useful contacts, who become increasingly important as unemployment rises. EVA 89 data show that less educated Maghrebin offspring rely on family members or family friends less than do their Portuguese peers, who also exploit the networks they have acquired from their apprenticeship opportunities (Silberman and Fournier 1999). More than 50 percent of less educated second-generation Portuguese found their first job in companies already employing a relative, whereas this was the case for only 40 percent of the Maghrebin boys. For related reasons, the Maghrebins are more involved in job programs in the civil service than are the Portuguese, who can enter the private sector through family relations.

Discrimination

Yet an ethnic penalty remains when education and other factors such as social capital are controlled, leaving room for discrimination as one of the mechanisms involved. Differences between attainments on the open market and in the public sector support this explanation. The ethnic penalty for first-time job seekers of Maghrebin or sub-Saharan origins on the open market contrasts sharply with the pattern in the public sector. For the different cohorts, there is no apparent penalty in the civil service, in which these two groups are overrepresented, whether as permanent civil servants or beneficiaries of new job programs for the underqualified (Silberman and Fournier 1999, 2006). Nor is there any negative effect on salaries for those who secure jobs in the private or public sector, as shown in a series of studies performed on the Génération 98 data (Dupray and Moulet 2004; Silberman and Fournier 2007a). Regardless of the reasons for these findings—in one case, exam-based government hiring, preference for the civil service because of perceived barriers in the private sector, or the high status of civil-service work among ex-colonial groups; and in the other, overqualification for a position or diminished aversion after hiring—the absence of an ethnic penalty seems indicative. It supports the idea that the ethnic hiring penalty on the open market is partly due to discrimination, even if it falls short of proof.

The perceptions of youth themselves also argue in favor of discrimination (Silberman and Fournier 2006, Silberman and Fournier 2007a). Asked "Have you ever been a victim of hiring discrimination?" 40 percent of Maghrebin males answered yes, as did 30 percent of their female peers. Sub-Saharans turned in equally numerous affirmative responses. This contrasts with rates of around 20 percent for Turkish and Southeast Asian offspring or 10 percent for Portuguese. Figures 14.1a and 14.1b show the reasons given by respondents for discrimination. Maghrebins of both genders give family name as the top reason, followed by skin color. Sub-Saharans cite the same two reasons but in the reverse order. These are exactly the same items that appear after anonymous testing in which job applications use different names and omit identification photos. Neighborhood address comes in third place and significantly so only for Maghrebin and sub-Saharan males but rarely for females, suggesting that employers perceive a domicile in a "tough" neighborhood as an indicator of a male's potential delinquency.

Responses obviously include a dose of subjectivity and do not prove discrimination in themselves. However, the perception is so widely held that it argues in favor of discrimination, that is, unfair hiring criteria. This does not preclude a sensitivity in youths that leads to what Goffman (1963) called "overinterpretation" and "hyperreactivity," stimulated by the social hostility they face. This sensitivity goes hand in hand with other negative perceptions these youth have about the jobs they are holding and about their careers in general. The data show the prevalence of negative perceptions among Maghrebins. Males as well as females are more pessimistic about their future than are their native French peers or members of other ethnic groups. Over 40 percent of the male Maghrebin job holders (twice the figure for their

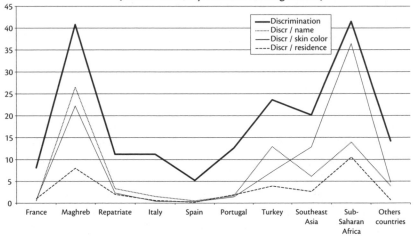

FIGURE 14.1A

Motive for discrimination according to men
(cohort 1998, 3 years after leaving school)

Discrimination
Discr / name
Discr / skin color
Discr / residence

France Maghreb Repatriate Italy Spain Portugal Turkey Southeast Asia Sub-Saharan Africa Others countries

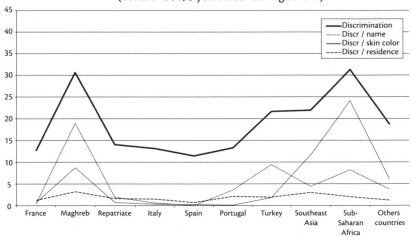

FIGURE 14.1B

Motive for discrimination according to women
(cohort 1998, 3 years after leaving school)

Discrimination
Discr / name
Discr / skin color
Discr / residence

France Maghreb Repatriate Italy Spain Portugal Turkey Southeast Asia Sub-Saharan Africa Others countries native French peers) report that they are already looking for another job, a strong indicator of job dissatisfaction. Higher shares also report wanting to go into business, which is one way around the hiring barrier. Southeast Asian males and sub-Saharan females present similarly negative perceptions, but less systematically so, while Portuguese and Turkish respondents show none (Silberman and Fournier 2006).

The extremely negative perceptions held in some groups obviously affect their social integration. The feelings are real, and their broad consequences require consideration. They may reinforce the process of downward integration on the job market and aggravate the mechanisms of discrimination.

The Vicious Circle of Insecure Jobs and Subjective Perceptions

The final set of factors that might explain the long-term entrenchment of the ethnic penalty for some groups involves a vicious circle of short-term insecure jobs and high unemployment and of pessimistic self-appraisals of employability.

Analysis of job histories[4] shows that affected youth enter a negative spiral of falling employability because of long periods of unemployment and/ or a record of short-term unskilled jobs, which sends negative signals at job interviews, discourages them, and adversely impacts their behavior. A retrospective review of the first four-year job calendars in the EVA 89 survey shows an accumulation of negative events that affects Maghrebin youth most. Once they lose a job, they have a harder time finding the next one (Silberman and Fournier 1999). The longitudinal data from the successive waves of the Génération 98 survey of school leavers show that respondents stood a higher chance of being unemployed in 2003 if they were already jobless in 2001, a trajectory more common for Maghrebins and sub-Saharans (see table 14.9).

The same longitudinal data also reveal the effects of how respondents perceive their situations. All else being equal, respondents were more likely to be unemployed in 2003 if they had reported suffering discrimination or had a bleak job outlook in 2001. This supports the finding from the retrospective EVA 89 data that, all else being equal, the high frustration expressed by Maghrebins over their channeling into vocational curricula increased their chances of being unemployed, especially when it remained strong at the time of job-market entry (Silberman and Fournier 1999).

Here we see something akin to the processes of downward assimilation identified by sociologists (Ogbu and Simons 1998; Portes 1995a; Rumbaut 1996) and economists (Barron, Black, and Loewenstein 1993), in which a per-

TABLE 14.9
Access to employment in 2003 for young persons on the labor market in 2001 (1998 cohort)

	Men				Women			
	Mod. 1	Mod. 2.	Mod. 3.	Mod. 4.	Mod. 1	Mod. 2	Mod. 3	Mod. 4
Origin (father's or mother's country of birth and citizenship)								
French	ref.	ref.	ref.	ref.	ref.	ref.	ref.	ref.
Maghrebin	-0,72***	-0,66**	-0,64**	-0,52**	-0,45*	-0,36	-0,34	-0,32
Situation in 2001								
Employed		ref.	ref.	ref.		ref.	ref.	ref.
Unemployed		-1,67***	-1,57***	-1,64***		-1,67***	-1,6***	-1,65***
Perceptions								
Discrimination				-0,47***				-0,27**
Worried			-0,56***				-0,37***	
N	10523	10523	10523	10523	9949	9949	9949	9949

Note: Other origins are not reported to conserve space
Source: Génération 1998 Survey, CÉREQ
Controls include educational qualification and generation

son's anticipations based on a self-appraisal of his or her situation can foster patterns of avoidance or aggression that send negative signals to hirers who may already have a discriminatory mindset.

The findings remain open to different interpretations. I cannot rule out undetected heterogeneity in the survey population. In that case, negative perceptions would come from individuals with more extreme job-market experiences, who are more aware of their exclusion. The perceptions would then be a spin-off of an increasingly selective job market that is most revealed in the job histories of the most vulnerable job seekers. Alternatively, it may be the job seekers' perceptions that produce patterns of avoidance or aggressive behavior, with negative signals to hirers that reinforce discriminatory attitudes, trigger overt discrimination, and then reinforce the applicant's original negative perceptions. Discrimination can be self-reinforcing.

Conclusion: Revisiting the Segmented-Assimilation Model in the French Context

Three second-generation groups, Maghrebins, sub-Saharan Africans, and, to a lesser degree, Southeast Asians, face serious barriers upon entry to a tight labor market and suffer ethnic penalties that an economic upturn failed to erode. Many respondents in the two first groups feel targeted by discrimination and worry about their future careers. Second-generation Maghrebins face as heavy a hiring penalty as their parents did, although this group is rather settled now. Nor do they have a better situation than the current first generation, that is, more recent immigrants still on the labor market, some of them also coming with better education. The consequences of this state of affairs reach beyond the issue of employment. They correspond with inequalities that reinforce ethnic divides as groups are shunted to large low-income housing projects and dilapidated neighborhoods. Given the generally poor medium-term outlook for the French job market, these findings constitute unavoidable elements in any diagnosis of early-twenty-first-century French society—a symptom is the November 2005 riots, in which sub-Saharan second generations appeared together with Maghrebins. The potential for durable job insecurity weighing on undereducated youth poses a serious threat to the Republican model. The data I have used refer to the end of the 1990s. Ten years later, in 2010, the level of unemployment is still quite similar in the segregated suburbs.

Are the French and U.S. situations comparable? What does an understanding of the French situation contribute to models of immigrant integration in the U.S. literature? France seems to host a process of downward assimilation that will last at least through the medium term, a symptom consistent with the segmented-assimilation model. One salient feature is that the most vulnerable groups originate in ex-colonial possessions. Their experiences are unlike those of groups such as the Portuguese but also, interestingly, the Turks. Well along on the path blazed by the Portuguese, the Turks are remarkable for a recent immigration wave with a large share of undereducated members and from a predominantly Muslim country, but one never ruled by France. Its members do express a perception of discrimination, but less consistently and intensely than the Maghrebins; and they face a milder hiring penalty. Thus, the religious factor—namely, Islam—cannot be seen as the main reason for the discrimination against Maghrebin youth. This is in line with perceptions of these youngsters, who do not rank religion as a major reason for discrimination encountered on the job market.

This picture suggests a reformulation of the U.S. model in more general terms. A generalization is necessary because of the specifics in the United States that situate racism and the consequences of slavery at the heart of the model's mechanisms—the Afro-Americans in inner-city ghettos acting as cultural models for the second generations from low-income immigrant groups. There is no analogue there to the Maghrebin case. We therefore face a more general problem of the relationship of ruler to ruled, wherein slavery and colonization are but two variants. Such a relationship can arise between a host society and its indigenous minorities or ethnic immigrant waves. It sets up a context of mutual hostility and reciprocal expectations that shape behavior and representations. All immigrants are "outsiders," but some stand further outside than others. Here, the individual colonial histories of each group could be an important factor. The histories may help explain why Maghrebins suffer a heavier penalty than sub-Saharans or Southeast Asians do. More research is needed into differences among Maghrebin countries and into the special case of Algeria, once legally an integral part of France that only achieved independence after a particularly violent war. We also need to investigate differences between sub-Saharans and black immigrants from overseas possessions still under French rule. Further, the values fostered by the colonizer during the colonial period might help explain the schooling strategies of certain ethnic groups, for example, why working-class immigrant parents prod their children to pursue academic programs and avoid gradual socio-professional mobility via the vocational route.

We also need to refine the U.S. model because our analysis shows that a history of domination does not suffice. It must graft itself onto the mechanisms of discrimination at play on the job market and amplify them. Its effects are more powerful on groups with low incomes, little social capital, and other disadvantages. Not all immigration waves from ex-French possessions suffer from discrimination to the same degree; for example, Southeast Asian youth complain of discrimination yet possess greater resources and experience an ethnic penalty less consistently.

These considerations call for longer-term follow-up of the more recent immigration waves, that is, Turks and sub-Saharans. They also call for new approaches to international comparisons: do the same migration waves lead to the same trajectories regardless of the presence or absence of previous domination by the host country? Of course, the conclusions here are only provisional, and the current situation may not compromise the assimilation process in the long term, as Alba and Nee (2003) argue. A persistent ethnic penalty may also coexist with some social mobility. The immediate situation in France, however, does point to the existence of a process of widespread and durable downward assimilation along ethnic lines that affects a large share of second-generation youth.

NOTES

'Ihis chapter synthesizes the results of Silberman and Fournier (1999, 2006, 2007b) and Silberman, Alba, and Fournier (2007) into a broader overview. All research includes analytical work undertaken together with Irène Fournier and has benefited from joint research and discussion with Richard Alba and Anthony Heath; but the author assumes full responsibility for all interpretations and conclusions.

1. It must be noted that Dominique Schnapper has changed her view, saying that the existence of ethnic frontiers in French society must now be acknowledged even if they are regrettable (Schnapper 2006).

2. One recent example is Rachida Dati, the former minister of justice of Sarkozy.

3. A new organization called CRAN (Conseil représentatif des associations noires) has appeared. It has conducted the first survey based on the color question and designed to estimate the number of black people in France. A national day has now been designated to commemorate the sufferings of slavery.

4. See CEREQ-LASMAS (1993–2004).

References

Achermann, Christin, and Stefanie Gass. 2003. *Staatsbürgerschaft und soziale Schliessung: Eine rechtsethnologische Sicht auf die Einbürgerungspraxis der Stadt Basel.* Zurich: Seismo.

Aguilera, Michael B., and Douglas S. Massey. 2003. "Social Capital and the Wages of Mexican Migrants: New Hypotheses and Tests." *Social Forces* 82:671–701.

Ahmad, Fauzia, Tariq Modood, and Stephen Lissenburgh. 2003. *South Asian Women and Employment in Britain: The Interaction of Gender and Ethnicity.* London: Policy Studies Institute.

Alba, Richard. 1998. "Assimilation's Quiet Tide." Pp. 327–335 in *Majority and Minority: The Dynamics of Race and Ethnicity in American Life,* 6th ed., edited by Norman Yetman. Boston: Allyn and Bacon.

———. 2005. "Bright vs. Blurred Boundaries: Second-Generation Assimilation and Exclusion in France, Germany, and the United States." *Ethnic and Racial Studies* 28:20–49.

———. 2008. "Why We Still Need a Theory of Mainstream Assimilation." *Kölner Zeitschrift für Soziologie und Sozialpsychologie* 48:37–56.

———. 2009. *Blurring the Color Line: The New Chance for a More Integrated America.* Cambridge, MA: Harvard University Press.

Alba, Richard, and Nancy Foner. 2009. "Entering the Precincts of Power: Do National Differences Matter for Immigrant Minority Political Participation?" Pp. 277–293 in *Bringing Outsiders In: Transatlantic Perspectives on Immigrant Political Incorporation,* edited by Jennifer Hochschild and John H. Mollenkopf. Ithaca, NY: Cornell University Press.

Alba, Richard, and Tariquel Islam. 2009. "The Case of the Disappearing Mexican Americans: An Ethnic-Identity Mystery." *Population Research and Policy Review* 28:109–121.

Alba, Richard, John Logan, and Brian Stults. 2000. "The Changing Neighborhood Contexts of the Immigrant Metropolis." *Social Forces* 79:587–621.

Alba, Richard, and Victor Nee. 1997. "Rethinking Assimilation Theory for a New Era of Immigration." *International Migration Review* 31:826–875.

———. 2003. *Remaking the American Mainstream: Assimilation and Contemporary Immigration.* Cambridge, MA: Harvard University Press.

Alba, Richard, and Roxanne Silberman. 2002. "Decolonization Immigrations and the Social Origins of the Second Generation: The Case of North Africans in France." *International Migration Review* 36:1169–1193.

———. 2009. "The Children of Immigrants and Host-Society Educational Systems: Mexicans in the United States and North Africans in France." *Teachers College Record* 111:1444–1475.

Aleinikoff, T. Alexander. 2001. "Policing Boundaries: Migration, Citizenship and the State." Pp. 267–291 in *E Pluribus Unum? Contemporary and Historical Perspectives on Immigrant Political Incorporation,* edited by Gary Gerstle and John Mollenkopf. New York: Russell Sage Foundation.

———. 2003. "Between National and Postnational: Membership in the United States." Pp. 110–129 in *Toward Assimilation and Citizenship: Immigrants in Liberal Nation-States,* edited by Christian Joppke and Ewa Morawksa. New York: Palgrave Macmillan.

Alexander, Claire. 1996. *The Art of Being Black.* Oxford, UK: Clarendon.

———. 2002. "Beyond Black: Re-thinking the Colour/Culture Divide." *Ethnic and Racial Studies* 25:552–571.

Alibhai-Brown, Yasmin. 2000. "A Magic Carpet of Cultures in London." *New York Times,* June 25.

Angel, Ronald, and Marta Tienda. 1982. "Determinants of Extended Household Structure: Cultural Pattern or Economic Need?" *American Journal of Sociology* 87:1360–1383.

Arrow, Kenneth. 1973. "The Theory of Discrimination." Pp. 3–33 in *Discrimination in Labor Markets,* edited by Orley Ashenfelter and Albert Rees. Princeton, NJ: Princeton University Press.

Attewell, Paul, and David Lavin. 2007. *Passing the Torch.* New York: Russell Sage Foundation.

Attinasi, Louis. 1989. "Getting In: Mexican Americans' Perceptions of University Attendance and the Implications for Freshman Year Persistence." *Journal of Higher Education* 60:247–277.

Aydemir, Abdurrahman, and Arthur Sweetman. 2008. "First and Second Generation Immigrant Educational Attainment and Labor Market Outcomes: A Comparison of the United States and Canada." *Research in Labor Economics* 27:215–270.

Back, Les. 1996. *New Ethnicities and Urban Culture: Racisms and Multiculture in Young Lives.* New York: St. Martin's.

Bade, Klaus. 1994. *Ausländer—Aussiedler—Asyl: Eine Bestandsaufnahme.* Munich: C. H. Beck.

Ballard, Roger. 1996. "The Pakistanis: Stability and Introspection." Pp 121–149 in *Ethnicity in the 1991 Census,* vol. 2, *The Ethnic Minority Populations of Britain,* edited by Ceri Peach. London: HMSO.

———. 1999. "Socio-Economic and Educational Achievements of Ethnic Minorities." Unpublished paper submitted to The Commission on the Future of Multi-Ethnic Britain. London: The Runnymede Trust.

Bankston, Carl L., and Min Zhou. 2002. "Social Capital as Process: The Meaning and Problems of a Theoretical Metaphor." *Sociological Inquiry* 72:285–317.

Barkan, E. R., and N. Khokhlov. 1980. "Socioeconomic Data as Indexes of Naturalization Patterns in the United States—a Theory Revisited." *Ethnicity* 7:159–190.

Barn, Ravinder. 2001. "Caribbean Families and the Child Welfare System in Britain." Pp. 204–218 in *Caribbean Families in Britain and the Trans-Atlantic World,* edited by Harry Goulbourne and Mary Chamberlain. London: Macmillan.

Barnett, W. Steven, Kenneth B. Robin, Jason T. Hustedt, and Karen L. Schulman. 2003. *The State of Preschool: 2003 Preschool Yearbook.* New Brunswick, NJ: National Institute for Early Education Research.

Barron, John, Dan Black, and Mark Loewenstein. 1993. "Gender Differences in Training, Capital and Wages." *Journal of Human Resources* 28:343–364.

Bartel, Ann P. 1989. "Where Do the New U.S. Immigrants Live?" *Journal of Labor Economics* 7:371–391.

Basch, Linda G., Nina Glick Schiller, and Cristina Szanton Blanc, eds. 1994. *Nations Unbound: Transnational Projects, Postcolonial Predicaments, and Deterritorialized Nation-States.* Montreux, Switzerland: Gordon and Breach.

Bashi Bobb, Vilna, and Averil Clarke. 2001. "Experiencing Success: Structuring the Perception of Opportunities for West Indians." Pp. 216–226 in *Islands in the City: West Indian Migration to New York*, edited by Nancy Foner. Berkeley: University of California Press.

Basit, Tehmina N. 1997. *Eastern Values, Western Milieu: Identities and Aspirations of Adolescent British Muslim Girls.* Aldershot, UK: Ashgate.

Bauböck, Rainer. 1994. *Transnational Citizenship: Membership and Rights in International Migration.* Aldershot, UK: Edward Elgar.

Baumann, Gerd. 1996. *Contesting Culture: Discourses of Identity in Multi-ethnic London.* Cambridge: Cambridge University Press.

Bean, Frank D., Susan K. Brown, and Rubén G. Rumbaut. 2006. "Mexican Immigrant Political and Economic Incorporation." *Perspectives on Politics* 4:309–313.

Bean, Frank D., Jorge Chapa, Ruth Berg, and Kathryn Sowards. 1994. "Educational and Sociodemographic Incorporation among Hispanic Immigrants to the United States." Pp 73–100 in *Immigration and Ethnicity*, edited by Barry Edmonston and Jeffrey Passel. Washington, DC: Urban Institute Press.

Bean, Frank D., Jeffrey S. Passel, and Barry Edmonston. 1990. *Undocumented Migration to the United States: IRCA and the Experience of the 1980s.* Washington, DC: Urban Institute Press.

Bean, Frank D., and Gillian Stevens. 2003. *America's Newcomers and the Dynamics of Diversity.* New York: Russell Sage Foundation.

Bean, Frank D., Georges Vernez, and Charles B. Keely. 1989. *Opening and Closing the Doors: Evaluating Immigration Reform and Control.* Santa Monica, CA, and Washington, DC: Rand Corporation and the Urban Institute.

Beaud, Stephane. 2002. *80% au bac? Et après? Les enfants de la démocratisation scolaire.* Paris: Éditions La Découverte.

Beijbom, U. 1971. *Swedes in Chicago: A Demographic and Social Study of the 1846–1880 Immigration.* Chicago: Chicago Historical Society.

Beller, Emily. 2009. "Bringing Intergenerational Social Mobility into the Twenty-First Century: Why Mothers Matter." *American Sociological Review* 74:507–528.

Bendix, Reinhard. 1964. *Nation-Building and Citizenship.* New York: Wiley.

Bernard, W. S. 1936. "Cultural Determinants of Naturalization." *American Sociological Review* 1:843–953.

Berthoud, Richard. 2005. "Family Formation in Multicultural Britain: Diversity and Change." Pp. 222–253 in *Ethnicity, Social Mobility, and Public Policy*, edited by Glenn C. Loury, Tariq Modood, and Steven M Teles. Cambridge: Cambridge University Press.

Berthoud, Richard, Mark Taylor, and Jonathan Burton, with contributions by Tariq Modood, Nick Buck, and Alison Booth. 2000. "Comparing the Transition from School to Work among Young People from Different Ethnic Groups." Institute for Social and Economic Research, University of Essex.

Bloemraad, Irene. 2004. "Who Claims Dual Citizenship? The Limits of Postnationalism, the Possibilities of Transnationalism and the Persistence of Traditional Citizenship." *International Migration Review* 38:5–42.

———. 2006. *Becoming a Citizen: Incorporating Immigrants and Refugees in the United States and Canada.* Berkeley: University of California Press.

Body-Gendrot, Sophie. 1999. "Ghetto, mythes et réalités." Pp. 279–284 in *Immigration et intégration: L'état des savoirs,* edited by P. Dewitte. Paris: La Découverte.

Body-Gendrot, Sophie, and Marco Martinello, eds. 2000. *Minorities in European Cities: The Dynamics of Social Integration and Social Exclusion at the Neighborhood Level.* Houndmills, UK: Macmillan.

Bogard, Kimber, and Ruby Takanishi. 2005. "PK3: An Aligned and Coordinated Approach to Education for Children 3 to 8 Years Old." *Social Policy Report Society for Research in Child Development* 19:1–23.

Bolzman, Claudio, Rosita Fibbi, and Marie Vial. 2003. *"Secondas—Secondos": Le processus d'intégration des jeunes issus de la migration espagnole et italienne en Suisse.* Zurich: Seismo.

Bonacich, Edna. 1973. "A Theory of Middleman Minorities." *American Sociological Review* 38:583–594.

Bonilla-Silva, Eduardo. 2003. *Racism without Racists: Color-Blind Racism and the Persistence of Racial Inequality in the United States.* Lanham, MD: Rowman and Littlefield.

Boos-Nünning, Ursula, and Yasemin Karakasoglu. 2004. *Viele Welten Leben: Lebenslagen von Mädchen und jungen Frauen mit griechischem, italienischem, jugoslawischem, türkischem und Aussiedlerhintergrund.* Berlin: Bundesministerium für Familien, Senioren, Frauen und Jugend.

Borjas, George. 1988. *International Differences in the Labor Market Performance of Immigrants.* Kalamazoo, MI: W. E. Upjohn Institute for Employment Research.

———. 1990. *Friends or Strangers: The Impact of Immigrants on the U.S. Economy.* New York: Basic Books.

———. 1994. "Long-Run Convergence of Ethnic Skill Differentials: The Children and Grandchildren of the Great Migration." *Industrial and Labor Relations Review* 47:553–573.

———. 1999. *Heaven's Door: Immigration Policy and the American Economy.* Princeton, NJ: Princeton University Press.

Borkowsky, Anna. 1991. *Enfants et jeunes d'origine étrangère dans le système de formation en Suisse.* Berne: Office fédéral de la statistique.

Bourdieu, Pierre. 1997. "The Forms of Social Capital." Pp. 46–58 in *Education, Culture, Economy, Society,* edited by A. H. Halsey, Hugh Lauder, Phillip Brown, and Amy Stuart Wells. Oxford: Oxford University Press.

Bourdieu, Pierre, and J. C. Passeron. 1977. *Reproduction in Education, Society and Culture.* London: Sage.

Boyd, Monica. 2002. "Educational Attainments of Immigrant Offspring: Success or Segmented Assimilation." *International Migration Review* 36:1037–1060.

———. 2003. "Educational Attainments of Immigrant Offspring: Success or Segmented Assimilation?" Pp. 91–117 in *Host Societies and the Reception of Immigrants,* edited by Jeffrey G. Reitz. San Diego: Center for Comparative Research, University of California.

Boyd, Monica, and Elizabeth M. Grieco. 1998. "Triumphant Transitions: Socioeconomic Achievements of the Second Generation in Canada." *International Migration Review* 32:853–876.

Boyd, Monica, and Michael Vickers. 2009. "The Ebb and Flow of Immigration in Canada." Pp. 258–272 in *Social Inequality in Canada: Patterns, Problems and Policies,* edited by James Curtis, Edward Grabb, and Neil Guppy. Toronto: Pearson Education Canada Prentice Hall.

Bradley, Steve, and Jim Taylor. 2004. "Ethnicity, Educational Attainment and the Transition from School." *Manchester School* 72:317–346.

Brandon, Peter. 2004. "The Child Care Arrangements of Preschool Children in Immigrant Families in the United States." *International Migration* 42:65–87.

Brauns, Hildegard, and Susanne Steinman. 1999. "Educational Reform in France, West-Germany, and the United Kingdom: Updating the CASMIN Educational Classification." *ZUMA Nachrichten* 44:7–44.

Breen, Richard, and Jan O. Jonsson. 2005. "Inequality of Opportunity in Comparative Perspective: Recent Research on Educational Attainment and Social Mobility." *Annual Review of Sociology* 31:223–243.

Brinbaum, Yaël, and Anick Kieffer. 2005. "D'une génération à l'autre, les aspirations éducatives des familles immigrées: Ambition et persévérance." *Education et Formations* 72:53–75.

Brown, Tamara Mose. 2010. *Raising Brooklyn: Nannies, Childcare, and Caribbeans Creating Community.* New York: New York University Press.

Brubaker, Rogers. 1989. "Membership without Citizenship: The Economic and Social Rights of Non-Citizens." Pp. 145–162 in *Immigration and the Politics of Citizenship in Europe and North America,* edited by Rogers Brubaker. Lanham, MD: German Marshall Fund of the United States and University Press of America.

———. 1992. *Citizenship and Nationhood in France and Germany.* Cambridge, MA: Harvard University Press.

Bühler, Elisabeth, and Corinna Heye. 2005. *Avancée et stagnation dans la problématique de l'égalité entre hommes et femmes de 1070 à 2000.* Neuchâtel, Switzerland: Office fédéral de la statistique.

Buruma, Ian. 2006. *Murder in Amsterdam.* New York: Penguin.

Butterfield, Sherri-Ann. 2004. "'We're Just Black': The Racial and Ethnic Identities of Second-Generation West Indians in New York." In *Becoming New Yorkers: Ethnographies of the New Second Generation,* edited by Philip Kasinitz, John H. Mollenkopf, and Mary C. Waters. New York: Russell Sage Foundation.

Camarota, Steven A. 2001. "Immigration from Mexico: Assessing the Impact on the United States." Washington, DC: Center for Immigration Studies. http://www.cis.org/articles/2001/Mexico/toc.html.

Camarota, Steven A., and Nora McArdle. 2003. "Where Immigrants Live: An Examination of State Residency of the Foreign Born by Country of Origin in 1920 and 2000." *Center for Immigration Studies Backgrounder,* September.

Carens, Joseph H. 1987. "Aliens and Citizens: The Case for Open Borders." *Review of Politics* 49:251–273.

Cassée, Paul, Ruth Gurny, and Hans Peter Hauser. 1981. "Les difficultés scolaires des enfants étrangers: Destin de la deuxième génération ou conséquence de la politique de l'immigration." Pp. 161–172 in *Être migrant,* edited by A. Gretler, R. Gurny, A. N. Perret-Clermot, and E. Poglia. Bern: Peter Lang.

Castles, Stephen, and Mark J. Miller. 1993. *The Age of Migration: International Population Movements in the Modern World.* London: Macmillan.

CÉREQ-LASMAS, ed. 1993–2004. *Journées d'analyses longitudinales du marché du travail.* Marseille: CÉREQ.

Cerutti, Mauro. 2005. "La politique migratoire de la Suisse, 1945–1970." Pp. 89–134 in *Histoire des politiques d'immigration, d'intégration et d'asile en Suisse,* edited by Hans Mahnig. Zurich: Seismo.

CFR. 1996. *La Commission fédérale contre le racisme (CFR) critique le modèle des trois cercles du Conseil fédéral sur la politique suisse à l'égard des étrangers.* Berne: Commission fédérale contre le racisme.

Chavez, Leo R. 2008. *The Latino Threat: Constructing Immigrants, Citizens, and the Nation.* Stanford, CA: Stanford University Press.

Chin, Margaret. 2005. *Sewing Women: Immigrants in the New York City Garment Industry.* New York: Columbia University Press.

Chiswick, Barry R. 1978. "The Effect of Americanization on the Earnings of Foreign-Born Men." *Journal of Political Economy* 86:897–921.

———. 1991. "Speaking, Reading, and Earnings among Low-Skilled Immigrants." *Journal of Labor Economics* 9:149–170.

Citro, Constance F., and Robert T. Michael. 1995. *Measuring Poverty: A New Approach.* Washington, DC: National Academy Press.

Cockburn, Andrew, and James Ridgeway. 1982. "The Revolt of the Underclass." *Village Voice,* January, pp. 6–12.

Coenen, L. 2001. *Word niet zoals wij: De veranderende betekenis van onderwijs bij Turkse gezinnen in Nederland.* Amsterdam: Het Spinhuis.

Coleman, James S. 1988. "Social Capital in the Creation of Human Capital." *American Journal of Sociology* 94:S95–121.

———. 1990. *Foundations of Social Theory.* Cambridge, MA: Belknap Press of Harvard University Press.

Collingwood, R. G. 1924. *Speculum Mentis.* Oxford: Oxford University Press.

Commission for Racial Equality. 2007. "Race Relations 2006: A Research Study." London Commission for Racial Equality.

Commission Nationale Consultative des Droits de l'Homme. 2008. "La lutte contre le racisme et la xénophobie." Paris.

Connor, Helen, Claire Tyers, Tariq Modood, and Jim Hillage. 2004. "Why the Difference? A Closer Look at Higher Education Minority Ethnic Students and Graduates." Research Report RR552. UK Department for Education. www.dfes.gov.uk/research/data/upload-files/RB552.pdf.

Corak, Miles. 2008. "Immigration in the Long Run: The Education and Earnings Mobility of Second-Generation Canadians." *IRPP Choices* 14:1–30.

Cortes, Carlos E. 1980. "Mexicans." Pp. 698–748 in *Harvard Encyclopedia of American Ethnic Groups,* edited by Stephan Thernstrom, Ann Orlov, and Oscar Handlin. Cambridge, MA: Belknap Press of Harvard University Press.

Crowder, Kyle, and Lucky Tedrow. 2001. "West Indians and the Residential Landscape of New York." Pp. 81–114 in *Islands in the City,* edited by Nancy Foner. Berkeley: University of California Press.

Crul, Maurice. 1994. "Springen over je eigen schaduw: De onderwijsprestaties van Marokkanen en Turken van de tweede generatie." *Migrantenstudies* 10:168–186.

———. 2000. *De sleutel tot succes: Over hulp, keuzes en kansen in de schoolloopbanen van Turkse en Marokkaanse jongeren van de tweede generatie.* Amsterdam: Het Spinhuis.

Crul, Maurice, and Jeroen Doomernik. 2003. "The Turkish and the Moroccan Second Generation in the Netherlands: Divergent Trends between and Polarization within the Two Groups." *International Migration Review* 37:1039–1065.

Crul, Maurice, Adel Pasztor, and Frans Lelie. 2008. *De tweede generatie: Last of kapitaal voor de stad.* The Hague: NICIS.

Crul, Maurice, and Jens Schneider. 2007. "TIES: The Integration of the European Second Generation." Working paper, Institute for Migration and Ethnic Studies (IMES), University of Amsterdam.

Crul, Maurice, and Hans Vermeulen. 2003. "The Second Generation in Europe: Introduction to the Special Issue." *International Migration Review* 37:965–986.

———. 2006. "Immigration, Education and the Turkish Second Generation in Five European Nations: A Comparative Study." Pp. 236–250 in *Immigration and the Transformation of Europe,* edited by C. Parsons and T. Smeeding. Cambridge: Cambridge University Press.

Davies, Scott, and Neil Guppy. 1998. "Race and Canadian Education." Pp. 131–156 in *Racism and Social Inequality in Canada: Concepts, Controversies and Strategies of Resistance,* edited by Vic Satzewich. Toronto: Thompson.

Davis, James, Tom Smith, and Peter Marsden. 2001. *General Social Surveys, 1972–2000: Cumulative Codebook.* Chicago: National Opinion Research Center.

Dayan, Jean-Louis, Annick Échardour, and Michel Glaude. 1996. "Le parcours professionnel des immigrés en France: Une analyse longitudinale." *Économie et Statistique* 259:107–128.

Dekovic, M., T. Pels, and S. Model, eds. 2006. *Child Rearing in Six Ethnic Families: The Multicultural Dutch Experience.* Lewiston, NY: Edwin Mellen.

DeNavas-Walt, Carmen, Bernadette D. Proctor, and Cheryl Hill Lee. 2005. "Income, Poverty and Health Insurance Coverage in the United States: 2004." Current Population Reports: Consumer Income P60-229. Washington, DC: U.S. Bureau of the Census.

DeSipio, Louis, Frank D. Bean, and Rubén G. Rumbaut. 2005. "Immigration Status and Naturalization across Generations: The Consequences of Parental Unauthorized Migration or Naturalization on the Civic and Political Behaviors of 1.5 and 2nd Generation Young Adults in Los Angeles." Paper presented at the annual meeting of the American Political Science Association, Washington, DC, September.

Diehl, Claudia, and Michael Blohm. 2003. "Rights or Identity? Naturalization Processes among 'Labor Migrants' in Germany." *International Migration Review* 37:133–162.

DiMaggio, Paul. 1982. "Cultural Capital and School Success: The Impact of Status Culture Participation on the Grades of High School Students." *American Sociological Review* 47:189–201.

DiPrete, Thomas, Dominique Goux, Eric Maurin, and Amelie Quesnel-Vallee. 2006. "Work and Pay in Flexible and Regulated Labor Markets: A Generalized Perspective on Institutional Evolution and Inequality Trends in Europe and the U.S." *Research in Social Stratification and Mobility* 24:311–332.

Doomernik, Jeroen. 1998. *The Effectiveness of Integration Policies towards Immigrants and Their Descendants in France, Germany and the Netherlands.* Geneva: International Labour Organisation.

Downey, Douglas B. 2008. "Black/White Differences in School Performance: The Oppositional Culture Explanation." *Annual Review of Sociology* 34:107–126.

Duncan, Otis Dudley, and Beverly Duncan. 1955. "A Methodological Analysis of Segregation Indexes." *American Sociological Review* 20:210–217.

Dupray, Arnaud, and Stéphanie Moulet. 2004. "Quelles discriminations à l'encontre des jeunes d'origine maghrébine à l'entrée du marché du travail en France?" Pp. 347–360 in *Marché du travail et genre, Maghreb-Europe,* edited by Lahcen Achy et al. Brussels: Actes du Colloque international de Rabat.

Eggerickx, T., C. Kesteloot, and M. Poulain. 1999. "De allochtone bevolking in België." Censusmonografie nr. 3. Brussels: National Institute of Statistics.

Eldering, Lotty, and Jo Kloprogge. 1989. *Different Cultures, Same School: Ethnic Minority Children in Europe.* Amsterdam: Swets and Zeitlinger.

Elliott, James. 2001. "Referral Hiring and Ethnically Homogeneous Jobs: How Prevalent Is the Connection and for Whom?" *Social Science Research* 30:401–425.

Erikson, Robert, and John H. Goldthorpe. 1992. "The CASMIN Project and the American Dream." *European Sociological Review* 3:145–166.

Erikson, Robert, John H. Goldthorpe, and Lucienne Portocarero. 1979. "Intergenerational Class Mobility in Three Western European Societies." *British Journal of Sociology* 30:415–441.

Erzan, R., and K. Kirisci. 2006. "Determinants of Immigration and Integration of Turkish Immigrants in the European Union." Special issue of *Turkish Studies* 1:7.

Esping-Andersen, Gosta. 1999. *Social Foundations of Post-Industrial Economies.* Oxford: Oxford University Press.

Esser, Hartmut. 1980. *Aspekte der Wanderungssoziologie.* Darmstadt and Neuwied, Germany: Luchterhand.

———. 2004. "Does the New Immigration Require a New Theory of Intergenerational Integration?" *International Migration Review* 38:1126–1159.

Faist, Thomas. 1995. *Social Citizenship for Whom? Young Turks in Germany and Mexican Americans in the United States.* Aldershot, UK: Avebury.

Farley, Reynolds, and Richard Alba. 2002. "The New Second Generation in the United States." *International Migration Review* 36:669–701.

Fase, Willem. 1994. *Ethnic Divisions in Western European Education.* Münster: Waxmann.

Favell, Adrian 1998. *Philosophies of Integration: Immigration and the Idea of Citizenship in France and Britain.* New York: St. Martin's.

———. 2004. "Eurostars and Eurocities: Free Moving Professionals and the Promise of European Integration." New York Council for European Studies at Columbia University. http://www.europanet.org/pub/Favell_jan04.html.

Favell, Adrian, Miriam Feldbaum, and Michael Peter Smith. 2006. "The Human Face of Global Mobility." *Comparative Urban and Community Research* 8:1–25.

Feld, Scott L. 1984. "The Structured Use of Personal Associates." *Social Forces* 62:640–652.

Feldblum, Miriam. 2000. "Managing Membership: New Trends in Citizenship and Nationality Policy." Pp. 475–500 in *From Migrants to Citizens: Membership in a Changing World,* edited by T. A. Aleinikoff and D. Klusmeyer. Washington, DC: Carnegie Endowment for International Peace.

Feliciano, Cynthia. 2005. "Educational Selectivity in U.S. Immigration: How Do Immigrants Compare to Those Left Behind?" *Demography* 42:131–152.

Fenton, Steve. 1999. *Ethnicity: Racism, Class and Culture.* Basingstoke, UK: Macmillan.

———. 2003. *Ethnicity.* Cambridge, UK: Polity.

Fibbi, Rosita, Philippe Wanner, Bulent Kaya, and Etienne Piquet. 2003. "Second Generation Immigrants from Turkey in Switzerland." *Zeitschrift für Türkeistudien* (Journal for Studies on Turkey) 16:217–239.

Fibbi, Rosita, and Gérard De Rham. 1988. "Switzerland: The Position of Second Generation Immigrants on the Labour Market." Pp. 24–55 in *Entering the Working World: Following the Descendants of Europe's Immigrant Labour Force*, edited by Wilpert Czarina. Aldershot, UK: Gower.

Fibbi, Rosita, Mathias Lerch, and Philippe Wanner. 2005. "Processus de naturalisation et caractéristiques socio-économiques des jeunes issus de la migration." Pp. 1–57 in *L'intégration des populations issues de l'immigration en Suisse: Personnes naturalisés et deuxième génération*, edited by OFS. Neuchâtel, Switzerland: Office fédéral de statistique.

Fishman, Joshua Aaron. 1964. "Language Maintenance and Language Shift as a Field of Inquiry: A Definition of the Field and Suggestions for Its Further Development." *Linguistics* 9:32–70.

Floge, Liliane. 1985. "The Dynamics of Child Care Use and Some Implications for Women's Employment." *Journal of Marriage and the Family* 4:143–154.

Foerster, Amy. 2004. "Isn't Anyone Here from Alabama? Solidarity and Struggle in a Mighty, Mighty Union." Pp. 197–226 in *Becoming New Yorkers: Ethnographies of the New Second Generation*, edited by Philip Kasinitz, John Mollenkopf, and Mary C. Waters. New York: Russell Sage Foundation.

Foner, Nancy. 1985. "Race and Color: Jamaican Migrants in New York and London." *International Migration Review* 19:708–727.

———. 1998a. "Towards a Comparative Perspective on Caribbean Migration." Pp. 47–60 in *Caribbean Migration: Globalised Identities*, edited by Mary Chamberlain. London: Routledge.

———. 1998b. "West Indian Identity in the Diaspora: Comparative and Historical Perspectives." *Latin American Perspectives* 25:173–188.

———. 2001. "West Indian Migration to New York: An Overview." Pp. 1–22 in *Islands in the City: West Indian Migration to New York*, edited by Nancy Foner. Berkeley: University of California Press.

———. 2003. "Immigrants and African Americans: Comparative Perspectives on the New York Experience across Time and Space." Pp. 45–71 in *Host Societies and the Reception of Immigrants*, edited by Jeffrey G. Reitz. San Diego: Center for Comparative Immigration Research, University of California.

———. 2005. *In a New Land: A Comparative View of Immigration.* New York: New York University Press.

Fredrickson, George M. 1997. *The Comparative Imagination: On the History of Racism, Nationalism, and Social Movements.* Berkeley: University of California Press.

Freeman, Gary. 2004. "Immigrant Incorporation in Western Democracies." *International Migration Review* 38:945–969.

Friedberg, Rachel M. 2000. "You Can't Take It with You? Immigrant Assimilation and the Portability of Human Capital." *Journal of Labor Economics* 18:221–251.

Gabaccia, Donna. 1994. *From the Other Side: Women, Gender, and Immigrant Life in the United States, 1820–1990.* Bloomington: Indiana University Press.

Gans, Herbert J. 1992. "Second Generation Decline: Scenarios for the Economic and Ethnic Futures of the Post-1965 American Immigrants." *Ethnic and Racial Studies* 15:173.

Ganter, Stephan. 2003. *Soziale Netzwerke und interethnische Distanz: Theoretische und empirische Analysen zum Verhältnis von Deutschen und Ausländern.* Opladen, Germany: Westdeutscher Verlag.

Ganzeboom, Harry H. G, Paul de Graaf, and Donald J. Treiman. 1992. "A Standard International Socio-Economic Index of Occupational Status." *Social Science Research* 21:1–56.

Garcia, Eugene. 2001. *Hispanic Education in the United States: Raíces y Alas.* Lanham, MD: Rowman and Littlefield.

Gates, Henry Louis, Jr. 1997. "Black London." *New Yorker,* April 28, pp. 194–205.

Gates, Henry Louis, Jr., and Cornel West. 2004. "Black, White and Brown." *New York Times Book Review,* May 16, p. 35.

Gibson, Margaret, Silvia Carrasco, Jordi Pàmies, Maribel Ponferrada, and Anna Ríos. 2009. "Different Systems, Similar Results: Immigrant Youth at School in California and Catalonia." Paper presented at the Children of Immigrants in Schools Conference, New York City, October 1–2.

Gilbertson, Greta. 1995. "Women's Labor and Enclave Employment: The Case of Dominican and Colombian Women in New York City." *International Migration Review* 29:657–667.

Gilbertson, Greta, and Audrey Singer. 2003. "The Emergence of Protective Citizenship in the USA: Naturalization among Dominican Immigrants in the Post-1996 Welfare Reform Era." *Ethnic and Racial Studies* 26:25–51.

Gillborn, David. 1998. "Race and Ethnicity in Compulsory Schooling." Pp. 11–23 in *Race and Higher Education,* edited by Tariq Modood and Tony Acland. London: Policy Studies Institute.

Gillborn, David, and Heidi Mirza. 2000. "Educational Inequality: Mapping Race, Class and Gender, A Synthesis of Research Evidence." London: UK Office for Standards in Education.

Gilroy, Paul. 1993. *Small Acts: Thoughts on the Politics of Black Cultures.* London: Serpent's Tail.

Girard, Alain, and Jean Stoetzel. 1953. "Français et immigrés: L'attitude française, l'adaptation des Italiens et des Polonais." *Travaux et Documents* 19. Paris: INED and PUF.

Glazer, Nathan. 1999. "Comment on London and New York: Contrasts in British and American Models of Segregation by Ceri Peach." *International Journal of Population Geography* 5:319–351.

Glazer, Nathan, and Daniel P. Moynihan. 1963. *Beyond the Melting Pot: The Negroes, Puerto Ricans, Jews, Italians, and Irish of New York City.* Cambridge, MA: MIT Press and Harvard University Press.

Glick Schiller, Nina, Linda Basch, and Cristina Blanc-Szanton. 1995. "From Immigrant to Transmigrant: Theorizing Transnational Migration." *Anthropological Quarterly* 68:48–63.

Goffman, Erving. 1963. *Stigma: Notes on the Management of Spoiled Identity.* New York: Simon and Schuster.

Goldthorpe, John H. 2000. *On Sociology.* Oxford: Oxford University Press.

———. 2003. "Outline of a Theory of Social Mobility Revisited: The Increasingly Problematic Role of Education." Paper presented at the Conference in Honour of Professor Tore Lindbekk, Trondheim, April.

González Baker, Susan. 1990. *The Cautious Welcome*. Santa Monica, CA, and Washington, DC: Rand Corporation and Urban Institute.

———. 1997. "The 'Amnesty' Aftermath: Current Policy Issues Stemming from the Legalization Programs of the 1986 Immigration Reform and Control Act." *International Migration Review* 31:5–27.

González, Gilbert. 1990. *Chicano Education in the Era of Segregation*. Philadelphia: Balch Institute Press.

Gordon, Milton M. 1964. *Assimilation in American Life: The Role of Race, Religion, and National Origins*. New York: Oxford University Press.

Gormley, William T., Ted Gayer, Deborah Phillips, and Brittany Dawson. 2005. "The Effects of Universal Pre-K on Cognitive Development." *Developmental Psychology* 41:872–884.

Goulbourne, Harry. 2002a. *Caribbean Transnational Experience*. London: Pluto.

———. 2002b. "Review of *Islands in the City: West Indian Migration to New York*." *Ethnic and Racial Studies* 25:1105–1106.

Goulbourne, Harry, and Mary Chamberlain. 2001. "Caribbean Families in the Trans-Atlantic World." Pp. 2–10 in *Caribbean Families in Britain and the Trans-Atlantic World*, edited by Harry Goulbourne and Mary Chamberlain. London: Macmillan.

Goux, Dominique, and Eric Maurin. 1998. "From Education to First Job: The French Case." Pp 103–142 in *From School to Work*, edited by Yossi Shavit and Walter Müller. Oxford, UK: Clarendon.

Granato, Nadia. 2004. *Ethnische Ungleichheit auf dem deutschen Arbeitsmarkt: Schriftenreihe des Bundesinstituts für Bevölkerungsforschung, Bd. 33*. Opladen, Germany: Leske+Budrich.

Granato, Nadia, and Frank Kalter. 2001. "Die Persistenz ethnischer Ungleichheit auf dem deutschen Arbeitsmarkt: Diskriminierung oder Unterinvestition in Humankapital?" *Kölner Zeitschrift für Soziologie und Sozialpsychologie* 53:497–520.

Granovetter, Mark S. 1973. "The Strength of Weak Ties." *American Journal of Sociology* 78:1360–1380.

———. 1983. "The Strength of Weak Ties: A Network Theory Revisited." *Sociological Theory* 1:201–233

———. 1995. *Getting a Job: A Study of Contacts and Careers*. Chicago: University of Chicago Press.

Grebler, Leo, Joan W. Moore, and Ralph C. Guzmán. 1970. *The Mexican American People: The Nation's Second Largest Minority*. New York: Free Press.

Greenman, Emily, and Yu Xie. 2008. "Is Assimilation Theory Dead? The Effect of Assimilation on Adolescent Well-Being." *Social Science Research* 37:109–137.

Groenendijk, Kees. 2008. *Local Voting Rights for Non-Nationals in Europe: What We Know and What We Need to Learn*. Washington, DC: Migration Policy Institute.

Hagell, Ann, and Catherine Shaw. 1996. *Opportunity and Disadvantage at Age 16*. London: Policy Studies Institute.

Haisken-DeNew, John P., and Joachim R. Frick. 2004. "Desktop Companion to the German Socio-Economic Panel Study (SOEP) Version 7.0 September 2003." DIW-Berlin. September.

Hall, Stuart. 1998. "Aspiration and Attitude: Reflections on Black Britain in the Nineties." *New Formations, Frontlines/Backyards* 33: 38–46.

———. 2000. "Old and New Identities, Old and New Ethnicities." Pp. 144–153 in *Theories of Race and Racism: A Reader,* edited by Les Back and John Solomos. London: Routledge.

Hämmig, Oliver. 2000. *Zwischen zwei Kulturen: Spannungen, Konflikte und ihre Bewältigung bei der zweiten Ausländergeneration.* Opladen, Germany: Leske+Budrich.

Hanson, Victor Davis. 2003. *Mexifornia: A State of Becoming.* San Francisco: Encounter Books.

Harzig, Christine. 2006. "Domestics of the World (Unite?): Labor Migration Systems and Personal Trajectories of Household Workers in Historical and Global Perspective." *Journal of American Ethnic History* 25:48–73.

Haskins, Ron, and Cecilia E. Rouse. 2005. "Closing Achievement Gaps: The Future of Children Policy Brief." Princeton, NJ, and Washington, DC: Princeton University and Brookings Institution.

Hassini, Mohamed 1996. *La réussite scolaire des filles d'origine maghrébine en France.* Paris: L'Harmattan.

Haug, Sonja. 2003. "Interethnische Freundschaftsbeziehungen und soziale Integration: Unterschiede in der Ausstattung mit sozialem Kapital bei jungen Deutschen und Immigranten." *Kölner Zeitschrift für Soziologie und Sozialpsychologie* 55:716–736.

Haug, Werner. 1995. *La Suisse: Terre d'immigration, société multiculturelle: Eléments pour une politique de migration.* Berne: Office fédéral de statistique.

———. 2002. "The Demography of Immigrant Populations in Europe." European Population Papers Series 8. DG III. Strasbourg: Council of Europe.

Heath, Anthony, and Sin Yi Cheung, eds. 2007. *Unequal Chances: Ethnic Minorities in Western Labour Markets.* Oxford: Oxford University Press for the British Academy.

Heath, Anthony, and J. Ridge. 1983. "Social Mobility of Ethnic Minorities." *Journal of Biosocial Science Supplement* 8:169–184.

Heath, Anthony, Catherine Rothon, and Elina Kilpi. 2008. "The Second Generation in Western Europe: Education, Unemployment and Occupational Attainment." *Annual Review of Sociology* 34:211–235.

Heckman, James J. 1997. "The Value of Quantitative Evidence on the Effect of the Past on the Present." *American Economics Association Paper and Proceedings* 87:404–408.

Heckman, James J., Jeffrey Smith, and Nancy Clements. 1997. "Making the Most Out of Programme Evaluations and Social Experiments: Accounting for Heterogeneity in Programme Impacts." *Review of Economic Studies* 64:487–535.

Heckmann, Friedrich, H. W. Lederer, and Susanne Worbs. 2001. "Effectiveness of National Integration Strategies towards Second Generation Migrant Youth in a Comparative European Perspective." Final Report to the European Commission. Bamberg, Germany.

HEFCE. 2005. "Higher Education Admissions: Assessment of Bias." HEFCE Research Paper 2005/47. December.

Héran, François. 2002. "Immigration, marché du travail, intégration." Commissariat Général du Plan, Paris, La Documentation Française.

Hernandez, Donald J. 1993. *America's Children: Resources from Family, Government, and the Economy.* New York: Russell Sage Foundation.

———. 2004. "Demographic Change and the Life Circumstances of Immigrants." *Future of Children* 14:16–47.

Hernandez, Donald J., and Evan Charney, eds. 1998. *From Generation to Generation: The Health and Well-Being of Children in Immigrant Families.* Washington, DC: National Academy Press.

Hernandez, Donald J., Nancy A. Denton, and Suzanne E. Macartney. 2007. "Child Poverty in the U.S.: A New Family Budget Approach with Comparison to European Countries." Pp. 109–140 in *Childhood, Generational Order and the Welfare State: Exploring Children's Social and Economic Welfare,* vol. 1 of *COST A19: Children's Welfare,* edited by Helmut Wintersberger, Leena Alanen, Thomas Olk, and Jens Qvortrup. Odense: University Press of Southern Denmark.

Herwijer, L. 2004. "Voortgezet onderwijs, beroepsonderwijs en hoger onderwijs." Pp. 111–142 in *In Rapportage Minderheden: Onderwijs, arbeid en sociaal-culturele integratie,* edited by J. Dagevos, M. Gijsberts, and C. v. Praag. Rijswijk, Netherlands: SCP.

Herzog-Punzensberger, B. 2003. "Ethnic Segmentation in School and Labour Market—40 Year Legacy of Austrian 'Guestworker' Policy." *International Migration Review* 37:1120–1144.

Hewitt, Roger. 1986. *White Talk, Black Talk: Inter-racial Friendship and Communication amongst Adolescents.* London: Cambridge University Press.

Hill-Scott, Karen 2004. "Universal Preschool Master Plan." Los Angeles: First 5 LA. http://www.laup.net./downloads/Proj_UPK_MasterPlanFinalDraft.pdf.

———. 2005a. "Facilities Technical Report." Los Angeles: First 5 LA.

———. 2005b. "Parents' Views on Universal Preschool: Summary Report on Parent Focus Groups." Los Angeles: First 5 LA.

Hirschman, Charles 2001. "The Educational Enrollment of Immigrant Youth: A Test of the Segmented-Assimilation Hypothesis." *Demography* 38:317–336.

Hofferth, Sandra L. 1996. "Child Care in the United States Today." *Future of Children* 6:41–61.

Hoffmann-Nowotny, Hans-Joachim, ed. 1992. *Chancen und Risiken multikultureller Einwanderungsgesellschaften.* Bern: Schweizerischer Wissenschaftsrat.

Holloway, Susan, and Bruce Fuller. 1999. *Through My Own Eyes: Single Mothers and the Cultures of Poverty.* Cambridge, MA: Harvard University Press.

Hondagneu-Sotelo, Pierrette. 1994. *Gendered Transitions: Mexican Experiences of Immigration.* Berkeley: University of California Press.

Hosmer, David, and Stanley Lemeshow. 1989. *Applied Logistic Regression.* New York: Wiley.

Hutmacher, Walo. 1987. "Le passeport ou la position sociale? Quelques données sur la réussite et l'orientation scolaire d'enfants suisses et étrangers compte tenu de la position sociale des familles." Pp. 228–256 in *Les enfants de migrants à l'école.* Paris: CERI OCDE.

Ihlanfeldt, Keith R, and David L. Sjoquist. 1998. "The Spatial Mismatch Hypothesis: A Review of Recent Studies and Their Implications." *Housing Policy Debate* 9:842–892.

Innocenti Research Centre. 2009. *Children in Immigrant Families in Eight Affluent Countries: Their Family, National and International Context.* Florence, Italy: UNICEF.

Ireland, Patrick. 1994. *The Policy Challenge of Ethnic Diversity: Immigrant Politics in France and Switzerland.* Cambridge, MA: Harvard University Press.

Jacobs, D., K. Phalet, and M. Swyngedouw. 2006. "Political Participation and Associational Life of Turkish Residents in the Capital of Europe." *Turkish Studies* 7:145–161.

Jacobs, D., and J. Tillie, eds. 2004. "Social Capital and the Political Integration of Migrants." Special issue of *Journal of Ethnic and Migration Studies* 30:419–559.

Jacobson, David. 1996. *Rights across Borders: Immigration and the Decline of Citizenship.* Baltimore: Johns Hopkins University Press.

Jasso, Guillermina, and Mark Rosenzweig. 1986. "Family Reunification and the Immigration Multiplier: U.S. Immigration Law, Origin-Country Conditions, and the Reproduction of Immigrants." *Demography* 23:294–311.

Jencks, Christopher. 1992. *Rethinking Social Policy: Race, Poverty, and the Underclass.* Cambridge, MA: Harvard University Press.

———. 2001. "Who Should Get In?" *New York Review of Books,* part 1: November 29; part 2: December 20.

———. 2002. "Who Should Get In? An Exchange." *New York Review of Books,* May 23.

Johnson, Julia Overturf. 2005. "Who's Minding the Kids? Child Care Arrangements 2002." Household Economic Studies P70-101. Washington, DC: U.S. Bureau of the Census. www.census.gov/population/socdemo/child/ppl-964/tab01.pdf.

Johnston, Ron, James Forrest, and Michael Poulsen. 2002. "Are There Ethnic Enclaves/Ghettos in English Cities?" *Urban Studies* 39:591–618.

Joppke, Christian. 1999. *Immigration and the Nation-State.* Oxford: Oxford University Press.

Kalmijn, Matthijs. 1994. "Mother's Occupational Status and Children's Schooling." *American Sociological Review* 59:257–275.

Kalter, Frank. 2003. *Chancen, Fouls und Abseitsfallen: Migranten im deutschen Ligenfußball.* Opladen, Germany: Westdeutscher Verlag.

———. 2005. "Ethnische Ungleichheit auf dem Arbeitsmarkt." In *Arbeitsmarktsoziologie: Probleme, Theorien, empirische Befunde,* edited by Martin Abraham and Thomas Hinz. Opladen, Germany: VS.

———. 2006. "Auf der Suche nach einer Erklärung für die spezifischen Arbeitsmarktnachteile von Jugendlichen türkischer Herkunft: Zugleich eine Replik auf den Beitrag von Holger Seibert und Heike Solga: 'Gleiche Chancen dank einer abgeschlossenen Ausbildung?' (ZfS 5/2005)." *Zeitschrift für Soziologie* 35:144–160.

Kalter, Frank, and Nadia Granato. 2002. "Demographic Change, Educational Expansion, and Structural Assimilation of Immigrants: The Case of Germany." *European Sociological Review* 18:199–226.

———. 2007. "Educational Hurdles on the Way to Structural Assimilation in Germany." Pp. 271–319 in *Unequal Chances: Ethnic Minorities in Western Labour Markets,* edited by Anthony Heath and Sin Yi Cheung. Oxford: Oxford University for the British Academy.

Kalter, Frank, Nadia Granato, and Cornelia Kristen. 2007. "Disentangling Recent Trends of the Second Generation's Structural Assimilation." Pp. 214–245 in *From Origin to Destination,* edited by Stefani Scherer. Frankfurt: Campus.

Kamerman, Sheila B., and Alfred J. Kahn. 1995. *Starting Right: How America Neglects Its Youngest Children and What We Can Do about It.* Oxford: Oxford University Press.

Kao, Grace. 1999. "Psychological Well-Being and Educational Achievement among Immigrant Youth." Pp. 410–477 in *Children of Immigrants: Health, Adjustment and Public Assistance,* edited by Donald J. Hernandez. Washington, DC: National Academy Press.

Kao, Grace, and Marta Tienda. 1995. "Optimism and Achievement: The Educational Performance of Immigrant Youth." *Social Science Quarterly* 76:1 19.

Karpat, Kemal. 1995. "The Turks in America." Pp. 612–638 in *Turcs d'Europe . . . et d'ailleurs*, edited by Stéphane de Tapia. Paris: ERISM.

Kasinitz, Philip. 1992. *Caribbean New York: Black Immigrants and the Politics of Race.* Ithaca, NY: Cornell University Press.

———. 2001. "Invisible No More? West Indian Americans in the Social Scientific Imagination." Pp. 257–275 in *Islands in the City: West Indian Migration to New York*, edited by Nancy Foner. Berkeley: University of California Press.

Kasinitz, Philip, Juan Battle, and Ines Miyares. 2001. "Fade to Black? The Children of West Indian Immigrants in South Florida." Pp. 267–300 in *Ethnicities: Children of Immigrants in America*, edited by Rubén Rumbaut and Alejandro Portes. New York and Berkeley: Russell Sage Foundation and University of California Press.

Kasinitz, Philip, John Mollenkopf, and Mary C. Waters. 2002. "Becoming Americans/ Becoming New Yorkers: Immigrant Incorporation in a Majority Minority City." *International Migration Review* 36:1020–1036.

———, eds. 2004. *Becoming New Yorkers: Ethnographies of the New Second Generation.* New York: Russell Sage Foundation.

Kasinitz, Philip, John Mollenkopf, Mary C. Waters, and Jennifer Holdaway. 2008. *Inheriting the City: The Children of Immigrants Come of Age.* Cambridge, MA, and New York: Harvard University Press and Russell Sage Foundation.

Kasinitz, Philip, and Jan Rosenberg. 1996. "Missing the Connection: Social Isolation and Employment on the Brooklyn Waterfront." *Social Problems* 43:180–196.

Kelek, Necla. 2005. *Die fremde Braut: Ein Bericht aus dem Inneren des türkischen Lebens in Deutschland.* Cologne: Kiepenheuer and Witsch.

Kelson, Gregory, and Debra De Laet, eds.1999. *Gender and Immigration.* Houndmills, UK: Macmillan.

Kim, Dae Young. 2004. "Leaving the Ethnic Economy: The Rapid Integration of Second-Generation Korean Americans in New York." Pp. 154–188 in *Becoming New Yorkers: Ethnographies of the New Second Generation*, edited by Philip Kasinitz, John Mollenkopf, and Mary C. Waters. New York: Russell Sage Foundation.

———. 2006. "Stepping-Stone to Intergenerational Mobility? The Springboard, Safety Net, or Mobility Trap Functions of Korean Immigrant Entrepreneurship for the Second Generation." *International Migration Review* 40:927–962.

Kim, Illsoo. 1982. *The New Urban Immigrants.* New Brunswick, NJ: Rutgers University Press.

Kogan, I., and F. Schubert. 2003. "Youth Transitions from Education to Working Life in Europe: A General Overview." Pp. 5–27 in *School-to-Work Transitions in Europe: Analyses of the EU LFS 2000 Ad Hoc Module*, edited by I. Kogan and W. Müller. Mannheim: MZES.

Konietzka, Dirk, and Holger H. Seibert. 2003. "Deutsche und Ausländer an der 'zweiten Schwelle': Eine vergleichende Analyse der Berufseinstiegskohorten 1976–1995 in Westdeutschland." *Zeitschrift für Pädagogik* 49:567–590.

Kristen, Cornelia. 2004. *School Choice and Ethnic School Segregation.* Munster: Waxmann.

Kwong, Peter. 1997. *Forbidden Workers: Illegal Chinese Immigrants and American Labor.* New York: New Press.

Lamont, Michele. 2000. *The Dignity of Working Men: Morality and the Boundaries of Race, Class, and Immigration.* Princeton, NJ: Princeton University Press.

Lamont, Michele, and Annette Lareau. 1990. "Cultural Capital: Allusions, Gaps and Glissandos in Recent Theoretical Developments." *Sociological Theory* 6:153–168.

Laughlo, Jon. 2000. "Social Capital Trumping Class and Cultural Capital? Engagement with School among Immigrant Youth." Pp. 142–167 in *Social Capital: Critical Perspectives,* edited by Stephen Baron, John Field, and Tom Schuller. Oxford: Oxford University Press.

Le Bras, Hervé. 1998. *Le démon des origines.* Paris: Éditions de l'Aube.

Leibowitz, Arleen, Linda J. Waite, and Christina Witsberger. 1988. "Child Care for Preschoolers: Differences by Child's Age." *Demography* 25:205–220.

Lein, Laura. 1979. "Parental Evaluation of Child Care Alternatives." *Urban and Social Change Review* 12:11–16.

Lesthaeghe, Ron, ed. 1997. *Diversiteit in sociale verandering: Turkse en Marokkaanse vrouwen in België.* Brussels: VUB Press.

———, ed. 2000. *Communities and Generations: Turkish and Moroccan Populations in Belgium.* Brussels: VUB Press.

Levitt, Peggy. 2001. *The Transnational Villagers.* Berkeley: University of California Press.

Liang, Xiaoyan, Bruce Fuller, and Judith D. Singer. 2000. "Ethnic Differences in Child Care Selection: The Influence of Family Structure, Parental Practices, and Home Language." *Early Childhood Research Quarterly* 15:357–384.

Liang, Zai. 1994. "Social Contact, Social Capital, and the Naturalization Process: Evidence from Six Immigrant Groups." *Social Science Research* 23:407–437.

Lieberson, Stanley. 1963. *Ethnic Patterns in American Cities.* New York: Free Press.

———. 1980. *A Piece of the Pie: Blacks and White Immigrants since 1880.* Berkeley: University of California Press.

Lieberson, Stanley, and Mary C. Waters. 1988. *From Many Strands: Ethnic and Racial Groups in Contemporary America.* New York: Russell Sage Foundation.

Light, Ivan, and Steven Gold. 2000. *Ethnic Economies.* San Diego, CA: Academic.

Lin, Nan. 1999. "Social Networks and Status Attainment." *Annual Review of Sociology* 25:467–487.

Lischer, Rolf. 2002. "Intégration réussie des étrangers? La réponse des statistiques: Les enfants et adolescents étrangers dans le système suisse d'éducation et de formation." Pp. 6–18 in *Le parcours scolaire et de formation des élèves immigrés à faibles performances scolaires—une présentation du problème,* edited by CDIP. Emmetten, Switzerland: Conférence suisse des directeurs cantonaux de l'instruction publique.

Lischer, Rolf, Paul Röthlisberger, and Beat Schmid. 1997. *Education and Integration in Switzerland: A Conflicting Picture Regarding the Situation of Foreigners.* Neuchâtel, Switzerland: Siena Group Meeting, Office fédéral de statistique.

Lobo, Peter Arun, and Joseph Salvo. 2004. *The Newest New Yorkers 2000.* New York: New York City Department of City Planning.

Logan, John R., Richard D. Alba, and Thomas McNulty. 1994. "Ethnic Economies in Metropolitan Regions: Miami and Beyond." *Social Forces* 72:691–724.

Logan, John R., and Glenn Deane. 2003. "Black Diversity in Metropolitan America." Report of the Lewis Mumford Center, University at Albany.

Lopes-Claros, Augusto, and Saadia Zahidi. 2005. *Women's Empowerment: Measuring the Global Gender Gap.* Geneva: World Economic Forum.

Lopez, David, and Ricardo Stanton-Salazar. 2001. "Mexican Americans: A Second Generation at Risk." Pp. 57–90 in *Ethnicities: Children of Immigrants in America,* edited by Rubén G. Rumbaut and Alejandro Portes. Berkeley: University of California Press.

Lopez, Nancy. 2003. *Hopeful Girls, Troubled Boys: Race and Gender Disparity in Urban Education.* New York: Routledge.

Loury, Glenn C. 1977. "A Dynamic Theory of Racial Income Differences." In *Women, Minorities, and Employment Discrimination,* edited by Phyllis A. Wallace and Annette Le Mund. Lanham, MD: Lexington Books.

Lucassen, Leo. 2002. "Immigration Now and in the Past: Integration Processes of Immigrants in America from a European Perspective." *Journal of American Ethnic History* 21:85–101.

Lynch, Robert G. 2004. "Exceptional Returns: Economic, Fiscal and Social Benefits of Investment in Early Childhood Development." Washington, DC: Economic Policy Institute.

Mahnig, Hans. 1998. *Integrationspolitik in Grossbritannien, Frankreich, Deutschland und den Niederlanden: Ein vergleichende analyse.* Neuchâtel: Swiss Forum for Migration and Population Studies.

Mahnig, Hans, and Etienne Piguet. 2003. "La politique d'immigration suisse de 1948 à 1998: Évolution et effet." Pp. 63–103 in *Les migrations et la Suisse: Résultats du PNR "Migrations et relations interculturelles,"* edited by Hans Rudolph Wicker, Rosita Fibbi, and Werner Haug. Zurich: Seismo.

Malkin, Victoria. 2004. "Who's Behind the Counter? Retail Workers in New York City." Pp. 115–153 in *Becoming New Yorkers: Ethnographies of the New Second Generation,* edited by Philip Kasinitz, John H. Mollenkopf, and Mary C. Waters. New York: Russell Sage Foundation.

Marie, Claude-Valentin. 2002. "Les Antillais en France: Une nouvelle donne, ADRI: Une nouvelle version de 'Les Antillais de l'Hexagone.'" In *Immigration et intégration: L'état des savoirs,* edited by P. Dewitte. Paris: La Découverte.

Marshall, T. H. 1964. *Class, Citizenship and Social Development.* Garden City, NY: Doubleday.

Massey, Douglas S. 1985. "Ethnic Residential Segregation: A Theoretical Synthesis and Empirical Review." *Sociology and Social Research* 69:315–350.

———. 1987. "Do Undocumented Migrants Earn Lower Wages than Legal Immigrants? New Evidence from Mexico." *International Migration Review* 2:236–274.

Massey, Douglas S., Joaquin Arango, Graeme Hugo, Ali Kouaouci, Adela Pellegrino, and J. Edward Taylor. 1993. "Theories of International Migration: A Review and Reappraisal." *Population and Development Review* 3:431–465.

Massey, Douglas S., Camille Z. Charles, Garvey Lundy, and Mary Fischer. 2003. *The Source of the River: The Social Origins of Freshmen at America's Selective Colleges and Universities.* Princeton, NJ: Princeton University Press.

Massey, Douglas S., Jorge Durand, and Nolan J. Malone. 2002. *Beyond Smoke and Mirrors: Mexican Immigration in an Era of Economic Integration.* New York: Russell Sage Foundation.

Matthews, Glenna. 1987. *Just a Housewife: The Rise and Fall of Domesticity in America.* New York: Oxford University Press.

Matthews, Hannah, and Danielle Ewen. 2006. "Reaching All Children? Understanding Early Care and Education Participation among Immigrant Families." Washington, DC: Center for Law and Social Policy.

Matute-Bianchi, Maria. 1991. "Situational Ethnicity and Patterns of School Performance among Immigrant and Nonimmigrant Mexican Descent Students." Pp. 205–247 in *Minority Status and Schooling: A Comparative Study of Immigrant and Involuntary Minorities,* edited by Margaret Gibson and John Ogbu. New York: Garland.

Mauco, Georges. 1932. *Les étrangers en France: Leur rôle dans l'activité économique.* Paris: Armand Colin.

May, Stephen. 1999. "Critical Multiculturalism and Cultural Difference: Avoiding Essentialism." Pp. 11–41 in *Critical Multiculturalism: Rethinking Multicultural and Antiracist Education,* edited by Stephen May. London: Falmer.

Mayer, N. 1994. "Racisme et xénophobie dans l'Europe des Douze: Étude sociologique." Pp. 65–70 in *La lutte contre le racisme et la xénophobie 1993: Exclusion et Droits de l'Homme.* Rapport de la Commission Consultative des Droits de l'Homme.

Mezey, Jennifer, Mark Greenberg, and Rachel Schumacher. 2002. "The Vast Majority of Federally Eligible Children Did Not Receive Child Care Assistance in FY2000." Washington, DC: Center for Law and Social Policy. http://www.clasp.org/publications/1in7full.pdf.

Min, Pyong Gap. 1996. *Caught in the Middle: Korean Merchants in America's Multiethnic Cities.* Berkeley: University of California Press.

———. 2002. *The Second Generation: Ethnic Identity among Asian Americans.* Walnut Creek, CA: AltaMira.

———. 2008. *Ethnic Solidarity for Economic Survival: Korean Green Grocers in New York City.* New York: Russell Sage Foundation.

Model, Suzanne. 1993. "The Ethnic Niche and the Structure of Opportunity: Immigrants and Minorities in New York City." Pp. 161–193 in *The "Underclass" Debate: Views from History,* edited by Michael Katz. Princeton, NJ: Princeton University Press.

———. 2008. *West Indian Immigrants: A Black Success Story?* New York: Russell Sage Foundation.

Model, Suzanne, and Gene Fisher. 2002a. "The Socio-economic Attainment of Second Generation Americans at the Turn of the Century." Paper presented at the RC28 Conference, Nuffield College, Oxford University.

———. 2002b. "Unions between Blacks and Whites: England and the U.S. Compared." *Ethnic and Racial Studies* 25:728–754.

Modood, Tariq. 1984. "RG Collingwood, MJ Oakeshott and the Idea of a Philosophical Culture." Swansea University College, University of Wales.

———. 1993. "The Number of Ethnic Minority Students in British Higher Education." *Oxford Review of Education* 19:167–182.

———. 1999. "New Forms of Britishness: Post-immigration Ethnicity and Hybridity in Britain." Pp. 77–90 in *Identity and Integration: Migrants in Western Europe,* edited by Rosemarie Sackmann, Bernhard Peters, and Thomas Faist. Aldershot, UK: Ashgate.

———. 2004. "Capitals, Ethnic Identity and Educational Qualifications." *Cultural Trends* 13:87–105.

————. 2005a. "The Educational Attainment of Minorities in Britain." Pp. 288–308 in *Ethnicity, Social Mobility, and Public Policy,* edited by Glenn C. Loury, Tariq Modood, and Steven M. Teles. Cambridge: Cambridge University Press.

————. 2005b. *Multicultural Politics: Racism, Ethnicity, and Muslims in Britain.* Minneapolis and Edinburgh: University of Minnesota Press and University of Edinburgh Press.

Modood, Tariq, and Tony Acland, eds. 1998. *Race and Higher Education.* London: Policy Studies Institute.

Modood, Tariq, Richard Berthoud, Jane Lakey, James Nazroo, Patten Smith, Satnam Virdee, and Sharon Beishon. 1997. *Ethnic Minorities in Britain: Diversity and Disadvantage.* London: Policy Studies Institute.

Mollenkopf, John. 1992. *A Phoenix in the Ashes: The Rise and Fall of the Koch Coalition in New York City Politics.* Princeton, NJ: Princeton University Press.

————. 1999. "Assimilating Immigrants in Amsterdam: A Perspective from New York." *Netherlands Journal of Social Science* 36:126–145.

————. 2001. "The Democratic Vote in Living Color." *New York Times,* March 14.

Mollenkopf, John, David Olson, and Timothy Ross. 2001. "Immigrant Political Participation in New York and Los Angeles." Pp. 17–70 in *Governing American Cities: Interethnic Coalitions, Competition, and Conflict,* edited by Michael Jones-Correa. New York: Russell Sage Foundation.

Montgomery, James D. 1991. "Social Networks and Labor-Market Outcomes: Toward an Economic Analysis." *American Economic Review* 81:1408–1418.

Morawska, Ewa. 2001. "Immigrants, Transnationalism, and Ethnicization: A Comparison of This Great Wave and the Last." Pp. 175–212 in *E Pluribus Unum? Contemporary and Historical Perspectives on Immigrant Political Incorporation,* edited by Gary Gerstle and John Mollenkopf. New York: Russell Sage Foundation.

————. 2003. "Immigrant Transnationalism and Assimilation: A Variety of Combinations and the Analytic Strategy It Suggests." In *Integrating Immigrants in Liberal Nation-States: From Post-national to Transnational,* edited by Christian Joppke and Ewa Morawska. New York: Palgrave Macmillan.

Morokvasic, Mirjana. 1984. "Birds of Passage Are Also Women." *International Migration Review* 68:886–907.

Mouw, Ted. 2003. "Social Capital and Finding a Job: Do Contacts Matter?" *American Sociological Review* 68:868–898.

Müller, Walter, Susanne Steinman, and Renate Ell. 1998. "Education and Labour-Market Entry in Germany." In *From School to Work,* edited by Yossi Shavit and Walter Müller. Oxford, UK: Clarendon.

Münz, Rainer, and Ralf Ulrich. 2003. "The Ethnic and Demographic Structure of Foreigners and Immigrants in Germany." Pp. 19–44 in *Germans or Foreigners? Attitudes toward Ethnic Minorities in Post-reunification Germany,* edited by Richard Alba, Peter Schmidt, and Martina Wasmer. New York: Palgrave.

National Equity Panel (NEP). 2010. *An Anatomy of Economic Inequality in the UK.* London: HMSO.

Nauck, Bernhard. 2001. "Intercultural Contact and Intergenerational Transmission in Immigrant Families." *Journal of Cross-Cultural Psychology* 32:159–173.

Neckerman, Kathryn M., Prudence Carter, and Jennifer Lee. 1999. "Segmented Assimilation and Minority Cultures of Mobility." *Ethnic and Racial Studies* 22:945–965.

Nee, Victor. 2003. "Institutional Change and Immigrant Assimilation in the United States." In *Host Societies and the Reception of Immigrants,* edited by Jeffrey G. Reitz. San Diego: Center for Comparative Immigration Research, University of California.

Nef, Rolf, Vera Herrmann, and Alex Martinovits. 1997. *"Die Ausländer" im Bild des schweizerischen Bevölkerung.* Zurich: Social Insight.

Neuman, Michelle, and John Bennett. 2001. "Starting Strong: Early Childhood Education and Care." Paris: Organization for Economic Co-operation and Development.

NICHD Early Child Care Research Network. 1997. "Familial Factors Associated with Characteristics of Nonmaternal Care for Infants." *Journal of Marriage and the Family* 59:581–591.

Noiriel, Gérard. 1988. *Le creuset francais: Histoire de l'immigration, XIXe–XXe siècles.* Paris: Le Seuil.

Oakeshott, Michael. 1933. *Experience and Its Modes.* Cambridge: Cambridge University Press.

———. 1962. *Rationalism in Politics and Other Essays.* London: Methuen.

OECD. 2001. *Knowledge and Skills for Life: First Results from the OECD Programme for International Student Assessment (PISA) 2000.* Paris: Organization for Economic Co-operation and Development.

———. 2004. *Learning for Tomorrow's World: First Results from PISA 2003.* Paris: Organisation for Economic Co-operation and Development.

———. 2006. "Early Childhood Education and Care Policy: Country Note for Mexico." OECD Directorate for Education. www.oecd.org/dataoecd/11/39/34429196.pdf.

Office of Immigration Statistics. 2008 *Statistical Yearbook of Immigration.* Washington, DC: Department of Homeland Security.

Ogbu, John, and H. D. Simons. 1998. "Voluntary and Involuntary Minorities: A Cultural-Ecological Theory of School Performance with Some Implications for Education." *Anthropology and Education Quarterly* 29:155–188.

Olneck, Michael, and Marvin Lazerson. 1980. "Education." Pp. 303–319 in *Harvard Encyclopedia of American Ethnic Groups,* edited by Stephan Thernstrom, Ann Orlov, and Oscar Handlin. Cambridge, MA: Belknap Press of Harvard University Press,

Omi, Michael, and Howard Winant. 1994. *Racial Formations: From the 1960s to the 1990s.* New York: Routledge.

Ong, Aihwa. 1999. *Flexible Citizenship: The Cultural Logic of Transnationality.* Durham, NC: Duke University Press.

ONZUS (Observatoire National des Zones Urbaines Sensibles). 2009. "Rapport 2009." Éditions du CIV.

Oppenheimer, Valerie Kincade. 1970. "The Female Labor Force in the United States." Population Monograph Series 5. Berkeley, CA: Institute of International Studies.

———. 1997. "Women's Employment and the Gain to Marriage: The Specialization and Trading Model." *Annual Review of Sociology* 23:431–453.

Orfield, Gary. 2001. "Schools More Separate: Consequences of a Decade of Resegregation." Civil Rights Project. http://www.civilrightsproject.ucla.edu/research/deseg/separate_schools01.php.

Ortiz, V., and R. Cooney. 1985. "Sex-Role Attitudes and Labor Force Participation among Hispanic Females and Non-Hispanic White Females." Pp. 174–182 in *The Mexican American Experience: An Interdisciplinary Anthology,* edited by R. de la Garza, F. D. Bean, C. Bonjean, R. Romo, and R. Alvarez. Austin: University of Texas Press.

Owen, David, Anne Green, Jane Pitcher, and Malcolm Maguire. 2000. "Minority Ethnic Participation and Achievements in Education, Training and the Labour Market." UK Department of Education and Employment.

Özüekren, Sule, and Ronald van Kempen. 1997. *Turks in European Cities: Housing and Urban Segregation*. Utrecht: ERCOMER.

Pager, Deborah. 2007. *Marked: Race, Crime, and Finding Work in an Era of Mass Incarceration*. Chicago: University of Chicago Press.

Passel, Jeffrey S., and D'Vera Cohn. 2008. *Trends in Unauthorized Immigration: Undocumented Inflow Now Trails Legal Inflow*. Washington, DC: Pew Hispanic Center.

Pathak, Shalini. 2000. "Race Research for the Future: Ethnicity in Education, Training and the Labour Market." Research Topic Paper. UK Department of Education and Employment.

Patterson, Orlando. 2005. "Four Modes of Ethno-somatic Stratification: The Experience of Blacks in Europe and the Americas." Pp. 67–122 in *Ethnicity, Social Mobility, and Public Policy: Comparing the US and the UK*, edited by Glenn C. Loury, Tariq Modood, and Steven Michael Teles. Cambridge: Cambridge University Press.

Peach, Ceri. 1998. "Trends in Levels of Caribbean Segregation, Great Britain, 1961–91." Pp. 210–225 in *Caribbean Migration: Globalised Identities*, edited by Mary Chamberlain. London: Routledge.

———. 2005. "Social Integration and Social Mobility: Spatial Segregation and Intermarriage of the Caribbean Population in Britain." Pp. 178–203 in *Ethnicity, Social Mobility, and Public Policy*, edited by Glenn C. Loury, Tariq Modood, and Steven M. Teles. Cambridge: Cambridge University Press.

Pease-Alvarez, Lucinda 2002. "Moving beyond Linear Trajectories of Language Shift and Bilingual Language Socialization." *Hispanic Journal of Behavioral Sciences* 24:114–137.

Pels, Trees. 2001. "Student Disengagement and Pedagogical Climate." Paper presented at the Sixth International Metropolis Conference, Rotterdam, November 26–30.

Perlmann, Joel. 1988. *Ethnic Differences: Schooling and Social Structure among the Irish, Italians, Jews and Blacks in an American City, 1880–1935*. New York: Cambridge University Press.

———. 2000. "The Persistence of Culture vs. Structure in Recent Work: The Case of Modes of Incorporation." Pp. 22–33 in *Immigrants, Schooling, and Social Mobility: Does Culture Make a Difference?* edited by Hans Vermeulen and Joel Perlmann. New York: St. Martin's.

———. 2003. "Polish and Italian Schooling Then, Mexican Schooling Now? U.S. Ethnic School Attainments across the Generations of the 20th Century." Annandale-on-Hudson, NY: Levy Institute, Bard College.

———. 2005. *Italians Then, Mexicans Now: Immigrant Origins and Second-Generation Progress, 1890 to 2000*. New York City: Russell Sage Foundation.

Perlmann, Joel, and Roger Waldinger. 1997. "Second Generation Decline? Children of Immigrants, Past and Present: A Reconsideration." *International Migration Review* 31:893–922.

Peterson, Trond, Ishak Saporta, and Marc-David L. Seidel. 2000. "Offering a Job: Meritocracy and Social Networks." *American Journal of Sociology* 106:763–816.

Pew Hispanic Center. 2009. "Mexican Immigrants in the United States 2008." http://pewhispanic.org/files/factsheets/47.pdf.

Phalet, Karen. 2007. "Down and Out: The Children of Migrant Workers in the Belgian Labour Market." In *Unequal Chances: Ethnic Minorities in Western Labor Markets*, edited by Anthony Heath and Sin Yi Cheung. Oxford: Oxford University Press.

Platt, Lucinda. 2005. *Migration and Social Mobility: The Life Chances of Britain's Minority Ethnic Communities*. London: Policy Press.

Portes, Alejandro. 1987. "The Social Origins of the Cuban Enclave Economy in Miami." *Sociological Perspectives* 30:340–372.

——. 1995a. "Children of Immigrants: Segmented Assimilation and Its Determinants." Pp. 248–279 in *The Economic Sociology of Immigration: Essays on Networks, Ethnicity, and Entrepreneurship*, edited by Alejandro Portes. New York: Russell Sage Foundation.

——. 1995b. "Economic Sociology and the Sociology of Immigration: A Conceptual Overview." Pp. 1–41 in *The Economic Sociology of Immigration: Essays on Networks, Ethnicity, and Entrepreneurship*, edited by Alejandro Portes. New York: Russell Sage Foundation.

——, ed. 1995c. *The Economic Sociology of Immigration*. New York: Russell Sage Foundation.

——, ed. 1996. *The New Second Generation*. New York: Russell Sage Foundation.

——. 1998. "Social Capital: Its Origins and Applications in Modern Sociology." *Annual Review of Sociology* 24:1–12.

——. 2006. "Italians Then, Mexicans Now: Immigrant Origins and Second-Generation Progress, 1890–2000." *Sociological Forum* 21:499–504.

Portes, Alejandro, and Josh DeWind. 2004. "A Cross-Atlantic Dialogue: The Progress of Research and Theory in the Study of International Migration." *International Migration Review* 38:828–851.

Portes, Alejandro, and Patricia Fernandez-Kelly. 2008. "No Margin for Error: Educational and Occupational Achievement among Disadvantaged Children of Immigrants." *Annals of the American Academy of Political and Social Science* 620:12–36.

Portes, Alejandro, Patricia Fernandez-Kelly, and William Haller. 2005. "Segmented Assimilation on the Ground: the New Second Generation in Early Adulthood." *Ethnic and Racial Studies* 28:1000–1040.

——. 2009. "The Adaptation of the Immigrant Second Generation in America: A Theoretical Overview and Recent Evidence." *Journal of Ethnic and Migration Studies* 35:1077–1104.

Portes, Alejandro, Luis Guarnizo, and Patricia Landolt. 1999. "Introduction: Pitfalls and Promise of an Emergent Research Field." *Ethnic and Racial Studies* 22:217–237.

Portes, Alejandro, and Robert D. Manning. 1986. "The Immigrant Enclave: Theory and Empirical Example." Pp. 47–68 in *Competitive Ethnic Relations*, edited by Joane Nagel and Susan Olzak. Orlando, FL: Academic Press.

Portes, Alejandro, and Rubén G. Rumbaut. 2001. *Legacies: The Story of the Immigrant Second Generation*. Berkeley and New York: University of California Press and Russell Sage Foundation.

——. 2005. "Introduction: The Second Generation and the Children of Immigrants Longitudinal Study." *Ethnic and Racial Studies* 28:983–999.

——. 2006. *Immigrant America: A Portrait*. Berkeley: University of California Press.

Portes, Alejandro, and Steven Shafer. 2007. "Revisiting the Enclave Hypothesis: Miami Twenty-Five Years Later; The Sociology of Entrepreneurship." *Research in the Sociology of Organizations* 25:175–190.

Portes, Alejandro, and Alex Stepick. 1994. *City on the Edge: The Transformation of Miami.* Berkeley University of California Press.

Portes, Alejandro, and Min Zhou. 1992. "Gaining the Upper Hand: Economic Mobility among Immigrant and Domestic Minorities." *Ethnic and Racial Studies* 15:491–521.

———. 1993. "The New Second Generation: Segmented Assimilation and Its Variants among Post-1965 Immigrant Youth." *Annals of the American Academy of Political and Social Science* 530:74–96.

Presser, Harriet B. 1989. "Some Economic Complexities of Child Care Provided by Grandmothers." *Journal of Marriage and the Family* 51:581–591.

Presser, Harriet B., and Wendy Baldwin. 1980. "Child Care as a Constraint on Employment: Prevalence, Correlates, and Bearing on the Work Fertility Nexus." *American Journal of Sociology* 18:1202–1213.

Pugh, Margaret. 1998. "Barriers to Work: The Spatial Divide between Jobs and Welfare Recipients in Metropolitan Areas." Washington, DC: Brookings Institution.

Putnam, Robert. 1995. "Bowling Alone: America's Declining Social Capital." *Journal of Democracy* 6:64–78.

———. 2000. *Bowling Alone: The Collapse and Revival of American Community.* New York: Simon and Schuster.

Quintini, Glenda, John Martin, and Sébastien Martin. 2007. "The Changing Nature of the School-to-Work Transition Process in OECD Countries." Bonn, Germany: Institute for the Study of Labor.

Raymann, Ursula. 2003. "Meinungen und Einstellungen gegenüber Ausländerinnen and Ausländern in der Schweiz." Zurich: GfS-Forschungsinstitut.

Reay, Diane. 2004. "'It's All Becoming a Habitus': Beyond the Habitual Use of Habitus in Educational Research." *British Journal of Sociology of Education* 25:431–444.

Reid, Ira De A. 1969 [1939]. *The Negro Immigrant: His Background, Characteristics, and Social Adjustments, 1899–1937.* New York: Columbia University Press.

Reitz, Jeffrey G. 1977. "Analysis of Changing Group Inequalities in a Changing Occupational Structure." Pp. 167–191 in *Mathematical Models of Sociology,* edited by P. Krishnan. Keele, UK: University of Keele.

———. 1998. *The Warmth of the Welcome: The Social Causes of Economic Success for Immigrants in Different Nations and Cities.* Boulder, CO: Westview.

———. 2001. "Terms of Entry: Social Institutions and Immigrant Earnings in American, Canadian and Australian Cities." Pp. 50–81 in *Globalization and the New City: Migrants, Minorities and Urban Transformations in Comparative Perspective,* edited by Malcolm Cross and Robert Moore. Houndmills, UK: Palgrave Macmillan.

———. 2003. "Host Societies and the Reception of Immigrants." La Jolla: Center for Comparative Immigration, University of California at San Diego.

———. 2004. "Canada: Immigration and Nation-Building in the Transition to a Knowledge Economy." Pp. 97–133 in *Controlling Immigration. A Global Perspective,* 2nd ed., edited by Wayne Cornelius, Takeyuki Tsuda, Philip Martin, and James Hollifield. Stanford, CA: Stanford University Press.

Reitz, Jeffrey G., and Raymond Breton. 1994. *The Illusion of Difference: Realities of Ethnicity in Canada and the United States.* Toronto: C. D. Howe.

Reitz, Jeffrey G., and Kara Somerville. 2004. "Institutional Change and Emerging Cohorts of the 'New' Immigrant Second Generation: Implications for the Integration of Racial Minorities in Canada." *Journal of International Migration and Integration* 5:385–415.

Reynolds, Tracey. 2006. "Caribbean Families, Social Capital and Young People's Diasporic Identities." *Ethnic and Racial Studies* 29:1087–1103.

Richard, J. L. 1997. "Dynamiques démographiques et socioéconomiques de l'intégration des jeunes générations d'origine immigrée en France." Paris: Economics Institut d'Etudes Politiques.

Richardson, Robin, and Angela Gluck Wood 1999. *Inclusive Schools, Inclusive Society: Race and Identity on the Agenda.* Stoke-on-Trent, UK: Trentham Books.

Rogers, William H. 1993. "Regression Standard Errors in Clustered Samples." *STATA Technical Bulletin Reprints* 3: 88–94.

Rothon, Catherine. 2005. "Black and Minority Ethnic Educational Attainment and Engagement with School in Britain." Ph.D. diss., Sociology Department, Oxford University.

Ruggles, Steven, Matthew Sobek, Trent Alexander, Catherine A. Fitch, Ronald Goeken, Patricia Kelly Hall, Mariam King, and Chad Ronnander. 2004. "Integrated Public Use Microdata Set: Version 3.0." Machine-readable database.

Rumbaut, Rubén G. 1996. "The Crucible Within: Ethnicity Identity, Self-Esteem, and Segmented Assimilation among Children of Immigrants." Pp. 119–170 in *The New Second Generation,* edited by Alejandro Portes. New York: Russell Sage Foundation.

———. 1999. "Passages to Adulthood: The Adaptation of Children of Immigrants in Southern California." Pp. 478–545 in *Children of Immigrants: Health, Adjustment, and Public Assistance,* edited by Donald J. Hernandez. Washington, DC: National Academy Press.

———. 2003. "Conceptual Issues, Methodological Problems, and New Empirical Findings in the Comparative Study of the 'Immigrant Second Generation' in the United States." Paper presented at the Conference on the Second Generation in Europe and North America, Bellagio, Italy, June.

Rumbaut, Rubén G., Frank D. Bean, Leo R. Chavez, Jennifer Lee, Susan K. Brown, Louis DeSipio, and Min Zhou. 2004. "Immigration and Intergenerational Mobility in Metropolitan Los Angeles (IIMMLA)." Computer file. ICPSR. http://dx.doi.org/10.3886/ICPSR22627.

Rumbaut, Rubén G., and Alejandro Portes, eds. 2001. *Ethnicities: Children of Immigrants in America.* Berkeley and New York: University of California Press and Russell Sage Foundation.

Salentin, Kurt, and Frank Wilkening. 2003. "Ausländer, Eingebürgerte und das Problem einer realistischen Zuwanderer-Integrationsbilanz." *Kölner Zeitschrift für Soziologie und Sozialpsychologie* 55:278–298.

Sanders, J. M., and Victor Nee. 1987. "Limits of Ethnic Solidarity in the Ethnic Enclave Economy." *American Sociological Review* 52:745–767.

———. 1996. "Immigrant Self-Employment: The Family as Social Capital and the Value of Human Capital." *American Sociological Review* 61:231–249.

Santelli, Emmanuelle. 2001. *La mobilité sociale dans l'immigration: Itinéraires de réussite des enfants d'origine algérienne.* Toulouse: Presses Universitaires du Mirail.

Sassen, Saskia. 1988. *The Mobility of Capital and Labor*. Cambridge: Cambridge University Press.

———. 1991. *The Global City: New York, London, Tokyo*. Princeton, NJ: Princeton University Press.

Savage, Mike, Alan Warde, and Fiona Devine. 2005. "Capitals, Assets, and Resources: Some Critical Issues." Paper presented at the Cultural Capital and Social Exclusion Workshop, Oxford, UK, January.

Schnapper, Dominique. 1991. *La France de l'intégration: Sociologie de la nation en 1990*. Paris: Éditions Gallimard.

———. 2006. "État des lieux, état des problèmes." In *Les Statistiques ethniques: éléments de cadrage*, report of Centre d'analyse stratégique. Paris: La documentation française.

Schuck, Peter H. 1998. *Citizens, Strangers, and In-Betweens: Essays on Immigration and Citizenship*. Boulder, CO: Westview.

Seibert, Holger H., and Heike Solga. 2005. "Gleiche Chancen dank einer abgeschlossenen Ausbildung? Zum Signalwert von Ausbildungsabschlüssen bei ausländischen und deutschen jungen Erwachsenen." *Zeitschrift für Soziologie* 34:364–382.

Seifert, W. 1992. "Die zweite Ausländergeneration in der Bundesrepublik: Längsschnittbeobachtungen in der Berufseinstiegsphase." *Kölner Zeitschrift für Soziologie und Sozialpsychologie* 44:677–696.

Shavit, Yossi, and Walter Müller, eds. 1998. *From School to Work: A Comparative Study of Educational Qualifications and Occupational Destinations*. Oxford: Oxford University Press.

Shiner, Mike, and Tariq Modood. 2002. "Help or Hindrance? Higher Education and the Route to Ethnic Equality." *British Journal of Sociology of Education* 23:209–230.

Shonkoff, Jack P., and Deborah A. Phillips, eds. 2000. *From Neurons to Neighborhoods: The Science of Early Childhood Development*. Washington, DC: National Academy Press.

Short, Kathleen, Thesia Garner, David Johnson, and Patricia Doyle. 1999. "Experimental Poverty Measures 1990 to 1997." Current Population Reports P60-205. Washington, DC: U.S. Bureau of the Census.

Silberman, Roxane. 2008. "Parler de la couleur de la peau: D'un côté de l'Atlantique à l'autre." *La Revue Tocqueville* 29.

Silberman, Roxane, Richard Alba, and Irène Fournier. 2007. "Segmented Assimilation in France? Discrimination in the Labor Market against the Second Generation." *Ethnic and Racial Studies* 30:1–27.

Silberman, Roxane, and Irène Fournier. 1999. "Les enfants d'immigrés sur le marché du travail: Les mécanismes d'une discrimination sélective." *Formation Emploi* 65:31–55.

———. 2006. "Les secondes générations sur le marché du travail en France: Une pénalité ethnique qui persiste; Contribution à la discussion sur l'assimilation segmentée." *Revue Française de Sociologie* 47:243–292. English version: "Second Generations on the Job Market in France: A Persistent Ethnic Penalty; A Contribution to Segmented Assimilation Theory." *Revue Française de Sociologie*, Suppl. no. 49 (2008): 45–94.

———. 2007a. "Discrimination in the Labour Market against the Second Generation." *Ethnic and Racial Studies* 30:1–27.

———. 2007b. "Is French Society Truly Assimilative? Immigrant Parents and Offspring on the French Labour Market." Pp. 221–269 in *Unequal Chances Ethnic Minorities in Western Labour Markets*, edited by Anthony Heath and Sin Yi Cheung. Oxford: Oxford University Press.

Simmons, Alan B., and Dwaine E. Plaza. 1998. "Breaking through the Glass Ceiling: The Pursuit of University Training among African-Caribbean Migrants and Their Children in Toronto." *Canadian Ethnic Studies* 30:99–120.

Simon, Patrick. 2003. "France and the Unknown Second Generation: Preliminary Results on Social Mobility." *International Migration Review* 37:1091–1119.

———. 2004. "Étude comparative de la collecte de données visant à mesurer l'étendue et l'impact de la discrimination aux Etats-Unis, Canada, Australie, Royaume-Uni et Pays-Bas." Rapport remis à la Commission Européenne, DG Emploi et Affaires Sociales.

———. 2008. "The Choice of Ignorance: The Debate on Ethnic and Racial Statistics in France." *French Politics, Culture, and Society* 26(1):7–31.

Singer, Audrey. 2004. "The Rise of New Immigrant Gateways." Washington, DC: Brookings Institution.

Skenderovic, Damir, and Gianni D'Amato. 2008. *Mit dem Fremden politisieren: Rechtspopulismus und Migrationspolitik in der Schweiz seit den 1960er Jahren.* Zurich: Chronos.

Smith, James. 2003. "Assimilation across the Latino Generations." *American Economic Review* 93:315–319.

Smith, Sandra. 2007. *Lone Pursuit: Distrust and Defensive Individualism among the Black Poor.* New York: Russell Sage Foundation.

Smyth, Emer. 2001. "Gender Differentiation in Education and Early Labour Market Transitions: A Comparative Analysis." In *A Comparative Analysis of Transitions from Education to Work in Europe (CATEWE): Final Report,* edited by Emer Smyth et al. Dublin: ESRI.

Song, Miri. 2003. *Choosing Ethnic Identity.* London: Polity.

Soysal, Yasemin N. 1994. *Limits of Citizenship: Migrants and Postnational Membership in Europe.* Chicago: University of Chicago Press.

Stata Corporation. 2001. *Stata User's Guide Release 7.* College Station, TX: Stata.

Steinbach, Anja. 2004. *Soziale Distanz: Ethnische Grenzziehung und die Eingliederung von Zuwanderern in Deutschland.* Opladen, Germany: VS.

Stier, Haya, and Marta Tienda. 2001. *The Color of Opportunity: Pathways to Family, Welfare, and Work.* Chicago: University of Chicago Press.

Suárez-Orozco, Carola, and Marcelo Suárez-Orozco. 1995. *Transformations: Immigration, Family Life, and Achievement Motivation among Latino Adolescents.* Stanford, CA: Stanford University Press.

Sudbury, Julia. 2001. "(Re)constructing Multiracial Blackness: Women's Activism, Difference, and Collectivity in Britain." *Ethnic and Racial Studies* 24:29–49.

Swyngedouw, M., K. Phalet, and K. Deschouwer. 1999. *Minderheden in Brussel.* Brussels: VUB Press.

Takanishi, Ruby. 2004. "Leveling the Playing Field: Supporting Immigrant Children from Birth to Eighteen." *Future of Children* 14:61–79.

Telles, Edward, and Vilma Ortiz. 2008. *Generations of Exclusion: Mexican Americans, Assimilation, and Race.* New York: Russell Sage Foundation.

Thomas, William Isaac, and Florian Znaniecki. [1918] 1927. *The Polish Peasant in Europe and America.* New York: Knopf.

Tizard, Barbara, and Ann Phoenix. 1993. *Black, White, or Mixed Race?* London: Routledge.

Toulis, Nicole Rodriguez. 1997. *Believing Identity: Pentecostalism and the Mediation of Jamaican Ethnicity and Gender in England.* Oxford, UK: Berg.

Tribalat, Michèle. 1995. *Faire France: Une enquête sur les immigrés et leurs enfants*. Paris: Découverte.

Trillo, Alex. 2004. "Somewhere between Wall Street and El Barrio: Community College as a Second Chance for Second-Generation Latino Students." Pp. 57–78 in *Becoming New Yorkers: Ethnographies of the New Second Generation*, edited by Philip Kasinitz, John Mollenkopf, and Mary C. Waters. New York: Russell Sage Foundation.

Tropp, L., S. Erkut, O. Alarcon, C. Garcia Coll, and H. V. Garcia. 1995. "Measuring Psychological Acculturation: An Expanded Approach with U.S. Hispanics." Wellesley Center for Research on Women.

U.S. Bureau of the Census. 2006a. "American Community Survey for Metropolitan Los Angeles." http://www.census.gov/acs/www/.

———. 2006b. Census 2000, Summary File 3, Table P19. American FactFinder. http://factfinder.census.gov.

U.S. Commission on Immigration Reform. 1994. "U.S. Immigration Policy: Restoring Credibility." Washington, DC.

Uttall, Lynet. 1999. "Using Kin for Child Care: Embedment in the Socioeconomic Networks of Extended Families." *Journal of Marriage and the Family* 61:845–857.

Vallet, Louis-André, and Jean-Paul Caille. 1996. "Les élèves étrangers ou issus de l'immigration dans l'école et le collège français." *Les Dossiers d'Éducation et Formation* 67.

Van Hook, Jennifer, and Frank D. Bean. 2009. "Explaining Mexican-Immigrant Welfare Behaviors: The Importance of Employment-Related Cultural Repertoires." *American Sociological Review* 74:423–444.

Van Hook, Jennifer, Susan K. Brown, and Frank D. Bean. 2006. "For Love or Money? Welfare Reform and Immigrant Naturalization." *Social Forces* 85:643–666.

Van Zanten, Agnès. 2001. *L'école de la périphérie: Scolarité et ségrégation en banlieue*. Paris: Presses universitaires de France.

Veenman, J. 1996. *Keren de kansen*. Assen, Netherlands: Van Gorcum.

Velez, William. 1989. "High School Attrition among Hispanic and Non-Hispanic White Youths." *Sociology of Education* 62:119–133.

Vermeulen, Hans. 2001. *Culture and Equality: Immigrant Cultures and Social Mobility in Long-Term Perspective*. Amsterdam: Het Spinhuis.

———. 2004. "Models and Modes of Immigrant Integration . . . and Where Does Southern Europe Fit?" Pp. 27–39 in *Immigration and Integration in Northern versus Southern Europe*, edited by Chrissi Inglessi, Antigone Lyberaki, and Hans Vermeulen. Athens: Netherlands Institute at Athens.

Vickerman, Milton.. 2001a. "Jamaicans: Balancing Race and Ethnicity." Pp. 201–228 in *New Immigrants in New York*, 2d ed., edited by Nancy Foner. New York: Columbia University Press.

———. 2001b. "Tweaking a Monolith: The West Indian Immigrant Encounter with 'Blackness'" Pp. 237–256 in *Islands in the City: West Indian Migration to New York*, edited by Nancy Foner. Berkeley: University of California Press.

Virdee, Satnam, Tariq Modood, and Tim Newburn. 2000. "Understanding Racial Harassment in School." A Project Report to the ESRC.

Virot, Marc. 2006. "Er kann assimiliert sein und trotzdem Olivenöl verwenden." *Terra Cognita* 9:28–29.

Waldinger, Roger 1996. *Still the Promised City? African Americans and New Immigrants in Postindustrial New York*. Cambridge, MA: Harvard University Press.

———. 2001. *Strangers at the Gates: New Immigrants in Urban America*. Berkeley: University of California Press.

Waldinger, Roger, Howard Aldrich, and Robin Ward. 1990. *Ethnic Entrepreneurs: Immigrant Business in Industrial Society*. Newbury Park, CA: Sage.

Waldinger, Roger, and Cynthia Feliciano. 2004. "Will the Second Generation Experience 'Downward Assimilation'? Segmented Assimilation Re-assessed." *Ethnic and Racial Studies* 27:376–402.

Waldinger, Roger, and Michael Lichter. 2003. *How the Other Half Works: Immigration and the Social Organization of Labor*. Berkeley: University of California Press.

Waldinger, Roger, and Joel Perlmann. 1998. "Second Generation: Past, Present and Future." *Journal of Ethnic and Migration Studies* 24:5–24.

Wallman, Sandra. 1979. *Ethnicity at Work*. London: Macmillan.

Wanner, Philippe, and Rosita Fibbi. 2002. "Familles et migration, familles en migration." Pp. 1–56 in *Commission fédérale de coordination pour les questions familiales*, edited by Commission fédérale de coordination pour les questions familiales. Neuchâtel: Forum suisse pour l'étude des migrations et de la population.

Warikoo, Natasha. 2007. "Racial Authenticity among Second Generation Youth in Multiethnic New York and London." *Poetics: Journal of Empirical Research on Culture, the Media, and the Arts* 35:388–408.

Warren, John Robert. 1996. "Educational Inequality among White and Mexican-Origin Adolescents in the American Southwest: 1990." *Sociology of Education* 69:142–158.

Waters, Mary C. 1994. "Ethnic and Racial Identities of Second-Generation Black Immigrants in New York City." *International Migration Review* 28:795–820.

———. 1999. *Black Identities: West Indian Immigrant Dreams and American Realities*. Cambridge, MA: Harvard University Press.

———. 2001. "Growing Up West Indian and African American: Gender and Class Differences in the Second Generation." Pp. 193–215 in *Islands in the City: West Indian Migration to New York*, edited by Nancy Foner. Berkeley: University of California Press.

Watkins-Owens, Irma. 2001. "Early-Twentieth-Century Caribbean Women: Migration and Social Networks in New York City." Pp. 25–51 in *Islands in the City: West Indian Migration to New York*, edited by Nancy Foner. Berkeley: University of California Press.

Werbner, Pnina. 1990a. *The Migration Process: Capital, Gifts and Offerings among British Pakistanis*. Oxford, UK: Berg.

———. 1990b. "Renewing the Industrial Past: British Pakistani Entrepreneurship in Manchester." *Migration* 8:7–39.

Wicker, Hans Rudolph. 2003. Introduction to *Les Migrations et la Suisse: Resultats du PNR Migrations et Relations Interculturelles*, edited by Hans Rudolph Wicker, Rosita Fibbi, and Werner Hadig, Zurich: Seismo.

Wilson, William Julius. 1987. *The Truly Disadvantaged: The Inner City, the Underclass, and Public Policy*. Chicago: University of Chicago Press.

———. 1996. *When Work Disappears: The World of the New Urban Poor*. New York: Knopf.

Wimmer, Andreas. 2004. "Does Ethnicity Matter? Everyday Group Formation in Three Swiss Immigrant Neighborhoods." *Ethnic and Racial Studies* 27:376–402.

Wittgenstein, Ludwig. 1968. *Philosophical Investigations*. Oxford, UK: Blackwell.

Wojtkiewicz, Roger, and Katharine Donato. 1995. "Hispanic Educational Attainment: The Effects of Family Background and Nativity." *Social Forces* 74:559–574.

Wooldridge, Jeffrey M. 2003. *Introductory Econometrics: A Modern Approach*, 2e. Mason, OH: Thompson.

Worbs, Susanne. "The Second Generation in Germany: Between School and Labor Market." *International Migration Review* 37:1011–1038.

Worrall, Simon. 2000. "London on a Roll." *National Geographic*, June, 6–23.

Worswick, C. 2001. "School Performance of the Children of Immigrants in Canada, 1994–98." Statistics Canada Ottawa Catalogue Number 11F0019MIE, No. 178. Analytical Studies Branch research paper series.

Yang, Phillip Q. 1994. "Explaining Immigrant Naturalization." *International Migration Review* 28:449–477.

Zahner Rossier, Claudia, Simone Berwerger, Christian Bruhwiler, Thomas Holzer, Myrte Mariotta, Urs Moser, and Manuela Nicoli 2004. *PISA 2003: Compétences pour l'avenir.* Neuchâtel, Switzerland: OFSCDIP.

Zeltzer-Zubida, Aviva. 2004. "Affinities and Affiliations: The Many Ways of Being a Russian Jewish American." Pp. 339–360 in *Becoming New Yorkers: Ethnographies of the New Second Generation,* edited by Philip Kasinitz, John H. Mollenkopf, and Mary C. Waters. New York: Russell Sage Foundation.

Zéroulou, Zaïhia. 1988. "La réussite scolaire des enfants d'immigrés: L'apport d'une approche en termes de mobilisation." *Revue Française de Sociologie* 29:447–470.

Zhou, Min. 1992. *Chinatown: The Socioeconomic Potential of an Urban Enclave.* Philadelphia: Temple University Press.

———. 1997. "Growing Up American: The Challenge Confronting Immigrant Children and the Children of Immigrants." *Annual Review of Sociology* 23:63–95.

———. 1999. "Segmented Assimilation: Issues, Controversies and Recent Research on the New Second Generation." Pp. 196–211 in *The Handbook of International Migration,* edited by Charles Hirschman, Philip Kasinitz, and Josh DeWind. New York: Russell Sage Foundation.

———. 2005. "Ethnicity as Social Capital: Community-Based Institutions and Embedded Networks of Social Relations." Pp. 131–159 in *Ethnicity, Social Mobility and Public Policy: Comparing the USA and UK,* edited by Glenn C. Loury, Tariq Modood, and Steven Michael Teles. Cambridge: Cambridge University Press.

Zhou, Min, and Carl L. Bankston. 1998. *Growing Up American: How Vietnamese Children Adapt to Life in the United States.* New York: Russell Sage Foundation.

Zhou, Min, and John Logan. 1989. "Returns on Human Capital in Ethnic Enclaves: New York City's Chinatown." *American Sociological Review* 54:809–820.

Zúñiga, Victor, and Ruben Hernández-León. 2005. *New Destinations: Mexican Immigration in the United States.* New York: Russell Sage Foundation.

About the Contributors

DALIA ABDEL-HADY is Assistant Professor at Southern Methodist University in Dallas, Texas. Her research focuses on issues of immigration and identity, cultural politics, religion, education, and social mobility. She has conducted field work in the United States, Canada, and France on Arab and Mexican immigrants and their children.

RICHARD ALBA is currently Distinguished Professor of Sociology at the Graduate Center of the City University of New York and previously held the same title at the University at Albany. He was educated at Columbia, where he received his undergraduate degree in 1963 and his Ph.D. in 1974. His teaching and research focus on ethnic and racial change, especially for immigrants and their children in the United States and Europe. His books include *Ethnic Identity: The Transformation of White America* (1990); *Italian Americans: Into the Twilight of Ethnicity* (1985); *Remaking the American Mainstream: Assimilation and Contemporary Immigration* (2003), written with Victor Nee; and, most recently, *Blurring the Color Line: The New Chance for a More Integrated America* (2009).

FRANK D. BEAN is Chancellor's Professor of Sociology and Director of the Center for Research on Immigration, Population, and Public Policy at the University of California, Irvine. He is the editor of *Immigration and Opportunity: Race, Ethnicity, and Employment in the United States* (with Stephanie Bell-Rose), the author of *America's Newcomers and the Dynamics of Diversity* (with Gillian Stevens; winner of the Otis Dudley Duncan award), and, most recently, *The Paradox of Diversity: Immigration and the Color Line in 21st Century America* (with Jennifer Lee).

SUSAN K. BROWN is Associate Professor of Sociology at the University of California, Irvine. Her research examines the socioeconomic and residential incorporation of immigrant groups across multiple generations. She is the author of *Beyond the Immigrant Enclave: Network Change and Assimilation* (2004).

MAURICE CRUL is working as a senior researcher at the Amsterdam Institute for Social Science Research of the University of Amsterdam. He has published on school careers of children of immigrants in a comparative European and transatlantic perspective. He is the international coordinator of the TIES (The Integration of the European Second Generation) project that compares second-generation Turkish, Moroccan, and former Yugoslavian youth in fifteen cities in eight European countries: http://www.tiesproject.eu/.

NANCY A. DENTON is Professor of Sociology at the University at Albany, State University of New York, where she is also Director of the Lewis Mumford Center for Urban and Regional Research and Associate Director of the Center for Social and Demographic Analysis. Her research interests include race, residential segregation, urban sociology, demography, and housing. Currently she is working on projects on the neighborhood contexts of children in immigrant families, homeownership, and immigration to upstate New York.

ROSITA FIBBI teaches Sociology of Migration at the University of Lausanne and works as a project manager at the Swiss Forum for Migration and Population Studies at the University of Neuchâtel. Recent publications include "Naturalisation and Socio-economic Characteristics of Youth of Immigrant Descent in Switzerland" (with Mathias Lerch and Philippe Wanner; *Journal of Ethnic and Migration Studies,* 2007); "Unemployment and Discrimination against Youth of Immigrant Origin in Switzerland: When the Name Makes the Difference" (with Mathias Lerch and Philippe Wanner; *Journal of International Migration and Integration,* 2006) and *"Secondas—Secondos": Le processus d'intégration des jeunes issus de la migration espagnole et italienne en Suisse* (with Claudio Bolzman and Marie Vial; 2003).

NANCY FONER is Distinguished Professor of Sociology at Hunter College and the Graduate Center of the City University of New York. She is the author or editor of more than a dozen books, including *From Ellis Island to JFK: New York's Two Great Waves of Immigration* (2000), *Not Just Black and White: Historical and Contemporary Perspectives on Immigration, Race, and Ethnicity in the United States* (edited with George Fredrickson; 2004), *In a New Land: A Comparative View of Immigration* (New York University Press, 2005), and, most recently, *Across Generations: Immigrant Families in America* (New York University Press, 2009).

ANTHONY HEATH is FBA, Professor of Sociology, University of Oxford. His recent books include *Diversity and Change in Modern India* (editor, with R. Jeffery; 2009); *Unequal Chances: Ethnic Minorities in Western Labour Markets* (editor, with Sin Yi Cheung; 2007); and *The Rise of New Labour* (2001). Professor Heath is also currently conducting studies on the affirmative-action program in Northern Ireland (funded by the Nuffield Foundation), on ethnoreligious diversity and social cohesion (funded by the Leverhulme Trust), and on ethnic minority political attitudes and behavior (funded by the ESRC).

DONALD J. HERNANDEZ is Professor of Sociology at Hunter College and the Graduate Center of the City University of New York. He is the author or editor of several publications, including *Children of Immigrants: Health, Adjustment, and Public Assistance* (1999), *From Generation to Generation: The Health and Well-Being of Children in Immigrant Families* (edited with Evan Charney; 1998), *America's Children: Resources from Family, Government, and the Economy* (1993), *Success or Failure? Family Planning Programs in the Third World* (1984), *National Statistics on Children, Youth, and Their Families: A Guide to Federal Data Programs* (with Nicholas Zill, James Peterson, and Kristin Moore; 1984), and *Child and Family Indicators* (edited with Harold W. Watts; 1982).

TARIQUL ISLAM is a graduate student in sociology at the University at Albany, State University of New York.

FRANK KALTER is Professor of Sociology at the Faculty of Social Sciences, University of Mannheim, Germany. He is the author of *Wohnortwechsel in Deutschland* (1997) and *Chancen, Fouls, and Abseitsfallen* (2003) (both in German) and is the editor of *Migration and Integration* (2008).

PHILIP KASINITZ is Professor of Sociology at the Graduate Center of the City University of New York. With Mary C. Waters and John Mollenkopf, he was coprincipal investigator of the New York Second Generation Study. He is coauthor (with Mollenkopf, Waters, and Jennifer Holdaway) of *Inheriting the City: The Children of Immigrants Come Age* and coeditor (with Waters and Mollenkopf) of *Becoming New Yorkers: Ethnographies of the New Second Generation*. His other publications include *Caribbean New York: Black Immigrants and the Politics of Race* and the *Urban Ethnography Reader*, which he edited with Mitchell Duneier.

MARK A. LEACH is Assistant Professor of Rural Sociology and Demography at the Pennsylvania State University, University Park. His research examines various aspects of Mexican immigration to the United States, including change in settlement patterns, labor-market outcomes, household structures, and child poverty.

MATHIAS LERCH is scientific collaborator at the Laboratory of Demography at the University of Geneva. As a geographer and demographer, he is interested in different topics of immigrant integration in Switzerland as well as in the impact of migration in the countries of origin, particularly in southeastern Europe.

SUZANNE MACARTNEY is completing her dissertation on Hispanic children in immigrant families and their neighborhoods. Currently, she is a Poverty Analyst with the U.S. Census Bureau in Washington, DC.

KAREN MAROTZ is a Ph.D. candidate in the Department of Sociology at the University of Albany, State University of New York. Her research interests include social demography, race and ethnicity, immigration, and residential segregation. Her dissertation examines the dynamics of race, ethnicity, and citizenship in the U.S. armed forces. Her most recent journal publication appeared in *Social Forces*.

NORIKO MATSUMOTO is a Ph.D. candidate at the Graduate Center of the City University of New York. Her dissertation focuses on the development of a contemporary ethnic suburb of New York City and its implications for immigrant assimilation and social relations.

TARIQ MODOOD is Director of the Centre for the Study of Ethnicity and Citizenship and Professor of Sociology at the University of Bristol, UK. His latest books are *Multiculturalism: A Civic Idea* (2007) and, as coeditor with G. B. Levey, *Secularism, Religion and Multicultural Citizenship* (2009).

JOEL PERLMANN is Senior Scholar at the Levy Economics Institute of Bard College and Research Professor at the college. He is the author of *Ethnic Differences: Schooling and Social Structure among the Irish, Italians, Jews, and Blacks in an American City, 1880–1935, Woman's Work? American Schoolteachers, 1650–1920* (with Robert A. Margo), and *Italians Then, Mexicans*

Now: Immigrant Origins and Second-Generation Progress, 1890–2000. He has coedited *Immigrants, Schooling, and Social Mobility: Does Culture Make a Difference?* (with Hans Vermeulen) and *The New Race Question: How the Census Counts Multiracial Individuals* (with Mary C. Waters).

KAREN PHALET is a professor of social and cultural psychology at the University of Leuven, Belgium, and a senior research fellow of the European Research Centre on Migration and Ethnic Relations (ERCOMER), Utrecht University, Netherlands. Her current work is mainly concerned with acculturation and identity construals of the European second generation and with ethnic educational inequalities.

JEFFREY G. REITZ is Professor and former Chair in the Department of Sociology, R. F. Harney Professor and Director of Ethnic, Immigration and Pluralism Studies (http://www.utoronto.ca/ethnicstudies), and research associate at the Munk Centre for International Studies at the University of Toronto. He has held visiting positions at nine universities in the United States, Australia, the United Kingdom, and Japan, including appointment as the William Lyon Mackenzie King Visiting Professor in Canadian Studies at Harvard University in 2000–2001. He received the Outstanding Contribution award from the Canadian Sociological Association in 2005. His books include *Multiculturalism and Social Cohesion: Potentials and Challenges of Diversity* (2009), *Host Societies and the Reception of Immigrants* (2003), *Warmth of the Welcome: The Social Causes of Economic Success for Immigrant in Different Nations and Cities* (1998), and *The Illusion of Difference: Realities of Ethnicity in Canada and the United States* (1994). Recent articles include "Tapping Immigrants' Skills: New Directions for Canadian Immigration Policy in the Knowledge Economy" (2005) and "Immigrant Employment Success in Canada: Individual and Contextual Causes, and Understanding the Decline" (2007).

RUBÉN G. RUMBAUT is Professor of Sociology at the University of California, Irvine. The Founding Chair of the Section on International Migration of the American Sociological Association, he is the coauthor, among other books, of *Immigrant America: A Portrait and Legacies: The Story of the Immigrant Second Generation,* which won the ASA's Distinguished Scholarship Award and the Thomas and Znaniecki Award for best book in the immigration field.

ROXANE SILBERMAN is senior researcher at the Centre Maurice Halbwachs (CNRS) and at the Paris School of Economics. She was a fellow in sociology at the École Normale Supériere in Paris and entered the CNRS in 1986. From 1998 to 2004, she was the director of LASMAS (Laboratoire d'analyse secondaire et de methods appliqués a la sociologie), a CNRS research center. She is currently in charge of the French National Data Committee for Humanities and Social Sciences and represents the researchers at the CNIS, the national council for statistical information. She has worked intensively on immigration and the second generation. Recent publications in English include "Second Generations on the Job Market in France: A Persistent Ethnic Penalty; A Contribution to Segmented Assimilation Theory" (*Revue Francaise de Sociologie,* 2008) and "Is French Society Truly Assimilative? Immigrants Parents and Offspring in the French Labor Market," in *Unequal Chances, Ethnic Minorities in Western Labor Markets* (2007), both coauthored with I. Fournier, as well as "The Children of Immigrants and Host Society Educational Systems: Mexicans in the United States and North Africans in France" (with Richard Alba; *Teachers College Record,* 2008).

PHILIPPE WANNER is Professor in Demography at the University of Geneva. He is the author of a number of books on the demographic impact of migration in Switzerland and the economic integration of migrants.

MARY C. WATERS is the M. E. Zukerman Professor of Sociology at Harvard University, where she has taught since 1986. She is the author or editor of numerous books and articles on immigration, ethnicity, race relations, and young adulthood, including *Ethnic Options: Choosing Identities in America* (1990), *Black Identities: West Indian Immigrant Dream and American Realities* (1999), and most recently, *Inheriting the City: The Children of Immigrants Come of Age* (with Philip Kasinitz, John Mollenkopf, and Jennifer Holdaway; 2008). Her current research examines the experiences over time of a cross-section of people displaced by Hurricane Katrina.

AVIVA ZELTZER-ZUBIDA received a Ph.D. in sociology from the Graduate Center of the City University of New York. Her research interests include social inequality, race and ethnicity, immigration, and labor markets. She has published several articles on identity formation among the children of Russian Jewish immigrants. Her research centers on the role of race and ethnicity in shaping labor-market trajectories of second-generation immigrants in the metropolitan New York area. She has worked as an assistant professor of sociology at Brooklyn College of the City University of New York. Currently, she lives in Israel and serves as the head of the research and planning division at the Jewish Agency for Israel.

YE ZHANG is a Ph.D. candidate in the Department of Sociology, University of Toronto. She is interested in the research area of the integration of immigrants.

Index

German-Turk ethnic penalty study, (*cont'd*):
German friends in, 171–72, *173*, 174, *175*,
176–77, *178–79*, 180–81, 184n6; German
language proficiency in, 172, *173*, 174,
177, *178*, 180–81; GSOEP for, 167, 170–72;
mothers' German friends in, *173*, 174,
179, 180–81; mothers' language in, 172,
173, *179*; research methods for, 170–72,
174, *175*, 183n1, 183n5, 184n6; results for,
172–81; salaried positions in, 172–74, *175*,
178–79, 180, 184n6; skills v. education,
168, 176; social assimilation and, 181–83;
subject selection for, 171; summary of,
181–83
Germany: citizenship in, 10; foreign-born
in, 2; immigrant social capital in, 22–23;
membership in, 12; model of differential exclusion for, 274; naturalization
in, 133n13; tracking in, 17–18, 275–76,
277–78; Turkish labor migration to, 270,
271
Globalization, immigration v., 1
Goffman, Erving, 309
Gogh, Theo van, 13
Goldthorpe, John H., 147–48, 183n2, 189, 295
Gordon, Milton M., 91
Goulbourne, Harry, 266
Granato, Nadia, 171
Granovetter, Mark S., 140, 198, 236
Grebler, Leo, 97
Gross Domestic Product (GDP), 63
GSEOP. *See* German Socio-Economic Panel
GSS. *See* General Social Survey
Guzmán, Ralph C., 97

Hall, Stuart, 262
Haller, William, 90
Heath, Anthony, 26, 135–65, 148, 166
HEIPRs. *See* Higher Education Initial Par-
ticipation Rates
Hernandez, Donald J., 46–66
Higher Education Initial Participation Rates
(HEIPRs), *188*
Hoffman-Nowotny, Hans-Joachim, 111
Human capital, 3, 40; ethnic penalties v.,
168–69; labor immigration v., 87–88

Identification, 15; of Afro-Caribbeans,
258–59; in Brussels regional/Turkish
study, 145–46; in early childhood educational programs study, *47*, *49*, 66nn2–3;
of French second generations, 292–93;
national models of integration v., 274–77,
282n6; opting out v., 109
Identity: in Afro-Caribbean Britain-U.S.
study, 255–56; for Afro-Caribbeans,
255–58; gender v., 256; segmented
assimilation v., 256–57
IIMMLA. *See* Immigration and Intergenerational Mobility in Metropolitan Los
Angeles
Immigrants, 1, 5–9, 17; citizenship v., 10–14,
44–45; "gateway cities" for, 211, 218–19,
220, 221, 225; global cities and, 210–11;
natives v. in preschool programs, 19–20;
stagnation v., 88–89; urban contexts and,
23–24. *See also specific ethnicities, studies*
Immigration and Intergenerational Mobility
in Metropolitan Los Angeles (IIMMLA),
11, 26; discussion/conclusions from,
43–45; findings of, *37–39*, *40–41*, *42–43*;
research for, 35–36; trajectories within, 35
Immigration and Nationality Act, U.S., 253
Immigration Reform and Control Act
(IRCA), 7–8, 32; legalization percent
from, 40
Income: ethnic enclave v., 232; Mexican
American parental legal status v., 34,
39–41, *42*, 43–44; total family income,
85–86. *See also specific studies*
Incorporation, 3–6, 33–34; of Mexican
immigrants, 31–32; national integration
paradigms v., 13
Indians, 187, *188*, 191, *195*; post-9/11, 192; self-
concept of, 199–200; whites v., 189–90
Indochinese: in early childhood education
programs, 47–48, *49*, *57*, 59–61; fathers'
occupations and, *49*, 53; Vietnamese, 199
INSEE. *See* Census and Labor survey
Institutional discrimination: Mexican
American parents' education and, 97, 103;
in United Kingdom ethnic minorities/
higher education study, 187–89, 203nn4–5

Mexican American citizenship trajectories: dropouts in, 71, *72*, 74, 79–80, 83–84; entry status v., 36, *37*, 40

Mexican American educational attainment study: college graduation in, *105*, 106; cross-sectional data v. intergenerational data in, 96; dropouts in, 99–100, *105*, 106, 108; GSS for, 96, 98–104, 106–7; mothers' education in, 102, *103*; NELS for, 96, 99, 104–7; NLSY for, 96, 98–99, 104–7; parents' education in, 97–98, 101–4; second-generation Mexican American men/women in, 100, *105*; some college in, 104, *105*, 106; third+-generation Mexican American men/women in, *105*; third-generation Mexican American men/women in, 99–100, *105*; third+-generation white men/women in, 101–3, *105*, 106–7; U.S.-born Mexican American men/women in, 104, *105*, 106; U.S.-born white men/women in, *105*, 106; white parents' education in, 101–3; whites in, 101–4, *105*, 106–8

Mexican American education/earnings study: black men in, 76–79, *81*, 82, 85, 92; black women in, 75–77, *79*, 91–92; dropouts in, 71, *72*, 74, 79–80, 83–84; earnings in, 80–81, *81*; employment full-time in, 75–76, *76–77*, 82, 93n3; ethnic classifications of, 70–71; fathers in, 80–82, 89; gender in, 71, *72–73*, 74; high school graduation v. college graduation in, 84; institutionalization in, 76–78, *79*, 92, 94n13; Mexican American dropouts in, 71, *72*, 74, 108; Mexican 1.53 group in, 71, *72*, 74–75, *76–77*, *79*, 79–85, 91–92; Mexican 1.56 group in, *76*, 77–78, *79*; single motherhood in, 75, *76*, 91; stay-at-home women in, 76, 93n3; teen pregnancy and, 91–92; total family income in, 85–86; white men in, *79*, 80–82, *81*, 83, 85; whites in, *70*, 71, *72–73*, 74–75, *76–77*, 79–80, *81*, 82–85

Mexican American fathers: in Mexican American education/earnings study, 80–82, 89; Mexican American moth-

ers v., *37–39*, 40–41, *42–43*; in Mexican immigrants legalization/naturalization study, 36, *37–38*, 39–41, *42–43*; socioeconomic status for, 39–40, 43, 45n1; statuses of, 36, *37–38*, 39–40

Mexican American mothers: as LPR, 36, *37–39*; Mexican American fathers v., *37–39*, 40–41, *42–43*; statuses of, 36, *37–39*, *39*, 40; as unauthorized parents, 36, *37–39*

Mexican American parental legal status, *37*; causation v. correlation of, 44; civic engagement v., 43; college education v., 38, *39–41*, 42, 43; education v., 38, *39–41*, 42, 43; English speakers v., *39*, 39–41, 42; gender v., *42–43*; human capital and, 40; income v., 34, 39–41, 42, 43–44; occupational socioeconomic prestige v., *39*, 39–40, 43, 45n1; second generation v., 11, 33–34; selectivity in, 44

Mexican American unauthorized parents, 35; immigrant underclass v., 44; income v., 41, *43*; percentages of, 36, 40

Mexican Americans: citizenship for, 11; downward assimilation v., 95–96, 108; dropouts and, 16, 71, *72*, 74, 108; in early childhood education programs, 47, 48, 49, *57*, 59–62; English speakers and, *39*, 40–41, 42, 49; gender and, *72–73*; higher education and, *72–73*, 74; older- v. newer populations, 92–93; poverty v., 49, 50; risky behaviors and, 16; school discrimination and, 78; stagnation among, 95–96; third generation of, 16, 99–100, *105*; upward-mobility patterns of, 86

Mexican immigrants: Chinese immigrants v., 227; early childhood education programs v., 47, 48, 49, 53–56, *57*, 58–62; incorporation of, 31–32; Los Angeles and, 32; number of, 31; unauthorization v., 31

Mexican immigrants legalization/naturalization study: citizenship trajectories in, 36, *37*, 40; data/approach for, 35; discussion/conclusion on, 43–45; English speakers in, *39*, 39–41, *42*; fathers in, 36, *37–38*, *37–39*, 39–41, *42–43*; findings of, 36, *37–39*, 39–41, *42–43*; gender in,

34, 39–41, 42–43; immigrant parents v. native parents in, 35–36; income in, 39, 39–41, 43, 43–44; incorporation/legalization/citizenship in, 32–34; Los Angeles for, 32; Mexican American college education in, 38, 39–41, 42, 43; mothers in, 36, 37–39, 40–41, 42–43; occupational prestige in, 39, 39–40, 43, 45n1; parental legal status in, 33–34, 37–39, 39–41, 42–43, 43–44; theme of, 31–32; unauthorized parents in, 35–36, 37–39, 39–41, 43, 44

Mexican 1.53 group, 80; high school graduation v. college graduation for, 84; total family income in, 85–86; whites' education/earnings v., 83, 85

Mexican 1.53 group men: black men's earnings v., 85; dropouts in, 71, 72, 74, 79–80, 83–84; earnings of, 80–82, 81; education/earnings of, 85; employment full-time and, 75, 77; higher education, 71, 72, 74; institutionalization of, 77–78, 79, 92; white men's earnings v., 83, 85

Mexican 1.53 women, 77, 79, 85, 92; higher education of, 71, 72, 74; single motherhood in, 75, 76, 91

Mexico, early childhood education programs in, 63–64

Minorities: "the system" v., 195–96; voluntary v. involuntary, 196. See also specific studies

Model, Suzanne, 227

Model of differential exclusion, 274

Modes of incorporation: in segmented assimilation, 3–4; trajectories v., 4–5

Modood, Tariq, 16–17, 137, 185–203, 268n6, 268n8

Mollenkopf, John, 213

Moore, Joan W., 97

Moroccans, 142–43, 149–53, 160–61, 287–88

Motherhood, single, 75, 76, 91

Müller, Walter, 147

Multicultural model, 274

Münz, Rainer, 2

Muslims, 123, 130, 137, 288–89, 313; post-9/11, 192; religious symbols controversy and, 292. See also Turkish immigrant youth

National context: in France's labor market study, 286–93; in research, 269–70

National Education Longitudinal Study (NELS), 96; analyses from, 104–7; nativity data from, 99

National integration paradigms, 11–12; incorporation v., 13

National Longitudinal Study of Youth (NLSY), 96; analyses of, 104–7; generations in, 99; labor markets and, 98–99

National models of integration: education v., 274–77; identification v., 274, 282n6; socioeconomic status v., 274

Nee, Victor, 112, 246, 258, 314

NELS. See National Education Longitudinal Study

Netherlands: integration in, 12–13; multiculturalist model and, 274; political rights in, 11. See also Turks

"New second generation," 135, 165n1

The New Second Generation, 269

New York, 25–26; African Americans in, 254–60, 267n2; African Americans v. Afro-Caribbeans in, 254–60; skills in, 210–11

New York labor force study: African Americans in, 229, 234–41, 242, 243, 246; career opportunities and, 243–44; Chinese in, 229, 231–32, 234–37, 239–46, 248n2; CILS results and, 247; coethnic employment in, 240–42, 245–46; dissimilarity/parents' industry in, 237–38, 239; Dominicans in, 229, 231–41, 242, 243–45, 248n2; downward assimilation v., 246–47; early employment in, 235; earnings in, 239–40, 248n2; ethnic niche occupations in, 230–34; family/employment in, 235–36, 238, 239; full-time employment in, 235; full-time school in, 234, 235; gender/work hours in, 238; history and, 247–48; job-finding method in, 236–37; Korean stores in, 231; labor force entry in, 234–37; mainstream in, 246–48; nationalities in, 229, 248n1; network expansion in, 244; New York natives in, 239, 240; no school/no work in, 234, 235;

Reitz, Jeffrey, 24, 141, 207–28, 270, 282n7

Religion: race v., 137. *See also* Muslims; Russian Jews

Republican model, 285, 291–92, 307, 313

Research: comparative approach in, 28, 252; cross-national, 28; cross-sectional data v. intergenerational data, 96, 101; for IIMMLA, 35–36; national context in, 269–70; social networks and, 233–34; in U.S., 269, 282n3. *See also* Afro-Caribbean Britain-U.S. study; Brussels regional/Turkish study; Early childhood education programs study; France's labor market study; German-Turk ethnic penalty study; Mexican American educational attainment study; Mexican American education/earnings study; Mexican immigrants legalization/naturalization study; New York labor force study; Swiss immigrants study; Turkish-European educational outcome study; United Kingdom ethnic minorities/ higher education study; U.S.-Canada urban education study

Reynolds, Tracey, 262

Ridge, J., 166

Rumbaut, Rubén G., 1, 3, 31–45, 88

Russian Jews: ethnic niches for, 232–33; in New York labor force study, 229, 234, 235, 236–37, 239–40, 241, 242, 244–45, 248n2

Sassen, Saskia, 140, 210

Savage, Mike, 185

Schnapper, Dominique, 283, 315n1

School discrimination, 78

School funding: in France, 19; inequalities v., 19; in Mexico, 63; in U.S., 19–20

Second generation: definitions of, 1, 146, 272; earnings v. occupations of, 89; enclaves v., 242; entrepreneurs v., 9; identification of, 15; "new second generation" v., 135, 165n1; 1.5 generation v., 1; Puerto Ricans, 66n2; stagnation v., 88–89; urban polarization and, 140–41. *See also specific studies*

Second Generation in Metropolitan New York Study, 229–30

Second-generation Mexican Americans: black discrimination v., 78; college for, *105*; dropout of, 99–100; fathers' earnings v., 89; high-school completion for, *105*; institutionalization v., 77–78, 92; men, 100, 105; origin of, 93n5; women, 100, 105

Second-generation progress, segmented assimilation v., 4

Segmentation, in U.S., 3–4

Segmented assimilation, 213; Afro-Caribbeans v., 210, 218, 227; Canada and, 4; cautions about, 90–92, 94n10; consonant/ dissonant acculturation and, 3; downward assimilation v., 86–87, 90–91, 95; dropout rates v., 74; ethnic social capital in, 138–40, 160–61; in Europe, 136–38; in France, 284; historical factors v., 91, 94n11; identity v., 256–57; immigration v., 2–4; labor immigration and, 88, 93n8; modes of incorporation in, 3–4; New York v. London, 25–26; occupations v., 230; Perlmann and, 90; predictions of, 88, 90; race v., 4, 86; revision of, 90–91; second-generation progress v., 4; selective acculturation and, 3, 180; social assimilation v., 169–70; social class v., 256–57; stagnation in, 90; upward mobility and, 258; urban economy and, 140–41; U.S. and, 137–38, 208–9; in U.S. cities, 137; young marriage v., 92

Seifert, W., 269

Selective acculturation, 3, 180

Self-employment, 141, *150*, 151, 158–59, 162, 164

Serbo-Croat-speaking Yugoslav immigrant youth, *117*, 118, 120; parents' education and, *121*, 125–26, *128*; school attainment and, *119*, 121, 122, 123–26, *128*

Settlement patterns: immigrant earnings v., 212; urban contexts and, 210–12, 218–19, *220*, 221; in U.S.-Canada urban education study, 210–12, 218–19, *220*, 221

Shavit, Yossi, 147

Silberman, Roxane, 4, 19, 20–21, 283–315
Simmons, Alan B., 212
Skills: education v., 8, 168, 176; in New York, 210–11
Slavery, 289, 315n3
Social assimilation: for Germany's Turkish second generation, 181–83; school-choice v., 182; segmented assimilation v., 169–70
Social capital: assimilation v., 169, 230; bonding/bridging/linking, 196–99; cultural capital v., 169–70, 186, 201; definition of, 138; enclaves and, 200–201; ethnic capital v., 17, 22–23, 138–40, 142–43, 160–61; ethnicity v., 197–201; Germany, 22–23; human capital v., 169; "intergenerational closure" in, 198; job-market entry v., 308; measurable behaviors and, 200; norms enforcement and, 198–200; Portes on, 197–98; Putnam and, 196–97; socioeconomic status v., 139–40; voluntary organizations and, 197
Social citizenship, 13–14
Social class, 44, 88–90, 202, 210; Britain's Afro-Caribbeans and, 256, 261, 263; cultural capital v., 139, 185–86; economics v., 226–27; education v., 15; ethnicity v., 185–86, 189–91, 193; occupation v., 190–91, 193; segmented assimilation v., 256–57; social mobility v., 189; Turks/Netherlands and, 279–80
Social democratic welfare state, 13–14
Social mobility: integration v., 27–28; social class v., 189
Social networks: ethnic niches and, 233; research and, 233–34
Social Position and Use of Facilities by Ethnic Minorities Survey (SPVA), 272
Social Services Block Grant (SSBG), 50
Social welfare: citizenship v., 14; welfare states v., 14
Socioeconomic status: cultural capital v., 139; early childhood education programs v., 50–51, 59–62, 65; in German-Turk ethnic penalty study, 173–74, 175, 176; for Mexican American fathers, 39–40, 43, 45n1; national model of integration v.,

274; preschool programs and, 20; social capital v., 139–40; Turkish labor migration v., 271–72. *See also specific studies*
South Americans: ethnic niches for, 232–33; in New York labor force study, 229, 231–34, 235, 237–41, 242, 248n2
South Asians, 191–94, 196–97, 199–200. *See also* Indians; Pakistanis
Southeast Asians: in France's labor market study, 293, *294, 296–97,* 298, *300–301, 303, 304–5, 310,* 312, 314; as French immigrants, 289, *290*
Spanish immigrant youth, *117,* 118; school attainment and, *119,* 120, *121–22,* 123, *124, 126, 128,* 129–30
SPVA. *See* Social Position and Use of Facilities by Ethnic Minorities Survey
SSBG. *See* Social Services Block Grant
State policies: immigration and, 5–6; IRCA, 7–8, 32, 40; labor immigration v., 6; migration v., 44; U.S. Immigration and Nationality Act, 253
Stevens, Gillian, 89
Strangers at the Gates: New Immigrants in Urban America (Waldinger), 282n7
Structural assimilation, cognitive assimilation v., 182
Sweetman, Arthur, 228n1
Swiss immigrants study: Albanian-speaking Yugoslav immigrant youth in, *117,* 118–20, *121–22, 124,* 125, *126, 128;* Bosnian immigrant youth in, *117, 119, 121–22,* 123, 125–26, *128,* 130; cantonal school system in, 127, *128,* 133n16; cultural distance in, 119–20, 130–31; demographics for, 116–18, 133nn6–7; dropouts in, 119–21, 123, 133n8; educational attainment in, 119–20, *124,* 125, *126,* 133nn7–8; French immigrant youth in, *117, 119, 121–22,* 123–24, *126, 128,* 129–30; gender gap in, 115, 123–25, 129–31, 133n11, 133n14; German immigrant youth in, *117, 119,* 120, *121–22,* 123–24, *126, 128,* 129–30; intergenerational mobility in, 125–26; Italian immigrant youth in, *117,* 118, *119,* 120, *121–22,* 123–24, *126, 128,* 129; language in, 127, *128,* 129, 133n18; Mace-

donian immigrant youth in, *117*, 118, *119*, 120, *121–22*, *124*, *126*, *128*, 130; migratory youths' background in, 118; native-born youth in, 129–30, 134n20; naturalization in, 121, *122*, 123–25, 131, 133n10, 133n13; parents' education in, 120, *121*, 127, *128*, 129, 133n9, 133n17; Portuguese immigrant youth in, *117*, 119, *121–22*, 124–25, *126*, *128*; residence length in, 121, *122*, 124, 131; school success factors in, 126–27, *128*, 129–30, 133nn15–18, 134n19; school system in, 129; Serbo-Croat-speaking Yugoslav immigrant youth in, *117*, 118–20, *121–22*, 123–26, *128*; Spanish immigrant youth in, *117*, 118, *119*, 120, *121–22*, 123, *124*, *126*, *128*, 129–30; Swiss language-speaking Yugoslav immigrant youth in, *117*, *119*, 120, *121–22*, 124, *126*, *128*, 130; tertiary education in, 123–27, *128*, 129–30, 133n12, 133nn15–18, 134nn19–20

Switzerland, 2; census data for, 113; convergent trend in, 114; cultural distance in, 21, 111–13, 131n1, 132n2; employment discrimination in, 21; labor immigration in, 110–12; naturalization in, 110, 116, 132n4; noncitizen percentages in, 110; "origin groups" in, 116, 118, 132n5; second generation in, 113, 132n3; U.S. v., 112–13

TANF. *See* Temporary Assistance for Needy Families
Teacher contact, 275
Teen pregnancy, 91–92; in whites, 75
Telles, Edward, 96
Temporary Assistance for Needy Families (TANF), 50
Temporary immigration, family reunification v., 7
Third+ generation: Mexican American men/women in, 99–100, *105*; white men/women in, 99–103, *105*, 106–7
Third generation, of Mexican Americans, 16, 99–100, *105*
Third-generation Mexican American men/women: college for, 100, *105*; dropouts of, 99–100, *105*

Thomas, William I., 24
TIES. *See* Integration of the European Second Generation Study
Tracking, 19, 27; in French school system, 290; in Germany, 17–18, 275–76, 277–78; Turkish-European educational outcome study and, 273, 275–76, 277–78; in U.S., 18
Transnational connection, 3
Transnational employment, 244–45
Transnationalism, U.S. citizenship v., 33
Tribalat, Michèle, 269
Tunisians, 287–88
Turkish-European educational outcome study: academic degrees and, 273; age and, 275; assistance/support and, 276; community development and, 280; conclusion on, 281; data sources for, 272, 276; difference factors in, 275; different scenarios and, 278–81; dropouts in, 273–74, 277–78, 279; elites and, 279–80, 282n8; Europe's Turkish community and, 270–72; homogeneity v. heterogeneity and, 280; language and, 275, 276–77, 279; national models of integration and, 274; outcome differences and, 273–78; school careers in, 272–78; school performance and, 273–74; second generation definitions and, 272; teacher contact and, 275; tracking and, 273, 275–76, 277–78; unemployment and, 278, 279, 281; university preparation in, 273; VBO and, 278
Turkish immigrant youth, in Swiss study, *117*, 118–20, *121–22*, 123–26, *128*, 130. *See also* Brussels regional/Turkish study
Turkish labor migration, 7; education v., 270–71; to Germany, 270, 271; socioeconomics v., 271–72; sources of, 271
Turks, 9; academic degrees and, 273; age and, 275; blue-collar work for, 280; cultural distance for, 168; dropouts and, 273–74, 277–78; ethnic social capital v., 22–23, 142–43; as French immigrants, 287; language and, 275, 276–77; local contexts for, 26; Moroccans v., 142–43, 160–61; polarization and, 279–80, 281; school performance and, 273–74, 279;

Turks (*cont'd*): social class and, 279–80; teacher contact and, 275; tracking and, 275–76, 277–78. *See also* German-Turk ethnic penalty study

2003 Formation Qualification Professionnnelle (FQP 2003), 285, 289

Ulrich, Ralf, 2

Undocumented immigrants: labor immigration v., 7–8; unauthorized parents as, 35–36, *37–39*, 39–41, *43*, 44

Unemployment: French school system v., 291. *See also specific studies*

United Kingdom ethnic minorities/higher education study: acceptances in, 186–87, *188*; A-levels in, 188, 203n3, 203n5; "Asian other" category in, 187–*88*, 203n2; black Caribbeans in, 187, *188*, 189–90, 194; Caribbeans in, 186–88, 190, *191*; Chinese in, 187–89, *191*, 193, 203n2; cultural capital and, 194–96; downward mobility and, 190–91; economics in, 226–27; ethnic strategies and, 193–94; gender gap in, 186, *187*; HEIPRs in, *188*; Indians in, 187, *188*, 189, 191, *195*; institutional discrimination in, 187–89, 203nn4–5; Pakistanis in, 187–*88*, 190, *191*, 192, 195; racial discrimination in, 190; racism in, 191–92; social class/ethnicity in, 185–86, 189–91, 193; social class in, 189–91, 226–27; social class v. occupation in, 190–91, 193; South Asians in, 191–94, 196–97, 199–200

United States (U.S.): Afro-Caribbean immigration to, 253; assimilation v., 12; bracero program in, 6; citizenship and, 32–33; family reunification in, 7; France's labor market study and, 284; France v., 286, 313–14; higher education in, 18; postsecondary education in, 209–10; research in, 269, 282n3; school funding in, 19–20; second generation numbers in, 2; segmentation in, 3–4; segmented assimilation and, 137–38, 208–9; social class in, 210; Switzerland v., 112–13; tracking in, 18; undocumented immigrants in, 7–8. *See also* African

Americans; Early childhood education programs study; Mexican American educational attainment study; Mexican American education/earnings study; New York; U.S.-Canada

Urban contexts: assimilation in, 24; educational attainment v., 221, *222–23*, 224; immigrants and, 23–24; settlement patterns and, 210–12, 218–19, *220*, 221

Urban economy, segmented assimilation and, 140–41

Urban polarization, 140–41

U.S.-born Mexican American men/women: college for, 104, *105*, 106; dropouts of, *105*, 106; high-school completion for, *105*, 106

U.S.-born Mexican origin men: black men v., 78–79; earnings of, *81*, 81–82; employment full-time and, 75, *76*, *77*; institutionalization of, 76–78, *79*

U.S.-born Mexican origin women, *77*; institutionalization of, *79*; single motherhood in, 75, *76*

U.S.-born white men/women, *105*, 106

U.S.-Canada, 5–6; education in, 211–13; equal treatment in, 208–9; unequal immigrant economics in, 209–11

U.S.-Canada urban education study, 207; African Americans in, 227, 228n8; Afro-Caribbeans in, 215, *216*, 217–19, *220*, 221, 222, 224–27, 228n7; Asians in, 214–15, *216*, 217–19, *220*, 221, 223, 224–27, 228n3; Chinese in, 214–19, *220*, 221, 223, 224–27, 228n3; conclusion of, 224–28; cross-national difference in, 214–15, 228n4; data sources/analytic framework for, 213–15, 228nn2–3; educational attainment in, 214–18, 221, *222–23*, 224–27, 228n5; equal minority treatment and, 208–9; findings of, 215–24; intergenerational mobility differences in, 217–18, 221, *222–23*, 224–26, 228nn6–7; national differences implications of, 208–10; previous research and, 212–13; racial categories for, 213–14, 228nn2–3; research methods for, 213–15, 228n5; second-generation national-level differences in,

215–17; settlement patterns in, 210–12, 218–19, *220*, 221; unequal economics and, 209–10; urban contexts in, 210–12, 218–19, *220*, 221, *222–23*, 224; whites in, 213–19, *220*, *222–23*, 224–27

VBO. *See* Vocational education
Veenman, J., 269
Vickerman, Milton, 256, 258, 264
Vietnamese, 199
Vocational education (VBO), 278

Waldinger, Roger, 4, 94n10, 231, 282n7
Wanner, Philippe, 110–34
Warde, Alan, 185
The Warmth of Welcome: The Social Causes of Economic Success for Immigrants in Different Nations and Cities (Reitz), 282n7
Waters, Mary, 1 28, 213, 255, 257, 259
Welfare reform act, 14
Welfare states: corporatist, 14; liberalism in, 13; social democratic, 13–14; social welfare v., 14
West Indians: African Americans v., 238; ethnic niches for, 231–32; in New York labor force study, 229, 231–32, 234–35, *237*, 238–41, *242*, 243, 248n1, 248n2
White men: earnings of, 80–82, *81*; education/earnings of, 85; institutionalization of, *79*, 92; in Mexican American education/earnings study, *79*, 80–82, *81*, 83, 85; Mexican 1.53 group men's earnings v., 83, 85; third/fourth generation, 99–100; third+ generation, in Mexican American educational attainment study, 101–3, *105*, 106–7; U.S.-born, in Mexican American educational attainment study, *105*, 106
White parents' education: gender v., 101–2; Mexican American parents' education v., 101–3; missing data on, 102

White women: earnings of, 85; education/earnings of, 85; institutionalization of, *79*; in Mexican American educational attainment study, 99–103, *105*, 106–7; single motherhood in, 75, *76*; third+ generation, 101–3, *105*
Whites: Caribbeans v., 192; college education for, 74; dropouts of, 71, *72*, 74, 84; in early childhood education programs, *47*, 48, *49*, 55, *57*, 65; employment full-time and, 82; higher education/gender and, *72–73*; immigrants' earnings v., 93n8; Indians v., 189–90; in Mexican American educational attainment study, 101–4, *105*, 106–8; in Mexican American education/earnings study, *70*, 71, *72–73*, 74–75, *76–77*, 79–80, *81*, 82–85; in New York labor force study, 229, 234, *235*, 236, *237*, 238–41, *242*; Pakistanis v., 189–90; teen pregnancy in, 75; total family income in, 85–86; in U.S.-Canada urban education study, 213–19, *220*, *222–23*, 224–27; voluntary minorities v., 196; "white" cultural capital, 201–2
Wittgenstein, Ludwig, 203n6
Working-class culture, 202

Yugoslavs: Albanian-speaking Yugoslav immigrant youth, *117*, 118–20, *121–22*, *124*, 125, *126*, *128*; Serbo-Croat-speaking Yugoslav immigrant youth, *117*, 118–20, *121–22*, 123–26, *128*; Swiss language-speaking Yugoslav immigrant youth, *117*, *119*, 120, *121–22*, 124, *126*, *128*, 130

Zelter-Zubida, Aviva, 229–48
ZEP. *See Zones d'éducation prioritaire*
Zhang, Ye, 24, 207–28
Zhou, Min, 86–87, 95, 138, 198–200, 241
Znaniecki, Florian, 24
Zones d'éducation prioritaire (Zones of Educational Priority) (ZEP), 19, 201